THE SELZNICK PLAYERS

THE SELZNICK PLAYERS

Ronald Bowers

Editorial Assistant:

C. Leigh Hibbard Church

SOUTH BRUNSWICK AND NEW YORK: A. S. BARNES AND COMPANY
LONDON: THOMAS YOSELOFF LTD

A.S. Barnes and Co., Inc.
Cranbury, New Jersey 08512

Thomas Yoselof Ltd
108 New Bond Street
London W1Y OQX, England

Library of Congress Cataloging in Publication Data

Bowers, Ronald L.
The Selznick players.

Bibliography: p.
Includes index.
1. Selznick, David O., 1902-1965. I. Title.
PN1998.A3S393 791.43'0232'0924 [B]
ISBN 0-498-01375-8 74-9278

PRINTED IN THE UNITED STATES OF AMERICA

for
Anne, Nathalie and Joan

CONTENTS

Dorothy McGuire, 1947

FOREWORD

David imposed upon himself the best in artistic tradition to apply himself totally—his knowledge, his judgment, his taste—to what he understood and loved so much—motion pictures; and he raised that medium to its highest peak. In addition, he was a wonderful human being.

DOROTHY McGUIRE
Beverly Hills, California
August, 1974

ACKNOWLEDGMENTS

For their courtesy and co-operation the author wishes to thank the following individuals and organizations (in alphabetical order).

Academy of Motion Picture Arts and Sciences
Gene Andrewski
Ingrid Bergman
Katharine "Kay" Brown
Joseph Cotten
Joan Crawford
George Cukor
Norma Ederhardt Dauphin
Alfred De Liagre Jr.
Drew Dudley
Anita Colby Flagler
Rhonda Fleming
Joan Fontaine
Olivia de Havilland
Arthur Hornblow Jr.
Ward Jackson
Ruby Keeler
Greta Keller
Vivien Leigh (posthumously)
Library of Performing Arts at Lincoln Center
Myrna Loy
Charles Reilly, Editor: "Films In Review"
Leon Van Dyke
Victoria and Albert Museum, London: Gabrielle Enthoven Theatre Collection
Doris Warner Vidor

THE SELZNICK PLAYERS

David O. Selznick accepting the Irving G. Thalberg Memorial Award for producing *Gone With the Wind*, Spring 1940.

1

DAVID O. SELZNICK THE INDEPENDENT PRODUCER

In that elite circle of independent Hollywood producers, David O. Selznick was undoubtedly the most creative. He brought to his position an innate love of the motion-picture industry, a knowledge of all aspects of film making, a genius for promotion and publicity, a nose for discovering outstanding new talent, and an executive ability to hire the best technicians and oversee every aspect of his product. Selznick cannily made use of these attributes to create that unique mosaic that is the motion picture.

While much of the myth that surrounds Hollywood men such as Irving G. Thalberg and David O. Selznick is exaggeration, it cannot be denied that Selznick's reputation as a brilliant independent producer is justified by the merits of *Gone With the Wind* and *Rebecca,* his two most accomplished productions. Selznick hated having *Rebecca* compared to *Gone With the Wind,* and once adamantly stated, "That makes me furious. I really am furious every time I hear that. And don't think I haven't heard it. At least fifty people have said it to me, and each time I go into a regular rage. There is nothing that infuriates me so much. It (*Gone With the Wind)* was such a stupendous undertaking. Anything else, no matter what we'll ever make, will always seem insignificant after that."

Unfortunately most of his career after these two films reveals considerable inconsistency, owing to his almost monomaniacal desire to top *Gone With the Wind,* his overly-protective preoccupation with Jennifer Jones' career, and his constant financial vicissitudes. In addition to these obstacles was his personal obdurateness and his refusal to delegate responsibility. When questioned about delegating authority, he once replied, "The point is I don't want to!"—thereby elevating himself to producer-*auteur*.

Of this autonomous production practice, Selznick, shortly before his death, explained, "The movie producer seems to have become an anachronism. In my day the leading producers were men who had mastered every detail of filmmaking. When they produced a picture it was really their picture, creative control was in their hands. Today most producers are not producers at all. The producing function has all but disappeared."

There are those who speculate that the reason for Selznick's obvious creative decline in the Forties was the dissolution of his dynastic, albeit compatible, marriage to Irene Mayer; a marriage, in the words of Arthur Hornblow Jr., one of Selznick's intimate friends, "that should never have ended." Hornblow goes on to propose that Selznick tried to justify his marriage to Jennifer Jones by making her career his personal *Gone With the Wind.*

These observations notwithstanding, Selznick did in fact during the Forties, establish his prestigious stock company of Selznick Players, and almost single-handedly, through his genius for promotion, launched the stellar careers of such personalities as Vivien Leigh, Ingrid Bergman, Joan Fontaine, Jennifer Jones, Dorothy McGuire, Joseph Cotten and Gregory Peck. Of his stock company, Selznick once commented, "I've had some luck in discovering newcomers and if I weren't honest with myself I might be pretty smug about it. But the real truth is that a producer can only find and put over new personalities when he has the patience and the money for the overhead, and the authority to refuse to be rushed into making judgments."

While Selznick realised the importance of having a big name to draw his audience, he, always the showman, said, "No amount of ballyhoo about the artistic function of the motion picture can affect the fact that the primary and guiding purpose of all film production is to provide entertainment for the greatest possible number of persons. All of us in the industry realise that the basis of good entertainment is a good story and that no array of box-office names can overcome weakness in the plot or in the treatment of the script."

While the Selznick legacy is certainly overshadowed by *Gone With the Wind* — his *chef d'oeuvre* — his position in film history is incontrovertible. It is not a question of Selznick's genius in a profession filled with geniuses, but a matter of a man who loved making motion pictures. In the words of Arthur Hornblow Jr., "The disappearance of the creative producer has demolished an American industry. It was people like Selznick who kept the product coming."

David Selznick was born on May 22, 1902, in Pittsburgh, Pennsylvania. He was the son of Lewis J. and Florence Sachs Selznick. There were two other children, Howard, a life-long invalid, and Myron (born October 5, 1898), who would become for a time the most powerful agent in Hollywood. The two boys' future clout in the motion-picture industry was a natural progression as they were following in their father's footsteps. However, David's motives were opposite to those of his father. His father was a man who thought the movies "silly and stupid," but an enterprising way in which to make a buck. Conversely, David, entirely aware of the monetary rewards, loved the medium.

Lewis J. Selznick was born in Kiev, Russia, on May 2, 1870, and his family name had been Zeleznick. One of thirteen children, he ran away to London at the age of twelve, where he worked in a factory long enough to earn passage to the United States. At thirteen he emigrated to America and settled in Pittsburgh. A born promoter, he had established a national bank and three jewelry stores in that city by the time he was twenty-four years old. He married Florence Sachs, an Orthodox German Jewess, and in 1910, feeling he had accomplished all he could in Pittsburgh, moved his family to New York City. There he opened what he tagged "the world's greatest jewelery store," but when that venture failed in 1912, he entered the motion-picture business at the suggestion of a boyhood friend named Mark Dintenfass. Dintenfass headed a small production company which released motion pictures through Universal. Lewis Selznick came home one evening and declared, "Today I met my old friend Mark Dintenfass. He is the dumbest man I ever knew. If he can make money in pictures, anybody can."

Lewis Selznick invested in Universal Pictures and in the middle of a power play between that company's two directors — Patrick A. Powers and Carl Laemmle — managed to set himself up in the newly created position of General Manager with both Powers and Laemmle thinking the other had named him to the post. When the war between these two opposing factions came to a head, they finally discovered that Selznick had finagled his way into the company at a sizeable profit. In 1914, Laemmle, who had won his battle over Powers, handed Selznick a letter saying, "Your resignation has been accepted."

Undaunted, Selznick joined World Film Corporation and by selling the company's stock, purchased a studio in Fort Lee, New Jersey, where, in an arrangement with Broadway's Shubert Brothers and theatrical producer William A. Brady, he purchased the rights to plays and produced them as motion pictures. He blatantly advertised these pictures as "Features Made From Well Known Plays by Well Known Players," a phrase he lifted from Adolph Zukor's Famous Players motto: "Famous Plays for Famous Players." It soon became apparent Selznick was more interested in promoting himself than the World Film Corporation and he was finally ousted from that company, but not before he absconded with the company's most valuable asset, actress Clara Kimball Young.

David O. Selznick with a portrait of his father, Lewis J. Selznick.

He formed Lewis J. Selznick Enterprises, Incorporated and made a fortune releasing this popular actress's films by charging the exhibitors astronomical fees. He also induced producer Joseph M. Schenck to release the pictures Schenck produced starring his wife, Norma Talmadge. In addition, Selznick produced *War Brides* (1916) starring Alla Nazimova which earned him a small fortune.

The Selznicks moved into a seventeen-room apartment at 270 Park Avenue where they had a staff of servants and a fleet of Rolls-Royces. This luxurious life-style enabled Lewis Selznick to court the pleasures of gambling and women.

In his rise to the top, Selznick had made a

number of enemies, most importantly the powerful Adolph Zukor. Also, as head of his own company, he had begun to hire stars indiscriminately and produced pictures which revealed less and less of a profit. To make this position even more tenuous, his gambling losses in one year amounted to one million dollars. Selznick found himself in need of a loan and ironically the man who offered him the money was his arch-enemy, Adolph Zukor. Zukor's terms were stiff and rankled the ego of the proud Selznick, who, however, could do nothing but accept. Zukor offered to buy one half of Selznick's company with two major stipulations — that the name Selznick would not appear in the company's name or on the screen credits and that the company would henceforth produce smaller pictures for less money. They decided that the company would be called Select Pictures Corporation. It marked the beginning of the end for Lewis J. Selznick. By 1923, through competition and over-extending himself financially, Selznick was again in a critical position. This time, hated by the film industry, Selznick found no help. His creditors were pounding on the doors and he was forced into bankruptcy. Simultaneously, he suffered a stroke which prevented him from working again and until his death in 1933, the elder Selznick was supported by his sons. There are still those in Hollywood who believe the tenacious and sometimes ruthless manner in which Myron and David Selznick gained their respective positions on the Hollywood scene was partly in an effort to vindicate their father's tainted reputation. This was more true of Myron than David. Myron made a regular practice of intimidating studio heads.

David Selznick was educated at the Hamilton Institute for Boys in New York, where, like his mother, he developed a passionate interest in literature. Each day after school he worked in his father's office as did his brother, Myron. By age nineteen, Myron was producing over fifty motion pictures a year for his father, while David was being trained in distribution, advertising, and promotion. Both boys attended Columbia University for a short time, but preferred working full-time in their father's business. In 1923, just as Select Pictures Corporation was suffering its decline, David Selznick began his own motion-picture production career. Setting his sights on fame, he added the middle initial "O" to his name because it looked good and because his parents had failed to give him a middle name.

At twenty-one, he took $2,000 to produce his first picture. It was a short subject entitled *Will He Conquer Dempsey*? for which he hired Argentine boxer, Luis Angel Firpo, known as the "wild bull of the Pampas," for $1,000 for one day's shooting. The picture cost $875 to make and Selznick sold it for $3,500. Following that he enlisted Rudolph Valentino, who was then in the middle of a contractual dispute with Paramount Pictures, to judge a beauty contest in Madison Square Garden. He filmed this event as a short subject and released it at a profit of $15,000. With this money he produced a small budget feature called *Roulette* (1924) for Aetna starring Montagu Love.

This spurt of success came just as his father's company folded, and the young Selznick made two business overtures outside the movie business. One found him trying to amass money for a publishing venture with Arthur Brentano Jr., and another was an ill-timed flirtation with the land boom in Florida. Both failed. He decided to return to producing motion pictures but could not raise enough capital. His brother, Myron, under the sponsorship of Joseph M. Schenck, was now employed on the West Coast by United Artists. David decided to follow his brother to Hollywood where he found production jobs were not open to him, largely because the name Selznick was so hated by the industry. Myron arranged an interview for David with Harry Rapf of Metro-Goldwyn-Mayer, and as a result, David was hired as a reader at $75.00 a week. When he showed up for work the next day, Rapf told him the studio head, Louis B. Mayer, had heard about his employment and recalling an old enmity with Lewis J. Selznick, declared, "Nobody named Selznick will ever work here!"

Fortuitously, David heard of Nicholas M. Schenck's arrival in town. Schenck was president of Metro-Goldwyn-Mayer and Loew's Incorporated and as an old friend of his father's, David implored him to intercede and give him a chance. Schenck consented and in October, 1926, David Selznick went to work for Metro-Goldwyn-Mayer.

Selznick feared he might be overlooked on the vast Culver City lot as a reader and therefore bombarded the executive offices of M-G-M with suggestions for producing films. He decided to use the memo form because he thought he was too young and inexperienced to be taken seriously if he were to talk to an M-G-M executive in person. This began his compulsive habit of writing voluminous memos.

This ploy was remarkably successful and he

soon became the head of the Writers Department, then rapidly progressed from assistant story editor, associate story editor, assistant to Harry Rapf, to assistant producer. This mercurial rise awarded him with his chance to produce and he ingeniously came up with two pictures at the same time. Rapf had assigned him to produce a western starring Tim McCoy. Selznick later recalled, "I went on location with two sets of stars, one director, one supporting cast and worked the director and the supporting cast twice." The result was two Tim McCoy westerns — *Spoilers of the West* (1927) and *Wyoming* (1928) — both directed by W.S. Van Dyke, who later became known as "quick-take Van Dyke."

Irving G. Thalberg, then creative head of M-G-M, was impressed by Selznick having produced these two westerns at the cost of $120,000, rather then the $90,000 allocated for the original project and assigned him as assistant producer to Hunt Stromberg on *White Shadows of the South Seas* (1928). This picture was to be co-directed by the "artistic" Robert Flaherty and the "rough and-ready" W.S. Van Dyke. Selznick, who had known Stromberg when he had been a publicity man for Selznick senior, knew that Stromberg was interested in "showing women's breasts," and maintained the co-direction plan would never work. He went to see Thalberg with his complaints but Thalberg was unreceptive and Selznick was fired. The picture was released with W.S. Van Dyke and not Flaherty as director, just as Selznick had surmised.

Selznick's brother Myron had also been fired from Universal and the two brothers were befriended by Lewis Milestone in whose Santa Monica beach house they lived for several weeks. At this time Myron decided to become an agent and, with the usual Selznick virtuosity, soon became the most powerful in Hollywood, the nemesis of all studio heads and the hero of his illustrious clients. By 1935, his list of stars included Fred Astaire, Mary Astor, Gary Cooper, Henry Fonda, Helen Hayes, Katharine Hepburn, Carole Lombard, Myrna Loy, Ida Lupino, Fredric March, Merle Oberon, Laurence Olivier, William Powell, Ginger Rogers, and Margaret Sullavan.

Director William A. Wellman, a personal friend of David's, suggested that B.P. Schulberg, Paramount's West Coast production chief, hire him. Schulberg despised M-G-M and, while not convinced he could get along with a Selznick, nonetheless hired him. When Selznick was first interviewed by Schulberg, they argued over salary and the arrogant young Selznick walked out of the office. His friends persuaded Schulberg to see him again and on that occasion, Schulberg asked Selznick how long it would take for him to prove himself, to which Selznick replied, two weeks. Later Selznick recalled, "During those two weeks, I did all sorts of things: I deluged him with my famous or notorious memoranda, I got the studio to accept about five or six story ideas; I named about ten of their pictures for which they were looking for new titles; (They provided in my contract, later, that I would no longer get the $100 bonus that was offered for new titles!) I gave them script critiques and preview critiques; I devised a whole new system of the work of the producers and writers."

Schulberg was impressed with Selznick's accomplishments and put him under contract. Variously as supervisor, associate producer or producer, Selznick was closely involved with over a dozen motion pictures released by Paramount between 1929-1930. This was during Paramount's transition from silents to talkies. At Selznick's suggestion, *Four Feathers* (1929), a silent film directed by Merian C. Cooper and starring Richard Arlen and Fay Wray, was provided with a sound track with music and sound effects and became one of the year's most popular pictures. *The Dance of Life* (1929) and *Honey* (1930) helped make Nancy Carroll the most popular star of 1930. *Street of Chance* (1930) was Kay Francis' first important role and the picture which made William Powell a star. Also noteworthy were *Sarah and Son* (1930) with Fredric March and Ruth Chatterton, *The Texan* (1930) with Gary Cooper and Fay Wray, and *Manslaughter* with Fredric March and Claudette Colbert.

Selznick's one aim from the beginning was to have his own production unit. Schulberg refused to acquiesce to Selznick's wishes because he felt it would interrupt the flow of Paramount's automated system. As Selznick put it, "Schulberg was a great factory foreman, with a picture being started every Monday and a picture being shipped every Saturday, without fail." Selznick found this atmosphere claustrophobic and on June 18, 1931, submitted his resignation.

While at Paramount, on April 29, 1929, Selznick married Irene Mayer, daughter of M-G-M's Louis B. Mayer. Earlier Selznick had been in love with actress Jean Arthur after which he began courting Irene against her father's wishes. Irene was as headstrong as her father and was not deterred.

David and Irene were married in Mayer's Santa Monica beach house with David's brother Myron as best man and Irene's sister Edith (Mrs. William Goetz) as matron of honour. Janet Gaynor was one of the bridesmaids. Many in Hollywood likened it to a dynastic marriage as though the Capulets and the Montagues had made up. While the marriage may have been a union of the Capulets and the Montagues, Mayer's feelings about his son-in-law were less than affectionate.

After Selznick resigned from Paramount, he endeavoured to form his own production company in collaboration with director Lewis Milestone. When he started putting out feelers to releasing companies, he found that Mayer "had asked all the companies to refuse me a release because if I were helped, every director and producer would want his own independent unit and the studios would break up."

Selznick's resignation from Paramount came to the attention of David Sarnoff, president of the Radio Corporation of America. That company had recently purchased the RKO-Radio and RKO-Pathé studios in California, and Sarnoff, a pioneer who did not fear the Hollywood moguls, hired Selznick as vice-president in charge of production and merged the RKO-Radio and RKO-Pathé companies. Selznick took over in October, 1931, and remained with the studio until February, 1933. During his tenure he originated the title "executive producer" and oversaw each of the company's feature films including *The Lost Squadron* (1932) with Richard Dix and Mary Astor; *State's Attorney* (1932) with John Barrymore; *Rockabye* (1932) with Constance Bennett and Joel McCrea, and *Christopher Strong* (1933) with Katharine Hepburn. Another picture with which he was closely involved and from which he would later draw script ideas for his production of *A Star Is Born* in 1937 was *What Price Hollywood*? (1932). This was the story of a waitress (Constance Bennett) in the Brown Derby restaurant who is catapulted to stardom under the tutelage of an alcoholic director (Lowell Sherman), one of the first self-revelatory pictures about the Hollywood milieu. To direct this film, Selznick hired George Cukor * from Paramount Pictures.

Of this early association with Selznick, Cukor recalls, "He had a kind of excitement about him, and he sprung me. I was doing rather badly at Paramount; my talent wasn't appreciated. But as is generally the way with people — Paramount didn't want me until someone else did; the whole thing became really complicated. But Selznick arranged for me to go to RKO and work with their biggest star at the time, Connie Bennett. It was rather early in the game. From then on Selznick and I worked together on a great many pictures. I think we had a salubrious influence on each other. I know that working with him had an effect on me, and I should think I had an effect on him. He had enthusiasm. He had a kind of gusto, and he would take a chance, and it was enormous fun to work with him. He was a real showman."

During his administration at RKO, Selznick said that despite the fact his name appeared on nearly twenty pictures, he personally produced only four: *Bird of Paradise* (1932), *A Bill of Divorcement* (1932), *The Animal Kingdom* (1932), and *Topaze* (1933).

For *Bird of Paradise*, Selznick borrowed the services of director King Vidor from his father-in-law, Louis B. Mayer. Vidor recalls in his autobiography, *A Tree Is a Tree*, that Selznick told him, "I want Dolores Del Rio and Joel McCrea in a South Seas romance. Just give me three wonderful love scenes like you had in *The Big Parade* and *Bardelys the Magnificent*. I don't care what story you use so long as we call it *Bird of Paradise* and Del Rio jumps into a flaming volcano at the finish."

A Bill of Divorcement was a picture Selznick said he had wanted to make for some time but everyone felt because of the father's insanity it would be taboo at the box-office. The theatre version a decade earlier had made a star of Katharine Cornell and now that Selznick was in charge of his own studio, he felt the time had come to produce this picture. He and George Cukor tested several young actresses for the part but Cukor was particularly impressed with only one — Katharine Hepburn. He recalled her screen test was a scene from "Holiday" and, "at the end, she placed a glass on the floor and something about the gesture

*George Cukor was born in New York City on July 7, 1899. By age twenty he was directing stage plays and came to Hollywood in 1929, where one of his first jobs was as a dialogue director on Lewis Milestone's *All Quiet on the Western Front* (1930). He went from dialogue director to co-director to director at Paramount when Selznick hired him to direct *What Price Hollywood?* at RKO in 1932. Selznick allowed his directorial finesse to blossom with *A Bill of Divorcement* at RKO in 1932, and *Dinner at Eight* (1933) and *David Copperfield* (1935) at MGM. Since that time his classic films include *Camille* (1937), *The Philadelphia Story* (1940), *Born Yesterday* (1950), *A Star Is Born* (1954) and he earned an Oscar for his direction of *My Fair Lady* (1964). A modest, charming and erudite man, he is a frank and positive exponent of Hollywood lore.

Constance Bennett and Neil Hamilton in *What Price Hollywood?* (1932).

Katharine Hepburn and John Barrymore in *A Bill of Divorcement* (1932).

was very, very moving. She was like no one I had ever seen." It took considerable persuasion on Cukor's part to convince Selznick that the unglamorous Miss Hepburn was right for the role. Selznick finally gave in to Cukor's intuition and during production became convinced that Cukor had been right all along. Later he said, "Not until the preview was the staff convinced we had a great screen personality. During the first few feet you could feel the audience's bewilderment at this completely new type, and also feel that they weren't quite used to this kind of face. But very early in the picture there was a scene in which Hepburn just walked across the room, stretched her arms, and then lay out on the floor before the fireplace. It sounds very simple, but you could almost feel, and you could definitely hear, the excitement in the audience. It was one of the greatest experiences I've ever had. In those few feet of film a star was born." That picture and its star created a sensation in 1932, and, today, while the plot appears superficial and dated, Miss Hepburn's performance comes alive on the screen.

The Animal Kingdom was an excellent screen version of Philip Barry's sophisticated marital comedy-drama starring Ann Harding, Leslie Howard, and Myrna Loy. Miss Loy played the bitch wife and Miss Harding played the faithful mistress in a clever reversal of the good wife vs. bitch-mistress plots. Miss Loy told the author that Selznick had wanted Karen Morley for the role of the wife because "she was hot then" but director Edward "Ned" H. Griffith tested Miss Loy and convinced Selznick she was right for the part. Griffith had cast Myrna Loy as the man-trap in *Rebound* (1931) at RKO against the objections of that picture's star, Ina Claire, and Griffith's faith in Miss Loy's abilities proved providential. *The Animal Kingdom* was Miss Loy's fifty-fifth motion picture — she had debuted in *Pretty Ladies* (1925) starring Norma Shearer, where she and another unknown, Joan Crawford, played chorines. All of these pictures had been mostly B's in which, for the most part, she played a variety of exotics and Orientals. *The Animal Kingdom* proved to be a transitional picture in Miss Loy's career — it was the end of her appearances in B's.

Also transitional in Myrna Loy's career was *Topaze*, produced by Selznick for RKO. This was one of her first opportunities to display her natural facility for comedy and her first time to do so in a first-rate picture. *Topaze* was a brilliant adaptation of Pagnol's play and starred John Barrymore. Miss Loy played Barrymore's mistress, Coco. This performance convinced Irving G. Thalberg of M-G-M, where Miss Loy was a contract player, that she had potential as a star, and the next year she became just that after her appearance in *The Thin Man* opposite William Powell. Miss Loy describes Selznick as a brilliant man with nerve, guts and intelligence, but says she was not aware of him being on the set frequently during the production of these two pictures, as was to be his habit later on.

Selznick was about to renew his contract with RKO, when its president, Hiram Brown, was succeeded by Merlin Hall Aylesworth. Aylesworth began making changes in Selznick's contract that reduced his autonomy and Selznick refused to sign. Instead, he chose, to the surprise of many, to accept an offer from his father-in-law to head his own unit as vice-president in charge of production at M-G-M. Mayer had made an overture to Selznick earlier in 1932, knowing that his powerful creative head, Irving G. Thalberg, was ill. But at that time, Selznick refused the offer saying he enjoyed the freedom and respect he had at RKO. Now it was indeed the Capulets and the Montagues under the same roof.

Selznick's two-and-a-half years with M-G-M resulted in some of the most memorable and profitable films in that company's history, and, for the most part, he was given complete artistic freedom.

Dinner at Eight (1933) was his initial production for M-G-M and its all-star cast included John and Lionel Barrymore, Marie Dressler, Wallace Beery, Jean Harlow, Billie Burke and Lee Tracy. It was a box-office blockbuster and is still as popular today. *Night Flight* (1933) was another attempt at all-star casting, this time with John and Lionel Barrymore, Helen Hayes, Robert Montgomery, Clark Gable and Myrna Loy, but the plot of this aerial adventure was very thin on characterisation and adventure and consequently was not popular. *Meet the Baron* (1933) was a ghastly mistake which Selznick undertook only at the pleading of his old friend Harry Rapf. It was little more than a vehicle to promote radio comedian Jack Pearl whom audiences found better suited to radio.

Selznick's next M-G-M release, *Dancing Lady* (1933), was another smashing success which again holds up well today. Selznick did not like musicals and this was the only one he ever produced, but it benefits from his expertise. It starred Clark Gable and Joan Crawford and revived Miss Crawford's

On the set of *Dinner at Eight* (1933). Left to right: *sitting:* Madge Evans, Louise Closser Hale, Billie Burke, Marie Dressler, Karen Morley, Grant Mitchell; *standing:* Edmund Lowe, Director, George Cukor, Lionel Barrymore, Jean Harlow, Phillips Holmes.

career which was then in a slump following the box-office failure of her last two pictures *Rain* (1932) and *Today We Live* (1933). Miss Crawford refers to such periodic declines as "the salt and pepper of one's career."

Dancing Lady was Fred Astaire's motion-picture debut and it was Kay Brown, RKO's East Coast talent representative and later Selznick's Eastern Representative, who had arranged for Astaire to be screen-tested for RKO before Selznick had resigned from that studio. Prior to his committing Astaire to a contract with RKO, Selznick wrote one of his famous memos to RKO executives, producer Louis Brock and director, Mark Sandrich, saying, "Astaire is one of the greatest artists of the day; a magnificent performer, a man conceded to be perhaps, next to Leslie Howard, the most charming in the American theater, and unquestionably, the outstanding young leader of American musical comedy. He would be, in my opinion, good enough to use in the lead of a million dollar Lubitsch picture — provided only that he photographs."

Astaire did photograph well and Selznick signed him to a contract with RKO, but before he could star him in a picture at that studio, Selznick had moved to M-G-M. When he decided to produce *Dancing Lady,* he borrowed Astaire, providing him with his debut vehicle. Joan Crawford, who was one of M-G-M's influential stars, consented to Astaire having star billing in the picture. When Louis B. Mayer asked her why, she replied, "He's been a star longer than me." Mayer's rebuttal was that no one knew theatre people.

In discussing *Dancing Lady*, one of her favourite pictures and her first dancing role in several years, Miss Crawford told the author, "I worked my you-know-what off for that picture. Selznick was on the set a lot and he was a taskmaster and likewise we became the same. I don't think he liked me. I don't think he was a genius. This myth about genius producers is so overblown. We have put him and Thalberg on a pedestal. I think Thalberg was overrated also. He did not really have foresight and he was not physically strong." When asked to comment on the picture's director Robert Z. Leonard, whom some young film historians refer to as a "hack," Miss Crawford forcefully replied, "He was one of the dearest, sweetest men I ever knew. If he was a hack I wish there were such hacks as he today, and there would be a helluva lot better movies than there are. And you can quote me on that!"

Viva Villa! (1934) provided Wallace Berry with his greatest screen performance and always remained one of Selznick's favorite pictures. *Manhattan Melodrama* (1934) was the picture which revived the waning career of William Powell and first cast him opposite Myrna Loy. This picture starred Clark Gable and was the film that John Dillinger went to see (allegedly because Miss

Joan Crawford and Fred Astaire in *Dancing Lady* (1933).

Wallace Beery in *Viva Villa!* (1934).

Loy was his favourite actress) when he was killed by the FBI as he came out of the theatre.

David Copperfield (1935) was a project particularly close to Selznick's heart. He supposedly wished to produce it because it had been one of his father's favourite novels, although biographies reveal it was his mother who possessed the literary bent. Whichever, Selznick took painstaking care in making this picture authentic and referred to it as one of the most difficult and satisfying pictures to make. Louis B. Mayer tried to persuade him to use M-G-M's money-making tow-head, Jackie Cooper, in the starring role, but Selznick insisted the title role required a sensitive, English child actor. In their search for such an actor, Selznick and Cukor went to London where Cukor discovered the beautiful Freddie Bartholomew and began that boy's brief but memorable childhood acting career.

Vanessa: Her Love Story (1935) was little more than slick soap-opera, but M-G-M had Helen Hayes under contract and did not know what to do with her. This was unfortunately their solution. *Reckless* (1935) was a melodrama with music in which Jean Harlow is pursued by Franchot Tone and William Powell. Not Harlow's best, it nonetheless cast her for the first time opposite William Powell, whom everyone assumed she would marry. She tragically died on June 7, 1937, aged twenty-six, before she and Powell could marry.

W.C. Fields and Freddie Bartholomew in *David Copperfield* (1935).

Greta Garbo, who had been under contract to M-G-M since 1925, had in one of her renewal contracts a clause stating that two of her pictures were to be produced by either Irving G. Thalberg or David O. Selznick. As it turned out, Selznick produced one, *Anna Karenina* (1935), and Thalberg the second, *Camille* (1937). When it became apparent that Garbo wished to star in a second version of the Tolstoy novel (she had appeared in a silent version entitled *Love* (1927), Selznick wrote her in an effort to change her mind. He contended it was not the time for her to do another period-piece following the small financial success of *Queen Christina* (1933) and *The Painted Veil* (1934) and suggested instead she do either a comedy (something she had never done) or an up-to-date woman's picture called *Dark Victory,* which he maintained he would purchase for her. He further added that Fredric March, who had been pencilled in as Vronsky, was adamantly against playing that role and would only do so if his company, 20th Century-Fox, insisted. Furthermore, Selznick said he preferred Clark Gable in the role if the picture were to be made at all. Whatever her reasons, Miss Garbo was adamant in her desire to play Anna, who in the words of venerable film critic James Agee is "literature's most vehemently average woman," and the picture was scheduled for production. The result was less than exciting but successful at the box-office.

Selznick's last picture under his contract with M-G-M was *A Tale of Two Cities* (1935), supposedly another of his father's favourite novels. The picture was exquisitely produced and Ronald Colman was splendid as Sidney Carton.

On June 27, 1935, Selznick wrote a lengthy letter of resignation to Louis B. Mayer. In it he emphasised his desire to form his own production company and he felt the time was now right. Mayer, who had come to respect his dynamic and talented son-in-law, reluctantly accepted his resignation but requested he stay with M-G-M until both *Anna Karenina* and *A Tale of Two Cities* were completed. Selznick agreed and left in the fall of 1935.

When Selznick left the studio, Irving G. Thalberg, who had once fired Selznick but who now

Guy D'ennery, Greta Garbo and Freddie Bartholomew in *Anna Karenina* (1935).

Ronald Colman in *A Tale of Two Cities* (1935).

had come to admire him as a producing colleague, graciously offered to invest $100,000 in Selznick's independent venture, and Thalberg's wife, Norma Shearer, invested the same amount. Thalberg had been planning to leave M-G-M himself for just the same purpose, but his health was becoming more impaired by tuberculosis, and he gave up the idea of leaving M-G-M. Selznick was overwhelmed by the Thalbergs' vote of confidence.

In his efforts to raise additional capital, Selznick's friend and former associate at RKO, Merian C. Cooper, suggested he see John "Jock" Hay Whitney. Cooper had been Selznick's executive assistant at RKO and there, under Selznick's encouragement, had created and co-directed the classic, *King Kong* (1933). Whitney, an old friend of Cooper's, had invested money in Cooper's Pioneer Pictures Company which produced Technicolor films. Whitney was receptive to Selznick's proposal and along with his brother, Cornelius Vanderbilt Whitney, and his sister, Mrs. Charles (Joan) S. Payson, became Selznick's principal investors. Other investors included Robert and Arthur Lehman, John Hertz, Dr. A.H. Giannini of the Bank of America and attorney Lloyd Wright; David's brother Myron, invested $200,000. The total capitalisation was $3,200,000 none of which was Selznick's own. The company was named Selznick International Pictures, Incorporated, and its formation was announced in September, 1935. Incorporated into this company was Merian C. Cooper's Pioneer Pictures. That company was not performing as well as Cooper had hoped. Although it had produced *Becky Sharp* (1935) and *Dancing Pirate* (1936), both were financial failures and Cooper felt that his company would be more successful under Selznick's management. Selznick International was housed in the old Pathé studio in Culver City. In his search for an emblem to represent the new company, Selznick decided to use a photograph of the front of the colonial Pathé building. The company's motto was "In a Tradition of Quality."

Selznick worked out a releasing deal with United Artists and his first project for his new company was another adaptation of a classic novel, *Little Lord Fauntleroy* (1936), starring Freddie Bartholomew. It was an expensively produced picture ($600,000) and was a critical and financial success, grossing $1,700,000, but the company's next project, *The Garden of Allah* (1936), was a flop. Based on Robert Hichens's Edwardian novel about an orphaned English seductress who meets a monk in the Algerian desert, it starred Marlene Dietrich and Charles Boyer, and was the first picture to be photographed in the three-colour Technicolor process. More attention was paid to the photography and Miss Dietrich's makeup and costumes than to the script. Miss Dietrich at the time was labelled box-office poison and the picture was a commercial failure.

In reviewing the picture, "Time" wrote: "Sad, serene and somewhat silly, *The Garden of Allah* belongs to that dignified class of pictures which reviewers customarily praise for the music and the photography. Unfortunately for Hollywood, cinemaddicts go to the theatre not to see the latest wonders of cinematography but to be entertained. That in this case both music by Max Steiner and color photography by cameraman, W. Howard Greene and Color Designer Lansing C. Holden, are genuinely superb, will doubtless not suffice to interest 1936 in two young lovers who, with money to burn, can apparently find nothing better to do than brood about the life hereafter. If *The Garden of Allah,* best example of color photography the cinema has so far contrived, is a box-office hit, it will be because of its stars." But the stars did not help. The picture cost $2,200,000 to make — $200,000 of which was Marlene Dietrich's salary — and failed at the box-office.

Selznick International was able to recoup some of its losses on *The Garden of Allah* with its next production, the excellent and dramatic, *A Star Is Born* (1937). Owing much to Selznick's RKO production of *What Price Hollywood?,* this time the story had Janet Gaynor as an aspiring actress whose career flourishes while that of her self-destructive, alcoholic, actor husband, Fredric March, is rapidly going down hill. Selznick hired his friend William A. Wellman to direct the picture and although Selznick was very much involved himself, credit for the original story went to Wellman and Robert Carson. The screenplay was written by Alan Campbell, Dorothy Parker and Robert Carson. Filmed in Technicolor, it remains the best of all the films about Hollywood. Both its stars, the director, the picture, the screenplay and the original story were nominated for Academy Awards. It was awarded the Oscar for the Best Screenplay and upon accepting it, Wellman walked over to Selznick and said, "Take it, you had more to do with winning it than I did." This picture contained the best performance of Miss Gaynor's career, a star who had received the first Academy Award as Best Actress in 1928, for her

Charles Boyer, Marlene Dietrich, Basil Rathbone and C. Aubrey Smith in *The Garden of Allah* (1936).

Janet Gaynor, Fredric March and Adolphe Menjou in *A Star Is Born* (1937).

combined performances in three films. *Seventh Heaven, Street Angel*, and *Sunrise*. This picture momentarily renewed interest in a career which had seen her as the number one box-office-star for 20th Century-Fox in the early Thirties, but after two more pictures, she resigned in 1938. She has returned to the films only once since to play the mother of Pat Boone in *Bernadine* (1957).

Ronald Colman had apprehensions about starring in a fourth re-make of *The Prisoner of Zenda* (1937) (a fifth version was made in 1952) but Selznick was convinced that Anthony Hope's adventurous war-horse was timely in view of the king of England's recent abdication to marry a commoner. Once again Selznick's foresight proved correct, and this picture remains the best of the five screen versions and countless imitations of this popular novel. The reason is easily explained. Selznick was a showman, but a talented showman with taste, and with this picture one can recognise his instinctive ability to hire the best people for each job. His cast was excellent — Ronald Colman, Madeleine Carroll, Douglas Fairbanks Jr., David Niven, C. Aubrey Smith. As director he hired John Cromwell, who had worked with him at Paramount and whose experience as a stage director allowed him to understand the needs of the actors and the dialogue and prevent his players from being lost amid the spectacle. The cinematographer was the able James Wong Howe, sets were designed by Lyle Wheeler (who later designed the sets for *Gone With the Wind*) and the script was by John L. Balderston, from an adaptation by Wells Root, with additional dialogue by Donald Ogden Stewart. All were experts in their fields and the picture reveals Selznick's ability to blend their talents at his creative best.

Ronald Colman and Madeleine Carroll in *The Prisoner of Zenda* (1937).

One of Myron Selznick's clients and one of the screen's brightest comediennes was Carole Lombard. Now free from her long association with Paramount, Miss Lombard convinced Selznick that he should use her in two pictures at Selznick International. Selznick was not particularly fond of comedy films but agreed. He produced two pictures with her, paying her $175,000 for each. The first and the better of the two was the zany farce, *Nothing Sacred* (1938), the story of a country girl who is told by a physician in error that she is about to die from radiation. Fredric March was her co-star and it is one of her best performances. The second production, *Made For Each Other* (1939), was a serious little drama about a young married couple struggling to attain a perfect marriage. Miss Lombard's co-star was James Stewart and while it was not what the public expected of her, she earned good notices as a serious actress.

Always more at home with the classics, Selznick's next production was *The Adventures of Tom Sawyer* (1938). Meticulously produced as always, it is a sincere piece of Americana but was never very popular. For the part of Tom, Selznick refused to accept a well-known actor and conducted a nation-wide search for an unknown. He chose Tommy Kelly, the son of a Bronx fireman, who after making a few more pictures did not wish to pursue an acting career.

Selznick followed *The Adventures of Tom Sawyer* with *The Young in Heart* (1938), a pleasant little story of a beneficient old lady (Minnie Dupree) who rehabilitates a family of crooks. The cast included Janet Gaynor, Roland Young, Billie Burke, Douglas Fairbanks Jr., and Paulette Goddard. Selznick had originally planned it as a vehicle for famed theatre star Maude Adams, but he could not convince that actress, then teaching drama, that she should return to acting and make her motion-picture debut.

At this point in Selznick's career, while he was regarded as a creative producer, he had not yet achieved the stature which would come to him in later years. However, his next three productions — *Intermezzo: A Love Story* (1939); *Gone With the Wind* (see separate chapter) (1939); and *Rebecca* (1940) — earned him the reputation as the genius of producers. Simultaneously with these productions he began to assemble The Selznick Players, his company of contractees.

The Selznick Players had actually begun to take

shape in 1937 when he signed Paulette Goddard to a seven-year contract with hopes of casting her as Scarlett O'Hara in *Gone With the Wind*. Selznick had purchased the rights to Margaret Mitchell's popular novel in 1936 and spent nearly three years bringing it to the screen and with that picture, he added Vivien Leigh to his stock company. The versatile Selznick found time to devote to two other productions simultaneously with *Gone With the Wind* — *Intermezzo: A Love Story* and *Rebecca* — adding two more illustrious names to his stock company — Ingrid Bergman and Joan Fontaine.

Early in 1938, Elsa Neuberger, Selznick's assistant story editor in New York, saw a Swedish picture called *Intermezzo* (1936) starring a well-known Swedish actress by the name of Ingrid Bergman, and she had a print of the picture shipped to Selznick in Hollywood. Selznick ran the picture in his home for a group of friends most of whom found it boring and some of whom walked out. With his perceptive eye for talent, Selznick ignored his friends' indifference and wired Kay Brown, his Eastern Representative, to obtain the re-make rights to the picture. She did so, and a short time later when he was certain he could fit the picture into his schedule, he decided he would also like to obtain the young actress who had made the original and wired Miss Brown saying, "Take the next boat to Sweden and do not come home without a contract with Miss Bergman." Miss Brown did just that and on May 6, 1939, Ingrid Bergman arrived in the United States to star in the re-make of *Intermezzo*. She refused to commit herself to a seven-year contract at that time saying she would only do so after the picture proved a success with the public.

Selznick began working on the pre-production planning of *Intermezzo: A Love Story* before Miss Bergman had arrived in Hollywood, and not being certain of this unknown quantity, he began to explore other casting possibilities among Hollywood actresses and, for a short time, considered Loretta Young as the young pianist, should Miss Bergman not photograph well. For the role of the violinist, Selznick briefly considered Charles Boyer after the part had been turned down by both Ronald Colman and William Powell. However, Selznick cast Leslie Howard in the part. William Wyler had been set to direct, but when the production was delayed because of script problems, Wyler, who was committed to direct *Wuthering Heights* (1939) for Samuel Goldwyn, was replaced by Gregory Ratoff.

Production began in June, and Selznick was thrilled by the way Miss Bergman photographed and the dedication with which she studied English and her part in the picture. The film was released in October, 1939, at New York City's Radio City Music Hall and while the romantic story was sentimental and hardly innovative, it was so expertly produced and acted that the public, if not the critics, thought it superb. It remains today one of the favourite movie love stories. Everyone, including the critics, was enchanted by the fresh, unmovie-star quality of Miss Bergman and agreed Selznick had created a star overnight. After completing the picture, Ingrid Bergman returned to her native Sweden, but when the American public's response to her performance proved so favourable, she agreed to sign a long-term contract with Selznick and returned to the United States in 1940. She became the sparkling gem in Selznick's elite little stock company and would, over the next seven years, be his most important commodity.

At the same time as Selznick had been negotiating for the re-make rights to *Intermezzo*, he signed a seven-year contract with England's most famous director, Alfred Hitchcock.* He told Hitchcock that he wished to produce a picture about the Titanic; Hitchcock liked the idea. However, when Selznick found his schedule occupied by *Gone With the Wind* and *Intermezzo: A Love Story*, he delayed Hitchcock's arrival at the Selznick studio. In the interim, Hitchcock directed *Jamaica Inn* (1939) in England; a picture based on the novel by Daphne du Maurier and starring Charles Laughton and Maureen O'Hara.

Always interested in period pictures, Selznick had read Daphne du Maurier's newest best-seller, "Rebecca," and decided that this should be Hitchcock's first American assignment. He wrote Hitchcock in London who agreed, and because of its English setting, Selznick had Hitchcock hire two English writers — Philip MacDonald and Michael Hogan — to adapt the novel for the

*Alfred Joseph Hitchcock was born in London, on August 13, 1899, and after a series of minor jobs in the film industry, made his directorial debut in 1921, with *Number Thirteen*. He soon gained a reputation as England's master of suspense with *The Lodger* (1926), *Blackmail* (1929), *The Thirty-Nine Steps* (1935) and *The Lady Vanishes* (1938). He signed with Selznick in 1940, and directed Selznick's Productions of *Rebecca* (1940), *Spellbound* (1945) and *The Paradine Case* (1947), and in between these assignments was loaned out to direct such memorable pictures as *Suspicion* (1941), *Shadow of a Doubt* (1943), *Lifeboat* (1944), and *Notorious* (1946). However, it was after the expiration of his contract with Selznick that he came in to his own as as "name" director with his own productions of *Dial M. For Murder* (1954), *To Catch a Thief* (1955), *Psycho* (1960), and *The Birds* (1963). He married Alma Reville in 1926, and they have a daughter, Patricia.[4]

Joan Fontaine, Laurence Olivier and Judith Anderson in *Rebecca* (1940).

screen. After reading the adaptation, Selznick, who was fanatical about keeping as much as possible of the original novel in the screenplay, was angered to find that the two writers had taken it upon themselves to make many critical changes. In one of his many memos to Hitchcock during this production, he wrote, "It is my unfortunate and distressing task to tell you that I am shocked and disappointed beyond words by the treatment of 'Rebecca.' I regard it as a distorted and vulgarized version of a provenly successful work, in which, for no reason that I can discern, old-fashioned movie scenes have been substituted for the captivatingly charming du Maurier scenes. I have never been able to understand why motion-picture people insist upon throwing away something of proven appeal to substitute things of their own creation. It is a form of ego which has very properly drawn upon Hollywood the wrath of the world for many years, and, candidly, I am surprised to discover that the disease has apparently also spread to England."

Hitchcock agreed with Selznick's criticisms and had the writers revise their adaptation. Selznick approved it and the two gentlemen were gratuitously retained. Playwright Robert E. Sherwood and Hitchcock's assistant, Joan Harrison, were assigned to write the screenplay. The one change from the novel that had to remain in the script was that Maxim did not kill Rebecca. This change was forced on Selznick much to his regret by the Hayes Office which felt the public would not accept a protagonist who had committed murder.

Hitchcock arrived in Hollywood in April, 1939. Work on the script continued and Selznick continued his search for the right cast, a search which had begun in 1938. William Powell wanted the role of Maxim but his fee was $100,000. Selznick preferred Laurence Olivier and also liked the fact that his fee was less than Powell's and Olivier was cast. Alla Nazimova had told George Cukor that she was interested in the part of Mrs. Danvers and Selznick considered her for a time, as he did Flora Robson, but settled on Judith Anderson, who turned in the best performance of her screen career. The role of the second Mrs. de Winter was, to Selznick, second only in importance to that of Scarlett O'Hara. He had approached Vivien Leigh about playing the part and she had refused. Then, after finding out that her fiancé, Laurence Olivier, was to play Maxim, changed her mind. Selznick, who had not really been that keen on her for the part, then refused to give it to her. Tossed about in the casting grab bag were the names of Joan Crawford, Bette Davis, Olivia de Havilland, and Anita Louise, with Miss de Havilland as the only serious contender. Another of Selznick's choices had been Loretta Young, but she was tested and ruled out. Selznick finally decided that Joan Fontaine, sister of Olivia de Havilland and a young actress who up to that time had had a mediocre career in B's, might be the actress for the part. Miss Fontaine was tested several times as were Margaret Sullavan and Anne Baxter. After many months of testing and indecision, these three ladies were the finalists, with Miss Baxter's tests regarded by most as the best. Hitchcock had been impressed with Miss Fontaine all along and she was cast. Hitchcock recalls, "The ironical thing about *Rebecca* is that it was an English picture, in effect. The only two — shall I call them foreigners — were Robert Sherwood, who did the main work on the script, and Selznick. Although Joan Fontaine was our first choice for the female lead, I had to go through the motions of testing every woman in town, because Selznick wanted to do the same publicity that he had done for Scarlett O'Hara. So, I was testing all these women — Loretta Young, Vivien Leigh even, Anne Baxter, Anita Louise, a whole lot of them, some of them totally unsuitable, although I'd already made up my mind that Fontaine was the best."

The production began in September, 1939, after shooting on *Gone With the Wind* had ended, and Selznick infused each aspect of the picture with his instinctive good taste, even down to deciding that it should not be given a surprise preview as was the habit for most major Hollywood productions. He stated, "*Rebecca* is a very tricky picture, with very peculiar moods and a very strange sort of construction and playing. I don't want to take the chance of finally editing it according to the reactions of an audience that has come in to see a Marx Brothers picture, or even a Joan Crawford picture, as might be the case at previews. I think the whole preview system is wrong, in that it is equivalent to trying out a Eugene O'Neill play on the road by advertising to the public that they are going to see the Zeigfeld Follies, and then having the reaction of a Follies audience determine how the O'Neill play should be cut."

Rebecca was released in 1940 to rave reviews and launched Joan Fontaine into stardom. The New York "Times" said, "*Rebecca* is an altogether brilliant film, haunting, suspenseful, handsome and handsomely played." Selznick received the Academy Award as producer of the Best Picture of the Year.

Selznick then halted production for two-and-a-half years. In his own words, "After *Gone With the Wind* and *Rebecca*, to draw down our profits, which were substantial, the only way I could see of getting myself some money that I needed and could keep was to liquidate Selznick International. The other stockholders agreed, and we thus created one of our lesser contributions to Hollywood, the introduction of capital gains. We made an agreement with the government under which we would complete our liquidation within three years. When the three years were up, my tax lawyers insisted upon a course which turned out to be extremely costly to me (and which also turned out to have been unnecessary, as was determined in a Supreme Court decision of years later) to the tune of many millions of dollars: they said that either the Whitneys or myself had to dispose of our respective interests in *Gone With the Wind* (we had previously cut up and sold to each other the other assets), or the government would challenge the liquidation. So in a quite simple meeting with my old friend Jock Whitney as to who would buy the other one out, I sold to Jock (for $2,000,000) for the simple reason that he didn't want to sell. Subsequently, Mr. Whitney and Mrs. Payson sold their original interest and what they had acquired from me, to M-G-M, for a huge profit." The result of this complicated transaction ironically gave Selznick's father-in-law, Louis B. Mayer, complete ownership of Selznick's *magnum opus* and Selznick would collect not a penny of the nearly $80,000,000 the picture has grossed to date.

Liquidation of Selznick International took place in August 1940, after which Selznick, with his own capital, established David O. Selznick Productions, Incorporated. On October 5, 1941, he purchased a one-fourth interest in United Artists for $1,200,000 and guaranteed to maintain production until he had delivered $20,000,000 worth of pictures to that company. In doing so, he also borrowed $1,000,000 to use for capital for these productions. Later on, when Mary Pickford, one of the major stockholders of United Artists, objected to the slow pace with which Selznick was producing films, his share was bought back by United Artists.

While sitting out his liquidation period, Selznick began to enlarge his stock company and prepare package deals to sell to other studios. He purchased the rights to the Broadway success, "Claudia," in 1941, and eventually signed its star, Dorothy McGuire, to a long-term contract. At the same time he signed a young actress named Phyllis Isley, who had come to his office to test for the screen version of "Claudia," and in February, 1942, introduced Miss Isley to the press as his new star — Jennifer Jones.

When 20th Century-Fox announced its film production of *The Song of Bernadette,* Miss Jones begged Selznick to allow her to test for the part, forgetting all about *"Claudia."* Selznick consented and the following December 20th, Century-Fox announced that Miss Jones had been cast in the picture. For that performance, she received the Academy Award as Best Actress of 1943. Selznick had by this time lost interest in personally producing *Claudia* and had sold the rights to that picture and Dorothy McGuire as its star to 20th Century-Fox; another Selznick Player was launched to stardom.

Ingrid Bergman was still Selznick's most important property and as long as he had no projects for her, she begged to be loaned out as often as he would allow, and by doing so, he profited considerably. He had originally been interested in producing the screen version of Ernest Hemingway's "For Whom the Bell Tolls," then changed his mind and Paramount Pictures purchased the screen rights. He had always considered Ingrid Bergman perfect for the part of Maria, and despite the fact that Paramount owned the project, kept planting stories in the press suggesting her as the only actress who could play the role. Coincidentally, Selznick's brother, Myron, was Hemingway's agent, and they arranged for the famous author to meet the Swedish actress and to have him personally endorse her for the part. When Paramount began the picture with ballerina Vera Zorina in the lead, they recognized their mistake immediately and reluctantly stopped the picture and paid Selznick's stiff loan-out fee of $150,000 for Miss Bergman. He also loaned Miss Bergman to Warner Brothers for *Casablanca* and *Saratoga Trunk*. For the latter, Warner Brothers paid him $125,000 and guaranteed him the services of Olivia de Havilland for one picture. Whereupon Selznick sold Miss de Havilland's services to RKO for $125,000 where she was forced against her wishes to make the forgettable *Government Girl* (1943).

Selznick also loaned Ingrid Bergman to M-G-M to star in *Gaslight* for which she won the Academy Award as Best Actress of 1944; the fourth Selznick Player to do so in five years, the other three being Vivien Leigh for *Gone With the Wind* in 1939; Joan Fontaine for *Suspicion* in 1941, and Jennifer Jones for *The Song of Bernadette* in 1944.

Arthur Hornblow Jr., who produced *Gaslight* for M-G-M, recalls how Miss Bergman came to be cast, "I was at a party at agent Charlie Feldman's home and we had bought the rights to the play "Angel Street," and I wanted Charles Boyer, Feldman's client, to play the husband. We settled that over drinks and David came in and said, 'Who are you casting in the female lead?' I said I would like to have Ingrid if he did not have her tied up in one of his loan-out deals. He said fine. As you see, in Hollywood, all deals for the most part are made over lunch or dinner or at parties. And the best ones were at parties. M-G-M groaned when they heard I had Bergman because they knew they would have to pay. Ben Thau, MGM's contract officer, handled the contract and I don't think David charged us any exhorbitant fee for Bergman's services. David was a kibitzer over the script, and made some very good suggestions at the preview. Some of his ideas were excellent and then others were simply over-meticulous."

Selznick added two more stars to the Selznick Players in 1943. He signed his first male lead,* Joseph Cotten, to a seven-year contract after Cotten was left stranded without a studio when Orson Welles was ousted from RKO. Cotten had been one of Welles' original Mercury Players in New York and had come to Hollywood to star in Wells' *Citizen Kane* (1941). Selznick's second acquisition in 1943, was the ex-curly-headed moppet who had captured the hearts of all America in the Thirties, Shirley Temple. Miss Temple was now fifteen and her career as a child star was over. Selznick hired her and put her in several respectable teenage roles, allowing her the opportunity to make the transition from child star to *ingenue* in a less painful and embarrassing manner than is the usual fate of such talents. Selznick had seen Miss Temple at a Hollywood Bowl affair honouring Madame Chiang-Kai-shek and observed, "I was watching the girls in the dressing room, and how they walked across to meet Madame. My reaction was that the two most wonderful personalities were Bergman and Temple. I think Shirley is enchanting."

After selling his option on another planned project, *Jane Eyre* (1944), to 20th Century-Fox with Joan Fontaine as its star, Selznick returned to production in the summer of 1943, with *Since You Went Away* (1944), his idealistic, all-star view of life on the American home front. The cast included his own players: Jennifer Jones, Joseph Cotten, Shirley Temple, and in bit parts, two young unknowns he had signed named Guy Madison and Rhonda Fleming. To these players he added Claudette Colbert, Robert Walker (Miss Jones's estranged husband), Monty Woolley, Lionel Barrymore, Agnes Moorehead, Nazimova, Craig Stevens and Keenan Wynn. The picture was a labour of love for which Selznick himself wrote the screenplay — a mistake — based on Margaret Buell Wilder's novel. *Since You Went Away* was popular wartime fare, but greatly over-produced

*In 1941, Selznick had hired what would have been the first male star of his pubescent stock company, Gene Kelly. Kelly, who was born Eugene Curran Kelly in Pittsburgh, Pennsylvania, on August 23, 1912, had been interested in gymnastics and dancing since childhood. From a hoofing act with his brother, Fred, he opened the Gene Kelly Studio of Dance in Pittsburgh, and arrived in New York City as a dance teacher in 1937. From the chorus of "Leave It to Me" (1938) starring Mary Martin, to summer stock, he finally was cast as the heel in the Broadway musical version of John O'Hara's "Pal Joey" (1940). Selznick saw his performance and offered him a contract. Kelly says, "After I did 'Pal Joey' on Broadway, David put me under contract. He said, 'You, you are a great actor. This nonsense about your doing musicals, that's fine. You can do them for a hobby.' I said, 'Wait a minute, I'm a dancer.' He said, 'No. I have a property for you. You are going to play the priest in *Keys of the Kingdom*.' David was, as everybody knows, a slow worker. Time went by. Finally he said, 'Well, all right, maybe you are not right for the priest in *Keys of the Kingdom*. But there is another great part. It is the role of the doctor, a Scotchman.' I said, 'My Scotch accent is like Harry Lauder. It sounds like a vaudevillian from Pittsburgh. It's just terrible. Forget it.' He said, 'No, I will get you a teacher.' So he got a guy who lived out in Pasadena, and three nights a week I would travel out there and take an hour lesson. About six weeks later, we made the test. David and I sat in the projection room looking at the test. We looked at each other and started to laugh. I still sounded like a vaudevillian doing the Scotch. Burgess Meredith played the part. The second year, David sold half my contract to M-G-M and loaned me out for *For Me and My Gal* (1942). He sold all of my contract finally." Kelly went on to become a star at M-G-M and a major creative force in motion-picture musicals, topping his achievements with *An American in Paris* (1951).

Shirley Temple, Craig Stevens, Joseph Cotten, Jennifer Jones, Alla Nazimova, Keenan Wynn, Claudette Colbert and Monty Woolley in *Since You Went Away* (1944).

and over-sentimental. James Agee, in his critique in the "Nation," best described it: "David O. Selznick's *Since You Went Away* is a movie about an American home in wartime. It is clear that Mr. Selznick thinks of it as *the* American home and that the Hiltons, who live in it, are supposed to be *the* American family. I even suspect that Selznick, who is nothing if not ambitious, hoped to make it a contemporary native equivalent to the home-front section of 'War and Peace.' What he managed, instead, is an immense improvement on a 'Ladies' Home Journal' story so sticky I couldn't get through it, which has, as he finished it, something of the charm of an updated and cellophaned 'Little Women'." Agee went on to say, "It is thus, too, in their wonderful blend of acute authenticity with authentic self-delusion, that I accept most of the things the Hiltons and their friends do, not to mention Mr. Selznick's masterpiece, the Hilton Home — one of those pitiful suburban brick things which is indeed *the* American home if you agree with me that seven out of ten Americans would sell their souls for it."

In 1944, just as shooting on *Since You Went Away* had finished, Selznick hired as his Feminine Director, Anita Colby, "The Face," then the world's most famous model. She was born Anita Catherine Counihan in New York City in 1914, the daughter of cartoonist Daniel "Bud" F. Counihan. In her twenties she became the world's highest paid model ($50 an hour) and was christened "The Face" by Quentin Reynolds. In 1935, she tired of modeling and made a stab at being an actress. RKO hired her and cast her in *Mary of Scotland* (1936) where her one line was, "Oh, this wretched fog!" A few more RKO B's followed after which she left RKO to become a pitch-man for "Harper's Bazaar." This led to her return to Hollywood where she was an actress, script adviser and Technical Adviser for Columbia's *Cover Girl* (1944). The ballyhoo over that successful picture and Miss Colby's growing reputation as an able lady executive led Selznick to hire her at his Feminine Director from 1944-1947.

On *Since You Went Away*, Miss Colby was only involved in the promotional publicity, but she helped create such a whirlwind of public interest that the Gallup poll gave the picture a ninety percent "Desire To See," which was almost as good as *Gone With the Wind*. During the next three years, Miss Colby became an integral part of the Selznick product because of her knack for grooming the Selznick Players for stardom and plotting their publicity campaigns. Of working with Selznick, she says, "David was my best man friend. He worked you hard — all hours, forgetting everything: food, sleep, appointments, and you did, too, when you were working on a project. One thing no one has been able to capture was his sense of humour — especially about himself. He was warm and thoughtful; he was cold and thoughtless, but aren't we all when we love the work we are doing. It is pretty obvious *Gone With the Wind* is still the greatest picture ever made — no one has been able to top it yet."

She left Selznick in 1947, to become Executive Assistant to Henry Ginsberg, vice-president in charge of production of Paramount Pictures where her salary was $150,000 a year, with a reputation as America's top lady executive. She went on to write a column for King Features called "Colby's Carousel;" published a book entitled "Anita Colby's Beauty Book;" performed a six-month stint as NBC television's anchor girl on the "Today" show (she hired Barbara Walters to write her scripts), and organised, with a financial share, Dr. Erno Laszlo's cosmetic firm. During her heyday as a trail-blazing lady executive she had no time for marriage. She turned down marriage proposals from Clark Gable and James Stewart and says, "I introduced them to their wives." And she once arranged for Sir Winston Churchill to meet his favourite actress, Greta Garbo. In 1969, she met Palen Flagler, corporate vice-president of J.P. Stevens and Company, and they were married on December 30, 1970. Retired, she now lives with her husband in Stockton, New Jersey, and is writing a second book of memoirs.

In addition to resuming his own production career with *Since You Went Away,* Selznick formed a partnership with screenwriter, Dore Schary, and established a subsidiary company called Vanguard Productions. Schary had formerly been employed by M-G-M, where he had written the screenplays for a number of that company's successful pictures, including *Boy's Town* (1938) for which he received the Academy Award. When Louis B. Mayer rejected several of Schary's story ideas as being too socially-

Dore Schary

conscious, Schary walked out. His agreement with Selznick allowed him to write and produce pictures of his choice and draw upon the Selznick Players for his casting. In 1963, Selznick said of Schary, "I thought more of him as a picture man than M-G-M apparently did at the time. I told him that we were miles apart politically — he was left-wing Democrat and I was a Republican — but that I never considered it my privilege to quarrel with the politics of an associate or employee and indeed had very few Republicans in my employ. I told him I didn't try to use my films to sell politics and wouldn't subscribe to his using his pictures to sell his, since we were using money that belonged to banks and their depositors to make pictures for audiences which presumably came to be entertained."

Their first co-production was *I'll Be Seeing You* (1944), an offbeat wartime romance between a shell-shocked soldier, Joseph Cotten, and a female ex-convict, Ginger Rogers. Selznick was not at all keen on the story, but when Schary bet him he could come up with a committment from a major actress, Selznick okayed the project and allowed him to borrow Joseph Cotten and Shirley Temple from the Selznick Players. Selznick handled the publicity campaign and obtained the title song. (The story had originally been called "Double Furlough.") It was a success despite the nature of its subject and Cotten turned in one of his best performances.

That picture was released through United Artists according to Selznick's releasing deal with that corporation, but shortly thereafter, Selznick sold back his share of United Artists, when its controllers, led by Mary Pickford, accused him of not delivering the goods. Selznick and Schary were associated on six more pictures which they released through RKO, and all but one used Selznick Players: Dorothy McGuire and Rhonda Fleming in *The Spiral Staircase* (1946); Dorothy McGuire and Guy Madison in *Till the End of Time* (1946); Joseph Cotten in *The Farmer's Daughter* (1947); Shirley Temple in *The Bachelor and the Bobby-Soxer* (1947); and Joseph Cotten and a new Selznick acquisition, Alida Valli, in *Walk Softly, Stranger* (1950). Only *Mr. Blandings Builds His Dream House* (1948) starring Cary Grant and Myrna Loy, did not use Selznick Players in the cast.

The last major star that Selznick added to his Players was Gregory Peck, in 1945. Selznick had tested the tall, handsome actor in 1942, at the time of his stage success in "The Morning Star" but felt he was not star potential, was too Lincolnesque, and his ears were too big. Shades of Clark Gable! However, by 1944, Peck had made a successful screen debut in *Days of Glory* at RKO, and all Hollywood studios were clamouring for his services. Peck's agent, the keen-minded Leland Hayward, kept him from signing an exclusive contract, but instead signed deals with several companies. Peck made a deal with producer-writer Casey Robinson, which Robinson shared with RKO, then Hayward had him sign multiple picture deals with M-G-M and 20th Century - Fox. Selznick also acquired him for a multi-picture deal and used him in his next three productions: *Spellbound* (1945), *Duel In the Sun* (1946) and *The Paradine Case* (1947).

Spellbound, one of the first psychiatric thrillers, was based on "The House of Dr. Edwards" by Francis Beeding. Selznick hired Ben Hecht to write the screenplay and Salvador Dali to create a surrealistic dream sequence. Directed by Alfred Hitchcock and using three of the Selznick Players, Ingrid Bergman, Peck and Rhonda Fleming, it was a Freudian melodrama about a psychiatrist, Ingrid Bergman, who suspects the head of a mental institution, Gregory Peck, is an amnesiac and possibly a murderer. Its psychology was more sophomoric than introspective but its over-produced special effects and haunting score made it immensely popular. Miklos Rozsa received the Academy Award for his music and the picture is listed by "Variety" as one of the all-time top grossers — $4,975,000.

Selznick also hired Ben Hecht to script another, and better, thriller, *Notorious* (1946) and sold the script, the director, Alfred Hitchcock, and the star, Ingrid Bergman, to RKO in 1945, for $800,000, twice the amount he had invested in the project.

That same year, in August, he signed an agreement with British film magnate J. Arthur Rank, to co-produce pictures in Great Britain under a new company to be called Selznick International Pictures of England, Ltd. Their first project was to have been a $5,000,000 production of *Mary Magdalene* starring Ingrid Bergman and Joseph Cotten and was to have been filmed on location in England and Palestine. At the same time, Rank over-committed himself by making a distribution deal with Universal-International and asked Selznick what it would cost for him to get out of his contract. Selznick, then busy with his production of *Duel In the Sun*, answered by tearing up the contract.

Selznick had purchased the rights to Niven Busch's lusty novel, "Duel In the Sun," and assigned its adaptation to screenwriter H.P. Garrett, saying, "I want this to be an artistic little western." Production began with Jennifer Jones as the star in March, 1945, and Selznick's obsession with having to top *Gone With the Wind* soon grew out of proportion and the picture became a colossal, Technicolor, all-star production that took twenty months to complete. Selznick wrote the screenplay himself and cast Joseph Cotten and Gregory Peck as the two brothers and completed the cast by hiring Walter Huston, Lionel Barrymore, Lillian Gish, Herbert Marshall, Harry Carey, Tilly Losch and Charles Bickford. He contracted King Vidor to direct and hired Josef von Sternberg, the director who had almost single-handedly created the image that *is* Marlene Dietrich, as lighting director to properly showcase Miss Jones. Selznick wrote and re-wrote the script, hired assistant directors for extraneous scenes and demanded that Vidor follow Selznick's interpretation of the script. Vidor finally quit under this harassment and William Dieterle was called in to finish the picture. The cost mounted to $4,255,000, more than had been spent on *Gone With the Wind*, and Selznick spent still another million dollars on one of the most extensive publicity campaigns ever conceived for a film. *Duel In the Sun* was a brutal, sadistic and fascinating western which critics hated and which the public flocked to see. It has grossed $11,300,000.

During production on this picture, on April 29, 1945 — his sixteenth wedding anniversary — Selznick came home to find his bags packed and waiting for him in the foyer. His wife, Irene, said she could no longer live with him. For some time all of Hollywood and Irene had been aware of Selznick's infatuation with Jennifer Jones. When Irene could no longer ignore the gossip, she demanded they separate. They were divorced in January, 1949, and Irene gained custody of their two sons — Lewis Jeffrey (born 1932) and Daniel Mayer (born 1936). (Both sons are now motion-picture producers.) Irene Mayer Selznick moved to New York City where she embarked upon a career as a theatrical producer. Two of her outstanding successes were "A Streetcar Named Desire" and "Bell, Book and Candle." When once discussing her dynamic father, Louis B. Mayer, and her equally dynamic husband, David O. Selznick, she remarked, "Where there are men like that around, a woman either withdraws completely into her shell and thickens it as fast as she can, or she sticks her neck out and develops muscle she never knew she had before."

Olivia de Havilland, a close friend of both Selznick and his wife, Irene, says of their marriage, "David and Irene were a unit. They gave a special warmth and affection to their friends while together which they were never able to give again after they were divorced. They never realised how right they were for each other."

To release his production of *Duel in the Sun*, Selznick set up the Selznick Releasing Organization. "It enabled me to practice what I had long preached and to prove that the whole method of distribution was wasteful and completely outmoded. Within a matter of weeks, I opened branch offices — not exchanges — in thirty key cities and arranged for the physical distribution of films through existing non-theatrical channels on a per shipment basis. I thereby cut the distribution costs sixty percent, even though I had extremely few pictures, and got far more efficient distribution. Moreover, it proved that it was unnecessary to make pictures no one wanted to see in order to absorb overhead, which in most cases was absurdly inflated. I effected similar savings in other countries. *Duel In the Sun*, which had attained one of the highest grosses, was distributed by my own sales department at a fraction of the distribution costs of other pictures. I also was able to make a large saving on print costs."

During this time, Selznick embarked upon a re-make of *Little Women* (1933), a picture on which he had done preliminary preparations before leaving RKO to join M-G-M. He obtained the re-make rights to this picture when he loaned Ingrid Bergman to RKO to star in *The Bells of St. Mary's*. His version was to star Jennifer Jones, Dorothy McGuire, Shirley Temple, Diana Lynn and Guy Madison, but he shelved the production after three months because of script problems. He sold the re-make rights to M-G-M who filmed it in 1949, starring June Allyson, Elizabeth Taylor, Janet Leigh and Margaret O'Brien.

Selznick released his next two productions — *The Paradine Case* (1947) and *Portrait of Jennie* (1948) — through his Selznick Releasing Organization.

The Paradine Case was Alfred Hitchcock's last directorial committment before his contract with Selznick expired, and through Selznick's over meticulous involvement, became an over-produced, all-star production. Alma Reville, Hitchcock's wife, adapted Robert Hichens's novel, and once again Selznick wrote the screenplay. He cast Gregory Peck, Ann Todd, Charles

On the set of *The Paradine Case* (1947). Left to right: *standing:* Alfred Hitchcock, Louis Jourdan, David O. Selznick, Charles Laughton, Charles Coburn, Gregory Peck, *sitting:* Joan Tetzel, Ann Todd and Ethel Barrymore.

Laughton, Ethel Barrymore, Charles Coburn, Leo G. Carroll and two new Selznick Players — Louis Jourdan and Alida Valli. It cost $4,000,000 to make and was a box-office flop.

Portrait of Jennie was another ode to Jennifer Jones and production on this picture similarly got out of hand. What was a charming fantasy about an artist, Joseph Cotten, and the ghost (Jennifer Jones) of his inspiration, became on film another expensive, superfluous motion picture. This time it was not because Selznick was too much involved in the project but just the opposite. He was busy completing *The Paradine Case,* unraveling the problems of the Selznick Releasing Organization and negotiating with Greta Garbo to make her comeback as Sarah Bernhardt. *Portrait of Jennie* was directed by William Dieterle but when Selznick saw the rushes he was disappointed and tacked on a new ending — a snow storm filmed in stereophonic sound. It didn't work; it was a flop in the United States, but in Europe it received favourable reviews and earned Joseph Cotten the Venice Film Festival Award as Best Actor of the Year. It also was the last picture Selznick would produce in this country and marked the end of the Selznick Players as a stock company.

Selznick had planned to enlarge his production schedule through arrangements with three producers, each of whom would deliver three pictures a year to the Selznick Releasing Organization. Some of these pictures would be used to develop the young talents he had under contract — Louis Jourdan, Rory Calhoun, Guy Madison, John Agar, Kim Hunter, Alida Valli, Joan Tetzel and Hildegarde Neff.

The three producers involved were Dore Schary, Mark Hellinger and M.J. Siegel (President of Republic Pictures). Hellinger and Siegel died suddenly, and Schary left Selznick's Vanguard Productions to become vice-president in charge of production for RKO, succeeding Charles W. Koerner. These incidents discouraged Selznick from continuing production, let alone expanding it. He said, "I stopped making films in 1948, because I was tired: I had been producing, at that time, for more then twenty years. I wanted to do some traveling that I had completely denied myself during my long concentration on work in Hollywood, and I felt I could combine business with pleasure by exploiting my backlog of films throughout the world."

He closed the Selznick studio, sold its physical inventory at public auction and the company's assets for $5,000,000. For an additional $1,500,000, he sold his remaining contractual committments to Warner Brothers for Gregory Peck, Joseph Cotten, Shirley Temple, Louis Jourdan and Rory Calhoun. The other members of his stock company had left the studio as their contracts had expired, and Vivien Leigh had broken her contract in 1945.

After closing the studio, Selznick signed a deal to co-produce with Alexander Korda. Their first production was the classic thriller, *The Third Man* (1950), a project with which Selznick was only slightly involved but which was exhibited in this country by the Selznick Releasing Organization. Their second venture was a film based on the novel "Gone to Earth" by Mary Webb, and despite the fact that Jennifer Jones was the star, Selznick again was not closely involved with the picture. After seeing the finished product, however, Selznick was appalled by the picture's mediocrity and filed a law suit against Korda. In May, 1950, the British courts ruled in favour of Selznick granting him 1) unconditional release rights to *The Third Man* and *Gone to Earth*, 2) world rights to *Gone to Earth* after ten years from its initial release, and 3) Korda's obligation to shoot additional scenes to *Gone to Earth* and pay half the cost of these scenes. Selznick had director Rouben Mamoulian come in to shoot these additional scenes. The picture was finally released in 1952, under the title, *The Wild Heart*, but the extra scenes were unable to give it any boost at the box-office.

In the spring of 1949, while Jennifer Jones was in England starring in *Gone to Earth,* Selznick persuaded her to marry him. Although there are those who say Miss Jones had set her sights on Selznick as a husband several years before, she was reluctant to say yes to his proposal because she thought it "unwise." But as always, Selznick's resolute determination won out. That summer he rented a yacht on the Riviera, and on July 13, 1949, they were married, with Mr. and Mrs. Leland Hayward and Mr. and Mrs. Louis Jourdan as witnesses. Later that day, to assure the legality of the marriage, they were married a second time in the city hall in Genoa, Italy. Their daughter, Mary Jennifer, was born on August 12, 1954.

After the failure of his association with Korda, Selznick remained inactive until the time of the death of Jennifer Jones' first husband, Robert Walker, on August 28, 1951. Miss Jones and Walker had divorced in 1945, and Walker's career had been ruined by his alcoholism. Miss Jones was so shaken by his death that Selznick felt it best for her to be busy working. His course of action was to form a partnership with Italian director, Vittorio De Sica, to produce a picture called *Terminal Station*, the story of a married American woman, Jennifer Jones, saying goodbye to her young Italian lover, Montgomery Clift, in the Rome railroad station. It was a static, talky, interminable bore which Selznick tried to salvage by editing it and releasing it under the marquee-less title — *Indiscretion of an American Wife* (1954). It was another disaster at the box-office for Miss Jones.

For the next three years, except for guiding Miss Jones' career, Selznick's only creative output was a two-hour televison special celebrating the 75th Anniversary of Thomas Edison's discovery of the electric light. Entitled "*Light's Diamond Jubilee,*" he hired Ben Hecht to write the script and King Vidor, William A. Wellman and Norman Taurog to direct. It was broadcast on October 24, 1954, simultaneously by CBS and NBC and was a great success. Joseph Cotten, an ex-Selznick Player, narrated.

Also in 1954, he oversaw the Broadway debut of his wife in Henry James' "Portrait of a Lady," a venture which proved unsuccessful. In the interim, there were frequent announcements regarding his future plans. He announced a production of "War and Peace" then cancelled it when both Mike Todd and Dino de Laurentiis announced their plans to film the same Tolstoy novel. There were also plans to produce two pictures for M-G-M, a Biblical series on television, and a three-year contract proposal with RKO. While these projects never materialised, Selznick nevertheless kept himself more than occupied by sending reams of memos to Jennifer Jones' directors. Some of the noteworthy recipients were John Huston on *Beat the Devil* (1954); Henry King on *Love Is a Many-Splendored Thing* (1955); Henry Koster on *Good Morning, Miss Dove* (1955); Nunnally Johnson on *The Man In the Gray Flannel Suit* (1956), and Sidney Franklin on *The Barretts of Wimpole Street* (1957).

Finally, with great ballyhoo, Selznick announced his return to producing with Ernest Hemingway's *A Farewell to Arms* (1957) with Jennifer Jones and Rock Hudson as the stars. He had acquired the rights to this novel from Warner Brothers by selling them the negative to his 1937 production of *A Star Is Born* (which they remade in 1954 starring Judy Garland) and by paying them an additional $25,000. He informed his public relations representative, Arthur Jacobs, that *A Farewell to Arms* would be publicised as a successor to *Gone With the Wind*. He chose to produce the picture in Italy, which he later admitted was a mistake, but even a bigger mistake, which he failed to acknowledge, was casting Jennifer Jones as Catherine Barkley. She was simply too old for the part. He hired John Huston to direct and, as in the old days, became personally involved in every aspect of the production. Huston, a strong-minded individualist, did not cotton to Selznick's meddling. They differed over interpretations and Selznick fired Huston saying, "In Huston I asked for a first violinist and instead got a soloist." He replaced Huston with Charles Vidor, and Vidor's widow, Doris Warner Vidor (daughter of Harry Warner and formerly married to Mervyn LeRoy), recalls the production vividly, "Charles accepted the job because he liked David and because we thought it would be fun to pack the children off to Rome. But as it turned out, it was anything but fun. It was *ghastly!* Every time a scene was shot, David would send Charles a memo dissatisfied over something involving Jennifer. No matter how small — such as there's a line under her chin — or those beautiful apple cheeks are not shown to full advantage. And, he kept rewriting the script, some times having it delivered to Charles' hotel after midnight, and many times I simply did not even wake him up. Also, Jennifer would move out of one villa and into a hotel, then into another villa, then another hotel; some close to the studio, some away from the studio. She could not make up her mind where she wanted to live. All during these delays and problems, Rock Hudson, who ate dinner with Charles and me almost every night, was a perfect gentlemen and never displayed any temperament and would have had the right to do so.

"When we first saw the picture in the United States, there were scenes that Charles had never shot, whole interludes that someone else had shot, and all the continuity was lost because of the emphasis on Jennifer, who was miscast from the beginning. During production Charles said, 'This picture is going to kill me.' (Vidor suffered a heart attack and died during production of *Song Without End* (1960) in 1959. George Cukor took over that picture.) Mrs. Vidor adds, 'When Charles died Rock was a great comfort to me.' "

A Farewell to Arms cost $3,500,000 and to-date has grossed $5,000,000. Ben Hecht's script took gross liberties with Hemingway's novel and the picture's failure at the box-office was a personal defeat which Selznick was never able to forget. It was the last film he ever produced.

One project both he and Jennifer had wanted to produce for many years was a film version of F. Scott Fitzgerald's *Tender Is the Night* (1961) with Miss Jones playing Nicole. Selznick owned the screen rights to the novel and had worked out many of the details of the picture with his wife. In first discussing the casting of Dick Diver, they listed several possibilities: Laurence Olivier, Cary Grant, Christopher Plummer, Robert Mitchum, Henry Fonda and Gregory Peck. When approached by Selznick about the picture, Peck said he saw "no point in making a picture about people who contributed nothing to the American scene." Miss Jones's choice for the male lead was William Holden, who had been her co-star in the very popular *Love Is a Many-Splendored Thing* in 1955. Finally, Selznick prepared the script himself with the help of screenwriter Ivan Moffatt and sold it to 20th Century-Fox with his wife as the star. Among the suggestions he made for casting were Richard Burton or Peter O'Toole as Dick Diver (played by Jason Robards Jr.); Montgomery Clift or Fred Astaire as Abe (played by Tom Ewell); Jane Fonda as Rosemary (played by Jill St. John); Louis Jourdan or Marcello Mastroianni as Tommy Barban (played by Cesare Danova), and either Peter Ustinov or Joseph Schildkraut in the role played by Sanford Meisner. Presumably Selznick's agreement with 20th Century-Fox allowed him approval of any script changes and casting, but Spyros Skouras's money-minded regime at 20th Century-Fox chose to ignore Selznick's advice and the picture was an inept dramatisation of Fitzgerald's work. In an angry but futile memo to the film's producer, Henry Weinstein, Selznick complained, "It just makes me sick at my stomach, and angers me to see the sloppiness with which pictures are made today, including, I'm sorry, to say, *Tender Is the Night*. In this, as in all other departments, these are the functions of the *producer*." When the picture was released, everyone concerned wished that Selznick had produced it himself.

In 1961, Selznick, along with Vivien Leigh and Olivia de Havilland, attended the Civil War Centennial in Atlanta, Georgia, where a screening of *Gone With the Wind* was the highlight of the festivities. Miss de Havilland recalled that occasion for the author: "David was an ebullient man. He had a radiant energy and a radiant manner. I met him at the Plaza Hotel in New York City to accompany him to Atlanta. His now-gray hair and those brown eyes made him more attractive but he seemed drained. He had an attitude of physical, emotional and psychological exhaustion. I was shocked by this alteration in his attitude. That evening in Atlanta, the applause was tremendous and he began to understand and appreciate *once again* the magnitude of that accomplishment and when he got up on stage, he came to life. That radiant energy and manner reappeared."

Selznick was never able to forget the disappointments of *A Farewell to Arms* and *Tender Is the Night,* and he knew that it was unlikely he would ever produce again. In the winter of 1964 , Jennifer Jones was in Florida appearing in a play by Patricia Joudry called "The Man With the Perfect Wife." In New York, Selznick attended a party at the home of his old friend, Arthur Hornblow Jr., at which his ex-wife, Irene, was present. In the middle of the party, guests noticed that Selznick was missing and found him slumped across a bed. He had suffered a mild heart attack. Irene accompanied him home to his suite in the Waldorf Towers and upon entering the hotel, he was stricken again. He was taken to the hospital where he remained ten days.

When he returned home, he knew his career was over. On the morning of June 22, 1965, he went to the Beverly Hills office of his attorney, Barry Brannan, where he was stricken with another attack. He was rushed to Mount Sinai Hospital, where, at 2:22 p.m., he was pronounced dead from a coronary occlusion.

In one of his memos, Selznick had dictated that he wanted a simple funeral so that no one would be bored. His sons, Jeffrey and Daniel, arranged the funeral at the Church of Recessional in the Forest Lawn Memorial Park. Joseph Cotten read the eulogy, "Greatness in a man makes him larger than life. This was not true of David Selznick. He was very much a part of life." Cary Grant read words written by William Paley: "I cannot help but think that our world will never be the same — nor will heaven. And if we are lucky enough to get there too, David will see that all the arrangements are made." George Cukor read words written by Truman Capote: "We have lost an irreplaceable individualist who was as tender as he was tenacious, as courageous as competitive, as inventive as ingenious, as sensitive as stalwart." At the request of Selznick's widow, Jennifer Jones, Katharine Hepburn recited Rudyard Kipling's

George Cukor

poem, "If." Irene Mayer Selznick remained in New York.

The New York "Herald-Tribune" editorialised: "David O. Selznick was one of that small band of film giants of whom it can truly be said that Hollywood — at its best — is their monument. A fierce attention to detail; a passionate devotion to his tasks; an unmistakable faith that better pictures were worth making, and worth whatever effort was needed to make them better; all these contributed to the Selznick legend and to the Selznick legacy. That legacy is measured, in part, by the extraordinary list of films he produced — *Gone With the Wind, Rebecca, A Star Is Born* and any number of other all-time classics."

And perhaps Selznick is better remembered by those who worked for him and with him than by any obituaries. Two of those people speak eloquently and respectfully.

His East Coast right arm for many years, Kay Brown, says, "Yes, he was a mad man at times, a monster — he never took no for an answer even if it were impossible, but while the work was hard, we were all working together and the results made the effort worth it. I remember one time we were all in Atlanta on the search for Scarlett O'Hara, and I got so angry at David for some reason I have now forgotten, and took the train back to New York. I came home, took out all his memos, threw them on the floor and walked on them in my spiked heels. Just then the telephone rang and it was David, and before I knew what happened, he had talked me into getting the next train back to Atlanta. He had a brilliant, inventive mind, and a great sense of humor."

George Cukor says, "He was a charming, warm, extraordinary man, not a monster. He was in the unfortunate position of always having to top *Gone With the Wind*. He was a tycoon, a showman with love and enthusiasm for movies. All this business about tycoons all being pants pressers is a lot of bullshit. They didn't intellectualise, but they were intelligent, and they had an instinct and they worked to gain experience which is reflected in their work. All of today's intellectualising is a bore."

The Feature Film Productions of David O. Selznick as Independent Producer

Little Lord Fauntleroy (Selznick International-United Artists, 1936). Screenplay by Hugh Walpole from the novel by Frances Hodgson Burnett. Directed by John Cromwell. *Cast:* Freddie Bartholomew, Dolores Costello, C. Aubrey Smith, Guy Kibbee, Mickey Rooney, Jessie Ralph, Jackie Searle, Helen Flint, Una O'Connor, E.E. Clive, Ivan Simpson.

The Garden of Allah (Selznick International-United Artists, 1936). Screenplay by W.P. Lipscomb and Lynn Riggs from the novel by Robert Hichens. Directed by Richard Boleslawski. *Cast:* Marlene Dietrich, Charles Boyer, Basil Rathbone, C. Aubrey Smith, Tilly Losch, Joseph Schildkraut, John Carradine, Alan Marshall, Lucile Watson, Henry Brandon, Helen Jerome Eddy, Charles Waldron, John Bryan, Nigel De Brulier, Pedro De Cordoba, Ferdinand Gottschalk, Adrian Rosely, "Corky," Robert Frazer, David Scott, Andrew McKenna, Bonita Granville, Marcia Mae Jones, Betty Jane Graham, Ann Gillis, Marion Soyers, Betty Van

Auken, Edna Harris, Frances Turnham, Leonid Kinsky, Louis Aldez, Barry Downing, Jane Kerr, Russell Powell, Eric Alden, Michael Mark, Harlan Briggs, Irene Franklin, Louis Mercier, Marcel De La Brosse, Robert Stevenson.

A Star Is Born (Selznick International-United Artists, 1937). Screenplay by Dorothy Parker, Alan Campbell and Robert Carson from a story by William A. Wellman and Robert Carson. Directed by William A. Wellman. *Cast:* Janet Gaynor, Fredric March, Adolphe Menjou, Andy Devine, May Robson, Lionel Stander, Owen Moore, Elizabeth Jenns, J.C. Nugent, Clara Blandick, A.W. Sweatt, Peggy Wood, Franklin Pangborn, Edgar Kennedy, Adrian Rosely, Arthur Hoyt, Edwin Maxwell, Quinn Williams, Vince Barnett, Paul Stanton, Robert Emmett O'Connor, Olin Howland, Irving Bacon, Jonathan Hale, Francis Ford, Pat Flaherty, Bill Dooley, Snowflake, Dennis O'Keefe, George Chandler, Jed Prouty, Trixie Friganza, Jane Barnes.

The Prisoner of Zenda (Selznick International-United Artists, 1937) Screenplay by John Balderston, adapted by Wells Root from Edward Rose's dramatisation of the novel by Anthony Hope, Directed by John Cromwell *Cast:* Ronald Colman, Madeleine Carroll, Douglas Fairbanks Jr., Mary Astor, C. Aubrey Smith, Raymond Massey, David Niven, Montagu Love, William von Brincken, Philip Sleeman, Torben Meyer, Byron Foulger, Lawrence Grant, Ian McLaren, Ralph Faulkner, Howard Lang, Ben Webster, Evelyn Beresford, Boyd Irwin, Emmett King, Al Shean, Charles Halton, Francis Ford, Spencer Charters.

Nothing Sacred (Selznick International-United Artists, 1937). Screenplay by Ben Hecht from a story by James H. Street. Directed by William A. Wellman. *Cast:* Carole Lombard, Fredric March, Charles Winninger, Walter Connolly, Sig Rumann, Frank Fay, Raymond Scott and his Quintet, Maxie Rosenbloom, Alex Schoenberg, Monty Woolley, Alex Novinsky, Margaret Hamilton, Troy Brown, Hattie McDaniel, Katherine Shelton, Olin Howland, Ben Morgan, Hans Steinke, George Chandler, Claire DuBrey, Nora Cecil, Hedda Hopper, John Qualen, Art Lasky, Ernest Whitman, Everett Brown, A.W. Sweatt, Vera Lewis, Ann Doran, Jinx Falkenburg, Bill Dunn, Lee Phelps, Cyril Ring, Mickey McMasters, Bobby Tracy.

The Adventures of Tom Sawyer (Selznick International-United Artists, 1938). Screenplay by John V.A. Weaver from the story by Mark Twain. Directed by Norman Taurog. *Cast:* Tommy Kelly, Ann Gillis, May Robson, Walter Brennan, Jackie Moran, Victor Jory, David Holt, Victor Kilian, Nana Bryant, Olin Howland, Donald Meek, Charles Richman, Margaret Hamilton, Marcia Mae Jones, Mickey Rentschler, Cora Sue Collins, Philip Hurlie, Spring Byington, David Holt, Georgie Billings, Byron Armstrong, Harry C. Myers.

The Young In Heart (Selznick International-United Artists, 1938) Screenplay by Paul Osborn and Charles Bennett from the novel, "The Gay Banditti" by I.A.R. Wylie. Directed by Richard Wallace. *Cast:* Janet Gaynor, Roland Young, Billie Burke, Douglas Fairbanks Jr., Richard Carlson, Minnie Dupree, Paulette Goddard, Henry Stephenson, Eily Maylon, Tom Ricketts, Irwin S. Cobb, Margaret Early, Lucile Watson, Ian McLaren, Billy Brown, Lawrence Grant, Walter Kingsford, Lionel Pape, George Sorrell, Georges Renevant.

Made For Each Other (Selznick International-United Artists, 1939). Screenplay by Jo Swerling from a story by Rose Franken. Directed by John Cromwell. *Cast:* Carole Lombard, James Stewart, Charles Coburn, Lucile Watson, Eddie Quillan, Alma Kruger, Ruth Weston, Donald Briggs, Harry Davenport, Esther Dale, Renee Orsell, Louise Beavers, Ward Bond, Olin Howland, Fern Emmett, Bonnie Belle Barber, Jackie Taylor, Mickey Rentschler, Ivan Simpson, Fred Ruller, Edwin Maxwell, Harry Depp, Robert Emmett O'Connor, Milburn Stone, Robert Strange, Perry Ivans, Gladden James, Arthur Hoyt, Harlan Briggs, Betty Farrington, Ruth Gillette, Jack Mulhall, Russell Hopton, Lane Chandler, Tom London, Harry Worth, Raymond Bailey, J.M. Sullivan.

Intermezzo: A Love Story (Selznick International-United Artists, 1939). Screenplay by George O'Neil from the Swedish scenario by Gosta Stevens and Gustaf Molander. Directed by Gregory Ratoff. *Cast:* Leslie Howard, Ingrid Bergman, Edna Best, John Halliday, Cecil Kellaway, Enid Bennett, Ann Todd, Douglas Scott, Eleanor Wesselhoeft, Moira Flynn.

Gone With the Wind (Selznick International-M-G-M, 1939). Screenplay by Sidney Howard from the novel by Margaret Mitchell. Directed by Victor Fleming. *Cast:* Clark Gable, Vivien Leigh, Leslie Howard, Olivia de Havilland, Hattie McDaniel, Thomas Mitchell, Barbara O'Neil. Laura Hope Crews, Harry Davenport, Ona Munson, Evelyn Keyes, Ann Rutherford, Butterfly McQueen, Alicia Rhett, Everett Brown, Eddie Anderson, Rand Brooks. Carrol Nye, Jane Darwell, Mary Anderson, Isabel Jewell, Victor Jory, Yakima Canutt, Cammie King, Lillian Kemple Cooper, Ward Bond, Paul Hurst, George Reeves, Fred Crane.

Rebecca (Selznick International - United Artists, 1940) Screenplay by Robert E. Sherwood and Joan Harrison from an adaptation by Philip MacDonald and Michael Hogan of the novel by Daphne du Maurier. Directed by Alfred Hitchcock. *Cast:* Laurence Olivier, Joan Fontaine, George Sanders, Judith Anderson, Nigel Bruce, Reginald Denny, C. Aubrey Smith, Gladys Cooper, Florence Bates, Melville Cooper, Leo G. Carroll, Leonard Carey, Lumsden Hare, Edward Fielding, Philip Winter, Forrester Harvey.

Since You Went Away (Selznick International-United Artists, 1944). Screenplay by David O. Selznick from the novel by Margaret Buell Wilder. Directed by John Cromwell. *Cast:* Claudette Colbert, Jennifer Jones, Joseph Cotten, Shirley Temple, Monty Woolley, Lionel Barrymore, Robert Walker, Hattie McDaniel, Agnes Moorehead, Guy Madison, Craig Stevens, Keenan Wynn, Albert Basserman, Nazimova, Lloyd Corrigan, Jackie Moran, Gordon Oliver, Jane Devlin, Ann Gillis, Dorothy (Cindy) Garner, Andrew McLaglen, Jill Warren, Helen Koford (Terry Moore), Robert Johnson, Dorothy Dandridge, Johnny Bond, Irving Bacon, George Chandler, Addison Richards, Barbara

Pepper, Byron Foulger, Edwin Maxwell, Florence Bates, Theodor Von Eltz, Adeline de Walt Reynolds, Doodles Weaver, Warren Hymer, Jonathan Hale, Eilene Janssen, William B. Davidson, Ruth Roman, Rhonda Fleming.

Spellbound (Selznick International-United Artists, 1945). Screenplay by Ben Hecht from Angus MacPhail's adaptation of the novel, "The House of Doctor Edwards," by Francis Beeding. Directed by Alfred Hitchcock. *Cast:* Ingrid Bergman, Gregory Peck, Michael Chekhov, Jean Acker, Donald Curtis, Rhonda Fleming, Leo G. Carroll, Norman Lloyd, John Emery, Paul Harvey, Steven Geray, Erskine Sanford, Janet Scott, Victor Kilian, Wallace Ford, Dave Willock, Bill Goodwin, George Meader, Matt Moore, Harry Brown, Art Baker, Regis Toomey, Joel Davis, Clarence Straight, Teddy Infuhr, Richard Bartell, Addison Richards, Edward Fielding.

Duel In the Sun (Selznick Releasing Organization, 1946). Screenplay by David O. Selznick from an adaptation by Oliver H.P. Garrett of the novel by Niven Busch. Directed by King Vidor. *Cast:* Jennifer Jones, Joseph Cotten, Gregory Peck, Lionel Barrymore, Lillian Gish, Walter Huston, Herbert Marshall, Charles Bickford, Joan Tetzel, Harry Carey, Otto Kruger, Sidney Blackmer, Tilly Losch, Scott McKay, Butterfly McQueen, Francis MacDonald, Victor Kilian, Griff Barnett, Frank Cordell, Dan White, Steven Dunhill, Lane Chandler, Lloyd Shaw, Thomas Dillon, Robert McKenzie, Charles Dingle, Kermit Maynard, Hank Bell, Johnny Bond, Bert Roach, Si Jenks, Hank Worden, Rose Plummer, Guy Wilkerson, Lee Phelps. *Narrated by Orson Welles.*

The Paradine Case (Selznick Releasing Corporation, 1947). Screenplay by David O. Selznick from an adaptation by Alma Reville and James Bridie of the novel by Robert Hichens. Directed by Alfred Hitchcock. *Cast:* Gregory Peck, Charles Laughton, Charles Coburn, Ann Todd, Ethel Barrymore, Louis Jourdan, Alida Valli, Leo G. Carroll, Joan Tetzel, Isobel Elsom, Lester Matthews, Pat Aherne, Colin Hunter, John Williams, John Goldsworthy.

Portrait of Jennie (Selznick Releasing Organization, 1948). Screenplay by Paul Osborn and Peter Berneis from the novel by Robert Nathan. Directed by William Dieterle. *Cast:* Jennifer Jones, Joseph Cotten, Ethel Barrymore, Cecil Kellaway, David Wayne, Albert Sharpe, Florence Bates, Lillian Gish, Henry Hull, Esther Somers, Maude Simmons, Felix Bressart, John Farrell, Clem Bevans, Robert Dudley.

The Third Man (Selznick Releasing Organization, 1950). Screenplay by Graham Greene from his own story. Directed by Carol Reed. *Cast:* Joseph Cotten, Trevor Howard, Alida Valli, Orson Welles, Bernard Lee, Ernest Deutsch, Erich Ponto, Siegfried Breuer, Wilfrid Hyde-White, Paul Hoerbiger, Hedwig Bleitreu, Frederick Schehcher, Herbert Mabik, Jenny Wermer, Nelly Amo, Alexis Chesnakov, Leo Rieber.

The Wild Heart (Selznick- RKO, 1952). Screenplay by Michael Powell and Emeric Pressburger from the novel "Gone To Earth," by Mary Webb. Directed by Michael Powell and Emeric Pressburger. *Cast:* Jennifer Jones, Cyril Cusack, David Farrar, Esmond Knight, Sybil Thorndyke, Hugh Griffith, George Cole, Beatrice Varley, Francis Clare, Raymond Rollett, Gerald Lawson. *Narrated by Joseph Cotten.*

Indiscretion of an American Wife (Selznick-Columbia, 1954). Screenplay by Cesare Zavattini, Luigi Chiarini and Georgia Presperi from a story by Cesare Zavattini and dialogue by Truman Capote. Directed by Vittorio De Sica. *Cast:* Jennifer Jones, Montgomery Clift, Gino Cervi, Dick Beymer.

A Farewell To Arms (Selznick-20th Century-Fox, 1957). Screenplay by Ben Hecht from the novel by Ernest Hemingway. Directed by Charles Vidor. *Cast,* Jennifer Jones, Rock Hudson, Vittorio de Sica, Albert Sordi, Kurt Kasznar, Mercedes McCambridge, Oscar Homolka, Elaine Stritch, Leopoldo Trieste, Franco Interlenghi, Jose Bieto, Georges Brehat, Memmo Carotenuto, Guido Martufi, Umberto Spadaro, Umbert Sacripanti, Victor Francen, Joan Shawlee, Alberto D'Amario.

Vivien Leigh and Clark Gable

2

THE STORY OF *Gone With the Wind*

David O. Selznick's
production of
Margaret Mitchell's
Story of the Old South

GONE WITH THE WIND

In Technicolor
A Selznick International Picture
Directed by Victor Fleming
Screenplay by Sidney Howard
Music by Max Steiner
A Metro-Goldwyn-Mayer Release

THE PLAYERS
in the order of their appearance

At Tara
The O'Hara Plantation in Georgia

Brent Tarleton .... Fred Crane
Stuart Tarleton .... George Reeves
Scarlett O'Hara .... Vivien Leigh
Mammy .... Hattie McDaniel
Big Sam .... Everett Brown
Elijah .... Zack Williams
Gerald O'Hara .... Thomas Mitchell
Pork .... Oscar Polk
Ellen O'Hara .... Barbara O'Neil
Jonas Wilkerson .... Victor Jory
Suellen O'Hara .... Evelyn Keyes
Carreen O'Hara .... Ann Rutherford
Prissy .... Butterfly McQueen

At Twelve Oaks
The nearby Wilkes Plantation

John Wilkes .... Howard Hickman
India Wilkes .... Alicia Rhett
Ashley Wilkes .... Leslie Howard
Melanie Hamilton .... Olivia de Havilland
Charles Hamilton .... Rand Brooks
Frank Kennedy .... Carroll Nye
Cathleen Calvert .... Marcella Martin
Rhett Butler .... Clark Gable

At the Bazaar in Atlanta

Aunt "Pittypat" Hamilton .... Laura Hope Crews
Doctor Meade .... Harry Davenport
Mrs. Meade .... Leona Roberts
Mrs. Merriwether .... Jane Darwell
Rene Picard .... Albert Morin
Maybelle Merriwether .... Mary Anderson
Fanny Elsing .... Terry Shero
Old Levi .... William McClain

Outside The Examiner Office

Uncle Peter .... Eddie Anderson
Phil Meade .... Jackie Moran

At The Hospital

Reminiscent Soldier . . . . Cliff Edwards
Belle Watling . . . . Ona Munson
The Sargeant . . . . Ed Chandler
A Wounded Soldier in Pain . . . . George Hackathorne
A Convalescent Soldier . . . . Roscoe Ates
A Dying Soldier . . . . John Arledge
An Amputation Case . . . . Eric Linden

During The Evacuation

A Commanding Office . . . . Tom Tyler

During the Seige

A Mounted Officer . . . . William Bakewell
The Bartender . . . . Lee Phelps

Georgia After Sherman

A Yankee Deserter . . . . Paul Hurst
The Carpetbagger's Friend . . . . Ernest Whitman
A Returning Veteran . . . . William Stelling
A Hungary Soldier . . . . Louis Jean Heydt
Emmy Slattery . . . . Isabel Jewell

During Reconstruction

The Yankee Major . . . . Robert Elliott
His Poker-Playing Captains . . . . George Meeker
Wallis Clark
The Corporal . . . . Irving Bacon
A Carpetbagger Orator . . . . Adrian Morris
Johnny Gallegher . . . . J. M. Kerrigan
A Yankee Businessman . . . . Olin Howland
A Renegade . . . . Yakima Canutt
His Companion . . . . Blue Washington
Tom, A Yankee Captain . . . . Ward Bond
Bonnie Blue Butler . . . . Cammie King
Beau Wilkes . . . . Mickey Kuhn
Bonnie's Nurse . . . . Lillian Kemble Cooper

The spirited and petite Margaret Mitchell—four feet, eleven inches—was born in Atlanta, Georgia, in 1900. Her father, Eugene Mitchell, was a lawyer and had been president of the Atlanta Historical Society. Miss Mitchell was a bright and witty conversationalist who was a welcome guest at dinner parties. She had been writing since childhood, but except for a four year stint as a reporter for the Atlanta "Journal," and an attempt at a novel about the Jazz Age, she never took her writing very seriously. Her one claim to fame was an interview she had conducted with Rudolph Valentino shortly after his flurry of success in *The Sheik*. Of Valentino she said, "He was a plain, nice-spoken, very weary sort of person. I don't think he quite understood why ladies acted the way they did."

After a brief first marriage, she married her ex-husband's best man, John Marsh, an advertising executive. Marsh encouraged his wife's affinity for writing and at his suggestion in 1926, while she was recovering from an accident which had left her walking on crutches, she secretly began work on a novel about the Civil War. Her heroine's name was Pansy O'Hara, and her tentative titles included—"Another Day," "Bugles Sang True," "Not in Our Stars," and "Tote the Weary Load." She began by writing the last chapter first, and during the next nine years, she continued with no particular pattern to add to the manuscript which she kept in a pile of envelopes in a closet. Lois Cole, a lifelong friend of Miss Mitchell's, had become an editor with the publishers Macmillan and Company, and she urged Miss Mitchell to submit the manuscript for publication. Margaret Mitchell refused, saying she was not interested, but finally, in April, 1935, Harold Latham, an editor for Macmillan who was visiting Atlanta, and having been told about the book by Miss Cole, asked to see it. Miss Mitchell replied that she had no book, but her husband pressed her into showing Latham the manuscript. She pulled the envelopes out of the closet and said, "Take the thing before I change my mind." Latham had to purchase an extra suitcase to carry the bulky mass of yellowed papers with him on his journey from Atlanta to New Orleans then back to New York. When he arrived at his hotel in New Orleans, a cable from Miss Mitchell demanded: "Send the manuscript back have changed my mind."

Fortunately, Latham did no such thing but read the manuscript on his way back to New York. Impressed, he began negotiations to have Miss Mitchell finish her incomplete work and ready it for publication. She reluctantly complied, and in her final revisions, made two major changes—one was to alter the name of her heroine to Scarlett, and the other was to chose the final title for the book from the poem "Cynara," by Ernest Dowson: "Gone With the Wind."

Macmillan originally planned to print 10,000 copies of "Gone With the Wind" in May, 1936, but when the Book-of-the-Month Club chose it as their July selection, Macmillan postponed the date until June 30th, and printed 50,000 additional copies. In May, well over one thousand review copies were in the mail to newspapers and editors across the country. One of these copies went to Kay Brown, the Eastern Representative for David O. Selznick.

Overwhelmed by the book, she wired Selznick on May 20, 1936, saying, "We have just air-mailed

Leslie Howard and Olivia de Havilland

detailed synopsis of "Gone With the Wind" by Margaret Mitchell, also copy of book. I beg, urge, coax and plead with you to read this at once. I know that after you read the book you will drop everything and buy it."

When Selznick received Miss Brown's telegram, he was less than enthusiastic about filming a picture about the Civil War, remembering very well the commercial failure of *So Red the Rose* the year before. Directed by the able King Vidor from Stark Young's popular novel and starring Margaret Sullavan, the failure of *So Red the Rose* was too recent to be ignored by the box-office-conscious Selznick. In addition, the asking price for the screen rights was an unprecedented $50,000, the highest ever paid for a book up to that time. However, when John Hay Whitney, chairman of the board of Selznick International, wired Selznick saying that he would buy the screen rights to "Gone With the Wind" if Selznick did not, Selznick said, "This was all the encouragement I needed, and rather than have Jock have the last laugh on me, we went ahead and bought 'Gone With the Wind'."

Doris Warner Vidor, daughter of Harry Warner and widow of director Charles Vidor, told the author that agent Annie Laurie Williams had offered her a two-week option on the screen rights to "Gone With the Wind" in 1936. She took the book to her father and to her uncle, Jack Warner, and they told her to leave the book alone. She later found out that the Motion Picture Producers Association had decided not to make bids on "Gone With the Wind" to prevent the already high asking fee from increasing. She suggested that her then husband, director Mervyn LeRoy, buy the property, but he told her that Civil War stories never sell. She telephoned Pandro S. Berman at RKO, and he said no because the only actress he had to play the part of Scarlett O'Hara was Katharine Hepburn and she was then box-office poison. Mrs. Vidor says she then went to Constance Bennett and remembers sitting up till three o'clock in the morning telling Miss Bennett the plot of the book. She suggested to Miss Bennett that they buy it together for $25,000 each, and that Miss Bennett was at first receptive to the idea, then changed her mind saying it was too much money to spend. Mrs. Vidor adds she is certain the fee paid by Selznick was $52,500.

Leslie Howard.

Selznick signed the contract for the book on July 30th, and took the 1,036 page novel with him on a voyage to Hawaii, during which time he read the book and began making notes for a possible film version. By this time, "Gone With the Wind" had hit the public and become a runaway best-seller, and by Christmas 1936, had already sold its first million copies at $3.00 a copy. Overwhelmingly received by the public, the reviews were not all unanimously favourable, but nonetheless the following April it was awarded the Pulitzer Prize as the best novel of the year. Since then, in countless editions and foreign language translations, it has sold twenty million copies.

Selznick immediately enlisted the aid of playwright Sidney Howard to prepare a shooting script from the book. Working with Selznick and director George Cukor, Howard devised a detailed script that ran to 30,000 words and if filmed verbatim would have made a six-hour motion picture. Selznick, Cukor and Howard revised this script then shelved it. Selznick then began to work on a script of his own and, over the next year, hired no less than nine writers to work on portions of the script for him. These included Oliver H. P. Garrett, Ben Hecht, John Van Druten, Michael Foster, Winston Miller, John Balderston, Edwin Justus Mayer and F. Scott Fitzgerald. Selznick ad-

Laura Hope Crews.

vised all these writers to keep as much of Miss Mitchell's original dialogue as possible and for the most part all they were required to do was to make suggestions as to cutting out unnecessary scenes and advising Selznick on transition from scene to scene. While assessment of the contributions of these men is almost impossible to evaluate, it was Sidney Howard who finally received sole credit for *Gone With the Wind's* screenplay.

After the picture was released, the film's credited director, Victor Fleming, said, "There were only two writers on this script: Margaret Mitchell and David Selznick."

From the beginning of his plans for a film of *Gone With the Wind*, Selznick was aware of two things: The public demanded Clark Gable in the role of Rhett Butler and if Selznick were to be able to acquire Gable for the part, he knew that Louis B. Mayer, his feisty little father-in-law and head of M-G-M who owned Gable's contract, would want a share in the picture; secondly, Selznick knew he would need additional capital to produce the picture.

While Selznick mentioned to Kay Brown the possibility of Ronald Colman playing the part of Rhett Butler, he never really waivered in his opinion that he must borrow Gable from M-G-M, and he knew that M-G-M would only consent to this if the picture were released through that company. In fact, Mayer had offered his son-in-law a casting package-deal: Gable, Joan Crawford as Scarlett O'Hara, Melvyn Douglas as Ashley Wilkes, and Maureen O'Sullivan as Melanie Hamilton. Selznick refused, saying Miss Crawford was not right for the role.

Warner Brothers offered Selznick full financial backing and twenty-five percent of the profits if he would release the picture through their company and cast Errol Flynn as Rhett and Bette Davis as Scarlett, with Olivia de Havilland as Melanie. Miss Davis was the public's first choice as Scarlett and Selznick approved, but since he insisted upon having Gable play Rhett, there was no way that Warner Brothers would allow Miss Davis to appear in a film released by M-G-M. And Miss Davis said she would never play the part if she had to play opposite a miscast Erroll Flynn.

Curiously, Gable did not want to play Rhett Butler and fought the idea. He said, "I never asked for the part. I was one of the last to read Margaret Mitchell's novel and did so only at the urging of friends who insisted that Rhett was so obviously written for me. To them I replied that when the book was being written I was a four-dollar-a-day laborer in Oklahoma and not in anybody's mind for anything, much less the hero in a Civil War novel. My reaction to Rhett was immediate and enthusiastic. 'What a part for Ronald Colman,' I said. I cannot say that I did not want to play Rhett. I did. But he was too popular. Miss Mitchell had etched him into the minds of millions, each of whom knew exactly how Rhett would look and act. It would be impossible to satisfy them all, or even a majority. I knew that. So when Dave Selznick offered me the part, I told him with some pleasure that I was sewed up by my M-G-M contract. And added that I didn't want the part for money, marbles or chalk. He said that he'd try to make a deal with the studio. And since my contract states that I have no choice in roles, I said nothing. I could see myself being sold down the river."

However, being under contract to M-G-M, Gable had no final say in what pictures he was to be cast. If M-G-M and Selznick worked out a deal whereby Selznick could borrow Gable, then Gable was, as all stars who are under contract, obliged to appear in the picture. That is exactly what happened and Gable reluctantly accepted his fate and was never totally happy throughout the filming.

Olivia de Havilland, in a conversation with the author, stated, "Gable was terrified but such fears are not uncommon among movie people. Hollywood people are preoccupied not with success, but with failure. There is a terror of failure. You are always in a state of vertigo. It is like a big black umbrella hovering over you." The main reason Gable could not refuse the part and thereby chance a suspension, was because he was then separated from his second wife, a thrice-divorced Texan named Mrs. Ria Langham, who was demanding a very large financial settlement because of his entanglement with Carole Lombard. Mrs. Langham finally settled for $265,000, and Gable married Miss Lombard on March 29, 1939.

Selznick finally had no choice but to make a deal with M-G-M. It stipulated that M-G-M would loan Gable for the part and 1) M-G-M would have exclusive distribution rights to *Gone With the Wind* and twenty-five percent of the profits for seven years, 2) M-G-M would finance the picture in the amount of $1,250,000, 3) Gable would begin work by February 15, 1939, and not be kept beyond a reasonable time.

While Selznick was negotiating with M-G-M, he knew he could not release the picture until December, 1939, because he was committed to release all his pictures through United Artists until then. This delay in the release of the picture gave Selznick the greatest publicity challenge of his career in deciding how to keep the public's interest alive in the project during that time. It was a challenge which Selznick met with his most famous publicity ploy—the search for Scarlett O'Hara. Selznick enlisted his Director of Advertising and Publicity, Russell Birdwell, in a national campaign to find the actress who would play the most coveted role in film history. Birdwell met his task enthusiastically, and the newspapers gave the campaign unending coverage and the public joined in the guessing game. Birdwell recalls, "When the book came out, the public got in on the so-called casting game which was furthered by starting the search for an unknown girl to play the role of Scarlett O'Hara. At one time we had 110 talent scouts going out across the country beating the bushes—little theatres, campuses, drama classes, night clubs, the stage—looking for an unknown girl. The beating of the bushes resulted in David Selznick looking at more than 2,000 girls, and the public began entering its choices."

During 1937, the public's first choice had been Miriam Hopkins, but by 1938, the race was between Bette Davis and Norma Shearer. When Warner Brothers refused to loan Miss Davis, she was out of the running; and when Miss Shearer's legion of fans wrote letters opposing the idea of the lady-like Miss Shearer playing such a bitchy role, she too relinquished the idea of playing Scarlett O'Hara.

Katharine Hepburn, who had worked with both director George Cukor and Selznick at RKO, said she *was* Scarlett O'Hara and Cukor agreed she would be right in the role. In 1937, Mrs. Ogden Reid, owner of the New York "Herald-Tribune," telephoned Margaret Mitchell in Atlanta, to ask her what she thought of Miss Hepburn as an actress. Miss Mitchell who had positively eschewed having anything to do with the film production of her novel (even refusing to help Sidney Howard in his request for aid in seeing to it that all the actors spoke the proper Southern accents) told Mrs. Reid she thought Miss Hepburn charming in hoop skirts and had enjoyed her performance in *Little Women*. The next day the wire services quoted Miss Mitchell as favoring Miss Hepburn as Scarlett. As a result, Miss Mitchell made a statement to the Associated Press saying, "I have never expressed a preference, and I never will. If Mrs. Reid understood me to say I felt a strong preference for Miss Hepburn in the role, I owe her and Miss Hepburn an apology." To complete the case against Miss Hepburn, Selznick told Cukor that he did not think she was sexy enough for Rhett Butler to pursue for years.

During 1937-38, nearly every actress in Hollywood was mentioned for the part, including Claudette Colbert, Carole Lombard, Margaret Sullavan, Ann Sheridan, Jean Harlow, Irene Dunne and Loretta Young. In addition, Birdwell was doing his best to create an interest across the country and countless unknowns were mentioned for the part. On Christmas Day, Selznick found a large package delivered to his front door, out of which stepped a young aspirant in crinolines, exclaiming, "Merry Christmas, Mr. Selznick! I am your Scarlett O'Hara!"

Concurrently with all this publicity, Selznick and Cukor were seriously testing, at the expense of $85,000, a number of contenders. Selznick had gone to San Francisco to see Tallulah Bankhead in "Reflected Glory," a part similar to Scarlett, after which he telephoned Cukor saying, "I've got our Scarlett." Miss Bankhead was whisked to Hollywood to make a test and Louella Parsons wrote in her column, "Tallulah Bankhead breezed into town last night to make a test for Scarlett O'Hara in *Gone With the Wind*. Her friend, George Cukor, is going to direct, Jock Whitney, another friend, is backing it, so I'm afraid she'll get the part. If she does, I, personally, will go home and weep, because she is *NOT* Scarlett O'Hara in any language, and if David Selznick gives her the part he will have to answer to every man, woman, and child in America." Miss Bankhead did not get the part, not because of Miss Parsons' tearful tirade, but because she was too old (34), and because she did not photograph well in colour. Jean Arthur, with whom Selznick had been in love several years before, was also tested, but similarly was too old and not right for the part. Cukor told the author that in their search for the right actress, he and Selznick kept three things in mind — suitablity, exposure and experience. They wanted someone suitable for the role, someone who had not had too much motion-picture exposure, yet someone who had enough acting experience to handle the part. Also tested were Joan Bennett, a nubile and unprepared Lana Turner, a young model named Edythe Marrener, who later became Susan Hayward,* Frances Dee, and an unknown from RKO, Lucille Ball, who, when asked to read for the part, exclaimed, "Are you kidding?"

As the starting date came closer, the leading finalist was Paulette Goddard. Miss Goddard, under contract to Selznick for a year, was the former Pauline Marion Goddard Levee (born on June 3, 1911, on Long Island) who at fifteen had been a blonde Ziegfeld Girl on Broadway in "No Foolin" (1926) and "Rio Rita" (1927). She had come to Hollywood in 1929, where she appeared in Hal Roach comedies and, in 1932, played a Goldwyn Girl in Eddie Cantor's *The Kid From Spain*. That same year she met Charles Chaplin, who became her mentor and cast her as the waif in *Modern Times* (1936). When Chaplin had no role for her to follow that picture, she signed with Selznick who cast her in *The Young at Heart* (1938) and loaned her to M-G-M for *Dramatic School* (1938) and *The Women* (1939). Cukor tested her for the part of Scarlett and it seemed that she was the one who would get the coveted role. Cukor recalls that despite her inexperience, she was "very promising." There was one hitch. Presumably Miss Goddard had married Chaplin on a world cruise in 1936. When Selznick announced that Miss Goddard might be the one cast, the public was outraged over her association with Chaplin, who already was being criticised for what were alleged to be un-American attitudes. In addition, Selznick insisted she produce a marriage license to avoid any further criticism about her romance-marriage to Chaplin. Apparently there was no license and Selznick, determined no scandal should surround his Scarlett, had to scrap the beautiful and vivacious actress.

By 1939, Selznick was no longer interested in Miss Goddard as a Selznick Player and she signed a contract with Paramount. The following year she obtained a Mexican divorce from Chaplin, but it was presumed she had only officially married him a few months before so she could go through with the legality of divorce.

The search for Scarlett O'Hara was still on and on October 30, 1938, Selznick told the press, "I still hope to give the American people a new girl as Scarlett, a girl whom they won't identify with a lot of other roles. But to find an unknown actress who has the talent for it is almost impossible. And to find an actress of sufficient experience who is at the same time, convincingly young, well, that's also a job. But we've got to find somebody soon."

Six weeks later, on the evening of December 10th, Selznick found his Scarlett O'Hara. He had decided that although his casting was incomplete, he must begin production. As the construction crew began building the set for Tara on the Culver City lot, they found the sets from other Selznick pictures had to be removed to make the necessary room. Selznick decided the old sets would be used to create the bonfire for the burning of Atlanta scene (where doubles were used for Rhett and Scarlett riding out of the burning city.) Preparations for this first scene turned into a minor festivity and that evening, to witness the fire, Selznick's brother Myron brought along two guests. One was Laurence Olivier, Myron's client and the star of the yet-to-be released *Wuthering Heights*. The other was Olivier's romantic interest, a young English actress named Vivien Leigh. The three

* Susan Hayward was born Edythe Marrener in Brooklyn, on June 30, 1918. While working as a model for a commercial artist, Cukor saw her photograph on the cover of the "Saturday Evening Post" and suggested that Selznick test her for *Gone With the Wind*. The inexperienced model's test was a flop. She recalls, "I looked like a snub-nosed teenager in it. What did I know about playing Southern belles?" Selznick dropped her option and said, "You'd better go back to Brooklyn and get some experience in stock." Whereupon she retorted, "I like the orange trees and I'm going to stay." She went to work for Warner Brothers, Paramount, Walter Wanger, and 20th Century-Fox, before winning her Academy Award in 1958, for *I Want to Live!*, produced by Wanger. Miss Hayward died of a brain tumor on March 14, 1975.

guests arrived after the fire had begun, and at one point during the evening, Myron, entranced by the reflection of the flames in Miss Leigh's green eyes, turned to his brother and said, "Dave, I want you to meet your Scarlett O'Hara."

Selznick talked to Miss Leigh about the part of Scarlett that evening and invited her to come to the studio the next day and read. From her reading, both Selznick and Cukor were convinced she was a serious contender and they arranged a test for her the following day. They used two scenes for their black and white test. The first was the scene in the library of Twelve Oaks where Scarlett tells Ashley she loves him, and instead of the sentiment which most of the other contenders had used, Miss Leigh played this scene with a near-hysterical laugh which impressed Cukor and Leslie Howard. The second scene had her being laced into her corset while dressing for the barbecue.

On Christmas Day, 1938, Miss Leigh was a guest for lunch at Cukor's elegant home on Cordell Drive. He took her aside and told her that the part of Scarlett had finally been cast. When Miss Leigh asked who, Cukor answered, "Well, I guess we're stuck with you." When Paulette Goddard heard of Miss Leigh's coup, she quipped, "Poor David! You really can't blame him. He was down to his last Whitney."

The major casting was now complete and Olivia de Havilland had been borrowed from Warner Brothers to play Melanie and Leslie Howard signed as Ashley. Even these two supporting roles had undergone many casting speculations. For the part of Melanie such actresses as Evelyn Keyes, Ann Dvorak, Janet Gaynor and Andrea Leeds had been considered. One of those tested for the role was Jane Wyman. Miss Wyman says she knew she was not right for the part and never even wanted it. Her good friend, Barbara Stanwyck, teases her still today, by saying, "Of course, you didn't want the part. You walked in with a hooped skirt and a picture hat and said, 'When are yooouall ready to start'." Stanwyck jokingly says of herself, "I was the *only* one never tested for Scarlett O'Hara."

Vivien Leigh and Hattie McDaniel.

Vivien Leigh and Leslie Howard.

For the part of Ashley the contestants included Melvyn Douglas, Robert Young, Ray Milland, Richard Carlson and Shepperd Strudwick. Miss de Havilland recalls her selection as Melanie, "It was through my sister, Joan Fontaine, that Melanie came. She had gone to see George Cukor, the director, to read for the part of Scarlett. When he asked her to read for Melanie instead, she declined and said, 'If it is a Melanie you are looking for, why don't you try my sister?' And he did. After I read for him the scene he had indicated, Geoge asked me to commit it to memory and meet him at the house of the producer, David Selznick, at three o'clock the following Sunday afternoon. I did so, and dressed in a black velvet afternoon dress with a round lace collar, and short puffed sleeves. I was ushered into the great man's drawing room for one of the most significant moments of my life. But destiny had a piquant humor, and the scene that ensued was pure comedy; it was George's role to play opposite me. He was at that time portly, his hair black, curly and closely cropped, his spectacles were large and thickly rimmed. To this day, I have claimed that it was his passionate portrayal of Scarlett O'Hara clutching the portieres that convinced David that afternoon he had finally found his Melanie. The part, however, was not yet mine, for I was under contract to Warner Brothers studios, renowned for keeping its players under discipline and on home ground. But during the suspenseful negotiations that followed, I found a friend and ally in Ann Warner, for it was Ann who persuaded her husband, Jack, to lend me to David. Then the afternoon came when I entered David's office to be photographed with a slight, beautiful, charming British actress as yet unknown to America, Vivien Leigh. An announcement went out to an expectant world and a bored and hostile Hollywood that a long search had ended and here, at last, were Scarlett and Melanie.''

Miss de Havilland explained to the author that the loan-out deal which enabled her to work for Selznick included Selznick's selling to Warner Brothers the one-picture services of James Stewart (then under contract to M-G-M) which Selznick owned, and that is how Stewart came to star opposite Rosalind Russell in *No Time For Comedy* (1940).

The public's response to the announcement, which came on January 13, 1939, was generally favourable regarding the unknown Miss Leigh, with only a few minor criticisms that a Britisher had got the part. Shooting on the picture began January 26th, and would end the following July 1st. Those short, action-packed five months resulted in not only the screen's most popular motion picture but also a true synthesis of all the various components of film production blended to entertainment perfection under the careful, watchful and meticulous eye of David O. Selznick.

There never really was a shooting script for the production in any completed form. Sidney Howard's script was the basis of the scenario to which Selznick himself daily added re-writes. It was soon apparent that he was not pleased with Cukor's directorial interpretation — the consensus being that he felt Cukor was emphasising the role of Scarlett to the detriment of the picture's overall scope. These differences between producer and director resulted in Cukor's release on

Leona Roberts, Vivien Leigh and Alicia Rhett.

Olivia de Havilland and Ona Munson.

February 13th. Cukor says today, calmly and with levity, that despite having been fired from the most important picture of all time, he recalls that he handled the whole affair like a gentleman and remained friends with Selznick.

Olivia de Havilland recalls that day vividly — "On the set of the bazaar sequence, Scarlett widowed, Melanie bereft of her brother, and both attired in black, Vivien and I learned that George would be leaving the picture and another director, Victor Fleming, would be taking his place. Of all the monumental tests of strength he met during the filming of *Gone With the Wind,* there was no greater test than David Selznick met that day. In our garb of deep mourning, Vivien and I stormed his office. For three solid hours we beseeched him not to let George go. As tears rained on David, he retreated to the haven of his window seat, and when we unfurled the forlorn banners of our black-bordered handkerchiefs, he nearly fled out the windows." Their plea was fruitless, and after a twelve-day hiatus in shooting, Victor Fleming, who had directed *Red Dust, Test Pilot* and *The Wizard of Oz,* took over the reins of the production.

Miss Leigh did not get on well with Fleming, but they treated each other with strained politeness. Both Miss Leigh and Miss de Havilland missed Cukor's guidance. Miss de Havilland says, "In spite of my confidence in the new director, however, there were moments in the months that followed when I felt the need of 'the talent strained through the finer sieve.' So I telephoned George Cukor and asked his help. Generously, at lunch in a restaurant or over a cup of tea in his house, George would give me black-market direction. I

Clark Gable and Vivien Leigh.

felt ever so slightly guilty toward Vivien about making these secret visits to George until, when the picture was finished, I learned that all during the filming, Vivien had been doing exactly the same thing."

One of the scenes for which Cukor tutored Miss de Havilland was the scene where Melanie is reading "David Copperfield" to the ladies who are waiting for their men to return from the political meeting. Miss de Havilland says, "When Ward Bond, the Yankee Captain, comes to the door, Melanie, who never simulated anything, who was *always* sincere, had to simulate the truth. I was uneasy about how to play that scene and George helped me and the scene worked. George's direction is like the silver of Cellini and Victor Fleming's was like the silver of Paul Revere. Both were excellent."

The production schedule was intense, with long working hours, and Selznick was constantly overseeing every detail of the picture, demanding perfection. At time humour failed and there were temperamental outbursts. On April 26th, in a disagreement with Miss Leigh, Fleming threw down his script and stalked off the set. The next day his wife reported that he had suffered a nervous breakdown. The breakdown was feigned; Fleming was just exhausted from the work load, but Selznick called in a third director, Sam Wood. Fleming returned to work after a two-week rest, but Selznick kept both directors on the job for the remainder of the picture, although the screen credit went to Victor Fleming.

When shooting ended in July, 449,512 feet of film had been exposed, and for the next two-and-a-half months, it was edited to its final 222 minutes

Clark Gable and Vivien Leigh.

and musically scored. There were some problems with the Hays Censorship office over the use of the famous "damn" at the end. One version had Gable say, "Frankly, my dear, I don't care," but after insisting on the line's importance, Selznick was allowed keep the original. "Frankly, my dear, I don't give a damn." One other line which was cut out entirely had him say to Scarlett, "May your mean little soul burn in hell for eternity," to which Scarlett responded by making the sign of the cross.

The picture was previewed in Santa Barbara and Riverside, California, in late September and premiered in Atlanta, Georgia, on December 15th, 1939. For citizens of Atlanta it was a major event, with the 2,051 seats of the Grand Theatre (the front of which had been made to look like Tara) selling at $10 each. Joining in the festivities were David and Irene Selznick, Vivien Leigh with Laurence Olivier, Clark Gable with Carole Lombard, and Olivia de Havilland. Following the screening, Margaret Mitchell, the real star of the evening, was asked to speak. She said, "It's not up to me to speak of the grand things these actors have done, for they've spoken so much more eloquently than I could ever do. But I just want to speak for one moment about Mr. David Selznick. He's the man that every one of you cracked that joke about, 'Oh, well, we'll wait till Shirley Temple grows up, and *she'll* play Scarlett.' I want to commend Mr. Selznick's courage and his obstinacy and his determination in just keeping his mouth shut until he got exactly the cast he wanted, in spite of everything everybody said. And I think you're going to agree with me — that he had the absolutely perfect cast."

Several days later *Gone With the Wind* opened in both New York and Los Angeles, and went into general release in 1940, with an admission fee of 75 cents for matinees and one dollar for evening performances.

Years later, Bosley Crowther assessed *Gone*

Vivien Leigh and Clark Gable.

Clark Gable and Vivien Leigh.

With the Wind as follows: "Its reception was tremendous. But for all the public enthusiasm and critical acclaim, no one then dreamed how popular and culturally momentous it would be. It has been the most widely circulated, the most often seen, the most profitable film ever made, and that includes *The Birth of a Nation,* to which it bears an astonishing resemblance in many significant ways. The eminence of this picture is in the richness with which it conveys a universally recognisable portrait of a many-faceted female character within a vast and tumultuous panorama of socially exciting events. But *Gone With the Wind* is more than the exposure of a vivid character, more than a superfluity of adventure, romance and spectacle. It is a superior illustration of a large chunk of American legend and myth, a grand illusion of imagined people living through a nostalgia-drenched experience."

In 1940, on February 28th, the Academy of Motion Picture Arts and Sciences bestowed its awards for the best film achievements of 1939, and *Gone With the Wind* earned ten awards, more than any picture up to that time — Best Picture, Best Actress (Vivien Leigh), Best Actress in a Supporting Role (Hattie McDaniel), Best Director (Victor Fleming), Best Screenplay (Sidney Howard*), Best Cinematography (Ernest Haller and Ray Rennahan), Best Art Direction (Lyle Wheeler), Best Editing (Hal Kern and James E. Newcom), Best Special Effects (John R. Cosgrove), and a Special Award to Cameron Menzies for his achievements in design and colour. To add to the historical occasion, David O. Selznick was presented with the Irving G. Thalberg Memorial

*Sidney Howard died in a tractor accident on his farm in Tyringham, Massachusetts, late in 1939. Sinclair Lewis accepted his Oscar.

Vivien Leigh and Clark Gable.

The burning of Atlanta.

Thomas Mitchell and Vivien Leigh.

Award "for the most consistent high level of production achievement by an individual producer." The picture's production cost was $3,700,000 and its final cost including publicity and promotion was $4,250,000. To date, it has grossed in the U.S.-Canadian markets $77,900,000 topped only by *The Sound of Music* ($83,000,000) and *The Godfather* ($85,000,000).

For the Centennial Celebration commemorating the onset of the Civil War, Atlanta, Georgia, sponsored a gala re-issue of *Gone With the Wind.* Attending that occasion were David Selznick, Vivien Leigh and Olivia de Havilland. As Miss Leigh was stepping off the plane, a young reporter asked her what part she had played in the picture. The elegant Miss Leigh sniffed, raised her feline head and haughtily walked off the plane like one of the several Siamese cats she owned.

In 1967, Atlanta sponsored a second re-issue of the film, and by that time all the major stars including the producer, David O. Selznick, were dead. Olivia de Havilland, the only exception, attended that screening, at which time she commented, "As Scarlett and Rhett and Ashley and Melanie and Mammy and Prissy and all the others told their story against the panorama of enormous struggle, defeat and renaissance, I looked at Scarlett, and knew she meant survival, the physical survival of a vanquished people; and I looked at Melanie, and knew she meant survival, the spiritual survival of the values and traditions of a lost civilization, and I understood why, for countries all over the world who have known conflict and defeat and survival, *Gone With the Wind* is their story."

When *Gone With the Wind* was re-issued for the sixth time in 1971, in a new 70mm version, Henry Hart of "Films In Review," commented, "For *Gone With the Wind,* he (Selznick) assembled and successfully utilized, more fine talent than had been employed on a single picture before, or has

Vivien Leigh and Harry Davenport.

Vivien Leigh and Oscar Polk.

been since. If a producer can ever be said to perform a creative function, Selznick did so on *Gone With the Wind.*"

On this same occasion, the author viewed *Gone With the Wind* for the second time and felt the last half, because of its preoccupation with Scarlett's tribulations, is largely soap-opera, not a full scale depiction of the South's struggle for its resurrection after the holocaust. This emphasis on Scarlett's personal melodrama was the very reason Selznick objected to George Cukor's interpretation.

For years there had been talk of a musical version of *Gone With the Wind.* Selznick once told producer, Arthur Hornblow Jr., that he would like to produce such a version himself and that if he did so he would produce the musical in two Broadway theatres across the street from each other with two casts. However, a musical version of the picture loomed such a formidable task and was so closely associated with the ultra-popular film version, that it was not until 1969, that such a version was attempted. Kay Brown, who had remained the representative of Margaret Mitchell's heirs for *Gone With the Wind's* rights, arranged for the musical version to be produced at the Imperial Theatre in Tokyo, Japan, in Japanese, with the co-operation of composer Harold Rome and director-choreographer Joe Layton. The book for this four-hour production was written by Kazuo Kikuta. Rehearsals began in October, 1969, and the show opened on January 2, 1970, with Sakura Jinguji as Scarlett O'Hara. It was very successful and when excerpts were shown on American television as part of the Tony Awards presentation, Miss Jinguji was delightful.

The success of that Japanese-American production prompted Rome and Layton to write an

Oscar Polk, Vivien Leigh, Hattie McDaniel and Butterfly McQueen.

Vivien Leigh.

Carroll Nye, Vivien Leigh and Hattie McDaniel.

Clark Gable and Vivien Leigh.

Vivien Leigh and Clark Gable.

Cammie King and Vivien Leigh.

English-speaking version. For this production, they used a new book written by Horton Foote. Rome wrote some new songs and again Layton staged and choreographed it. It opened at the Drury Lane Theatre in London on May 3, 1972, with June Ritchie and Harve Presnell in the leads. Unfortunately it was too long, too fragmented and contained no show-stopping songs. Its reviews were only modestly affirmative but the three-and-a-half hour show ran for 397 performances.

Following the London run, the show went on tour in the United States opening at the Chandler Pavilion of the Los Angeles Music Center on August 8, 1973. Budgeted at $500,000 and scheduled to tour for a year, it closed on November 24th, in San Francisco. The leads in this version were Leslie Ann Warren and Pernell Roberts.

In May, 1974, it was announced that *Gone With the Wind* would finally be seen on television screens, when the National Broadcasting Company purchased the television leasing rights from M-G-M for an unprecedented $5,000,000. It is scheduled to be shown during 1976, as part of the United States Bicentennial and is expected to draw an estimated 130 million viewers.

John Hay Whitney, Irene Selznick, Olivia de Havilland, David O. Selznick, Vivien Leigh and Laurence Olivier attending the Hollywood premiere of *Gone With the Wind*.

With Barry Fitzgerald and Bing Crosby, accepting her Oscar for *Gaslight* (1944).

3

INGRID BERGMAN

Perhaps the greatest performance of Ingrid Bergman's career was the valiant manner in which she maintained her dignity throughout *le scandale*, an event which adversely coloured the last two-and-a-half decades of her career. What at the time was considered a blatant breach of behavior, now seems trivial. Yet, no discussion of this lady's career is complete without that chapter.

As an actress, the most convincing image that Ingrid Bergman effortlessly projects is that of *selfless idealism*. When David O. Selznick brought her to this country in 1938, he first thought of her as a successor to Greta Garbo, Louis B. Mayer's Swedish find, and an actress whom Selznick greatly admired. Selznick immediately realised, however, that Miss Bergman was unique in the annals of Hollywood and not a successor to anyone. Her uniqueness lay in her complete naturalness, her radiant beauty, her vitality, her freshness and her uncontrived sexuality.

With these characteristics in mind, Selznick spun a web of shrewd publicity around her that supplied her public image with everything but a neon halo. And, during the ten years which she was a reigning Hollywood star, the public gullibly believed this publicity ploy. After the Rossellini affair, it was Selznick who admitted, "I'm afraid I'm responsible for the public image of her as St. Ingrid. I hired a press agent who was an expert at shielding stars from the press and we released only stories that emphasised her sterling character. We deliberately built her up as the normal, healthy, non-neurotic career woman, devoid of scandal and with an idyllic home life. I guess that backfired later."

During her first seven years in Hollywood, there were no provocations to cause a backfire. While under personal contract to Selznick, she became the most important member of his select stock company, providing him with more bargaining power in loan-out deals than any of his other players. It was not however, a one-sided business deal, because Selznick's influence upon the Bergman career was benign and through him, she entered the Hollywood arena under the best possible auspices, and gained, thanks to his promotional prowess, a position it takes most actresses who lack such backing, years to attain. It can however be argued that after she and Selznick separated, her career went into a decline.

Selznick personally produced only two of her films during this time: *Intermezzo, A Love Story* (1939) and *Spellbound* (1945). He was nevertheless closely involved with all details of the remaining ten pictures she made while under contract to him, even if it was nothing more than carefully choosing the proper vehicle for loan-out. His interest in her career is verified by the number of projects he held under consideration for her, although they eventually never materialised or were cast with other actresses. These projects included a biography of Sarah Bernhardt, re-makes of

Garbo's *Anna Christie* and *Anna Karenina, Joan of Arc* (which she later did independently), *The Spiral Staircase* (Dorothy McGuire), *To Each His Own* (Olivia de Havilland), *The Farmer's Daughter* (Loretta Young), *The Valley of Decision* (Greer Garson,) *A Tree Grows in Brooklyn* (Dorothy McGuire), and a "spectacular" about Mary Magdalene to be co-produced with England's J. Arthur Rank. While Selznick's output was not as prolific as these projects indicate, the films he assigned to Miss Bergman were the foundation for a remarkable screen career.

What Selznick did not take into account was that she was more than a one-dimensional human being despite her natural *gemütlich* character. During her early film days in Sweden, one of her colleagues described her as possessing an "iron willpower and an unbelievable memory." And once, Sam Wood, who directed her in *For Whom the Bell Tolls* and *Saratoga Trunk*, replied, when a friend expressed concern because she was swimming so far out from Wood's Malibu beach house, "No, she wouldn't like it if we signalled the lifeguards. Some day she's going to start swimming straight out. She's going to start swimming, and never come back." And Miss Bergman herself explained, "When I work, I concentrate completely, and I have not husband, nor children. I cannot divide myself. I have to do one thing at a time. I was born to be an actress, and if they ever take it away from me, I shall just lie down and die."

When her sterling image became boring to her, she said, "Here in the United States it is the personality that they like, more than the performance. People popped all of us into little boxes. If they wanted someone to be a bad woman, they opened a little box marked *Bette Davis*. If they wanted a saintly woman, they opened a little box marked *Ingrid Bergman.*" Thus, the other Ingrid Bergman, the wilful, impulsively human side of the coin, dared to defy Hollywood security and stardom, and go to Europe to make films with the then *avant-garde* Roberto Rossellini. That venture proved economically and artistically disastrous because "the scripts were not good and most of the time I was pregnant." She was still however, able proudly to hold her head up high and declare, "Happiness depends on two assets which fortunately I have. They are good health and a poor memory."

Ingrid Bergman was born on August 29, 1915, in an apartment on the top floor of a six-story Stockholm building in which her father, Justus, a frustrated painter, owned a photographer's shop. Aged thirty-seven, his artistic aspirations alluding him, he married a native of Hamburg, named Freidel Adler, who was eighteen years younger than he. Ingrid, their only child, was named after Sweden's two-year old princess who later became Queen of Denmark. At her father's request, Miss Bergman was given no middle name because he felt it was bothersome when filling out passports and official papers, an experience he had encountered with his wife who had four names.

When Ingrid was only two, her mother died at the age of thirty-seven from inflamation of the liver, and her father's spinster sister became her surrogate mother.

As her father was interested in music as well as painting, he endeavoured to introduce his little girl to the delights of the operatic world and provided her with music and vocal lessons. When she was ten, he organised a mixed chorus which toured the Swedish communities of the United States. A year later, back in Sweden, he took his daughter to see the play "Patrasket" by Hjalmar Bergman (no relation) about which Miss Bergman said, "I knew then that I would be an actress and there wasn't any question about it."

Justus Bergman died of stomach cancer when Ingrid was twelve and seven months later her spinster aunt died in her arms of a heart attack. While the orphaned child was packing up the family belongings, she discovered some of her parents' letters which led her to conclude that their opposite personalites — she practical and methodical, he bohemian and artistic — had influenced her father to compromise his deepest ambitions as an artist to sustain a solvent marriage. During these early years with her father and aunt, Miss Bergman later said, "The days and years were filled with a terrible sense of aloneness. I became extremely shy and withdrew into a dream world of my own imagination, with creatures of fantasy who were less oppressive than the people around me. To amuse myself, I began inventing characters — villains and heroes, witches and fairies, and even animals. I made up stories as I went along, and all these characters became familiar and friendly. At school my abnormal height and clumsy shyness prevented me from making friends. I barely passed from grade to grade, due partly to boredom with the regular subjects. but mostly because of my inability to stand up before the class and answer the teacher's questions. Self-consciousness would choke the words in my throat. ''

After the deaths of her father and her aunt, she went to live with an uncle, her father's elderly brother, who had five children, four of them older than Ingrid. A small inheritance from her father's estate paid the tuition to a private school, the Lyceum for Flickor, where, still ''all arms and legs'' the shy teenager continued to withdraw into her fantasies and discovered for herself a heroine in Joan of Arc. Her obsession with Joan of Arc continued for many years, and she would later say that she chose Joan not only for her ''dignity, courage, faith, and humour,'' but also for ''never being trapped by the questions of her inquisitors.'' Gradually, she was able to relax enough to perform before her schoolmates and subsequently decided that acting was definitely the way out of the labyrinth of personal fantasy.

Despite her uncle's protestations, she took the necessary examination to obtain a scholarship to Stockholm's Royal Dramatic Theatre School (Garbo had been an earlier pupil). For her auditions, she said, ''I chose three subjects — the crazy boy from Rostand's *'L'Aiglon,'* the goddess in Strindberg's *'The Dream Play,'* and a big, fat, country-girl part from something I've forgotten.'' She passed the auditions and entered the 1933-34 term.

Two months later on a blind date she met Petter Aron Lindstrom, a successful dentist nine years her senior. His car, his nice apartment, and his maturity impressed her. On July 10, 1937, Miss Bergman and Lindstrom were married in a Lutheran church, after which they spent a brief honeymoon in England. On September 20, 1938, Miss Bergman gave birth to a daughter, Freidel Pia, named after her mother. The Pia was derived from the initials of the child's parents — P (Petter), I (Ingrid), A (Aron).

Lindstrom entreated his wife to leave the Royal Dramatic Theatre School towards the end of her first term to sign a contract with Svensk Film Industri. Miss Bergman willingly complied.

Her motion-picture debut was in *Munkbrogreven* (1934), a comedy in which she played a maid in a cheap hotel and was billed seventh. Her second assignment as the heroine of *Branningar* (1935), a melodrama in which she played the daughter of a fisherman who is impregnated by a minister. These two films earned her good notices from the critics who found her ''beautiful and statuesque,'' ''self-assured,'' ''gracious and true,'' and she was voted the most promising newcomer in Swedish films.

As a result of her success, she was brought to the attention of Gustaf Molander, one of Sweden's most important directors, and he cast her in six films which offered her a variety of roles and made her one of the most popular Swedish stars of the day. Her two most important pictures with Molander were *Intermezzo* (1936) and *En kvinnas ansikte* (1938). *Intermezzo* was a polished soap-opera co-starring Gösta Ekman, one of Sweden's matinee idols, who played the violinist who interrupts his life with his wife and children for an affair with a beautiful young pianist played by Miss Bergman. Molander's direction elicited from her a performance which revealed that in additon to acting ability, Ingrid Bergman possessed star quality, i.e., personality. The composition of the latter has been much debated. The consensus is that her face, her voice, and her bearing, harmonise and suggest sincerity, idealism, peasant strength.

En kvinnas ansikte (re-made in this country in 1941, as *A Woman's Face* starring Joan Crawford) was a successful and unflinchingly stark story of a facially scarred woman, played by Miss Bergman, who lives in the criminal underworld, undergoes plastic surgery, becomes a governess and is blackmailed by her criminal friends. When reviewed in the United States in 1939, the New York ''World-Telegram'' called Miss Bergman another Garbo. Of the American version with Joan Crawford, Miss Bergman said, ''It is a more romantic version.''

When the dubbed version of *Intermezzo* was shown in this country, David O. Selznick sent his East Coast Representative, Kay Brown, career-woman *à outrance,* to Stockholm with orders to sign her to a contract for an American version of the same picture. Despite the fact that when Selznick had screened the original version of *Intermezzo* in his home and half of his guests had walked out, he nevertheless wired Miss Brown ''to take the next boat to Sweden and do not come home without a contract with Miss Bergman.''

Earlier, Miss Bergman had received several offers to appear in motion pictures outside Sweden, but had been reluctant to leave her child and her husband, upon whom she relied for all advice in her contractual dealings. She had already gone to Germany to make one picture for UFA, entitled *Die vier gesellen* (1938), the story of four girls just out of art school who form an advertising agency. One marries, one has to marry, one turns to seri-

With Gösta Ekman in the Swedish *Intermezzo* (1936).

With Leslie Howard in *Intermezzo: A Love Story* (1939).

ous painting, and Miss Bergman gets the agency and an architect husband. It was verbose and only moderately popular.

Miss Brown arrived in Stockholm to find herself dealing not only with Miss Bergman, but also her husband, Petter Lindstrom. Selznick's offer was a seven-year contract, but on Lindstroms' advice Miss Bergman agreed to a one-picture deal with the proviso to do more only if her first was acceptable to the American public.

She arrived alone in the United States aboard the "Queen Mary" on May 6, 1939, leaving Lindstrom behind to care for their daughter and continue his medical studies. Within a month she was at work on the re-make of *Intermezzo,* now called *Intermezzo: A Love Story*, and studying English under M-G-M's vocal coach, Ruth Roberts. Selznick later told the press, "When the girl arrived, my wife (Irene Mayer) and I took her into our own home as a house-guest. The minute I looked at her, I knew I had something. She had an extraordinary quality of purity and nobility and a definite star personality that is very rare. But she acted like a movie-struck teenager. I remember having a party for her at my home. Spencer Tracy, Charles Boyer and a dozen other movie stars were there. She just sat in a corner staring at them in awe. She was so shy she couldn't stop blushing." At that same party, director Ernst Lubitsch told Selznick that he felt he had made a mistake, that this was "just a great big peasant." Selznick, however, disagreed and saw her as another Garbo (he was obsessed with either having Garbo work with him again — after *Anna Karenina* — or discovering a replacement for her in Hollywood's stellar system). Ultimately both opinions proved incorrect.

Almost immediately, Selznick, with his usual genius for publicity, determined there would be one course and only one course to follow in exploiting his new find. In one of his famous memos he wrote to William Herbert, Director of Advertising and Publicity for Selznick International, "Miss Bergman is the most completely conscientious actress with whom I have ever worked, in that she thinks of absolutely nothing but her work before and during the time she is doing a picture, and makes no engagements of any kind and no plans that for one minute would distract her from her picture work. She practically never leaves the studio, and even suggested that her dressing room be equipped so that she could live here during the picture. She never for a minute suggests quitting at six-o'clock or anything of the kind, and on the contrary, is very unhappy if the company doesn't work until midnight, claiming that she does her best work in the evenings after a long day's work. All of this is so completely unaffected and completely unique and I should think would make a grand angle of approach to her publicity, so that her natural sweetness and consideration and conscientiousness become something of a legend." He further dictated that there would be no comparisions to other imports such as Garbo or Dietrich, and for the time being, he conveniently avoided mention of her husband and her daughter. Before this dictum was issued, one reporter asked Miss Bergman to raise her skirts for a photograph of her legs. She refused, saying, "But I came here to act, not to dance."

Intermezzo: A Love Story opened at New York City's Radio City Music Hall in October, 1939, and scored a box office and critical success. The New York critics were unanimous in commenting upon her freshness, her naturalness, her vitality, her beauty and her acting ability. Frank S. Nugent of the New York "Times" wrote, "There is that incandescence about Miss Bergman, that spiritual spark which makes us believe that Selznick has found another great lady of the screen." Graham Greene, with minor reservations about the romanticism of the picture, wrote, "But the film is most worth seeing; for the new star, Miss Ingrid Bergman, who is as natural as her name. What star before has made her first appearance on the international screen with a high-light gleaming on her nose-tip? That gleam is typical of a performance that doesn't give the effect of acting at all, but of living without make-up."

In the interim, Miss Bergman had returned to Sweden and her family at the end of August. She was elated by the success of the picture because it meant that Selznick would want her for more pictures.

By this time, World War II had begun, and when Selznick's offer came it was for a seven-year contract and this time Lindstrom advised his wife, "Take Pia and go. As for me, it won't be long before I join you." Accordingly, he drove them to Genoa, from where mother and daughter sailed aboard the "Rex" on New Year's Day, 1940.

Before Miss Bergman had left Hollywood the previous August, she had confided to Selznick her interest in playing Joan of Arc and he tentatively promised to fulfill her ambition and even cabled her aboard the "Rex" to advise her of his plans for the production. The ecstatic actress disembarked in the United States on January 12, 1940, only to find that Selznick had changed his plans because he felt that World War II made it inadvisable to revive the fact that the British had burned Joan at the stake. Furthermore, her contract notwithstanding, he stated he had no immediate plans for her.

Her friend and confidant, Kay Brown, suggested she remain with her in Miss Brown's New York apartment until Selznick called her to Hollywood. Miss Bergman's inactivity and separation from her husband depressed her and she decided to seek out a role on the stage. Legend has it that when producer Vinton Freedley sent her the script of Molnar's "Liliom," she returned it saying she was not right for the second lead, and Freedley supposedly replied he had meant her to star in the play as the volatile Viennese girl who falls in love with a carousel barker. Miss Brown, however, refutes this story saying that the only question regarding the choice of Miss Bergman was whether or not she could speak English well enough to appear on the Broadway stage.

Selznick gave his permission for her to do the role, and the play opened to excellent reviews on March 25, 1940, at the Forty-Fourth Street Theatre, for a limited three-month engagement. The cast included Burgess Meredith, Elia Kazan, Margaret Wycherly and John Emery.

When the play closed, Miss Bergman rented an apartment in Beverly Hills and resumed her English lessons with coach, Ruth Roberts. Meanwhile, her husband had succeeded, with Selznick's help, in enrolling in the medical school of the University of Rochester, and in September, 1940, Lindstrom began the studies which would enable him to qualify as a neurological surgeon. He rented a house in Rochester at 985 South Avenue, where, for the next three years, his wife would spend her time between pictures.

Between September, 1940, and January, 1941, Selznick loaned Miss Bergman to other producers on three occasions—once to Columbia for a programmer called *Adam Had Four Sons* (1941), in

Ingrid Bergman and Susan Hayward in *Adam Had Four Sons* (1941).

In *Dr. Jekyll and Mr. Hyde* (1941).

ed a governess who confronts her ns who oppose their father's love for -M for *Rage In Heaven* (1941), in as the secretary who contends with or her affections (Robert Montgomery an... Sanders); and again to M-G-M for the Spencer Tracy re-make of *Dr. Jekyll and Mr. Hyde* (1941), in which she played the erotic barmaid who is murdered. Although this was the smaller of the two female roles in this picture, Miss Bergman elected to play it because she felt it the more interesting and meatier part, thereby allowing the "nice *fiancée*" part to go to M-G-M's own Lana Turner. Speaking about this role as the barmaid, Miss Bergman stated, "It's a nice change; you know, in Hollywood, it's like being in a cage. They thrust the parts through the bars and you take what they give you." Already she was savvy to Hollywood's machinations.

Dr. Jekyll and Mr. Hyde was directed by Victor Fleming, the six-foot-three, silver-maned, part-Cherokee who had directed *Gone With the Wind*. Joseph Henry Steele, for some years Miss Bergman's press agent at Selznick International and author of "Ingrid Bergman: An Intimate Portrait" (McKay, 1959) says, "She experienced an emotion for Fleming I doubt she ever felt for any other man." This was contrary to the opinion held by others who felt that she was enamoured with co-star, Spencer Tracy. Nonetheless, rumours would persist that she was frequently and temporarily infatuated with her leading men—the strong woman in search of a stronger man. At the same time, Hungarian-born Gregory Ratoff, who had directed her in *Intermezzo: A Love Story* and *Adam Had Four Sons*, made a more amusing comment on the Swedish actress, "Haffing diracted Meese Boergmann in her foerst two American peetures, I vould say puzzitiffly I hope I do de same tvanty-two timeps more. She is sansahtional!"

After a year-and-a-half Selznick still had no projects for her and Miss Bergman took her daughter, Pia, to Rochester, a town which she found "unbearably dull." She began singing lessons and frequently went to New York City to stay with Kay Brown, while hounding Selznick to put her to work. In the summer of 1941, he backed a stage revival of O'Neill's "Anna Christie" to keep Miss Bergman's name before the public. Directed by John Houseman, it played Santa Barbara's Lobero Theatre, San Francisco's Geary, and the Maplewood Theatre in Maplewood, New Jersey. The critical reception was good for both the play and Miss Bergman, although some felt her "cleanliness of body and spirit" prevented her from getting down to the degradation of Anna. It was for just that reason, Alfred de Liagre Jr., Houseman's associate on this production, had wanted Ilona Massey to play Anna.

After her appearance in "Anna Christie," Selznick felt it was time to expose his property to the public in first-class vehicles. Although Paramount Pictures had acquired the motion-picture rights to Ernest Hemingway's "For Whom the Bell Tolls," both Miss Bergman and Selznick decided she should play Maria. Selznick's brother Myron, coincidentally was Hemingway's agent, and Selznick had considered purchasing the rights to the book himself but could not fit it into his production schedule. Nevertheless, for nearly two years, Selznick had been cleverly releasing bits to the press proclaiming Miss Bergman as the only "proper" choice for the part of Maria and was even instrumental in having Hemingway personally endorse her for the part.

Realising Selznick's strategy, Paramount went

With Humphrey Bogart in *Casablanca*.

ahead with the picture, casting ballerina and sometime actress, Vera Zorina, as Maria. Whereupon Selznick countered by lending Miss Bergman to Warners for *Casablanca* (1943), in the part presumably meant for Hedy Lamarr. *Casablanca* is a stussel-bussel in wartime Morocco which was made up as it was being shot, which Michael Curtiz ably directed, which had Humphrey Bogart and an exceptional supporting cast, and which revived the song "As Time Goes By." It enjoyed a success of unexpected proportions and made Miss Bergman the "hot property" Selznick had predicted she would be and Hollywood had begun to doubt even he could make her.

This success prompted Paramount to turn to Miss Bergman when it became apparent that Miss Zorina was not right as Maria. Paramount released to the press a statement saying Miss Zorina could not physically cope with the rarefied atmosphere of the High Sierras where the film was being shot, and subsequently met Selznick's stiff fee of $150,000 for Miss Bergman's services. "Time" magazine gave her a cover story and the production resumed on August 6, 1942.

Both *Casablanca* and *For Whom the Bell Tolls* were released in 1943, and although not everyone thought Miss Bergman right as Maria, her performance was liked by a sufficient number for it to be nominated for an Academy Award. In the "Nation," James Agee wrote, "She really knows how to act, in a blend of poetic grace with quiet realism which almost never appears in American pictures."

That year's Best Actress Award went to Selznick's wife-to-be, Jennifer Jones, for *The Song of Bernadette* and its significance was not lost on Miss Bergman.

When shooting ended on *For Whom the Bell Tolls*, in late October of 1942, Miss Bergman returned once again to Rochester and except for a

With Fortunio Bonanova, Katina Paxinou and Gary Cooper in *For Whom the Bell Tolls* (1943).

few weeks work in Minnesota on a propaganda film for the Office of War Information entitled *Swedes in America* (1943), she was free from work until March, 1943.

At that time she was once again teamed with Gary Cooper, her co-star in *For Whom the Bell Tolls*, this time in the film of Edna Ferber's "Saratoga Trunk," on loan to Warner Brothers. In a role refused by Vivien Leigh, another Selznick contractee, Miss Bergman played Clio Dulaine, the willful, Creole courtesan who stalks New Orleans society. Eyebrows raised at the prospect of Miss Bergman playing the vengeful, black-wigged Clio, but she enjoyed doing it and rose grandly to the challenge. As this picture's subject matter was not relevant to the war, as was Warner Brothers policy, it was not released in the United States until March, 1946, after being shown for two years to our servicemen abroad.

Following *Saratoga Trunk*, she immediately began work on *Gaslight* (1944) at M-G-M, based on Patrick Hamilton's play, "Angel Street," and directed by George Cukor. This had originally been purchased by Columbia Pictures as a vehicle for Irene Dunne, then was sold to M-G-M who had planned to make it starring Hedy Lamarr. When Louis B. Mayer, M-G-M's production head, lost interest in Hedy Lamarr as a first-rate property, Miss Bergman was borrowed from Selznick for the role. In a lushly claustrophobic setting, Miss Bergman gave a subtle and moving portrayal of the wife who is driven to the brink of insanity by her husband, Charles Boyer. In preparation for the role, Cukor arranged for her to visit a neuropsychiatric clinic. Her eerie credibility as the tormented wife prevented *Gaslight* from being just another soap-opera-ish melodrama and brought her the Academy Award which had eluded her the year before.

With Dame May Whitty in *Gaslight* (1944).

In his desire to join his successful wife in California, Petter Lindstrom transferred his studies to Stanford University in Palo Alto, California, for post-graduate work; his wife visited him on weekends from Hollywood. She spent Christmas and the New Year of 1943 in Alaska entertaining United States servicemen for the USO. Early in 1944, Lindstrom took a position at the Los Angeles County Hospital whereupon he and his wife bought a house at 1220 North Benedict Canyon Drive in Beverly Hills. Now that Lindstrom was finished with his studies he became involved in the management of his wife's business affairs as he had been wont to do earlier in Sweden.

Later in 1944, RKO director, Leo McCarey, came to Miss Bergman with the suggestion she play opposite Bing Crosby as the sensible, outgoing nun in his original screenplay, *The Bells of St. Mary's* (1945), his sequel to the tremendously popular *Going My Way* (1944) which had starred Bing Crosby and Barry Fitzgerald. She liked the idea but Selznick vetoed it saying sequels were never box-office. She insisted on doing the picture and threatened, "If you don't let me do this, I'll go back to the Old Country."

Selznick acquiesed, but only after feeling compelled to make several script changes as well as one of the most astute and financially profitable loan-out deals in film history. For Miss Bergman's services he demanded and received —1) a commitment for the use of an ace RKO director, 2) all re-make rights to two of his previous RKO successes: *A Bill of Divorcement* (1932) and *Little Women* (1933), 3) $175,000 in cash—an estimated $410,000 in market value. At the time, Miss Bergman was earning $2,000 weekly.

In preparation for the role of the nun, Miss Bergman worked three weeks with the Sisters of the Holy Cross in Los Angeles. The resultant picture was a box-office smash which earned Miss Bergman her third Academy Award nomination.

The second and last picture that Selznick personally produced with Ingrid Bergman was the psychiatric thriller, *Spellbound* (1945). It was a glossy, over-produced film commercially scripted by Ben Hecht, with a surrealistic dream sequence by Salvador Dali and directed by Alfred Hitchcock. It was nominated for six Academy Awards and won one for the beautiful score by Miklos

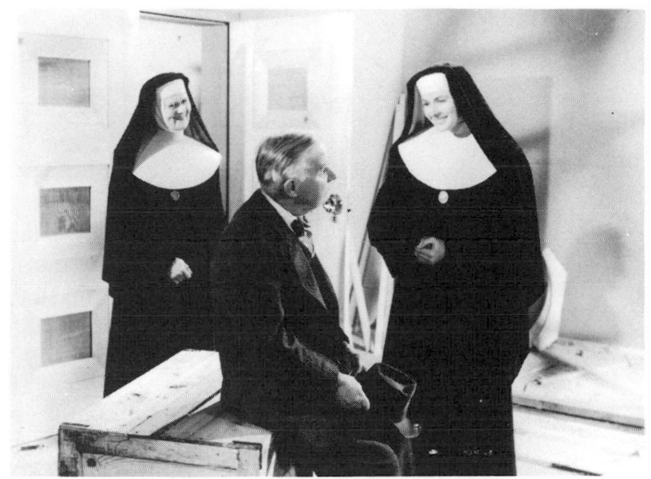

With Ruth Donnelly and Henry Travers in *The Bells of St. Mary's* (1945).

Rozsa. Miss Bergman played a psychiatrist who helps prove amnesia-victim Gregory Peck innocent of murder. For all of the production values, the picture never really made sense. Nonetheless, her performance in that film and *The Bells of St. Mary's* earned her the New York Film Critics Award, and with the release of those two pictures and the delayed release of *Saratoga Trunk*, it was

In *Spellbound* (1945).

a "Bergman Year," of which one Hollywood quipster said, "I saw a picture *without* Ingrid Bergman in it."

The last picture under her Selznick contract was *Notorious* (1946), a production scripted and directed by Alfred Hitchcock which Selznick sold as a package deal to RKO along with the services of Miss Bergman and Hitchcock. It was as much a character study of Hitchcock's famous love-duty theme as it was a thriller and Miss Bergman gave her best Hollywood performance as the daughter of a traitor who expiates her father's guilt by helping to uncover a Nazi spy ring in Rio de Janiero.

With Gary Cooper in *Saratoga Trunk* (1945).

Ingeniously photographed by Ted Tetzlaff, Miss Bergman and Cary Grant, who played the U. S. government agent, made a memorably erotic screen team, and performed what was then advertised as the longest kiss in movie history.

When negotiations began for Miss Bergman to renew her contract with Selznick, out of habit she relied upon her husband's advice. Lindstrom was of the opinion that Selznick was making far too much profit from Miss Bergman's services without properly compensating her monetarily. In addition to the phenomenal loan-out deal on *The Bells of St. Mary's*, Selznick had received $125,000 for her loan to Warner Brothers in *Casablanca*, and $150,000 for Paramount's *For Whom the Bell Tolls*. As Selznick later put it, "At the last minute, just as she was about to sign, Lindstrom got into the act. He decided that I was making too much money out of her and that they could do better elsewhere. After that, I offered them two pictures, both of which they turned down." One was *The Farmer's Daughter* for

With Cary Grant in *Notorious* (1946).

which Loretta Young earned an Academy Award and the other was *To Each His Own* for which Olivia de Havilland received her first Academy Award. Negotiations came to a stalemate; Miss Bergman refused to renew her contract which had expired on December 29, 1945.

Her first independent production was the film of Erich Maria Remarque's "Arch of Triumph" (1948). The motion-picture rights to this novel were owned by a small producing company called Enterprise Pictures, formed by Charles Enfield, who had been head of Warner Brothers' advertising and publicity department, and David Loew, son of Marcus Loew, the founder of the Loew theatre chain and one of the founders of Metro-Goldwyn-Mayer. Although Miss Bergman was not enthusiastically impressed with this particular script, she consented to star in the picture when Enterprise obtained the venerable Lewis Milestone as director. Milestone was most famous for his direction of the classic *All Quiet on the Western Front* (1930) also adapted from a Remarque novel. Lindstrom predictably arranged the financial matters. Miss Bergman was to be paid $175,000, plus twenty-five percent of the profits.

Arch of Triumph turned out to be an expensive, dull and repetitious melodrama in which Miss Bergman was miscast as Joan Madou, the Parisian chanteuse-courtesan who falls in love with wartime refugee-surgeon, Charles Boyer, but unable to overcome the degradation and deprivation of her past takes on a wealthy lover and is finally shot by Boyer. To turn the saintly Ingrid Bergman into this creation of immorality, Milestone photographed her somberly wearing a beret and languidly smoking a cigarette. Shooting on the picture ended in October, 1946, but it was so long and confused a project that a two-hour version was not edited and released until 1948. It was her first box-office failure and instead of gaining any percentage of the net profits for her, the picture lost $2,000,000.

With Charles Boyer in *Arch of Triumph* (1948).

Unsuspected by most of her friends and all of her public, the Lindstrom marriage was not as idyllic as reported; and during the filming of *Arch of Triumph*, Miss Bergman requested a divorce from her husband, then head neuro-surgeon at Los Angeles County Hospital. Years later, she recalled her reasons as being "we had grown apart and did not have much in common." Lewis Milestone observed, "Lindstrom had old-fashioned European ideas. He took the attitude that he had bestowed his name on a poor orphan girl and therefore she should be grateful to him for the rest of her life. There were implications all the time. He was the solid citizen who had rescued a poor waif. He never let her forget it. But how long can you operate on gratitude?"

During this one of many unhappy periods in her marital life, she sought solace in other male friends, this time photographer Robert Capa. Simultaneously Maxwell Anderson offered her the title role in his stage production of "Joan of Lorraine." Her elation over being cast in the part she had always wanted to play allayed, for a time, her feeling that her marriage was preventing her "growth."

"Joan of Lorraine" went into rehearsal on October 5, 1946, and opened in New York City's Alvin Theatre six weeks later on November 18th, for a limited engagement that ran until May 10, 1947. The play grossed $860,000, fifteen percent of which was Miss Bergman's salary. Said Brooks Atkinson in the New York "Times," "Miss Bergman gives an exalting performance...Her part is wholly becoming, both as Maid of Orleans and as an actress brooding over her role...She was excellent in 'Liliom' six years ago. She is superb now in the much grander part of Joan. Anyone can see that she comes to the stage bearing gifts of extraordinary splendour. In the first place, she is beautiful, which is no handicap on the stage or anywhere else. She is also magnetic, which is more essential than beauty on the stage...And she endows Joan with a spiritual aura that is reflected in the audience as well as in the play. It is a quality of sentience that, among the younger actresses, only Miss Bergman possesses — putting her in the category of Cornell and Hayes." And, Helen Hayes, in presenting Miss Bergman with the Antoinette Perry Award (Tony) as Best Actress of the Broadway season said, "Thank you, Miss Bergman, for bringing the theatre back to Broadway."

While Miss Bergman was starring on Broadway, Paramount Pictures offered her a contract for a film version of "Joan of Lorraine," to be directed by William Wyler, but she and her husband, together again, decided to do the film version themselves with Victor Fleming directing. "Themselves" meant the En Corporation ("en" meaning one in Swedish and Ingrid Bergman being the company's only property), which Miss Bergman and Lindstrom had recently formed with producer, Walter Wanger. Wanger invested heavily in the company and was its head. The picture was made in the first three months of 1948, at the Hal Roach studio in Culver City, and Lindstrom, who had now entered private medical practice, involved himself in all aspects of the production, and even requested approval of publicity releases. Maxwell Anderson collaborated with script writer Andrew Solt, but the final product lacked the wit and emotionalism of Anderson's play, and Miss Bergman, although a sturdy-looking Joan, was lost amid the spectacle of many pictorially beautiful scenes. However, she did receive her fourth nomination for an Academy Award and the Academy also cited Wanger with a special award for "distinguished service to the industry in adding to its moral stature in the world community by his production of the picture, *Joan of Arc*." Wanger refused the award because the Academy had failed to include the picture among the nominees as Best Picture of the Year. The film had cost $5,000,000 and was almost as great a critical and financial failure as had been *Arch of Triumph*. Victor Fleming died of a heart attack a few weeks after it opened.

With John Emery and Hurd Hatfield in *Joan of Arc* (1948).

Ingrid Bergman's friendship with Robert Capa had introduced her to the films of Roberto Rossellini, father of the postwar, Italian neo-realist school of films, and supposedly after seeing his *Open City*, she exclaimed, "Christ, what an experience!" Shortly after she finished work on *Joan of Arc* in the spring of 1948, she wrote, allegedly at the suggestion of Irene Mayer Selznick, by now divorced from David, the following letter to Rossellini: "I saw your films, *Open City* and *Paisan*, and enjoyed them very much. If you need a Swedish actress who speaks English very well, who has not forgotten her German, who is not very understandable in French, and who in Italian knows only '*ti amo*,' I am ready to come and make a film with you. Best regards, Ingrid Bergman." George Sanders, who co-starred with Miss Bergman in *Viaggio in Italia* in 1954, maintained in his memoirs, that she had written similar letters to several directors seeking challenging projects.

At any rate, Rossellini received this astonishing letter auspiciously on his forty-third birthday and, from Rome's Excelsior Hotel, cabled the following reply: "I have just received with great emotion your letter which happens to arrive on the anniversary of my birthday on the most precious gift stop It is absolutely true that I dreamed of making a film with you and from this very moment I will do everything that such a dream becomes a reality as soon as possible stop I will write you a long letter to submit to you my ideas stop With my admiration please accept the expression of my gratitude together with my best regards."

Miss Bergman's work schedule next took her to England to make *Under Capricorn* (1949) in which she played a dipsomaniac murderess. Despite Alfred Hitchcock's direction, it proved to be her third box-office failure in a row.

With Margaret Leighton and Michael Wilding in *Under Capricorn* (1949).

While in England, she arranged to meet Rossellini in Paris. Her husband flew over and together, through interpreters, they discussed a project called "After the Storm" later released under the title *Stromboli*, after the island on which it was filmed.

In January, 1949, Rossellini came to the United States to accept the New York Film Critics Award for *Paisan*, after which he travelled to California where he visited the Lindstrom's as a house guest. Negotiations for their project had first included producer, Samuel Goldwyn, but he withdrew and the financing was arranged through Howard Hughes. Hughes had recently purchased RKO Radio Pictures Corporation and for several years, had supposedly displayed an interest in Miss Bergman, part of a ubiquitous pursuit which had him dating nearly every feminine star of the screen except Marjorie Main. The deal with Hughes had forty percent of the profits go to En Corporation and twenty percent to Rossellini. Rossellini returned to Italy in February and Miss Bergman arrived in Rome on March 20th, to begin work on the picture.

Miss Bergman's romance with Rossellini was instantly apparent and she wrote Lindstrom for an immediate divorce. He refused, saying he would discuss the matter once she had returned to California.

The production of *Stromboli* was chaotic from the beginning. The press relentlessly followed the now famous couple everywhere. To add to the chaos, Rossellini had not even a prepared script—just the story line—a refugee woman marries a fisherman from an impoverished island to escape a concentration camp. The rest of the story was provided by Rossellini's "spontaneous" film technique. Amidst this turmoil, Miss Bergman continued her plea for a divorce, and when Lindstrom made a business trip to London, she urged him against Rossellini's protests, to meet her in Messina where their meeting reached an *impasse*.

Stromboli was completed in August and on December 12th, Hollywood columnist, Louella Parsons, headlined the news that Miss Bergman was expecting a child in three months. A new furor of publicity ensued, much more blatant and accusing than any that had preceded, and unable to come to terms with Lindstrom, Miss Bergman filed for divorce in Mexico.

erto Gisuto Guiseppe Rossellini (cal- io) was born on February 2, 1950. ned a banal campaign to release coincide with the birth of Robertino, the public on February 15th, what Rossellini called "a ruthlessly edited version," which was predictably condemned by the critics.

Public indignation mounted against Miss Bergman with protests from innumerable religious and "morally-minded" organisations and on March 14th, on the floor of the United States Senate, Senator Edwin C. Johnson of Colorado, made a lengthy declamation against the Bergman-Rossellini professional and personal relationship and vindictively called her "one of the most powerful women on earth...I regret to say a powerful influence for evil...Out of the ashes of Ingrid Bergman will grow a better Hollywood."

Recalling these moral judgments later, Miss Bergman said, "I was thrown out so completely that people couldn't hear my voice on the radio asking for money for the Red Cross. That generation of people does not exist anymore. And if they do exist, they must feel embarrassed."

After obtaining her Mexican divorce, Ingrid Bergman was married to Roberto Rossellini by proxy in Juarez, Mexico, on May 24, 1950. Shortly thereafter, Lindstrom successfully sued for divorce in California, which granted him custody of their daughter, Pia, and made provisions for his ex-wife to see their child during one half of her school vacations. In 1952, Miss Bergman unsuccessfully petitioned the California courts to force Lindstrom to allow Pia, whose name had now been changed to Jenny Ann, to visit her in Italy. At the hearing, the child said she did not love her mother, although she liked her, and wished to remain in the United States. (In 1954, Lindstrom married a pediatrician, Dr. Agnes Rovenek, in Pittsburgh, Pennsylvania, by whom he now has a son.)

Five years later, in the summer of 1957, Miss Bergman was reconciled with her daughter in Europe, and in interviews to the press thereafter, Pia, now resuming her christened name, told reporters that at the court petition in 1952, she had said things she did not understand. She said she had changed her name to Jenny Ann because she wanted to be like other children and did not like her unusual name. She told "Good Housekeeping" magazine, "Like all children, and I was no exception, I didn't like or want to be different. I ached to be *normal* like everyone else. Now, thinking back, I even loathed the way we lived. Our house was surrounded by an electronically-wired fence for protection against autograph seekers and jewel thieves. I dreamed we were imprisoned like convicts." And on another occasion she said, "This much I know. Mama and I are no longer afraid. We were strangers. Now we are sisters. It's too difficult to be bitter about bygone days. Mama has taught me that only when you try to understand others can you forgive."

Subsequently Pia attended the University of Colorado, Mills College and Stanford University studying dramatics, government and history; and while at Stanford, on February 21, 1960, she married Fuller E. Callaway III, a Harvard graduate and son of a Georgia textile manufacturer. They divorced eighteen months later. After attempting to act in several European-made otion pictures (*Marriage Italian Style* (1964), *Zorba the Greek* (1965) Pia became a news reporter for a San Francisco television station. She later transferred to New York City where she is employed by NBC as a news correspondent. On December 12, 1971, she married Joseph Daly, a New York real estate broker. Petter Lindstrom gave the bride away, and Ingrid Bergman attended. The Dalys have two children.

Ingrid Bergman continued to live in Europe and on June 18, 1952, she gave birth to twin daughters — Isabella Fiorella Elettra Giovanna and Issotta Ingrid Freida Giuliana; and she and Rossellini continued to produce motion pictures without attaining artistic or financial success.

In *Europa '51 (The Greatest Love* - (1951), she was implausible as a socially prominent matron who, after the tragic death of her son, turns to helping the poor, becomes too emotionally involved and is finally committed to a mental institution. *Siamo donne* (*We, the Women* - (1953) was an episodic film consisting of five stories allegedly based on actual incidents in the lives of five actresses. Miss Bergman, in the episode called *The Chicken*, wages a serio-comic war with a chicken that has been eating her roses. *Viaggio in Italia* (*Journey to Italy* - (1954) was the story of a bored businessman (George Sanders) and his wife (Miss Bergman) who travel to Italy, decide to divorce, but reconcile after being caught up in the fervour of a religious festival. *Giovanna D'Arco al rogo* (*Joan at the Stake*—(1954) was a choppy film version of the Arthur Honnegger-Paul Claudel oratorio in which Miss Bergman had performed on the stage from 1953 to 1955, in Milan, San Carlos, Palermo, Stockholm, Paris, Barcelona, and London. While performing "Joan at the Stake" in her native Sweden, she received a very cool reception from the press, and when she was invited to attend a charity benefit in Stockholm, she took that opportunity to vindicate herself. "For the past six years I have been slandered, condemned, judged by people who know nothing of my life. They have hurt me badly, but they can't get me down. Someday I'll be judged by Somebody who knows better. That is the only judgment that matters."

Her last film in association with Rossellini was *Angst* (Fear -1954) in which she played a wife who submits to blackmail to prevent her scientist husband from learning of her illicit affair with an artist.

After these disasters, the Rossellinis were strapped for money and the European press began to turn against them for their failure to come up with an artistic success. Rossellini reluctantly obliged when his wife proposed doing a film with another director, and in November, 1955, she began work in Paris on an ineptitude entitled *Paris Does Strange Things,* directed by Jean Renoir. The working titles for this failure included *Elena and the Men, The Red Carnation*, *Black Satin, The Strange Night,* and *The Night Does Strange Things*. The script, also by Renoir, for this cinematic confusion cast Miss Bergman as an impoverished Polish princess with three men awaiting her beck and call. The picture was finally released in the United States by Warner Brothers two years later, after her successful comeback in *Anastasia*.

While making that pointless film, she contracted to do Robert Anderson's "Tea and Sympathy" on the Paris stage in French, and Rossellini contracted to journey to India to make documentaries for the Indian government.

It was also while she was filming *Paris Does Strange Things* that her friend, Kay Brown, arrived in Paris with an offer from 20th Century-Fox to play the title role in *Anastasia;* for which they were willing to pay her $200,000. Buddy Adler, 20th's new president of production, contended that whatever feeling against Miss Bergman there may have been during the last seven years had subsided, and Darryl F. Zanuck, 20th's head, agreed. Filming began in London in the spring of 1956, and television M.C., Ed Sullivan, visited London and acquired film clips of Miss Bergman in a scene with Helen Hayes. On his widely-viewed Sunday evening variety show on July 29th, he announced his intention to show the clips at a future date and also possibly have Miss Bergman appear in person, but he stated, however, that that decision should be made by the public and requested they write him giving their opinion. He ended his speech in a lapse of good taste by stating that Ingrid Bergman had "had seven and a half years time for penance." The New York "Times" declared that Sullivan's comments sounded like the "sanctimonious dogmatism of a modern day Pharisee." 20th Century-Fox cancelled permission to use the film clips and Miss Bergman denied ever having had intentions of appearing on the show. When an accounting of the letters received was made, the majority were against her returning to the United States.

With Helen Hayes in *Anastasia* (1956).

When *Anastasia* was released in the United States in late 1956, it revealed an exquisite performance by Miss Bergman as the amnesia victim who bears a striking resemblance to the Grand Duchess Anastasia, daughter of Nicholas II, Russia's last Czar, who had presumably been murdered with the rest of the Imperial Family in 1918. The film was a personal triumph for Ingrid Bergman and she was awarded the New York Film Critics Award and the Academy Award — each for the second time.

On December 1st of that year, she opened in Paris in a very popular stage version of "Tea and Sympathy." Rossellini, whose masculine pride had been crushed by the failures of his professional ventures with his wife, called the play "trash" and refused to see it; one week after the opening night, he departed for India. He had planned the trip the year before, but postponed it to start work as director of an English film entitled *The Sea Wife* (1957) starring Richard Burton and Joan Collins. Filming had begun in Jamaica, but after several weeks of dissent over script interpretation, he quit. Later Miss Bergman commented on his departure for India. "We knew then that it was over. If only Roberto had accomplished something successfully, the marriage might have been saved. I understood him, but I was powerless to alter the way things were. Roberto's pride was hurt. Everything seemed to go against him — very hard for a man of his talent and ability to swallow. And *Anastasia* and "Tea and Sympathy" didn't help any."

During the run of "Tea and Sympathy," 20th Century-Fox bought up three performances of the play to enable Miss Bergman to fly to New York and accept her award from the New York Film Critics. She arrived on the morning of January 19, 1957, attended that award ceremony at Sardi's restaurant, saw a matinee of "My Fair Lady," received "Look" magazine's award from Joan Crawford, telephoned her daughter at school in Colorado, and returned to Paris the next day.

In October, 1957, Rossellini returned to Paris from India. His arrival was preceded three weeks by the arrival of his *amarota*, Sonali Dus Gupta, a scenarist who was also the wife of an Indian film director and the mother of two sons. The following December she gave birth to a daughter and shortly thereafter, Miss Bergman and Rossellini set Italy's legal machinery in motion to annul their marriage on the ground that Miss Bergman's divorce from Lindstrom had not been registered in Sweden.

On December 21, 1958, Miss Bergman married Lars Schmidt, a Swedish theatrical impresario whom she had met through her long-time friend, Kay Brown. The Schmidts established permanent residence in a remodeled chateau in the small village of Choisel, twenty-five miles from Paris, where Schmidt had business headquarters.

In the spring of 1959, Schmidt and Pia Lindstrom accompanied an apprehensive Ingrid Bergman on her first visit to Hollywood in ten years, where the Academy of Motion Picture Arts and Sciences had invited her to present their award for the Best Picture of the Year on their live television broadcast. She arrived on April 3rd, and three days later received the warmest ovation of the evening as she stepped forward to present producer Arthur Freed with his award for the motion-picture, *Gigi*.

Since *Anastasia,* Ingrid Bergman has appeared in only ten films and while not all of them have been good choices, they are not without interest. *Indiscreet* (1958), based on Norman Krasna's play "Kind Sir," was well-mounted *frou, frou* reuniting her with Cary Grant, her co-star in *Notorious*. *The Inn of the Sixth Happiness* (1958) cast her as Gladys Aylward the English missionary in China who leads children to safety during the 1934 invasion by Japan, and allowed her to project the selfless idealism she can so effortlessly make believable and earned her the Best Actress accolade from the National Board of Review of Motion Pictures.

Goodbye Again (1961) was an attempt at sophisticated soap-opera which asked us to believe in Miss Bergman as a fortyish Parisian interior decorator who leaves her middle-aged lover (Yves Montand) for the love of a bewildered youth played by, of all people, Anthony Perkins. Based on Francoise Sagan's novel "Aimez-Vous Brahms?" it created little stir this side of the Atlantic, but picked up a European award for Anthony Perkin's "emoting" as the young lover.

Her performance in "*The Visit*" (1964), from the play by Friedrich Durrenmatt cast her as a villainess, one of Europe's richest women who offers an enormous benefaction to her native village if it will turn upon one of its leading citizens (Anthony Quinn) and condemn him to death for having "ruined" her in her youth. However, the ending was changed so the human sacrifice in the play is not brought to fruition thereby making it less dramatic than the theatre version magnificently performed by Alfred Lunt and Lynn Fontanne during their last appearance together on Broadway in 1958. Nonetheless, Miss Bergman's performance astounded her admirers as well as her enemies. Her projection of implacable hatred and vengeance was so unlike anything she had done on the screen before but was just as convincing as her previous depictions of selfless idealism.

The Yellow Rolls-Royce (1965) was a three-part international production in which she was miscast as an American millionairess, who during World

In *The Inn of the Sixth Happiness* (1958).

With Anthony Quinn in *The Visit* (1964).

War II, has an affair with a Yugoslav patriot, Omar Sharif.

Stilmulantia (1967) was an eight part film, this time a Swedish production which has yet to be released in this country. Here she plays the wife in an episode that is based on de Maupassant's "The Necklace," and interestingly, this episode was directed by the same man who had directed many of her first Swedish films, Gustaf Molander: the man who made the Ingrid Bergman career possible.

In 1969, she contracted with Columbia Pictures for two pictures to be made in the United States. *Cactus Flower* (1969) was the film version of the Lauren Bacall Broadway comedy in which Miss Bergman played the shy, unnoticed, and essentially unappreciated assistant to a bachelor dentist. Not always at ease with comedy, she was for the most part believable, but was overshadowed by comedienne Goldie Hawn, who walked off with an Oscar.

Her second commitment for Columbia was *A Walk in the Spring Rain* (1970), a romantic story of a middle-aged love affair released at a time when such sentimentality was hardly acceptable screen fare.

Three years later she performed an almost cameo role in *From the Mixed-Up Files of Mrs. Basil E. Frankweiler* (1973). Based on the wonderfully entertaining book of the same title by E.L. Konigsburg, this family picture was a bit too precious and Miss Bergman was miscast at the septuagenarian recluse. Still much too beautiful for this kind of role, the make-up and wardrobe technicians were taken to task by Vincent Canby in the New York "Times" for allowing Miss Bergman to wear "a white wig and long black dress of the sort usually worn by the male lead in "Charley's Aunt."

While her output on the screen has not been as prolific in the last decade-and-a-half — Miss Bergman, like all middle-aged actresses, has suffered a demise of good scripts — she has made appearances on television and on the stage in parts which have received international attention. She received an Emmy Award for her first venture into television, playing Henry James's governess in "The Turn of the Screw" (NBC-1959). She was beautiful but lost in the tedious soap-opera called "24 Hours in a Woman's Life" (CBS-1961). In 1963, she starred in a stellar production of Ibsen's "Hedda Gabler" (CBS) with Michael Redgrave, Ralph Richardson and Trevor Howard. She had performed this role on the stage in French in Paris the year before and the critical reaction to each version was that she was beautiful and competent, but did not elicit the vanity and destructiveness of Ibsen's heroine. Her last television appearance was the dramatic "The Human Voice" (ABC-1967) based on Jean Cocteau's monologue about a woman trying to save her love affair via a telephone conversation. Miss Bergman, a friend of Cocteau, recorded this playlet several years before, and her televison version was none other than a *tour de force*.

Between television roles, in June, 1965, she starred in a London stage version of Ivan Turgenev's "A Month in the Country," where her stage presence compensated for the dated play. In the fall of 1967, she returned to the American stage for the first time in twenty-one years in O'Neill's "More Stately Mansions," with Colleen Dewhurst and Arthur Hill. Playing first in Los Angeles' Ahmason Theatre, then opening on Broadway on October 31st, O'Neill's static verbosity took its knocks from the critics. Miss Dewhurst won kudos for her emoting, but it was Ingrid Bergman the star who had Clive Barnes exclaiming in the New York "Times," "Ingrid Bergman is a woman so beautiful that she is herself a work of art."

In April, 1972, she again appeared on the Broadway stage in George Bernard Shaw's "Captain Brasshound's Conversion" after performing it in London and on tour in the States. Years before Miss Bergman had met the inimitable Shaw; he asked her which of his plays she had done and she replied none, to which he countered, "Oh, my dear girl, you haven't even begun yet." However, "Captain Brassbound's Conversion" was not an appropriate vehicle and she was no more than decorative as Shaw's irrepressibly charming heroine, Lady Cicely.

During the Washington, D.C., engagement of this play, on April 19th, Senator Charles H. Percy of Illinois, entered into the Congressional Record a tribute that named her "one of the world's loveliest, most gracious and most talented women...the victim of bitter attack in this chamber twenty-two years ago. Today, I would like to pay tribute to Ingrid Bergman, a true star in every sense of the word...I know that across the land millions of Americans would wish to join me in expressing their regrets for the personal and professional persecution that caused Ingrid Bergman to leave this country at the height of her career." Miss Bergman responded by saying Senator Percy's remarks came as a "complete surprise," and that the earlier comments in 1950, by Senator Johnson were "never forgotten. They were hard to forget."

The legal imbroglio over the Bergman-Rossellini divorce did not end in 1958. Two years later the Italian courts challenged the annulment and after it was finally recognised, the two parties were still involved in litigation over custody of the children and their education. They ultimately compromised by allowing the children to establish their own apartment in Rome under the supervision of a housekeeper. Miss Bergman and her ex-husband both visited their children when their work schedules permitted, all the while maintaining an equitable, personal friendship. Not incidentally, Pia, frequently also joined her half-brother and sisters. None of Miss Bergman's children by Rossellini have chosen to follow in their parents footsteps professionally. During her adolescence Isabella, who has the face of a Botticelli Venus, wore a cast to cure a deformed spine diagnosed as scoliosis.

Recently Miss Bergman expressed a certain pessimism when, speaking of her future in films, she said, "After more than thirty years as a film star a woman loses her appeal," but that statement proved quite premature, for her most recent film role — *Murder On the Orient Express* — brought her yet another personal triumph. Joining the all-star cast of Sidney Lumet's stylishly evocative adaptation of Agatha Christie's famous mystery novel, Miss Bergman was nothing short of brilliant as Greta, the humble, Swedish missionary. This performance, along with her performance in *Notorious* in 1946, are probably her finest work on the screen and it earned her a third Academy Award, this time as Best Supporting Actress.

At the award's ceremony on April 8, 1975, Miss Bergman was the highpoint of an otherwise dull evening when she confidently walked on stage and expressed her confusion at competing with Valentina Cortese's excellent performance in *Day For Night*, a film which the year before had been named the Best Foreign Film, and now was eligible for acting nominations a year later.

Her acceptance speech was one of the most forthright in Academy history: "It's so ironic that this year she's nominated when the picture won last year. I don't quite understand that but here I am and I don't like it at all. Please forgive me, Valentina. I didn't mean to."

Miss Bergman joins Helen Hayes as the only ladies to have won Awards for both Best Actress and Best Supporting Actress. There is some irony in Miss Bergman's richly deserved prestige in Hollywood today; it's not too long ago that Hollywood had rejected her for her romance with Roberto Rossellini.

While film roles may not have seemed all that accessible to Miss Bergman (the new Oscar could change that situation) she continues her career in the theatre preferring revivals of established works over modern plays because, "I don't think most modern plays are worth learning by heart." Her most recent theatrical venture was a revival of Somerset Maugham's "The Constant Wife," directed by Sir John Gielgud. The play opened in London in the fall of 1973, where reviewers praised her beauty more than her facility for drawing-room comedy. Following the London engagement, the play toured the United States during the spring of 1975 — Los Angeles, Denver, Washington, D.C., Boston — prior to opening on Broadway on April 14th for a limited four-week run. Once again critics were enthralled by her stage presence, her graciousness and her beauty.

Miss Bergman lives her life with no apparent regrets over the turmoil of the Fifties. As she once told columnist Dorothy Kilgallen, "I wanted success, a big success as an actress and a home and children. I have them. So I am happy. If the price I paid was too high I wish only I had paid it alone. My children paid for it too. Their paths were strewn with broken homes." Later only when her unorthodox move to Europe had become less newsworthy, she said, "I don't think my children are unhappy. I think the situation is as good as it can be for the children of divorced parents. Roberto takes good care of them, I take good care of them. That's as good as you can hope for in this world."

Without apologies, she states, "I have had a wonderful life. I have never regretted what I did. I regret the things I didn't do. My life has been rich and full of interesting things. All my life I've done things at a moment's notice. Those are the things we remember. I was given courage, a sense of adventure and a little bit of humor."

Always outspoken, she told the press in the Sixties, "Times have changed since 1949. No one objects to the Beatles having a holiday with their girls, perhaps because everyone is so pleased thay are not taking boys with them." And, during her return to Broadway in "More Stately Mansions," she told the New York "Times," I am the way I am, I can't help it. People say to me, 'You don't have to tell everything. Can't you learn from Garbo? She never says anything, and you are talking your head off.' But I'm terribly frank, and I don't have the restraint to think, 'Maybe I shouldn't say that.' Usually people hide behind some kind of facade. Usually people are much more careful, I am not careful. I throw it right out, and I never say anything that is not the truth."

Throughout her battle with public opinion and the press, a number of Miss Bergman's friends remained her loyal supporters, including Ernest Hemingway, Joan Crawford, Helen Hayes, Irene Mayer Selznick, Kay Brown, Ruth Roberts, Alfred Hitchcock, John Steinbeck, David O. Selznick, Jennifer Jones, Van Johnson, Gary Cooper, Elizabeth Bergner, Leonard Lyons, Billy Rose, and Cary Grant, who summed up her lifestyle very succinctly, "She dares to live truthfully."

The Feature Film Appearances of Ingrid Bergman

Munkbrogreven (The Count of the Monk's Bridge) (Svensk Filmindustri, 1934). Screenplay by Gosta Stevens from the play, "Greven fran Gamla Sta'n," by Arthur and Sigfried Fischer. Directed by Edvin Adolphon and Sigurd Wallen. *Cast*: Valdemar Dahlquist, Sigurd Wallen, Eric Abrahamson, Weyler Hildebrand, Arthur Cederborg, Edvin Adolphson, Ingrid Bergman, Tollie Zellman, Julia Caesar, Arthur Fischer, Emil Fjellstrom, Viktor "Kulorten" Andersson.

Branningar (Ocean Breakers) (Svensk Filmindustri, 1935) Screenplay by Ivar Johansson from an idea by Henning Ohlssen. Directed by Ivar Johansson. *Cast:* Tore Svennberg, Sten Lindgren, Carl Strom, Ingrid Bergman, Bror Ohlsson, Knut Frankman, Carin Swenson, Weyler Hildebrand, Georg Skarstedt, Henning Ohlsson, Vera Lindby, Viktor Ost,Emmy Albiin, Viktor Andersson, Helga Brofeldt, Carl Browallius, Olle Grenberg, Holger Lownadler, E. Rosen.

Swedenhielms (Svensk Filmindustri, 1935). Screenplay by Stina Bergman from the play by Hjalmar Bergman. Directed by Gustaf Molander. *Cast:* Gösta Ekman, Karin Swanström, Bjorn Berglund, Häkan Westergren, Tutta Rolf, Ingrid Bergman, Sigurd Wallén, Nils Ericsson, Adele Söderblom, Mona Geijer-Falkner, Hjalmar Peters.

Valborgsmässoafton (Walpurgis Night) (Svensk Filmindustri, 1935). Screenplay by Oscar Rydquist and Gustaf Edgren from their story. Directed by Gustaf Edgren. *Cast:* Lars Hanson, Karin Carlsson, Victor Seastrom, Ingrid Bergman, Erik Berglund, Sture Lagerwall, Georg Rydeberg, Georg Blickinberg, Rickard Lund, Stig Järrel, Marie-Louise Sorbon, Gabriel Alw, Carl-Gunnar Wingard, Aino Taube, Torsten Hillberg, Anders Henriksson, Torsten Winge, Greta Berthels, Ake Uppström, Linnea Hillberg, Ivar Kage, Lill-Acke, Olaf Widgren, Hjalmar Peters, Pecka Hagman, Harry Hednoff.

På solsidan (On the Sunny Side) (Svensk Filmindustri, 1936). Screenplay by Oscar Hemberg and Gösta Stevens from the play by Helge Krog. Directed by Gustaf Molander. *Cast:* Lars Hanson, Ingrid Bergman, Karin Swanstrom, Edvin Adolphson, Einar Axelson, Marianne L'ofgren, Carl Browallius, Bullen Berglund, Eddie Figge, Olga Andersson, Viktor Andersson, Eric Gustafsson.

Intermezzo (Svensk Filmindustri, 1936). Screenplay by Gustaf Molander and Gösta Stevens from the story by Molander. Directed by Gustaf Molander. *Cast:* Gösta Ekman, Inga Tidblad, Hasse Ekman, Britt Hagman, Erik Berglund, Ingrid Bergman, Hugo Bjorne, Emma Meissner, Anders Henrikson, Millan Bolander, George Fant, Folke Helleberg, Margit Orth, Carl Strom.

Dollar (Svensk Filmindustri, 1938) Screenplay by Stina Bergman and Gustaf Molander from the play by Hjalmar Bergman. Directed by Gustaf Molander. *Cast:* Georg Rydeberg, Ingrid Bergman, Kotti Chave, Tutta Rolf, Håkan Westergren, Birgit Tengroth, Elsa Burnett, Edvin Adolphson, Gösta Cederlund, Eric Rosen, Carl Ström, Alex Hogel, Millan Bolander, David Eriksson, Erland Colliander, Nils Dahlgren, Gustav Lagerberg, Richard Lindström, E. Dethorey, Dickson, Aina Elkman, Hester Harvey, Helge Kihlberg, Allan Linder.

En Kvilnnas ansikte (A Woman's Face) (Svensk Filmindustri, 1938). Screenplay by Gösta Stevens from the play "Il était une fois" by Francois de Croisset. Directed by Gustaf Molander. *Cast:* Ingrid Bergman, Anders Henrikson, Erik Berglund, Magnus Kesster, Gösta Cederlund, Georg Rydeberg, Tore Svennberg, Goran Bernhard, Gunnar Sjöberg, Hilda Borgstrom, John Ericsson, Karin Carlsson - Kavli, Sigurd Wallen, Bror Bugler.

En enda natt (Only One Night) (Svensk Filmindustri, 1938). Screenplay by Gösta Stevens from the story "En eneste natt" by Harald Tandrup. Directed by Gustaf Molander. *Cast:* Ingrid Bergman, Edvin Adolphson, Aino Taube, Olof Sandborg, Erik "Bullen" Berglund, Marianne Löfgren, Magnus Kesster, Sophus Dahl, Ragna Breda, John Eklof, Tor Borong, Viktor "Kulorten" Andersson, Ka Nerell, Folke Helleberg, Nila Nordstahl.

Die vier gesellen (The Four Companions) (UFA, 1938) Screenplay by Jochen Huth from his play. Directed by Carl Froelich. *Cast:* Ingrid Bergman, Sabine Peters, Ursula Herking, Carsta Lock, Hans Sohnker, Leo Slezak, Heinz Weizel, Willi Rose, Erich Ponto, Karl Haubenreiber, Wilhelm P. Kruger, Lotte Braun, Hugo Froelich, Rudolf Klicks, Max Rosenhauer, Ernst G. Schiffner, Hans Jurgen Weidlich

Juninatten (A Night in June) Svensk Filmindustri, 1939)Screenplay by Ragnar Hylten-Cavallius from a story by Tora Nordstrom-bonnier. Directed by Per Lindberg. *Cast:* Ingrid Bergman, Marianne Löfgren, Lill-Tollie Zellman, Marianne Aminoff, Olof Widgren, Gunnar Sjöberg, Gabriel Alw, Olof Winnerstrand, Sigurd Wallen, Hasse Ekman, Maritta Marke, Gudrun Brost, John Botvid, Karin Swanström, Carl Strom, Mimi Pollack, Charlie Paterson, Ernst Brunman, Alf Kjellin, Karin Nordgren, Mona Geijer-Falkner, David Eriksson, Douglas Hage, Carl Deurell, Sven-Goran Alw, Richard Lund, Nils Jacobsson, Sol-Britt Agerup, Kerstin Ekwall, Britta Larsson, Viran Rydkvist, Erik Forslund.

Intermezzo: A Love Story (Selznick International-United Artists, 1939) Screenpaly by George O'Neil from the Swedish scenario by Gosta Stevens and Gustaf Molander. Directed by Gregory Ratoff. *Cast*: Leslie Howard, Ingrid Bergman, Edna Best, John Halliday, Cecil Kellaway, Enid Bennett, Ann Todd, Douglas Scott, Eleanor Wesselhoeft, Moria Flynn.

Adam Had Four Sons (Columbia, 1941). Screenplay by William Hurlbutt and Michael Blankfort from the novel, "Legacy," by Charles Bonner. Directed by Gregory Ratoff. *Cast:* Ingrid Bergman, Warner Baxter, Susan Hayward, Fay Wray, Richard Denning, Johnny Downs, Robert Shaw, Charles Lind, Helen Westley, June Lockhart, Pietro Sasso, Gilbert Emery, Renie Riano, Clarence Muse, Billy Ray, Steven Muller, Wallace Chadwell, Bobby Walberg.

Rage in Heaven (M-G-M, 1941). Screenplay by Christopher Isherwood and Robert Thoeren from the novel by James Hilton. Directed by W.S. Van Dyke II. *Cast:* Robert Montgomery, Ingrid Bergman, George Sanders, Lucile Watson, Oscar Homolka, Philip Merivale, Matthew Bolton, Aubrey Mather, Fredric Worlock, Francis Compton, Gilbert Emery, Ludwig Hart.

Dr. Jekyll and Mr. Hyde (M-G-M, 1941). Screenplay by John Lee Mahin from the story by Robert Louis Stevenson. Directed by Victor Fleming, *Cast:* Spencer Tracy, Ingrid Bergman, Lana Turner, Ian Hunter, Donald Crisp, Barton MacLane, C. Aubrey Smith, Sara Allgood, Peter Godfrey, Fredric Worlock, William Tannen, Frances Robinson, Denis Green, Billy

Bevan, Forrester Harvey, Lumsden Hare, Lawrence Grant, John Barclay.

Casablanca (Warner Brothers, 1943). Screenplay by Julius J. and Philip G. Epstein and Howard Koch from the play "Everybody Comes to Rick's" by Murray Burnett and Joan Alison. Directed by Michael Curtiz. *Cast:* HumphreyBogart, Ingrid Bergman, Paul Henreid, Claude Rains, Conrad Veidt, Sydney Greenstreet, Peter Lorre, S.Z. Sakall, Madeleine Le Beau, Dooley Wilson, Joy Page, John Qualen, Leonid Kinsky, Helmut Dantine, Curt Bois, Marcel Dalio, Corinna Mura, Ludwig Gruning, Ilka Gruning, Charles La Torre, Frank Puglia, Dan Seymour.

Note: **Casablanca** was released without fanfare in November, 1942, but not officially released until after the first of the following year, qualifying it as a 1943 picture and enabling it to earn the Best Picture Academy Award for 1943.

For Whom the Bell Tolls (Paramount, 1943). Screenplay by Dudley Nichols from the novel by Ernest Hemingway. Directed by Sam Wood. *Cast:* Gary Cooper, Ingrid Bergman, Akim Tamiroff, Katina Paxinou, Joseph Calleia, Vladimir Sokoloff, Arturo de Cordova, Mikhail Rasumny, Eduardo Ciannelli, Fortunio Bonanova, Duncan Renaldo, Alexander Granach, Leonid Snegoff, George Coulouris, Frank Puglia, Pedro de Cordoba, Michael Visaroff, Konstantin Shayne, Martin Garralaga, Jean Del Val, Jack Mylong, Feodor Chaliapin, Mayo Newhall, Michael Delmatoff, Antonio Vidal, Robert Tafur, Armand Roland.

Gaslight (M-G-M, 1944) Screenplay by John Van Druten, Walter Reisch, and John L. Balderston from the play "Angel Street" by Patrick Hamilton. Directed by George Cukor. *Cast:* Charles Boyer, Ingrid Bergman, Joseph Cotten, Dame May Whitty, Angela Lansbury, Barbara Everest, Emil Rameau, Edmund Brean, Halliwell Hobbes, Tom Stevenson, Heather Thatcher, Lawrence Naismith, John Gimpel.

The Bells of St. Mary's (RKO, 1945). Screenplay by Dudley Nichols from a story by Leo McCarey. Directed by Leo McCarey. *Cast:* Bing Crosby, Ingrid Bergman, Henry Travers, William Gargan, Ruth Donnelly, Joan Carroll, Martha Sleeper, Rhys Williams, Dickie Tyler, Una O'Connor, Bobby Fresco, Aina Constant, Gwen Crawford, Matt McHugh, Edna Wonacott, Jimmy Crane, Minerva Urecal, Pietro Sasso, Cora Shannon, Joseph Palma, Jimmy Dundee, Dewey Robinson.

Spellbound (Selznick International-United Artists, 1945). Screenplay by Ben Hecht from Angus MacPhail's adaptation of the novel "The House of Doctor Edward's" by Francis Beeding. Directed by Alfred Hitchcock. *Cast:* Ingrid Bergman, Gregory Peck, Michael Chekhov, Jean Acker, Donald Curtis, Rhonda Fleming, Leo G. Carroll, Norman Lloyd, John Emery, Paul Harvey, Steven Geray, Erskine Sanford, Janet Scott, Victor Kilian, Wallace Ford, Dave Willock, Bill Goodwin, George Meader, Matt Moore, Harry Brown, Art Baker, Regis Toomey, Joel Davis, Clarence Straight, Teddy Infuhr, Richard Bartell, Addison Richards, Edward Fielding.

Saratoga Trunk (Warner Brothers, 1946). Screenplay by Casey Robinson from the novel by Edna Ferber. Directed by Sam Wood. *Cast:* Gary Cooper, Ingrid Bergman, Flora Robson, Jerry Austin, Florence Bates, John Warburton, John Abbott, Curt Bois, Ethel Griffies, Minor Watson, Louis Payne, Fred Essler, Adrienne D'Ambricourt, Helen Freeman, Sophie Huxley, Marla Shelton, Sarah Edwards, Jacqueline DeWit, Thurston Hall, William B. Davidson, Theodore Von Eltz. Glenn Strange, Monte Blue, Georges Renevant, Alice Fleming, Alan Bridge, Ruby Dandridge, Ralph Dunn.

Note, **Saratoga Trunk**, while made in 1943, and shown abroad to our servicemen and in a few cities in the United States in 1945, is given the official release date of March 30, 1946.

Notorious (RKO, 1946) Screenplay by Ben Hecht from a story by Alfred Hitchcock. Directed by Alfred Hitchcock. *Cast:* Cary Grant, Ingrid Bergman, Claude Rains, Louis Calhern, Madame Konstantin, Ivan Triesault, Reinhold Schunzel, Moroni Olsen, Alexis Minotis, Wally Brown, Ricardo Costa, Lenore Ulric, Sir Charles Mendl, Ederhard Krumschmidt, Fay Baker, Peter Von Zernack, Ramon Nomar.

Arch of Triumph (Enterprise-United Artists, 1948). Screenplay by Lewis Milestone and Harry Brown from the novel by Erich Maria Remarque. Directed by Lewis Milestone. *Cast:* Ingrid Bergman, Charles Boyer, Charles Laughton, Louis Calhern, Roman Bohner, Stephen Bekassy, Ruth Nelson, Curt Bois, J. Edward Bromberg, Michael Romanoff, Art Smith, John Laurenz, Leon Lenoir, Franco Corsaro, Nino Pepitoni, Vladimar Rashevsky, Alvin Hammer, Jay Gilpin, Ilia Khmara, Andre Marsauden, Hazel Brooks, Byron Foulger, William Conrad, Peter Virgo, Feodor Chaliapin.

Joan of Arc (RKO, 1948) Screenplay by Maxwell Anderson and Andrew Solt from Anderson's play, "Joan of Lorraine." Directed by Victor Fleming. *Cast:* Ingrid Bergman, Jose Ferrer, George Coulouris, Richard Derr, Ray Teal, Roman Bohnen, Selena Royle, Jimmy Lydon, Robert Barrat, Francis L. Sullivan, Rand Brooks, Nestor Paiva, Irene Rich, Gene Lockhart, Nicholas Joy, Frederic Worlock, Tom Browne Henry, Vincent Donahue, Richard Ney, Colin Keith-Johnston, Leif Erikson, John Emery, John Ireland, Ward Bond, Gregg Barton, Henry Brandon, Dennis Hoey, J. Carroll Naish, Hurd Hatfield, Cecil Kellaway, Ethan Laidlaw, Morris Ankrum, Philip Bourneuf, Shepperd Strudwick, Taylor Holmes, Stephen Roberts, Frank Puglia, Houseley Stevenson, Alan Napier, David Bond, Bill Kennedy, Victor Wood, George Zucco, Jeff Corey, John Parrish, Mary Currier, Aubrey Mather, Herbert Rudley, William Conrad, Frank Elliott, Roy Roberts, Barbara Wooddell, Greta Granstedt, Julia Faye, Marjorie Wood, Arthur Space, Eve March.

Under Capricorn (Warner Brothers, 1949). Screenplay by James Bridie from Hume Cronyn's adaptation of the play by John Colton and Margaret Linden and the novel by Helen Simpson. Directed by Alfred Hitchcock. *Cast:* Ingrid Bergman, Joseph Cotten, Michael Wilding, Margaret Leighton, Cecil Parker, Denis O'Dea, Jack Watling, Harcourt Williams, John Ruddock, Bill Shine, Victor Lucas, Ronald Adam, Francis de Wolff, G.H. Mulcaster, Olive Sloane, Maureen Delaney, Julia Lang, Betty McDermott, Roderick Lovell.

Stromboli (RKO, 1950). Screenplay by Roberto Rossellini in collaboration with Art Cohn, Renzo Cesana,

Sergio Amidei, and G. P. Callegari. Directed by Roberto Rossellini. *Cast:* Ingrid Bergman, Mario Vitale, Renzo Cesana, Mario Sponza.

Europá '51 (the Greatest Love) (I.F.E. Releasing Corporation, 1951). Screenplay by Roberto Rossellini, Sandro de Leo, Mario Pannunzio, Ivo Perilli and Brunello Rondi. Directed by Roberto Rossellini. *Cast:* Ingrid Bergman, Alexander Knox, Ettore Giannini, Giulietta Masina, Teresa Pellati, Sandro Franchina, William Tubbs, Alfred Browne.

Siamo donne (We, The Women) (Titanus, 1953). Screenplay by Cesare Zavattini from his stories with collaboration by Luigi Chiarini, Georgia Prosperi and Suso Cecchi D'Amico. Directed by Alfredo Guarini, Gianni Francioli, Roberto Rossellini, Luigi Zampa, Luchino Visconti. *Cast:* Ingrid Bergman, Anna Magnani, Isa Miranda, Alida Valli, Emma Danieli, Anna Amendola.

Viaggio in Italia (Journey to Italy) (Titanus, 1954). Screenplay by Roberto Rossellini and Vitaliano Brancati. Directed by Roberto Rossellini. *Cast:* Ingrid Bergman, George Sanders, Paul Muller, Anna Proclemer, Maria Mauban, Leslie Daniels, Natalia Rai, Jackie Frost.

Giovanna D'Arco al rogo (Joan at the Stake) (ENIC, 1954). Screenplay by Roberto Rossellini based on the story and dialogue of Paul Claudel and the oratorio by Claudel and Arthur Honegger. Directed by Roberto Rossellini. *Cast:* Ingrid Bergman, Tullio Carminati, Giacinto Prantelli, Augusto Romani, Plinio Clabassi, Saturno Meletti, Agnese Dubbini, Pietro de Palma, Aldo Tenossi, Voices of Pina Esca, Marcella Pillo, Giovanni Acolati, Miriam Pirazzini.

Angst (Fear) (Minerva Films, 1955). Screenplay by Roberto Rossellini, Sergio Amidei and Franz Graf Treuberg from the novel "Der Angst" by Stefan Zweig. Directed by Roberto Rossellini. *Cast:* Ingrid Bergman, Mathias Wiemann, Renate Mannhardt, Kurt Kreuger, Elise Aulinger.

Anastasia (20th Century-Fox, 1956). Screenplay by Arthur Laurents from Guy Bolton's adaptation of Marcel Maurette's play. Directed by Anatole Litvak. *Cast:* Ingrid Bergman, Yul Brynner, Helen Hayes, Akim Tamiroff, Martita Hunt, Felix Aylmer, Sacha Piteoff, Ivan Desny, Natalie Schafer, Gregoire Gromoff, Karel Stepanek, Ina De La Haye, Katherine Kath.

Paris Does Strange Things (Elèna et les hommes) (Warner Brothers, 1957). Screenplay by Jean Renoir from his story. Directed by Jean Renoir. *Cast:* Ingrid Bergman, Mel Ferrer, Jean Marais, Juliette Greco, Marjane, George Higgins, J. Richard.

Indiscreet (Warner Brothers, 1958). Screenplay by Norman Krasna from his play, "Kind Sir." Directed by Stanley Donen. *Cast:* Cary Grant, Ingrid Bergman. Cecil Parker, Phyllis Calvert, David Kossoff, Megs Jenkins, Oliver Johnston, Middleton Woods.

The Inn of the Sixth Happiness (20th Century-Fox, 1958). Screenplay by Isobel Lennart from "The Small Woman," by Alan Burgess. Directed by Mark Robson. *Cast:* Ingrid Bergman, Curt Jurgens, Robert Donat, Michael David, Athene Seyler, Ronald Squire, Moultrie Kelsall, Richard Wattis, Peter Chong, Tsai Chin, Edith Sharpe, Joan Young, Lian-Shin Yang, Noel Hood, Burt Kwouk.

Goodbye Again (United Artists, 1961). Screenplay by Samuel Taylor from the novel "Aimez-vous Bramhs?," by Françoise Sagan. Directed by Anatole Litvak. *Cast:* Ingrid Bergman, Yves Montand, Anthony Perkins, Jessie Royce Landis, Jackie Lane, Pierre dux, Jean Clarke, Peter Bull, Michele Mercier, Uta Taeger, André Randall, David Horne, Lee Patrick, A. Duperoux, Raymond Gerome, Jean Hebey, Michel Garland, Paul Uny, Colin Mann, Diahann Carroll.

The Visit (20th Century-Fox, 1964). Screenplay by Ben Barzman from the play by Friedrich Dürrenmatt. Directed by Bernhard Wicki. *Cast:* Ingrid Bergman, Anthony Quinn, Irina Demick, Valentina Cortese, Ernest Schroeder, Paolo Stoppa, Hans-Christian Bleck, Romolo Valli, Claude Dauphin, Eduardo Ciannelli, Leonard Stoeckel, Richard Munch, Mario Guglielmi, Jacques Dufilho, Fausto Tozzi, Dante Meggio, Reno Palmer, Lelia Luttozzi.

The Yellow Rolls-Royce (M-G-M, 1965). Screenplay by Terence Rattigan. Directed by Anthony Asquith. *Cast:* Episode One - Rex Harrison, Jeanne Moreau, Edmund Purdom, Moira Lister, Isa Miranda, Roland Culver, Episode Two - Shirley MacLaine, Alain Delon, George C. Scott, Art Carney; Episode Three - Ingrid Bergman, Omar Sharif, Joyce Grenfell, Wally Cox.

Stimulantia (Omnia Film, 1967). An episodic film directed by Hans Abramson, Jörn Donner, Lars Gorling, Ingmar Bergman, Arne Arnbom, Tage Danielsson-Hans Alfredson, Gustaf Molander, and Vilgot Sjöman. Miss Bergman appeared in the segment called *Smycket* (The Necklace) directed and written by Molander from the story by Guy de Maupassant. Co-starring in that segment were Gunnar Björnstrand and Gunnel Broström.

Cactus Flower (Columbia, 1969). Screenplay by I.A.L. Diamond from the play by Abe Burrows from the French play by Varillet and Gredy. Directed by Gene Saks. *Cast:* Ingrid Bergman, Walter Mathhau, Goldie Hawn, Jack Weston, Rick Lenz, Vito Scotti, Irene Hervey, Eve Bruce, Irwin Charone, Matthew Saks.

A Walk in the Spring Rain (Columbia, 1970). Screenplay by Stirling Silliphant from the novel by Rachel Maddux. Directed by Guy Green, *Cast:* Ingrid Bergman, Anthony Quinn, Fritz Weaver, Katherine Crawford, Tom Fielding, Virginia Gregg, Mitchell Silberman.

From the Mixed-Up Files of Mrs. Basil E. Frankweiler (Cinema 5, 1973). Screenplay by Blanche Hanalis from the novel by E.L. Konigsburg. Directed by Fielder Cook. *Cast:* Ingrid Bergman, Sally Prager, Johnny Doran, George Rose, Richard Mulligan, Georgann Johnson, Madeline Kahn, Donald Symington, Linda Selman, Brucie Conover, Mike Hammett, Peter Turgeon, Robert Packer.

Murder on the Orient Express (Paramount, 1974). Screenplay by Paul Dehn from the novel by Agatha Christie. Directed by Sidney Lumet. *Cast:* Albert Finney, Lauren Bacall, Martin Balsam, Ingrid Bergman, Jacqueline Bisset, Jean Pierre Cassel, Sean Connery, John Gielgud, Wendy Hiller, Anthony Perkins, Vanessa Redgrave, Rachel Roberts, Richard Widmark, Michael York, Colin Blakely, George Coulouris, Denis Quilley, Vernon Dotbcheff, Jeremy Lloyd, John Moffatt.

Accepting her Oscar for *Gone With the Wind* (1939).

4

VIVIEN LEIGH

The role of Scarlett O'Hara in *Gone With the Wind* was undoubtedly sought after by more actresses than any other role in movie history. There is no doubt that the actress who was finally chosen epitomised Margaret Mitchell's conception of her head-strong heroine. Vivien Leigh's portrayal of Scarlett O'Hara enabled us to see pathos as well as malevolence in an unloving heart. Miss Leigh continued to exhibit and develop those qualities in each of the nine films she made after *Gone With the Wind*. Although her stage roles were more versatile, and occasionally less neurotic, on the screen, she portrayed those emotions which are concomitant with feminine egotism and womanly incompletion. For example, her last two films — *The Roman Spring of Mrs. Stone* and *Ship of Fools* — resembled Dante-esque excursions into the hell experienced by mature women who in youth, loved only themselves.

While everyone acknowledged her delicate beauty and grace, there were those who felt her achievements were more the result of her twenty-odd years professional and personal association with Laurence Olivier, than the result of innate artistry. In 1946, British critic, James Agate, wrote, "She's heavenly to look at, and is an equisite, charming, delightful, witty, entrancing little actress. She is, indeed, everything except what I should call a good actress, and can be played off the screen any time by any number of actresses with one-tenth of her looks, exquisiteness, charm, delightfulness, etc."

It could be said that her acting was more cerebral than heart-felt, and her limited vocal range sometimes prevented her from achieving greatness in the classics. Nevertheless, several of her screen portrayals, and in particular, Blanche Du Bois in *A Streetcar Named Desire,* are major accomplishments. In 1970, Olivier told a reporter, "It always made me so angry when people said that Vivien Leigh wasn't talented. A person has to have talent to be beautiful on the stage or on the screen."

Her public was largely unaware that there were those elements in her personal life which were not unlike those of some of the women she portrayed on the screen. From the Forties on, she was wracked by recurring attacks of tuberculosis, the disease which finally killed her; her later years were interrupted by frequent depressions, serious enough to require shock treatments. There is no doubt these depressions severely hampered her ability to cope with personal as well as professional vicissitudes, for example her obsession with aging and its imagined effects on her career, and more importantly, her despondency over the dissolution of her marriage to Sir Laurence Olivier. These two factors successfully sapped her emotional will-power to combat her tuberculosis, and given these ingredients, she was able to will herself to die.

Following Miss Leigh's death, Paula Lawrence a friend and co star on Broadway in "Ivanov" in 1966, said, "She operated on a very thin edge, a great part of her energy spent in self-control. Her epic journeys through the dark labyrinths of her spirit were never far distant. But she rose from them like a phoenix, immortal and regenerated. She schooled herself not to react to disturbances, to block them out. And so her acting was always careful, always safe, always dainty. It never reflected the roaring furnaces of her inner turbulence."

An only child, Miss Leigh was born on November 5, 1913, in Darjeeling, India, and was christened Vivian Mary. Her father, Ernest Richard Hartley, was a partner in the Calcutta stock-brokerage firm of Piggot, Chapman and Company. He and his wife, Gertrude Robinson, lived in Alipore, a Calcutta suburb, but summered in Darjeeling, a resort in the lower Himalayas.

Being a British Commonwealth outpost, the British community was obliged to create its own entertainments. At one of these, at the age of three-and-a-half, Vivien gave her first public performance in a children's concert. Daintily decked out, she was to have sung "Little Bo-Peep," which her mother had taught her for the occasion. But instead of singing it, she sedately and firmly informed the audience she would recite it.

Shortly after her sixth birthday, her parents took her "home" and enrolled her in the school of the Convent of the Sacred Heart at Roehampton, just outside London. Mrs. Hartley, a native of Ireland, was a Roman Catholic and had also been educated in a convent.

Vivien entered the school in September, 1920, and almost at once developed an interest in dramatics. She eagerly participated in the school's production of "A Midsummer Night's Dream." A year later, she informed a fellow-student and friend by the name of Maureen O'Sullivan, that she was going to be an actress. Miss O'Sullivan, who at that time wanted to be a pilot, later said, "Vivien was so beautiful, I can't tell you. She always wanted to be an actress and she was the only girl in the school who took ballet. Viv was the most beautiful girl in the school. We thought she was ravishing."

Until Vivien was thirteen, and her father retired, her mother made visits to England every summer, and her father had visited every other year. Knowing of Vivien's love for the theatre, and coupled with her parents own interests in the dramatic arts, during these visits to England, her parents frequently took Vivien to the theatre to expose her to the multifarious pleasures of the London stage.

After her father's retirement, during the pre-war years of 1927-1931, the Hartleys, *en famille,* made the grand tour of Europe. During these years, Vivien attended a variety of schools including the convent of the Sacred Heart in San Remo, the private Mademoiselle Manileve's School for Young Ladies in Paris where one instructor, Mademoiselle Antoine, was an actress from the Comédie Française, and Baroness von Roeder's finishing school in the Bavarian Alps near Bad Reichenhall.

In 1931, the Hartleys summered in Ireland and settled in England that autumn. Vivien, who by this time had blossomed into a young beauty, spent the winter collecting beaux, one of whom was a handsome, young barrister named Herbert Leigh Holman. However, Vivien had never lost her love of the stage and the following May, she enrolled in the Royal Academy of Dramatic Art.

Considering her upbringing and the suitably romantic ideas of a proper, young English lady in the prosperous thirties, Vivien's theatrical ambitions were overshadowed by the prospects of marriage to her dashing young barrister and two months after her enrollment in the Royal Academy of Dramatic Art, she became engaged to Holman and shelved her dramatic studies.

On December 20, 1932, Vivien and Holman were married, and as was suitable for upper-middle-class Britishers, spent their honeywoon in Kitzbühel, that pristine Alpine village fifty miles from Salzburg. They returned to a small flat in London, where Vivien found her household duties did not occupy her full time. Her thoughts soon returned to acting and the Royal Academy of Dramatic Art, and her husband consented to her attending one or two classes a week. Several months later, however, she discovered she was pregnant and was forced to drop out once again.

A daughter, Suzanne Holman, was born on October 12, 1933, and needing larger quarters, the Holmans moved to a comfortable house on Little Stanhope Street. The following summer found Holman planning a cruise on the Baltic Sea, and Vivien still entertaining the thought of becoming an actress. By chance she had heard of a small part in a film called *Things Are Looking Up* (1934) and she was determined to have it. The film was a minor comedy about a girls' school, and the director, Albert de Courville, told her it would be several weeks before he knew whether or not he could use her. But on August 12th, she received a wire saying they could use her in the picture. Overjoyed by the news, she hurried back to London, leaving her husband to continue on alone. As it turned out, her part had only one line of dialogue: "If you are not made headmistress, I shan't come back next term." It was a beginning.

Soon after, she met actor-turned-agent, John Gliddon, and engaged him as her manager for a year. Because he suggested she change her name she consulted an actress friend, Beryl Samson, and they decided Vivien should use her husband's middle name, thereby becoming Vivien Leigh.

Her second film opportunity was the feminine lead in a picture called *The Village Squire* (1935), a quickie in which she worked for only one week, at five guineas a day. In a subsequent quickie, *Gentlemen's Agreement* (1935), she played a typist-heroine. Her leading man in both of these films had been David Horne, who suggested she try out for the part of the flirtatious wife in "The Green Sash," a play set in Fifteenth-century Florence. This vehicle became her stage debut on February 25, 1935, when it opened at the Q Theatre. After a short run in that play and a small part in a Gracie Fields picture called *Look Up and Laugh* (1935), producer Sydney Carroll signed her for one of the four leads in "The Mask of Virtue," a stage comedy by Ashley Dukes. This proved to be Vivien's lucky break, because her agent had heard through the casting grapevine that Carroll was looking for a beautiful girl, though not necessarily an actress with experience. Vivien won the audition and when the play opened on May 15, 1935, her notices were such raves that Carroll distributed posters throughout London proclaiming her "Vivien Leigh, The Fame in a Night Girl." Carroll had changed the spelling of her name because he thought Vivien with an "e" more feminine. Of her performance, Willson Disher of the London "Daily Mail" said, "She has youth, beauty and the assurance the part of Henrietta requires. In addition, she has a boldness in attack which wins our whole-hearted admiration. She should go a long way indeed." Stardom was no longer a dream.

Among those who saw Miss Leigh on opening night was producer Alexander Korda of London Films, who signed her to a five year contract calling for two films a year, allowing her time off for stage work, and paying her 1,300 pounds the first year with yearly increments to 18,000 pounds.

Korda first thought of casting her as Roxanne in a film version of "Cyrano de Bergerac," in which Charles Laughton was to have the title role. But Laughton rejected the script, the costumes, and the casting of the inexperienced Miss Leigh, and the picture was therefore never made. Meanwhile Korda became preoccupied with the opening of his new studios at Denham, and it was a year before he made any use of his new starlet.

During this year, she appeared in three stage productions—a one-week engagement with the Oxford University Dramatic Society as the Queen in "Richard III" directed by John Gielgud; as Jenny Mere in Max Beerbohm's "The Happy Hypocrite," a play adapted by Clemence Dane which was not well received and closed after a few weeks; and as Anne Boleyn in an outdoor theatre version of Shakespeare's "Henry VIII," produced by Sydney Carroll.

Finally, in August, 1936, Korda renewed his interest in Miss Leigh and cast her in *Fire Over England* (1936), a story of Queen Elizabeth I and the Spanish Armada, produced by Erich Pommer from A.E.W. Mason's novel. Flora Robson was Elizabeth and Vivien was one of her ladies-in-waiting. Fortuitously, Laurence Olivier was also in the cast. Olivier was then married to actress, Jill Esmond, by whom, that year, he had a son, Tarquin. By the end of the three-and-a-half months of production, Olivier and Miss Leigh had become very good friends.

Miss Leigh's next film for Korda was *Dark Journey* (1937), a melodrama about an international spy ring in which she played a French girl in a dressmaking shop in Stockholm who is supposedly giving information to Germany, while actually spying for France. The script also had her attempt to outwit and fall in love with German spy, Conrad Veidt.

She appeared on stage in the spring of 1937, in a short-lived play called "Because We Must"; and

With Laurence Olivier and Flora Robson in *Fire Over England* (1936).

With Conrad Veidt in *Dark Journey* (1937).

as an opening-night gift to her co-players, she gave them each copies of a book she had just finished reading, "Gone With the Wind."

After "Because We Must" closed, Korda assigned her to a third film, *Storm In a Teacup* (1937). It was a successful version of the James Bridie light comedy about a Scottish town and its newspaper reporter (Rex Harrison) who falls in love with the daughter of the town's wealthiest citizen and opposes her father in court when the father refuses to help a charwoman whose unlicensed dog has been impounded.

Korda then cast her opposite Olivier in John Galsworthy's *The First and the Last,* for which Graham Greene had written the script. It was the story of a youth who accidentally kills the evil husband of the girl he loves and spends three weeks with her before deciding to give himself up. Greene was so dissatisfied with the picture he vowed never to adapt another author's work for the screen (He did attempt it once more with Shaw's "St. Joan" for Otto Preminger, and the result was again disastrous.) Korda shelved the film and held its release until 1940, after both of its stars had become famous. Re-titled *21 Days Together,* it opened in New York where Bosley Crowther of the New York "Times" thought it a "trim and haunting melodrama" well acted by both stars.

While *The First and the Last* was still shooting, Miss Leigh and Olivier accompanied the Old Vic Company to Elsinore, Denmark, for a presentation of "Hamlet" at Kronberg Castle. Olivier played Hamlet, Miss Leigh was Ophelia, and Tyrone Guthrie directed. Interestingly, the critics singled her out for praise. Upon returning to London, Miss Leigh and Olivier felt obligated to inform their spouses that they were in love — a fact their friends had known for some time. Although divorce proceedings were not finalised for approximately three years, they both decided to continue their careers and maintain what was then considered an unorthodox life-style.

Shortly after the completion of *The First and the Last*, Korda loaned Miss Leigh to Metro-Goldwyn-Mayer for that company's first English production at its Denham studio. The picture was *A Yank At Oxford* (1938), starring Robert Taylor and Miss Leigh's erstwhile schoolmate, Maureen O'Sullivan. Her part was much smaller than Miss O'Sullivan's — she played the philandering wife of the Oxford bookseller — but she was highly visible as the vivacious coquette.

Because of her performance as Ophelia in "Hamlet," Tyrone Guthrie invited Miss Leigh to appear as Titania in an Old Vic production of "A Midsummer Night's Dream." This production was memorable for its having been staged "in the Victorian manner with Mendelssohn's music, painted gauze drops, and a flying ballet of fairies in Victorian ballet skirts." The production was also

With Laurence Olivier in *21 Days Together* (1940.)

With Robert Taylor in *A Yank at Oxford* (1938).

noteworthy because it was the first Shakespearean production that the present Queen of England attended.

As her next film assignment, Miss Leigh appeared in *St. Martin's Lane* (1938), a Charles Laughton vehicle produced by Erich Pommer. Laughton played a London street singer and Miss Leigh was the selfish, unscrupulous waif he helps become a musical star. It presented an austere view of London life and was not a commercial success. For its release in the United States it was re-titled *The Sidewalks of London*.

Upon completion of this film, Miss Leigh and Olivier took a romantic vacation on the Riviera, where they met with William Wyler to discuss Samuel Goldwyn's production of *Wuthering Heights* (1939). The tentative casting for that film had Olivier and Merle Oberon in the leads and Miss Leigh in the supporting role of Isabella. Although Wyler told Miss Leigh she could not expect a better part in her first American film, Miss Leigh decided not to accept the part as she felt she would suffer, *vis-à-vis* Olivier, both professionally and personally. Instead, she chose to do a stage presentation of "Serena Blandish" co-starring Stewart Granger.

Ten days after Olivier had sailed for the United States to begin production for *Wuthering Heights*, Miss Leigh impetuously followed him. She told Olivier she could only stay five days because she had to start rehearsals for a revival of "A Midsummer Night's Dream." The five days extended into quite a visit, during which time Olivier asked his agent, Myron Selznick, to suggest to David O. Selznick that he consider Miss Leigh for the part of Scarlett O'Hara in *Gone With the Wind*, as Olivier felt she was the perfect choice.

On December 10, 1938, with cast and script still incomplete, Selznick shot the burning of Atlanta scene and among the spectators were Myron Selznick, Olivier and Miss Leigh. Myron presented her to his brother, stating, "Dave, I want you to

In *St. Martin's Lane* (1938).

meet your Scarlett O'Hara.'' After a probing conversation with her later that evening, David O. Selznick agreed to screen test her.

Two scenes were used for the test. The first was the one in the library of Twelve Oaks, in which Scarlett tells Ashley Wilkes she loves him and therefore he must love her. Other actresses had done this scene with sentiment, but Miss Leigh used a near-hysterical laugh which impressed both Leslie Howard and director George Cukor. The second scene had Scarlett being laced into a corset by Mammy (Hattie McDaniel).

On Christmas Day, Miss Leigh and Olivier attended a party at Cukor's home at which time Cukor secretly told her she had landed the coveted role. On Friday, January 13th, Selznick announced publicly that he had found his Scarlett O'Hara. Selznick purchased her contract from Korda and had her sign the usual seven-year contract. Her salary for *Gone With the Wind*, according to the consensus of ''Hollywood film historians,'' was set at $30,000. Miss Leigh's English biographer, Gwen Robyns, however, maintains it was $15,000, and David O. Selznick, in a letter to the author, simply stated it was a ''confidential matter.'' Miss Leigh's own comment to the press in later years was simply that she could not remember what she had been paid.

Shooting on *Gone With the Wind* began on January 26, 1939, and Miss Leigh and the film's director, George Cukor, got on very well. However, Selznick felt that Cukor did not grasp the scope of the story and replaced him with Victor Fleming. Whereupon Miss Leigh and Olivia de Havilland, who played Melanie, tearfully pleaded Cukor's cause in vain. Will Price, at that time Maureen O'Hara's husband, was employed to tutor Miss Leigh's development of a Southern accent, and, in addition, unbeknownst to Selznick, she spent the majority of her Sunday afternoon's at Cukor's home discussing the role and its interpretations, even after Cukor had been replaced as the director. Whenever she found shooting out of sequence confusing, which she sometimes did, she would consult the book on the set, whereupon Selznick would invariably exclaim, ''Vivien, put away that damned book.''

There were times when Vivien Leigh differed with Selznick over her interpretation of the role of Scarlett. Needless to say, Selznick's interpretation invariably won. However, Miss Leigh did insist upon retaining one specific line which was delivered by Scarlett after her mother's death: ''I've always wanted to be like my mother'' (i.e. gentle, kind and sweet). Miss Leigh, in letters to the author shortly before her death, wrote, ''To me this was one of the finer points of Scarlett's character, that she did indeed want to be like her mother more. The Civil War had made that impossible if one were to survive. It seemed a most important detail, indicating something of Scarlett's true nature.''

With Clark Gable in *Gone With the Wind* (1939)

Of the less subtle characteristics of Scarlett, Miss Leigh further explained, "It's the rebel in her that draws us to a girl like Scarlett. Most of us have compromised in life. Those who fight for what they want will always thrill us." And on another occasion in discussing the role, she said, "I never liked Scarlett. I knew it was a marvelous part, but I never cared for her. I couldn't find anything of myself in her except that one line." However, contrary to that statement, Miss Leigh was on occasion known to display emotions quite similar to those of a Scarlett O'Hara — indignation, opinionatedness and an undaunted wilfulness.

She told one reporter, "when I was a little girl, and I was going to a party, my mother always said, 'Now do what the hostess wants to please her,' and when I was the hostess my mother used to say, 'now, do what the guests want to please them.' And I asked, 'When can I do what I want'."

Another reference to Miss Leigh's "wilfulness" was made by "Variety's" Wolfe Kaufman on March 5, 1969, "When the actress first came to attention internationally in Metro's (sic) *Gone With the Wind,* she already was well-known in London but was not yet a star. And yet, when David O. Selznick brought her to Hollywood (sic) she made life hell for everybody near her, unless they did everything she wished, as she wished, and when she wished. Despite which she was surrounded by people who worshipped her and were ready to carry out her wishes."

Shooting on *Gone With the Wind* ended on July 1st, and a sneak preview was held in September in Riverside, California. The premiere, in Loew's Grand Theatre in Atlanta, Georgia, on December 15th, was something of a Southern event. The New York premiere was held in the Capitol and Astor Theatres simultaneously four days later. Miss Leigh's performance as Scarlett O'Hara won her the Academy Award and the New York Film Critics Award as Best Actress of the Year. The New York "Times" said, "She is so perfectly designed for the part by art and nature that any other actress in the role would be inconceivable. She is the very embodiment of the selfish, hoydenish, slant-eyed miss who tackled life with both claws and a creamy complexion, asked no odds of any one or any thing — least of all her conscience — and faced at last a defeat which, by her very inconquerability, neither she nor we can recognize as final."

After her success as Scarlett O'Hara, Vivien Leigh tried to be cast opposite Laurence Olivier in Jane Austen's *Pride and Prejudice*, but M-G-M's reigning queen, Greer Garson, was given that part and Selznick had Miss Leigh assigned to M-G-M's *Waterloo Bridge* opposite Robert Taylor. That Robert Sherwood play had previously been filmed by Universal in 1931, with Mae Clarke. S.N. Behrman was hired to write the screenplay for the 1940 version, and Miss Leigh gave an enchanting portrayal of the ballerina who becomes a prostitute when she believes her soldier-fiancé (Taylor) has been killed. The London "Evening News" reviewer wrote, "Vivien Leigh gives a performance of beauty, inspiration and sensitivity which I do not expect to see surpassed this year." A musical version entitled *Gaby* was made in 1956 with Leslie Caron as the ballerina.

While he was working in *Pride and Prejudice,* Laurence Olivier promoted the idea of doing "Romeo and Juliet" on stage with Miss Leigh and himself in the title roles. They put up their entire savings of $60,000 as half the cost and assembled a cast which included Dame May Whitty as the nurse, Alexander Knox as Friar Laurence, and Edmond O'Brien as Mercutio. The play opened in San Francisco and then played Chicago, where they had a generally favourable response. But in New York, where their publicity screamed "See the real lovers make love in public," the reviews were caustic and the play lasted only twelve days. Brooks Atkinson for the New York "Times" wrote, "Let it be said in her favor that she makes an earnest attempt to act the part as it is written. But she is not yet accomplished enough as an actress to go deep into the heart of an imaginative character wrought out of sensuous poetry."

Financially stricken, Olivier and Miss Leigh thought of returning to England. It was the summer of 1940, when the Luftwaffe's "battle for Britain" was at its height. Olivier wrote to friends in England expressing a desire to join the British Navy's air arm but was told they were not accepting men without prior flying experience. He arranged to take flying lessons at Sneden's Landing, on the Hudson River a few miles above New York City, where he and Miss Leigh were occupying Katharine Cornell's home.

Alexander Korda then offered them the leads in *Lady Hamilton* (1941). Entitled *That Hamilton Woman* in the United States, it was made to hearten the British in "their finest hour," and was a film Winston Churchill saw over and over. Olivier as Nelson and Vivien Leigh as Lady Hamilton were equally believable. "Variety" said of her perfor-

With Robert Taylor in *Waterloo Bridge* (1940).

mance, "Miss Leigh hits the peak with her delineation of Lady Hamilton, a vivacious girl who is pictured as a victim of men but whose ingenuity in state craft saves the Empire."

In Hollywood, shortly before shooting had begun on *Lady Hamilton,* both Miss Leigh and Olivier received word of their divorce decrees with custody of their children going to their ex-spouses. They were married at Ronald Colman's ranch in Santa Barbara at one minute after midnight on August 30, 1940. Garson Kanin and Katharine Hepburn were the only guests. The Oliviers spent their brief honeymoon on the Colman's yacht with Colman and his wife, Benita Hume.

After completion of *Lady Hamilton*, they returned to England in January, 1941, and Olivier immediately joined the British Navy. Miss Leigh, at that time, had refused Selznick's suggestion of her playing Clio, the volatile Creole courtesan in Edna Ferber's *Saratoga Trunk*, and also an offer from the Theatre Guild in New York to do George Bernard Shaw's "Caesar and Cleopatra" with Cedric Hardwicke, saying, "I am not going to let any film offers from Hollywood or plays on Broadway attract me away from my own country. My place is here beside Larry." She chose instead to appear in another of Shaw's plays, "The Doctor's Dilemma." It was an elaborate production which toured the British provinces for six months before opening in London in March, 1942, where it stayed for thirteen months. Her reviews, while not overtly enthusiastic, were much better than those she had received for "Romeo and Juliet." The Manchester "Guardian" said, "Miss Leigh comes to the part (of Jennifer Dubedat) with

In *That Hamilton Woman* (1941).

a good many initial advantages and played the earlier scenes with a quiet beauty and simplicity which she would do well to substitute for her mannered treatment of the last scene."

In the summer of 1943, Miss Leigh toured the Middle East with Beatrice Lillie in a revue for the troops called "Spring Party." She recited nonsense verse and a poem satirising Scarlett O'Hara. The following year she began work on J. Arthur Rank's film version of *Caesar and Cleopatra* (1946), which was directed by Gabriel Pascal. Because Shaw's approval of all important casting was obligatory, Pascal arranged a meeting between Miss Leigh and Shaw. Shaw had personally chosen Claude Rains for Caesar and upon meeting Miss Leigh he gave his approval by saying, "You look just like a Persian kitten and that is how I want my Cleopatra."

During production when Shaw wished to change a line, which described Caesar as being "thin and stringy" because he felt Rains wasn't, Miss Leigh said she preferred the original dialogue and thought she could make Rains appear "thin and stringy" by the manner in which she spoke the line. Unimpressed, Shaw sent her one of his famous postcards saying, "No, Rains is not stringy, and would strongly resent any deliberate attempt to make him appear so. Besides, 'you are hundreds of years old' is a much better line, as it belongs to the childishness of Cleopatra in the first half of the play. I never change a line except for the better. Don't be an idiot. Why don't you put your address in your letters? G.B.S."

Wartime England was not the easiest place in which to make a motion picture and there were many problems during the filming of *Caesar and Cleopatra,* including strikes and an unusually cold November. To further complicate the production schedule, Miss Leigh suffered the first of her two miscarriages. The resultant film was a major cinematic effort, but not a box-office success. It was the most expensive motion picture made up to that time, costing $5,000,000. The reviews were mixed.

Miss Leigh and Oliver then started preparing a stage production of Thornton Wilder's "The Skin of Our Teeth," which had been such a triumph with Tallulah Bankhead in the United States. Miss Leigh was enthusiastic about doing the play, particularly because everything she had done in the past six years invariably brought about comparisons with Scarlett O'Hara. She had said, "No matter what I do, after Scarlett, it is going to be difficult to startle anybody. I'll try, naturally. But in case I don't succeed, I want to have something to show for my efforts. I want to be sure that, meanwhile, I'm learning more about acting." Both she and Olivier felt "The Skin of Our Teeth" would be an important vehicle for her and Olivier planned to produce and direct it himself. When David O. Selznick heard about it, he obtained an injunction to prevent the production saying Miss Leigh has refused to leave England to play several roles which he had suggested. J. Arthur Rank had paid dearly for her use in *Caesar and Cleopatra* and Selznick had prevented her from playing Katharine in Olivier's film, *Henry V,* on the grounds that the part was too insignificant for the Oscar-winning actress. Renée Asherson, wife of actor Robert Donat, was cast in her stead. The British courts ruled in favour of Miss Leigh and her association with Selznick was ended.

"The Skin of Our Teeth" opened on May 18, 1945, and the London critics thought her performance her best to date. Beverly Baxter in the "Evening Standard" wrote, "Miss Vivien Leigh

With Flora Robson in *Caesar and Cleopatra* (1946).

is startlingly good. Forget about her Scarlett O'Hara, and her stiff performance of the artist's wife in 'The Doctor's Dilemma.' We see her as she really is — part gamine, part woman, a comedienne, an artist.'' This was a particularly meaningful personal triumph for Vivien Leigh, who had been determined to make critics accept her on stage as something more than a film star and the wife of Laurence Olivier. This, along with Blanche Du Bois in *A Streetcar Named Desire,* remained her favourite role.

After playing the role for only two months, Miss Leigh's physicians informed her she had tuberculosis. She left the play and spent six months in a hospital and recuperated for almost eight months at Notley Abbey, the Oliviers' home in Buckinghamshire.

In the summer of 1946, she accompanied Olivier to New York and appeared with him and the Old Vic Company in a six-week engagement of ''Henry IV.'' When they returned to London, she briefly revived ''The Skin of Our Teeth.''

She and Olivier then vacationed on the Riviera, after which, early in 1947, Olivier began work on his film version of ''Hamlet,'' and Miss Leigh accepted an offer from Alexander Korda to star in

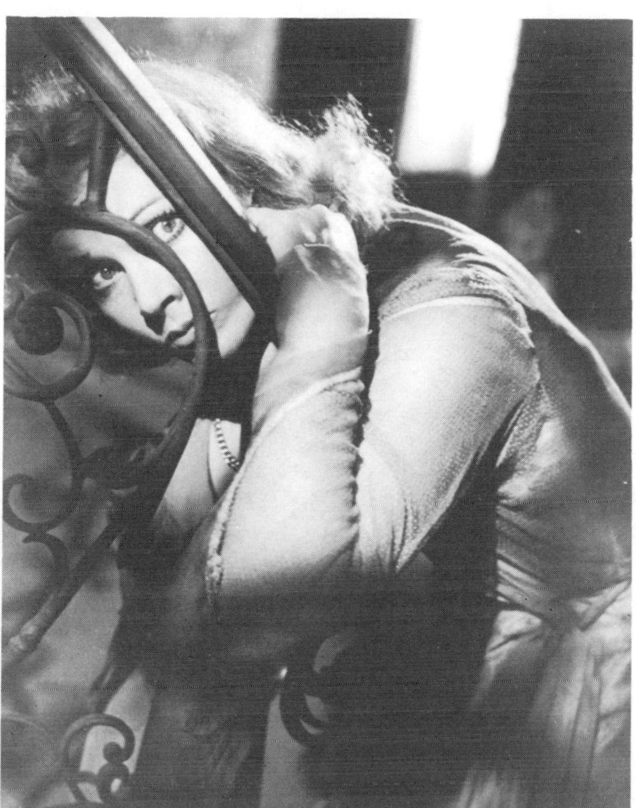

In *A Streetcar Named Desire* (1951).

Anna Karenina (1948) with Kieron Moore as Vronsky and Ralph Richardson as Karenin. Jean Anouilh, Guy Morgan, and Julien Duvivier wrote the script to this version of *Anna Karenina*, and to emphasize the role of Anna omitted most of Tolstoy's sub-plots. The result was a saccharine script which tried to make a heroine out of what critic James Agee called, ''one of fiction's most vehemently average women.'' Ralph Richardson received the best notices and Moore was miscast as Vronsky. Both of Greta Garbo's ''Karenina'' films (*Love* in 1927 and the Selznick-produced *Anna Karenina* in 1935) were superior adaptations of Tolstoy's novel.

Laurence Olivier was knighted on July 8, 1947, and in the following February, he and his wife headed an Old Vic tour of Australia and New Zealand. Their repertory consisted of ''Richard III'' with Miss Leigh as Lady Anne, Sheridan's ''The School for Scandal'' with Miss Leigh as Lady Teazle, and Wilder's ''The Skin of Our Teeth.'' They returned to England the following November, and remained with the Old Vic but changed their repertory. ''Richard III'' and ''The School For Scandal'' stayed, but in place of ''The Skin of Our Teeth'' they produced Anouilh's version of ''Antigone,'' starring Miss Leigh, with Olivier as the Chorus. Olivier had at first objected to ''Antigone,'' but capitulated when his wife alleged the part was as important to her as that of Scarlett O'Hara had been. ''Antigone'' became the first play in which the Oliviers appeared together on the London stage.

Several months after Olivier had been knighted, America's masterful playwright, Tennessee Williams, had seen his play, ''A Streetcar Named Desire,'' open on Broadway with Jessica Tandy as Blanche Du Bois. The play was awarded the Pulitzer Prize and the Drama Critics Circle Award, and Olivier, feeling that the role of Blanche Du Bois would be the perfect vehicle for his wife, arranged to purchase the British rights from its producer, Irene Mayer Selznick, the ex-wife of Miss Leigh's former employer, David O. Selznick. Olivier's foresight provided his wife with the most important role of both her stage and screen career. Miss Leigh's portrayal of Blanche Du Bois was the zenith of her acting career.

The British stage version opened in October, 1949, and ran for eight months. The film version of *A Streetcar Named Desire,* released in 1951, was both a critical and box-office success, and Miss Leigh's interpretation of the psychotic Blanche

In *Anna Karenina* (1948).

was imbued with such understanding of the character's psychopathology that she again won both the Academy Award and the New York Film Critics Award.

Miss Leigh had studied the role of Blanche Du Bois meticulously and at one point during the production of the film, she was ready to call it quits. The one line in William's play that she felt explicated the motivation for Blanche's behavior was the one that indicated her young husband had been a homosexual. The line in the play read, "I came into a room and found my husband with an older man who had been his friend for years," and the resulting confrontation with Blanche precipitated the young man's suicide. Film censorship, however, would not permit that line intact, and director Elia Kazan and Williams, over Miss Leigh's objections, finally changed the line to read, "He wasn't like other people." Miss Leigh told critic John Gruen, "Larry directed 'Streetcar' with such uncanny insight. It was an early directorial effort for him, and both of us learned a tremendous lot from it. I'm absolutely convinced that my screen performance turned out well more through Larry's remembered direction than through Elia Kazan's film direction. I recall having had a bit of a row with Gadge over Blanche's characterisation. He didn't really like the character — preferred Kowalski, the Brando part. He kept robbing Blanche of her poignancy and vulnerability thus making her more and more unsympathetic. Finally we had a *very* serious talk — and luckily I won out on a good many points."

London's C.A. Lejeune said of Miss Leigh's Blanche, "One would have to be blind not to appreciate the brillance of Vivien Leigh's performance. It is impossible not to be touched by her, inconceivable not to be impressed and dazzled. Her Blanche is a woman shimmering in a sheath of gold, never very clearly seen, but taking glint and radiance from every facet." And Pauline Kael, the dean of contemporary American film critics, stated, "Vivien Leigh gives one of those rare performances that can truly be said to evoke pity and terror. No one since the early Lillian Gish and the almost unknown, exquisite Nadia Sirbirskaya of *Menilmontant* has had this quality of hopeless feminine frailty; Shakespeare might have had women like this in mind when he conceived Ophelia. Blanche's plea, 'I don't want realism — I want magic!' is central to *Streetcar*."

With the success of *Streetcar* behind them, the Oliviers appeared in stage versions of Shaw's "Caesar and Cleopatra" and Shakespeare's "Anthony and Cleopatra" on alternate nights. They opened in London in May, 1951, after which they brought the two plays to New York where they stayed for four months.

In 1953, Miss Leigh began work on the film *Elephant Walk*, a story of a British tea plantation in Ceylon directed by William Dieterle. Olivier had been offered the lead opposite her but had declined because of commitments connected with the coronation of Queen Elizabeth II. Peter Finch was cast in his stead. This was one of the rare times that the Oliviers had been separated and when rumours concerning the solidity of their marriage reached Miss Leigh's ears, she collapsed hysterically on the Hollywood set. Olivier hurried to Hollywood to take her back to England, where she was placed under medical care. Her depression was serious enough to require shock treatment. As a result, Elizabeth Taylor replaced her in the picture.

After recuperating, Miss Leigh, with her husband as co-star, opened in London late in 1953 in "The Sleeping Prince," a play which Terence Rattigan had written especially for them. 'The Sleeping Prince" was a charming comedy about the romantic involvement of a prince with an American actress and the London critics welcomed Miss Leigh's return to the stage. Cecil Wilson wrote, "Miss Leigh is the most disarming little demon who ever upset a royal applecart. She minces around the legation in a wide-eyed daze of innocence and guile and carries her American accent with a practised ease. It is the teasing sing-song accent of Blanche du Bois suddenly aware that all that neurotic nonsense was only a nightmare."

Three years later the play was filmed as *The Prince and the Showgirl* with Laurence Olivier and Marilyn Monroe as the stars. When asked why she did not star in the film version, Miss Leigh replied candidly, "I'm forty-three, and Marilyn Monroe is thirty-one, and it is much harder to disguise one's age on the screen than on stage."

In 1955, she again appeared with her husband and the Shakespeare Memorial Company at Stratford-upon-Avon playing Lady Macbeth, Viola in "Twelfth Night," and Lavinia in "Titus Andronicus." While her performance in "Macbeth" created only a minor stir, one critic, Alan Pryce-Jones, thought her portrayal had "an icy, serpentine quality" which made her the most dangerous Lady Macbeth he had ever seen.

That same year, Vivien Leigh returned to the

screen in *The Deep Blue Sea* after a four-year absence. Her co-stars were Kenneth More, Eric Portman and Emlyn Williams. The film was based on Terence Rattigan's play of the same name, and Miss Leigh portrayed a middle-aged, suicidal woman who leaves the boredom of her secure marriage to become the mistress of a shiftless airplane test-pilot. It was static, melodramatic, and contrived, and more popular abroad than here.

After completing *The Deep Blue Sea,* Miss Leigh signed to appear in the stage version of a bit of *frou-frou* by Nöel Coward entitled "South Sea Bubble," co-starring Alan Webb. Concurrently she discovered that at the age of forty-six, she was pregnant and that the baby was due in December of 1956. She continued in her non-too-taxing role of Lady Alexander, the governor's lady, in "South Sea Bubble," and told the press, "I will be continuing my part in "South Sea Bubble" for several more weeks — no, I am not taking any special precautions — yes, I do feel very excited and well and naturally we are very happy." Her last scheduled performance in the play took place on Saturday, August 13th. The next day she took ill, and she lost the child that both she and Olivier very much desired. Their marriage never recovered from that disappointment.

France awarded Vivien Leigh the Knight's Cross of the *Légion d'Honneur* in May, 1957, and shortly thereafter, she and Olivier let it be known that they had decided to take separate vacations. Olivier traveled to Scotland to spend a few weeks with his son, Tarquin; Miss Leigh embarked on a tour of Europe accompanied by her daughter Suzanne and her ex-husband, Herbert Leigh Holman. Holman had never remarried and he and Miss Leigh had remained good friends since the time of their divorce. When asked by reporters if these separate vacations implied a divorce, Miss Leigh replied, "Of course not. It's just something we've never done before. We thought it would be a good idea to try something new." When a female member of the Labour party in Parliament publicly criticised the vacation as a "terrible example," Miss Leigh cabled, "Criticism illconsidered and unmannerly. Presence of our daughter gives reasonable explanation of holiday to any reasonable person."

In 1958, Vivien Leigh opened in London in Christopher Fry's version of Jean Giradoux's "Duel of Angels," a play about good versus evil as represented by two women. Miss Leigh played the evil woman, Paola, and it was to become one of her favourite roles. Her reviews were excellent.

Her next stage appearance was a less fortunate one. The vehicle she chose was a minor comedy by her good friend, Nöel Coward, entitled "Look After Lulu," which Coward had adapted from a farce by Georges Feydeau. It had failed earlier in New York where it had starred Tammy Grimes, and its London reception was only lukewarm when it opened at the Royal Court Theatre on July 29, 1959. The London "Times" commented, 'If "Look After Lulu" is only half a success, the reasons are more than complimentary. The trouble is that Mr. Nöel Coward is too witty and Miss Vivien Leigh too beautiful. For the kind of play that "Look After Lulu" is, beauty and wit are as unnecessary as a peach melba at the North Pole. In her costume in the second act, Miss Leigh does not, as Feydeau intended, look ridiculous, absurd, grotesque. On the contrary, she looked ravishing, for she cannot look anything else. She moves with extreme grace, and the timing and intelligence of her performance are perfect."

"Look After Lulu" closed after sixteen weeks and Miss Leigh readied a revival of "Duel of Angels" to be produced in New York. The cast included Mary Ure and John Merivale, Gladys Cooper's stepson, and the play opened on April 19, 1960.

In reviewing her performance as Paola in the New York "Times," Walter Kerr wrote, "Miss Leigh is devastating as she turns on the cool porcelain soul of moralising Mary Ure and sends all sorts of little cracks shattering through it, with speech that flickers as rapidly as the tongue of an iguana, yet with every syllable ruthlessly clear, she raises the temperature of the summer air about her as though an improbable thermostat were lodged deep in her throat. For my modest money, this is Miss Leigh's most controlled and captivating performance." In "Newsday," George Oppenheimer wrote, "She is as insidious an advertisement for evil as has been loosed on our stage in many a day."

A month after her arrival in New York, Miss Leigh issued the following announcement: "Lady Olivier wishes to say that Sir Laurence has asked for a divorce in order to marry Miss Joan Plowright. She will naturally do whatever he wishes."

However, she was not always able to maintain such dignity where her marriage was concerned. There were quotes at the time which indicate that her marriage to Olivier had been a professional arrangement for at least three years. There were also stories of Miss Leigh's obsession with her age. On one occasion when discussing the possibility of doing a television show about the life of Eva Peron, she suddenly exclaimed, "She was lucky. She died at thirty-two. I'm already forty-six." And once, during an interview when the subject of Alfred Lunt and Lynn Fontanne's successful marriage was mentioned, Miss Leigh exclaimed tearfully, "The Lunts worked it out, why couldn't Larry and I?"

She was granted a divorce on December 2, 1960, on grounds of adultery, naming Miss Plowright co-respondent. The latter's husband, Robert Gage, was granted a similar decree after naming Olivier co-respondent.

Olivier married Miss Plowright on March 17, 1961. A week before that event occurred, Miss Leigh had attended a publicity "do" in Atlanta, Georgia, celebrating the re-issue of *Gone With the Wind* as part of the Civil War Centennary. David O. Selznick and Olivia de Havilland also attended.

Rather than return to London and the memories of her failed marriage to Olivier, Vivien Leigh signed with the Old Vic Company for a tour which from July, 1961, through May, 1962, took her to Australia, New Zealand, South America, and Mexico. Her repertory consisted of "Twelfth Night," "Duel of Angels," "The Lady of the Camellias," and a recital of Shakespearean excerpts, and John Merivale, her friend and companion, was signed as her leading man. Those who saw her in "The Lady of the Camellias" regard her performance among the best she ever gave.

While in New Zealand, she agreed to appear as the penniless Grand Duchess who becomes the domestic of an American family in the Paris of the Twenties in the musical version of "Tovarich" opposite Jean-Pierre Aumont. The play opened in New York on March 9, 1963, and both Miss Leigh's dancing (the Charleston) and her singing were favourably reviewed; she was awarded the Broadway Tony as the season's Best Actress in a Musical.

After 224 performances, she missed the September 28th performance, and the next day was flown to England suffering from what was called "exhaustion." She later said "The heat of New York in summer" had prevented her from getting her proper rest thereby causing her collapse. She was replaced in the Broadway production by Eva Gabor.

She did not perform again professionally until April 23, 1964, when, as part of the celebration of the 400th Anniversary of Shakespeare's birth, she joined Diana Wynyard, Michael Redgrave, and Robert Helpmann at Guildford, in readings from the works of the Bard. Among the passages she recited were Portia's "Quality of mercy" lines from "The Merchant of Venice."

On the set of *The Roman Spring of Mrs. Stone* (1961).

Her last two screen performances depicted two more unhappy and neurotic women. The first was the decadent actress-widow in *The Roman Spring of Mrs. Stone* (1961) who hopes a male-whore will kill her. At the time she was making this picture, which was based on the novella by Tennessee Williams, Williams told a "Life" magazine reporter, "Her beauty is as delicately flamboyant as an orchid. Vivien, above all else, is incomparably graceful. When she takes the stage she commands it as if she first arrived there suspended from the bill of a stork. She moves like a marvelous dancer, both on and off stage. All these wonderful gifts she has with no apparent regard for her personal vulnerability, in other words, she is not only a stunning actress but a lady with the most important part of that intricate composition, which is kindness of heart."

Her last film role was little more than a cameo

In *Ship of Fools* (1965).

part in *Ship of Fools* (1965) where she played the divorcee who teases pick-ups into desire and then walks out on them. It was a strikingly chilling portrait of an embittered woman for which the French named her Best Actress of the Year. American critic, Judith Crist said, "There is perfection in Vivien Leigh's forty-six-year-old woman with a sixteen-year-old heart, terrified at the loveless aging that is driving her toward degradation."

Miss Leigh told the author in 1965 that she had decided at the age of seven that she wanted to be an actress. "I cannot say precisely why. I simply, perhaps intuitively, knew I had to be one. I recall seeing "Hamlet" and remember liking the ghost, which is a most impressive part in that play, and that I always liked the theatre. Acting is most rewarding when one feels one has captured a characterisation and is either entertaining or enlightening the public."

In an interview for the New York "Times" she observed, "From the actor's standpoint film works call for much more concentrated effort. On the stage the audience contributes by telling you when you are building logically toward a mood. In films you may have to start out with a big emotional scene the first thing in the morning, and perhaps keep doing it over all day. You have to learn to conserve your energy. If an actor can do that, I see no reason, other things being equal, a given interpretation can't be as telling on the screen as on the stage."

This lucid observation of film work was the antithesis of a quote she had tossed off back in 1937, after a friend had described her as a "film star." "Oh," she countered, "*Never* call me a film star. I'm an actress, I hate the films."

In comparing acting in England and the United States, she told the author, "I sometimes feel that the English approach to all facets of the theatre is more direct, concise and economical in achieving the co-ordination of the end result. The American approach however, is to be commended for its vitality and enthusiasm."

In the spring of 1965, Vivien Leigh toured with an unsuccessful play by Paul Osborn entitled, "La Contessa." She played a seventy-seven-year-old Italian countess reliving her past glories in the obscurity of a hotel room. The play never reached London's West End, the first time this had ever occured during her career. During that tour, when a reporter asked her to name her favourite actor, she devotedly replied, "Sir Laurence is the greatest I have ever seen."

She appeared briefly in 1966, on Broadway with Sir John Gielgud in Chekhov's "Ivanov." It was during this limited engagement that her biographer, Gwen Robyns, maintains her depressed emotional state was such that she required shock treatments each morning to enable her to perform in the evening. When the play closed, she returned to London to prepare for the English stage production of Edward Albee's "A Delicate Balance."

Early in 1967, X-rays showed a recurrance of tuberculosis and rehearsals on the play were halted. Urged by her physicians to remain under the hospital's intensive care facilities, she, according to columnist, Sheilah Graham, "with what seemed a frantic compulsion," held court in the bedroom of her flat at 54 Eaton Square. Miss Graham said, "She dazzled her friends with her gaiety and vivacity, and like a queen, presided over her adoring subjects."

On July 8, 1967, after one such convivial evening, her friend John Merivale returned from a theatre performance, greeted her, retired briefly to the kitchen for refreshment, heard a noise, and returned to the room to find her slumped on the floor. She died at the age of fifty-three, exactly twenty years to the day that she had officially become "Lady Olivier."

Her close friends had been cognizant of her inability to completely accept her divorce, nor healthfully combat her fits of depression. She had maintained her Rolls-Royce with its VL0123 license plate and continued to sign her name Vivien Olivier or Vivien, Lady Olivier. Some opined that she was indeed "tired" and wished to die. George Cukor, Miss Leigh's closest friend in America, said that upon hearing of Miss Leigh's death, Katharine Hepburn exclaimed, "Oh, Thank God!" And Viennese *chanteuse,* Greta Keller, told the author that she always felt that Miss Leigh had committed suicide by simply not wishing to live. Perhaps Vivien Leigh said it best, "I'm a Scorpio. We eat ourselves up and burn ourselves out."

On the evening of her death, the lights of the West End theatre marquees were darkened for one hour in tribute to the beautiful actress. Funeral services in the form of a Requiem Mass were private, with only twelve mourners. The services were held in St. Mary's Roman Catholic Church on Cadogan Street, after which, according to her instructions, she was cremated at Golders Green Crematorium and her ashes were scattered over the lake beside her country home, Tickeridge Mill, in Sussex.

A little more than a month later, on August 10th, a memorial service was held in the Royal Parish Church of St. Martin's-in-the-Fields. John Gielgud eulogised, "Her marriage to Laurence Olivier was an inspiration to her qualities, not only as a devoted pupil but also as a brilliant partner." In attendance were her daughter, Suzanne, (Mrs. Robin Farrington); her mother, Mrs. Gertrude Hartley, two of her three grandsons, her first husband, Herbert Leigh Holman, and friends including John Merivale, Dame Peggy Ashcroft, Anna Neagle, Cicely Courtneidge with husband Jack Hulbert, Robert Coote, Lady Redgrave, and in the back of the church, quietly and alone, Laurence Olivier. He had elected not to attend the earlier funeral services.

Miss Leigh's daughter was chief beneficiary to her net estate of $365,000. Her bequest that her eyes be used for corneal grafting was unable to be granted because of her tuberculosis.

In the spring of 1968, friends of Miss Leigh's in America, including Joseph Cotten, Dame Gladys Cooper, Dame Judith Anderson, Greer Garson, Mervyn LeRoy, Stanley Kramer, Brian Aherne, gathered in California for An Evening of Appreciation of Vivien Leigh, benefitting the Library of the University of Southern California. In London, friends and the British Film Institute established the Vivien Leigh Award, which annually sponsors young people making their first films.

When Rhett Butler responds to Scarlett O'Hara's final pleadings with "Frankly, I don't give a damn," Scarlett wistfully, yet willfully muses "Tomorrow is another day. For me tomorrow will always be exciting and worth fighting for." Conversely, Blance Du Bois poignantly pleaded for magic instead of reality. These two roles unquestionably establish the immortality of Vivien Leigh, the actress. Perhaps a more fitting tribute to Vivien Leigh, the woman, is Shelley's "She walks in beauty like the night."

The Feature Film Appearances of Vivien Leigh

Things Are Looking Up (Gainsborough, 1934). Screenplay by Stafford Dickins and Con West from a story by Albert de Courville and Daisey Fisher. Directed by Albert de Courville. *Cast:* Cicely Courtneidge, Max Miller, William Gargan, Mary Lawson, Gillian Maude, Mark Lester, Henrietta Watson, Cicely Oates, Judy Kelly, Dick Henderson, Dick Henderson Jr., Charles Mortimer, Hay Plums, Denny Green, Vivien Leigh, Suzanne Langlen, Hazel Terry, Wyn Weaver, Alma Taylor.

The Village Squire (British and Dominions, 1935). Screenplay by Sherard Powell from the play by Arthur Jarvis Black. Directed by Reginald Denham. *Cast*: David Horne, Vivien Leigh, Leslie Perrins, Moira Lynd, Margaret Watson, Ivor Barnard, David Nichol, Haddon Mason.

Gentlemen's Agreement (British and Dominions, 1935). Screenplay by Basil Mason from the story, "The Wager," by Jennifer Howard. Directed by George Pearson. *Cast:* Frederick Peisley, Vivien Leigh, Anthony Holles, David Horne, Victor Stanley, Vera Bogetti, Ronald Shiner, Kate Saxon.

Look Up and Laugh (Associated Talking Pictures, 1935). Screenplay by Gordon Wellesley from a story by J.B. Priestley. Directed by Basil Dean. *Cast:* Gracie Fields, Alfred Drayton, Douglas Wakefield, Billy Nelson, Harry Tate, Huntley Wright, D.J. Williams, Morris Harvey, Norman Walker, Tommy Fields, Robb Wilton, Arthur Hambling, Kenneth Kove, Jack Melford, Vivien Leigh, Maud Gill, Helen Ferres.

Fire Over England (London Films-United Artists, 1936). Screenplay by Clemence Dane and Sergei Nolbandov from the novel by A.E.W. Mason. Directed by William K. Howard. *Cast:* Flora Robson, Raymond Massey, Leslie Banks, Robert Newton, Tamara Desni, Laurence Olivier, Vivien Leigh, Morton Seiten, Lynn Harding. George Thirwell, Henry Oscar, Robert Rendell, Donald Calthrop. Charles Carson, James Mason.

Dark Journey (London Films-United Artists, 1937). Screenplay by Lajos Biro from a story by Arthur Wimperis. Directed by Victor Saville. *Cast:* Conrad Veidt. Vivien Leigh, Joan Gardner, Anthony Bushell, Ursula Jeans, Margery Pickard, Austin Trevor, Sam Livesey, Edmund Eillard, Charles Carson, Phil Ray, Henry Oscar, Lawrence Hanray, N. Martin Harvey, Robert Newton, Laidman Browne, Anthony Holles, William Dewhurst, Percy Walsh, Cecil Parker, Reginald Tate.

Storm In a Teacup (London Films-United Artists, 1937). Screenplay by Ian Dalrymple and Donald Bull from the adaptation by James Bridie (pseudonym for Osborne Henry Mavor) of the play, "Stürm im wasserglass" by Bruno Frank. Directed by Victor Saville. *Cast:* Rex Harrison, Vivien Leigh, Cecil Parker, Sara Allgood, Ursula Jeans, Gus McNaughton, Arthur Wontner, Eliot Makeham, George Pughe, Arthur Seaton, Cecil Mannering. Ivor Barnard, Cyril Smith, W.G. Fay.

A Yank At Oxford (M-G-M, 1938). Screenplay by Malcolm Stuart Boylan, Walter Ferris and George Oppenheimer from a story by Leon Gordon, Sidney Gilliatt and Michael Hogan from an idea by Jack Conway. Directed by Jack Conway. *Cast:* Robert Taylor, Lionel Barrymore, Maureen O'Sullivan, Vivien Leigh, Edmund Gwenn, Griffith Jones, C.V. France, Edward Rigby, Morton Seiten, Claude Gillingwater, Tully Marshall, Walter Kingford, Robért Coote, Peter Croft, Nöel Howlett, Edmund Breen.

St. Martin's Lane (U.S. Title: The Sidewalks of London (Mayflower-Paramount, 1938). Screenplay by Clemence Dane. Directed by Tim Whelan. *Cast:* Charles Laughton, Vivien Leigh, Rex Harrison, Larry Adler, Tyrone Guthrie, Gus McNaughton, Bart Cormack, Edward Lexy, Marie O'Neill, Basil Gill, Claire Greet, David Burns, Cyril Smith, Helen Hayes, Ronald Ward.

Gone With the Wind (Selznick International M-G-M, 1939). Screenplay by Sidney Howard from the novel by Margaret Mitchell. Directed by Victor Fleming. *Cast:* Clark Gable, Vivien Leigh, Leslie Howard, Olivia de Havilland, Hattie McDaniel, Thomas Mitchell, Barbara O'Neil, Laura Hope Crews, Harry Davenport, Ona Munson, Evelyn Keyes, Ann Rutherford, Butterfly McQueen, Alicia Rhett, Everett Brown, Eddie Anderson, Rand Brooks, Carrol Nye, Jane Darwell, Mary Anderson, Isabel Jewell, Victor Jory, Yakima Canutt, Cammie King, Lillian Kemple Cooper, Ward Bond, Paul Hurst, George Reeves, Fred Crane.

Waterloo Bridge (M-G-M, 1940) Screenplay by S.N. Behrman, Hans Rameau and George Froeschel from the play by Robert E. Sherwood. Directed by Mervyn LeRoy. *Cast:* Vivien Leigh, Robert Taylor, Virginia Field, Maria Ouspenskaya, Steffi Dane, Lucile Watson, C. Aubrey Smith, Janet Shaw, Janet Waldo, Virginia Carroll, Leda Nicova, Florence Baker, Margery Manning, Frances MacInerney, Eleanor Stewart.

21 Days Together (Columbia, 1940). Screenplay by Basil Dean and Graham Greene from the story "The First and the Last" by John Galsworthy. Directed by Basil Dean. *Cast:* Laurence Olivier, Vivien Leigh, Leslie Banks, Francis L. Sullivan, David Horne, William Dewhurst, Frederick Lloyd, Robert Newton, Esme Percy, Elliot Mason, Arthur Young, Hay Petrie, Meinhart Maur, Morris Harvey, Lawrence Hanray, Fred Groves, Aubrey Mallalieu.

That Hamilton Woman (Korda-United Artists, 1941) Screenplay by Walter Reisch and R.C. Sherriff. Directed by Alexander Korda. *Cast:* Laurence Olivier, Vivien Leigh, Alan Mowbray, Sara Allgood, Gladys Cooper, Henry Wilcoxin, Heather Angel, Halliwell Hobbes, Gilbert Emery, Miles Mander, Ronald Sinclair, Luis Alberni, Norma Drury, Georges Renavent, Leonard Carey, Alec Craig, George Davis, Olaf Hytten, Juliette Compton, Guy Kingsford.

Caesar and Cleopatra (Rank-United Artists, 1946). Screenplay by George Bernard Shaw from his play. Directed by Gabriel Pascal. *Cast:* Vivien Leigh, Claude Rains, Stewart Granger, Flora Robson, Francis L. Sullivan, Basil Sydney, Raymond Lovell, Anthony Eustrell, Ernest Thesiger, Anthony Harvey, Robert Adams, Olga Edwards, Harda Swanhilde, Michael Rennie, James McKechnie, Esme Percy, Stanley Holloway, Leo Genn, Felix Aylmer, Jean Simmons.

Anna Karenina (London Films-20th Century-Fox. 1948) Screenplay by Jean Anouilh, Guy Morgan and Julien Duvivier from the novel by Tolstoy. Directed by Julien Duvivier. *Cast:* Vivien Leigh, Ralph Richardson, Kieron Moore, Hugh Dempster, Mary Kerridge, Marie Lohr, Frank Tickle, Sally Ann Howes, Niall MacGinnis, Michael Gough, Martita Hunt, Heather Thatcher, Helen Haye, Mary Martlew, Ruby Miller, Austin Trevor, Guy Verney, John Longden, Leslie Bradley, Beckett Bould, Judith Nelmes, Theresa Giehse, Helen Campbell, Michael Medwin, John Salew, Patrick Skipworth, Gino Cervi, Jeremy Spenser.

A Streetcar Named Desire (Warners, 1951.) Screenplay by Tennessee Williams, adapted by Oscar Saul from Williams' play. Directed by Elia Kazan. *Cast:* Vivien Leigh, Marlon Brando, Kim Hunter, Karl Malden, Rudy Bond, Nick Dennis, Peg Hillias, Wright King, Richard Garrick, Anne Dere, Edna Thomas, Mickey Kuhn, Chester Jones, Marietta Canty, Charles Wagenheim, Maxie Thrower, Lyle Latell, Mel Archer.

The Deep Blue Sea. (London Films-20th Century Fox, 1955). Screenplay by Terence Rattigan from his play. Directed by Anatole Litvak. *Cast:* Vivien Leigh, Kenneth More, Eric Portman, Emlyn Williams, Moira Lister, Arthur Hill, Dandy Nichols, Jimmy Hanley, Miriam Karlin, Heather Thatcher, Bill Shine, Brian Oulton, Sidney James, Alex McCowen, Gibb McLaughlin.

The Roman Spring of Mrs. Stone (Warners, 1961) Screenplay by Gavin Lambert from the novella by Tennessee Williams. Directed by José Quintero *Cast:* Vivien Leigh, Warren Beatty, Lotte Lenya, Coral Browne, Jill St. John, Jeremy Spenser, Stella Bonheur, Josephine Brown, Peter Pyneley, Carl Jaffee, Harold Kasket, Viola Keats, Cleo Laine, Bessie Love, Elspeth March, Henry McCarthy, Warren Mitchell, John Phillips, Paul Stassino, Ernest Thesiger, Mavis Villiers, Thelma D'Aguir.

Ship of Fools (Columbia, 1965). Screenplay by Abby Mann from the novel by Katherine Anne Porter. Directed by Stanley Kramer. *Cast:* Vivien Leigh, Simone Signoret, Jose Ferrer, Lee Marvin, Oskar Werner, Elizabeth Ashley, George Segal, Jose Greco, Michael Dunn, Charles Korvin, Heinz Ruehmann, Lilia Skala, Barbara Luna, Christiane Schmidtmer, Alf Kjellin, Werner Klemperer, John Wengraf, Olga Fabian, Gila Golan, Oscar Beregi, Stanley Adams, Karen Verne, Charles dc Vries, Lydia Torea, Henry Calvin, Paul Daniel, David Renard, Rudy Carrella, Silvia Marino, Anthony Brand.

Accepting her Oscar for *Suspicion* (1941.)

5

JOAN FONTAINE

After appearing as the virginal, restringent ingenue in fourteen pictures during the first four years of her career (1935-39), Joan Fontaine was catapulted into full-fledged stardom via two excellent Alfred Hitchcock vehicles — *Rebecca* and *Suspicion* — both under the aegis of David O. Selznick. Although *Rebecca* was the better picture and contained the better performance, she was only nominated for the Academy Award, but for *Suspicion,* she was awarded the coveted Oscar. This fortuitous casting made her into a hot motion-picture property, but since that time, her ensuing assignments were never as prestigious as these two pictures; and not a few critics regarded her as a fluke who became a star only through sex appeal.

While never a great actress, she was nonetheless an intelligent one, even if she sometimes appeared methodical and mannered. Her appeal was not simply that of her subtle beauty, but that of gentility — a combination of a lady of quality with impeccable manners and poise. Film historian, John Carlyle, described her, "Her facial beauty is quite interesting. An almost masculine structure — vide the square jaw and prominent cheekbones — is softened by a blonde aura, blue eyes, fair skin, light brown hair. And her face is definitely feminised by the fetching concatenation of a droop of the upper right eyelid and an up-curve of the right corner of a full-lipped mouth. This lucky fillip has enabled her to suggest, to the libido of the beholder, a warmth the rest of her face belies, and enabled her to make audiences believe she is shy and well-bred as easily as she has made them believe she is the beautiful external covering of corruption."

Early in her career, she was the perfect, mousy, fragile, wistful, proper English lady that was to become later on the *forte* of Deborah Kerr. And it is for these roles that she is best remembered, but she was also equally convincing as a worldly sophisticate with more than a touch of bitchery in *Tender Is the Night.*

The final result however, can be considered as more than just a fluke as she developed into a thoroughly professional, appealing actress. The quality that she best projected was a cool worldliness, and sitting and talking with Joan Fontaine today, one perceives the screen image an actuality of the personal woman. She is sleek and slim, and luckily that facial structure and those luminescent eyes provide her with an appeal that can last for many years to come. As composer, Virgil Thomson, once remarked to her, "You will be a beautiful older woman."

Joan de Beauvoir de Havilland was born on October 22, 1917, in the International Settlement in Tokyo, Japan. Her English father, Walter A. de Havilland was the head of a firm of patent attorneys in that feudalistic city and also taught English and French at the Tokyo Imperial University. Her father's family was descended from Sir Peter de

Havilland, a supporter of Cromwell against England's Charles I. Other family noteables included Lord and Lady Nolesworth, patrons of Gilbert and Sullivan, and the French segment of the de Havillands, the china manufacturers and Sir Geoffrey de Havilland of de Havilland Aircraft.

At an embassy tea in Tokyo, Walter de Havilland made the acquaintance of Lillian Ruse, a young Britisher from Berkshire, who was on a world tour with her brother. Attracted to the lovely Lillian, he courted her and proposed, but she refused his offer of marriage and returned instead to England with her brother to continue her music and vocal lessons at Sir Herbert Beerbohm Tree's Dramatic Academy. In 1914, Walter de Havilland returned to England to enlist in the military service during World War I. His attempt was unsuccessful and he renewed his acquaintance with Lillian and persuaded the aspiring young actress to marry him and return to Japan. She accepted his offer and the de Havillands' first child, Olivia, was born on July 1, 1916. Fifteen months later, their second daughter, Joan, was born.

The couple soon saw that their marriage was a mistake and they separated in 1919. Joan was a frail, sickly child and a doctor had suggested to Mrs. de Havilland she select a climate better than Japan in which to bring her up, and in the fall of 1919, the three de Havillands arrived in San Francisco, and settled shortly thereafter in nearby Saratoga, a small town on the Monterey Peninsula.

Mrs. de Havilland raised her daughters in the hope that they would pursue the theatre, a dream she had never fulfilled. To encourage them, she gave them lessons in diction and required daily recitations from Shakespeare. "We were nauseating," recalls Miss Fontaine. While the girls were attending primary school in Saratoga, Mrs. de Havilland met a French-Canadian by the name of George M. Fontaine, who managed a local department store. She obtained a divorce from Walter de Havilland and married Fontaine in 1925. He was a disciplinarian as a step-father to Olivia and Joan and referred to them as his "thoroughbreds." He also opposed his wife's theatrical aspirations for them with the result that at the ages of sixteen and fifteen, the two aspiring actresses left home and went to live with one of their mother's bridge-club friends. They attended high school in Los Gatos, and supported themselves by working after school as waitresses.

Olivia was the first to decide to pursue an acting career in earnest. Throughout their childhood, it has always been Olivia who excelled in school activities and sports, whereas Joan hid her I.Q. of 160 and her independence behind an inferiority complex. Miss Fontaine recalls one of Olivia's expressions when they were growing up was, "I can, but Joan can't." Of her childhood maladies, Miss Fontaine says, "I was always sick. We don't know what it was. I still have it. I'd had rheumatic fever and I've had pneumonia seventeen times. I had terrible mastoids every winter and would be in bed for months and months. I even had a nervous breakdown when I went to school in a convent once, the convent of Notre Dame in Belmont, California. I remember fainting in chapel and being sent home after four months. We would get up at five-thirty in the morning and kneel at the altar for an hour. It was mad, rugged stuff, and I remember my hair falling out and being kept in bed for two months."

Miss Fontaine was less determined in her aspirations towards acting than her sister and consequently cabled her father for financial support. He replied that he would send the girls money if his favourite daughter, Joan, would come to Japan to visit him. The frail teenager left for Japan in 1932 and stayed a year during which time she attended school and blossomed into a young beauty, returning to the United States, as legend has it, with five engagement rings. At the mention of the five engagement rings, Miss Fontaine laughs and says, "Two engagement rings! I was there for a year. I went to school at the American school and studied everything. I was very young. I had some friends of my mother's in the diplomatic corps and my mother wrote and said, 'Look after Joan and take care of her. She is in boarding school and will be very lonely.' So, they asked me immediately to all their dances which was gorgeous and I felt like an American debutante. I had a few charming beaux and one I was engaged to was an Englishman in Shell Oil. I later became godmother to his son and helped send the son through Oxford. The other engagement was to a vice-consul whom I met on the boat coming back. We were engaged until he came out to Hollywood and called me a bit of fluff. And that wouldn't work. I was determined I wasn't a bit of fluff at all. That was the end of him!"

Back in California, she discovered that her sister was enjoying a modest success on the California stage and set out on her own in pursuit of stardom. Not wishing to capitalise on her sister's good fortune, she chose the name Joan St. John for its euphonious sound and joined a theatre group in San José. Finally, her mother took the girls to Hollywood, where soon Olivia attracted attention as Hermia in Max Reinhardt's Hollywood Bowl production of Shakespeare's "A Midsummer Night's Dream" and as a result was signed to a seven-year contract by Warner Brothers. Determined more than ever to pursue her own theatrical career, the young Joan changed her name again when she discovered her English friends pronounced St. John as "Sinjen." This time she chose the name of Burfield, after a Los Angeles street, and was cast in Homer Curran's stage production of Edward Chodorov's "Kind Lady," which starred May Robson and Ralph Forbes. Supposedly Miss Robson's observation was that the young lady would "never be an actress." Miss Fontaine told the author, "I never heard that until this day. I don't think she would have said such a thing. It doesn't sound like her at all. She would have been much too gracious to have said it even if she had thought it."

Miss Fontaine's next job was as the thirty-five-year-old rival to Joan Crawford for Robert Montgomery in the M-G-M comedy, *No More Ladies* (1935). She was eighteen years old and this was her motion-picture debut. The part was small and the M-G-M executives ignored her. Her tactic was to change her name for a third and final time, and in doing so, adopted her step-father's name because a numerologist recommended that her name should end with an "e." Shortly thereafter, as Joan Fontaine, she was cast as the daughter in a stage production of Dodie Smith's "Call It a Day," a comedy about a day in the life of an English family. The production starred Violet Heming and Conway Tearle and opened in Los Angeles' El Capitan Theatre. Producer Jesse L. Lasky, who was releasing films through RKO, saw her, was impressed by her performance, and signed her to a contract at $200 a week.

RKO gave her the small role of the army officer's wife in James M. Barrie's *Quality Street* (1937), starring Katharine Hepburn and Franchot Tone, where she was listed thirteenth in the cast. While her role was insignificant, RKO followed that assignment by giving her the lead in a B-picture called *You Can't Beat Love* (1937) opposite Preston Foster, in which Foster portrayed a playboy dabbling in politics and proves the father of his sweetheart (Miss Fontaine) innocent of corruption. It was an unimportant picture, but RKO liked her well enough to give her starring roles in two pictures, both musicals.

Music For Madame (1937), which Lasky produced, had her as a Hollywood extra who helps an Italian tenor (Nino Martini) gain fame, and *A Damsel in Distress* (1937) cast her as the daughter of an English earl who falls in love with an American dancer, Fred Astaire. Astaire's history-making partnership with Ginger Rogers had come to a halt, and supposedly Ruby Keeler was pencilled in as star of this picture until Astaire said no. Interestingly, Miss Keeler told the author that she never even knew she was being considered for the role or any role opposite Astaire. RKO's choice of Miss Fontaine as Astaire's partner was by no means a quest for a dancing replacement for Miss Rogers, but merely logical casting — Miss Fontaine played a proper British lady and to prevent comparisons to Astaire's former partner, she was given but one dance.

Despite these starring roles, her next four assignments were all perfunctory routine B's — as Hedda Hopper's daughter in *Maid's Night Out* (1938); an actress in *Blonde Cheat* (1938); John Beal's flight nurse-girl friend in *The Man Who Found Himself* (1938); and the sweetheart of both Richard Dix and Chester Morris in *Sky Giant* (1938). Even worse was a British-made loan-out called *A Million to One* (1938), in which she was a society doll in love with Olympic champion Herman Brix (Bruce Bennett). A somewhat better loan-out was *The Duke of West Point* (1938) in which she was Louis Hayward's amour; after which RKO director, George Stevens, chose her for the only female role in the memorable male cast of *Gunga Din* (1939). She was Douglas Fairbanks Jr.'s fiancée. Stevens had directed her in both *Quality Street* and *A Damsel in Distress* and believed she would one day be a star. RKO, however, seemed to have lost interest in her, and after one more loan-out, as the unloving wife of Richard Dix in Republic's *Man of Conquest* (1939), they released her from her contract. That picture is noteworthy only because it contained her first appearance in a bitchy role.

At this point she was offered a contract by Warner Brothers, but she turned it down, preferring not to be under contract to the same studio as her sister Olivia. In the meantime, she was momentarily considered, as was almost everyone in Hollywood except Lassie, for the role of Scarlett O'Hara. Never really a serious contender for the part, David O. Selznick, however, did request that director, George Cukor, invite her to read for the part of Melanie. One story maintains that when she received Cukor's invitation, she said, "Certainly not. Melanie doesn't interest me. If you want someone to play Melanie, I suggest you call my sister." Miss Fontaine's version of this is, "I didn't say, 'Certainly not.' I would have loved to have played it. But what happened was, I came in beautifully dressed and Cukor said, 'You are much too chic for the part.' So I said, 'Have you ever thought of my sister, for it?' And he said, 'Who is your sister?' And I said, 'Olivia de Havilland.' Cukor replied, 'That's a marvelous idea.' "

Cukor was impressed with her enough to cast her as the petite, well-groomed, lovely young wife who cancels her divorce when she discovers she is pregnant in M-G-M's *The Women* (1939). Cukor directed her in this picture and told her to "simply think and feel" and her performance would capture the character. His advice, which Miss Fontaine thinks the best she ever received from a director, proved correct and she held her own in a cast that included Norma Shearer, Joan Crawford, Rosalind Russell and Paulette Goddard.

Although her acting career was still in the shadow of her sister, she had one-upped Olivia by being the first to obtain a husband — Brian Aherne.* But she had not, as the gossip columns intimated, stolen him from her sister. She had for a time been escorted by actor Conrad Nagel, who

* Aherne was born Brian de Lacy Aherne on May 2, 1902, in King's Norton, Worcestershire, England, and began his acting career as a child star on the English stage at the age of eight. He established himself as a leading man in London, and made his American theatrical debut as Robert Browning in "The Barretts of Wimpole Street" in 1931. Other New York stage vehicles included "Romeo and Juliet" and "Saint Joan," both with Katharine Cornell. He made his American film debut opposite Marlene Dietrich in *Song of Songs* (1933) and was nominated for an Academy Award for playing Maximilian in *Juarez* (1939). After divorcing Miss Fontaine, he married Eleanor de Liagre Labrot in 1946. His last feature film appearance was in *Rosie* (1968) with Rosalind Russell.

With Norma Shearer, Rosalind Russell, Paulette Goddard and Mary Boland in *The Women* (1939).

was twenty years her senior. And it was through Nagel that she was introduced to Aherne, when Nagel took her to a party at Aherne's home. Aherne was fifteen years older than Miss Fontaine and already a successful theatre actor and rising motion-picture star. They were married in an Episcopal church in Del Monte, California, on August 20, 1939, with Olivia as Miss Fontaine's bridesmaid. The Ahernes' honeymoon was cut short by a summons from David O. Selznick which informed Miss Fontaine that she had been selected to play the second Mrs. de Winter in his production of *Rebecca* (1940).

Aherne recalled in his autobiography, "A Proper Job" (Houghton-Mifflin Company, 1969), "Almost on impulse, I married Joan Fontaine, sister of Olivia de Havilland, young, pretty, gay, and utterly charming - and no actress, thank God, or at least so I thought until the fifth day of our honeymoon in the Oregon woods, when my dream was abruptly shattered by a phone call from David Selznick, offering her the lead in his picture *Rebecca* with Laurence Olivier. Over my despairing protests, the honeymoon was instantly abandoned, and we rushed back to Hollywood, where she was launched into orbit as a big new motion-picture star."

Selznick's production of *Rebecca* occurred simultaneously with that of *Gone With the Wind*. Vivien Leigh had refused the role, then changed her mind when she found that Selznick wanted Laurence Olivier as Maxim, but Selznick said no. Loretta Young and Margaret Sullavan were also tested, and Olivia de Havilland was likewise an early choice, but Jack Warner could not see his way to loaning Miss de Havilland to Selznick. Selznick met Miss Fontaine at a dinner party early in 1939, and asked, "How would you like to test for *Rebecca?*" Miss Fontaine said she would and during the next six months he subjected her to several tests. He regarded the starring role in *Rebecca* as second in importance only to that of Scarlett O'Hara in *Gone With the Wind,* and with minor reservations, considered Miss Fontaine the strongest contender for the part.

In *Rebecca* (1940).

Before he had decided to personally produce *Rebecca*, Selznick had endeavoured to interest Samuel Goldwyn and Hal Roach in a three-way producing deal with Miss Fontaine as the star, but their response was, as was Hollywood's in general at the time — she is a "wooden woman." The competition finally narrowed down to Margaret Sullavan, Anne Baxter, and Miss Fontaine, with Miss Baxter's tests being the most successful, but Selznick still held out for Miss Fontaine. His one question being her ability to sustain the part. On the eve of her wedding day, Selznick had asked her to do still another test, but she declined saying, her face was swollen from an impacted wisdom tooth, a condition Selznick regarded as "not so good for a honeymoon." She said he could telephone her during her honeymoon if he decided she was right for the part.

Selznick reached his decision on the observation that, "Her inferiority complex endowed her with an innocence and incandescence that made her the perfect choice for the part of the second Mrs. de Winter." Commenting on the role, Miss Fontaine said, "When I was a little girl unable to hold my own with those who should have been my friends, I knew the same quality of unhappiness the second Mrs. de Winter knew. I was fearful and timid. And I lived in constant horror of criticism." And after completion of the picture she told the press, "We did so hope that David Selznick would want Brian for the role of Max. It would have been wonderful if we could have played it together." (The Ahernes did perform together on radio's Lux Radio Theatre in "Suspicion" on May 4, 1941).

Production of *Rebecca* began in September, 1939. Miss Fontaine and Olivier did not get on well together, and he, like May Robson, was quoted as saying that she would never be an actress. Miss Fontaine was very much aware that this picture was her testing ground and fortunately Selznick never faltered in his belief that she was properly cast. In a memo to the picture's director, Alfred Hitchcock, he said, "I am aware that it takes time to get the performance out of Joan Fontaine, but every picture I have ever worked on had some such difficulty, and you are fortunate in having a completely competent cast of highly expert actors (Laurence Olivier, Judith Anderson, Gladys Cooper, George Sanders). Miss Fontaine requires work, but so has every other girl who has been aimed at stardom and who requires an enormous amount of work in her first big opportunity.'' During production of the film, Miss Fontaine recalls, ''Hitch was rather intimidated by most of the cast. He had an inferiority complex with that usual caste system in England — he being a Cockney. I was probably the least intimidating to him, so we used to sit and talk quite a lot. And he was very dear. He would have me over to his house for dinner with his wife, Alma, whom I adored. He also used to draw what he wanted. He would draw that chair and say, 'I want your face half hidden behind that chair.' And that makes it much better for an actor. It gives you a visual aspect of what he wants from your performance.''

When the picture was released, Selznick was proved right. He received an Academy Award proclaiming *Rebecca* the Best Picture of the Year, and Miss Fontaine almost reached the pinnacle of stardom with a nomination as Best Actress. She lost the award to Ginger Rogers for *Kitty Foyle*. Suddenly critics were aware of Joan Fontaine, the actress. W.H. Mooring said, ''Hitchcock has succeeded in transforming Joan Fontaine from an unsatisfying feminine decoration into a great screen actress.'' The New York ''Times'' Frank S. Nugent wrote, ''Miss de Maurier never really convinced me that any one could behave quite as the second Mrs. de Winter behaved and still be sweet, modest, attractive and alive. But Miss Fontaine does it — and does it not simply with her eyes, her mouth, her hands and her words, but with her spine. Possibly it's unethical to criticize performance anatomically. Still we insist Miss Fontaine has the most expressive spine — and shoulders! — we've bothered to notice this season.'' Of her sister's performance, Olivia de Havilland said, ''Joan wouldn't have been as wonderfully good as she was in *Rebecca* if she hadn't been married to Brian and her home foremost in her life. She was able to be objective about her work. She didn't get too intense. We try hard in our family. We get too anxious about things.''

Despite the box-office success of *Gone With the Wind* and *Rebecca, Rebecca* was the only picture Miss Fontaine acted in under Selznick's personal supervision, for he was advised to liquidate his Selznick International Productions in order to gain financial fluidity, after which he formed David O. Selznick Productions, Incorporated. Selznick allowed Miss Fontaine to appear in a West Coast stage production of Noel Coward's ''Tonight at 8:30'' starring Gladys Cooper. Miss Fontaine appeared in the ''Family Album'' sequence. For her next motion-picture assignment, Selznick had planned to loan her to Columbia for *The Howards of Virginia* (1940) based on Elizabeth Page's novel, ''The Tree of Liberty.'' She was to play the aristocratic daughter of a Tidewater family who marries a backwoodsman (Cary Grant.) Abdominal surgery caused her to be replaced by Martha Scott, after which Selznick proposed another loan-out, this time to Universal for a re-make of *Back Street* (1941) opposite Charles Boyer. Miss Fontaine refused this role saying it was not of the caliber of *Rebecca,* so Selznick chose another Hitchcock vehicle, *Suspicion* (1941) based on Frances Iles' novel, ''Before the Fact,'' casting her as the young, provincial, innocent general's daughter who fears for her life after marrying a dashing young Englishman (Cary Grant) who lives by his wits.

Selznick sold Miss Fontaine, Hitchcock, and the picture as a package deal to RKO. While this picture was less successful than Hitchcock's *Rebecca,* Miss Fontaine once again came in for her share of acclaim. The New York ''Times'' said, ''This young lady has unquestionably become one of the finest actresses on the screen and one of the most beautiful, too; and her development in this picture of a fear-tortured character is fluid and compelling all the way.'' The New York

With Cary Grant in *Suspicion* (1941).

Film Critics named her Best Actress of the year, and she was again nominated for an Academy Award. Her competition that year — Bette Davis for *The Little Foxes,* Greer Garson for *Blossoms in the Dust,* Barbara Stanwyck for *Ball of Fire,* and her sister, Olivia de Havilland for *Hold Back the Dawn.*

At the awards dinner the two sisters shared a table, and when Miss Fontaine was announced the winner, Olivia exclaimed, "We got it!" There were those who maintained that it was an award in compensation for Miss Fontaine's loss of the Oscar the year before, and in a full-page picture in "Life" magazine, Miss Fontaine did look surprised. While Olivia's "we" was undoubtedly sincere, there were naturally elements of competition between the two sisters long before the famous "feud" that would follow several years later. Before she had become established as a first-rate actress, Miss Fontaine frequently felt she had gained many "friends" in Hollywood who were only using her to get to Olivia. On one occasion, when an escort asked to see her for a second time, Miss Fontaine quipped, "He probably wants to ask me for Liv's new phone number!" And Miss de Havilland in discussing the loss of the Oscar to her sister, told the press, "If *Suspicion* had been delayed just a little, it wouldn't have gotten under the wire for this year's award and I might have won. I think that voters are inclined to remember with the highest favor the picture they have seen most recently. By the time they saw *Suspicion,* they had almost forgotten about *Hold Back the Dawn.*"

While Miss Fontaine has never been considered as "dedicated" an actress as Bette Davis, or even her sister, she had certainly by now become convinced that acting would give her the kind of life she desired and she would use it as a means to an end. She commented, "Oh, it's a hectic calling, the movies, but there is money in it." And it was over money matters that she refused to accept Selznick's next assignment, *This Above All* (1941) on loan to 20th Century-Fox opposite Tyrone Power. She chose instead suspension. On October 26, 1941, the New York "Times" entertainment

With Tyrone Power in *This Above All* (1942).

section carried an article about what it called "Trouble in Paradise." The trouble being the disputes by three stars with their employers — Deanna Durbin with Universal Pictures, Victor Mature with Hal Roach, and Miss Fontaine with Selznick. Miss Durbin's vicissitudes were unexplained but those of Mr. Mature and Miss Fontaine were allayed to that "orthodox and sordid root of evil:, money." Miss Fontaine was quoted in the article, "No, the problem was not the script, it was money trouble. I adored the role, but I'm only getting $1,000 a week for six weeks work on this picture. My producer, David Selznick, is getting $75,000. I don't see why I should kill myself when he makes that terrific amount of money." Selznick told her she should be grateful for the $6,000, but she only consented to do the picture when he promised her a substantial bonus. Miss Fontaine further explained, "I think that after a certain point it should be fifty-fifty. That seems fair for the opportunity given, and for his guidance, which is very important. However, I've gone on suspension several times because I turned down pictures I didn't think right for me. I was sure about *Suspicion*." She received no bonus. When recalling these incidents today, Miss Fontaine remembers that for the first Christmas she celebrated under contract to Selznick he sent her some lovely Lowestoft china. On the second Christmas, after they had gone through some financial disputes, he sent her a geranium plant with the $5.00 price tag still attached.

This Above All was appropriate wartime movie fare about a conscientious objector-deserter (Tyrone Power) and an aristocratic member of the Women's Auxiliary Air Force (Miss Fontaine) who reforms him. The picture's highlight was Miss Fontaine's explanation of why she loved England enough to fight for her, one of the longest screen monologues ever spoken by a woman.

Miss Fontaine's personal wartime loyalties were evidenced by her training as a Red Cross nurse's aid and conducting War Bond tours. She became a citizen of the United States on February 23, 1943.

Warner Brothers had wanted Miss Fontaine to play opposite her sister Olivia de Havilland in 1942, in *Devotion,* but they were unable to come to terms with David O. Selznick and Ida Lupino was cast in her stead. However, Selznick did loan Miss Fontaine to Warner Brothers for *The Constant Nymph* (1943), not only one of her best performances but also her favourite picture. For this portrayal she earned her third nomination for an Academy Award. She played an adolescent urchin, the daughter of the musical mentor of composer, Charles Boyer. At the end, she dies of a heart ailment during the first performance of the love music which he had composed from her inspiration. The New York "Times" review said, "For Joan Fontaine, the role of Tessa is another superb achievement. As the delicate little girl, severed from Dodd (Charles Boyer) by years between them, she wrings from the part its humor and pathos." Miss Fontaine says, "I loved Charles Boyer. I think he is my favorite actor of all of them because first of all he is a gentlemen. Secondly, he is objective, and thirdly, he cared about the texture of the film rather than of his own performance. He was a great and sympathetic help to me. Oh, what a sweet man he is. And it's a beautiful film and the music is superb."

In *The Constant Nymph* (1943).

Still another loan-out sent her to 20th Century-Fox for *Jane Eyre* (1944) an elaborate re-make of Charlotte Bronte's novel adapted by Aldous Huxley, John Houseman and Robert Stevenson. It was not an entirely satisfying picture but Miss Fontaine was well cast as the bewildered governess who falls in love with Edward Rochester (Orson Welles), the brooding and unpredictable master of Thornfield.

That same year, on June 2nd, Miss Fontaine's marriage to her "perfect husband" ended in divorce. She alleged she was allergic to the dust on their ranch and, "His butler ran the home to such an extent that I felt like sort of a guest." And, "I am not strong. And whenever I make a picture, I am so weary I can't even carry on a conversation

With Orson Welles in *Jane Eyre* (1944).

after I finish at the studio. Brian is bitterly opposed to my working."

The emotional upheaval of her divorce thrust her into her next role as Lady St. Columb, a red-haired pirate in the lavish Paramount production of *Frenchman's Creek* (1945). The Selznick press releases quoted Miss Fontaine as saying it was a picture, "Where I could really throw myself into the part. I had to learn so many new things, singing and fencing and a Cockney accent — maybe it's Lancashire — and oh, all sorts of things." She was indeed never more beautifully photographed on the screen but the picture was no more than a well-mounted swashbuckling roustabout. Again Selznick's press department went to work, "Usually I'm in a psychological drama. They do take it out of one. You have to hold your breath all day to play those parts. You play them all inside yourself, really play them with your stomach. Then you come home and you are all in. You can't hold your breath all day and forget about it at night. I've never finished a picture yet without having a nurse on the set for at least the last two weeks. Those parts just tear me to pieces." While these comments make it appear that the picture was a great deal of fun for Miss Fontaine, in an interview with the author, she refutes those press releases by saying, "*Frenchman's Creek!* I hated it and I hated it all the way through. And David persuaded me to do it and said, 'I will do marvelous things for you. I'm not even going to tell you what I'll do for you if you do this one.' And I, like a stupid ass, didn't ask what he was going to do. I took him on faith. May I say, nothing ever happened. I think David was wrong to put me into *Frenchman's Creek* and I knew it and it became just a flamboyant color film and I think faultily cast. When I heard it was to be in colour I was horrified because it was a mood thing and should have remained one; and there was more attention given to the set than to the acting, unfortunately. I was *miserable* on it."

Selznick did manage to make her somewhat happier by allowing her to appear in her first comedy, the delightful *The Affairs of Susan* (1945), in which she changed costumes and personalities to match her four suitors — George Brent, Dennis O'Keefe, Don DeFore, Walter Abel. She was aptly cast and exclaimed, "I was sick of being the sad-sack of the screen. I've shed gallons of tears and moped all over the place. I wanted to play comedy, and now that I've done it, I'm happier than I've ever been in Hollywood."

***In Frenchman's Creek* (1945).**

That happiness was short-lived, however. After she provoked Selznick's ire by turning down the Ginger Rogers part in *I'll Be Seeing You,* he put her on suspension for eighteen months.

The year before, Miss Fontaine's sister Olivia de Havilland had spent her own money and nearly two years of her career fighting Warners against adding time spent on suspension to extend the normal seven-year contract. She finally won her suit, the same that Bette Davis had lost to Warner Brothers in 1936. Miss Fontaine applauded her sister's courage, "Liv has not made a picture for two years (no other studio would hire her while she was in litigation with Warners) and it's too bad. I think she is one of the finest actresses on the screen. I don't think I've ever seen such a moving, carefully worked-out performance as her Melanie in *Gone With the Wind.* I hope she wins her court case." Today, Miss Fontaine says of her sister's fight, "I think the Academy should recognize Olivia for what she has done for all actors and producers and directors and writers and everybody else. We, if not for her, would be impinged still. And I hope the Academy will have a special award for her. We certainly owe it to her. All of us."

During those eighteen months, on November 18, 1945, Miss Fontaine starred as Elizabeth Bennett on Theatre Guild on the Air, in a radio version of "Pride and Prejudice."

Miss Fontaine appeared in three more pictures, all on loan-out, before the termination of her contract with Selznick. She was miscast as the impoverished, young Bronx housewife in *From This Day Forward* (1946), but was seen to better advantage as the unsavoury, malevolent, Edwardian heroine in *Ivy* (1947), the story of a woman who poisons her lovers in her effort to obtain the richest of husbands. *Ivy* was a beautifully appointed costume drama and one critic felt it used to advantage the artificial streak in Miss Fontaine's acting. Playing her friend, Bella Crail, in the picture, was Lillian Fontaine, Joan's mother. Lillian Fontaine had made her motion-picture debut as Jane Wyman's mother in *Lost Weekend* (1945), and had small parts in *Time Out of Mind* and *Suddenly It's Spring,* both released in 1947. She never appeared in a picture with her older daughter Olivia. Lillian Fontaine died on February 20, 1975, at age 88.

Miss Fontaine's last loan-out was to Paramount where she proved merely decorative as the Hapsburg countess pursued by Bing Crosby in *The Emperor Waltz* (1947), a bit of musical *frou-frou,* directed by Billy Wilder. This was Wilder's first critical flop and the New York "Times" regarded it as a pastiche of "A dash of *The Prisoner of Zenda*, a twist of Old Vienna corn, and plenty of any roadshow." For his loan-out deal on this picture, Selznick received $225,000 for Paramount's use of Miss Fontaine. This ended their professional association.

Miss Fontaine gloried in the termination of her contract. She and Selznick had never got along as producer and star, and in 1969, when interviewed for the television special, "Hollywood: The Selznick Years," she spoke candidly, "I admired his tremendous ability and good taste, but he became a peddler in horse-flesh rather than a creative movie-maker. Selznick in many ways was a remarkable man. He was the first one to have a star under contract to him personally rather than to a studio. He would make a picture with you or loan you to some other producer. Doing this, he would collect a high price, but would pay you only the contract minimum. Oh, he made our lives an absolute hell, unless we acceded to his demands. And that's why I repeat that he became a peddler in horse-flesh. He was known as a Chinese War Lord, you know 'Off with their heads!'. Once when I wouldn't sign a release, he said, 'Tell her I'll blackball her from Hollywood for ten years.' " She described Selznick as very volatile, loving debates, arguments and fist fights and also said he had his tender and romantic side. "He wore heavy glasses, was six feet high, slightly overweight and had curly, iron-gray hair. He was a giant-sized Irving G. Thalberg. He didn't have a refined accent, it was just pure American. I think he had a burning ambition to avenge himself for his father who was ruined by Hollywood. When he married Louis B. Mayer's daughter, Irene, it was a dynastic marriage as though the Capulets and the Montagues had made up. David Selznick had a sense of quality, he raised the quality of movies from the nickelodeon days. He bought things of worth, hired people he thought were genuine actors instead of personalities only." In talking with the author, Miss Fontaine explained her relationship with Selznick further, "I wanted to do 'The Swan,' for instance, on the stage for Gilbert Miller. He wouldn't let me do that. I think he was wrong again. It would have built me up tremendously. I was offered *Claudia* to do with Brian. I don't remember whether Brian felt the part wasn't big enough, but it would have been superb for us. And of course, made Dorothy McGuire a star as a

In *Ivy* (1947).

matter of fact. And the man's part is a lovely part. So, I have had many frustrations along the line and most of all I had endless telegrams — just like paper towels — delivered by Western Union. They practically camped at the doorstep. Everytime I'd come back from a trip, I could hardly open the door for the yellow envelopes stuffed underneath. I wish I still had those memos. And I wish I had his early letters, because he wrote me very beautiful letters before he signed me up under contract. He, I think, fancied I was a romantic, English virgin and he glorified me and wrote almost Browningesque poems to me. Really very, very beautiful. Then, of course, the moment he had me under contract, it was quite different. As a boss, he was not romantic in any way."

Shortly before her contract had expired, on May 2, 1946, Miss Fontaine eloped to Mexico with Universal-International producer, William Dozier. They took up residence in a large house at 404 Fordyce Road in the Santa Monica mountains, and she, along with her new husband, became part of Rampart Productions, with Dozier as president and Miss Fontaine as vice-president. She exclaimed, "Oh, it's wonderful to be free. For the first time in my life, I'm independent. All those years, yes, seven of them, I was under contract to David Selznick, he only made one picture with me, *Rebecca*. All the others I made on loan-out to some other company. Now I am free to make the kind of pictures I want to make and it's wonderful. What a difference when I go on the set now! They don't say, 'Get the girl,' anymore. Now it's 'See if Miss Fontaine is ready,' and there is always somebody around with a chair when I want to sit down. And when I come on the set in the morning everyone gives me a cheery hello, and I also get flowers and sometimes a basket of fruit. There are a lot of advantages in being a producer of one's own pictures. David made lots of money loaning me to other studios, but he never paid me a big-time salary." Dozier interjected, saying the most she had received from Selznick for any picture had been $40,000. Miss Fontaine's contractual agreement with Rampart Productions involved a seven-year exclusive contract requiring one picture for Rampart and one on loan-out per year. She and Dozier were to have approval of the director, leading man, supporting players, and script. And Rampart would also produce two pictures annually not starring Miss Fontaine.

Their first project was to have been a loan-out of Miss Fontaine to Samuel Goldwyn to star opposite Gregory Peck in *Earth and High Heaven*, based on a novel by Gwethalyn Graham, about the marriage of a Jew and a Gentile. Supposedly, Goldwyn had delayed the project a year and a half awaiting Miss Fontaine's availability. The screenplay was to have been written by Howard Koch with production to begin in the spring of 1947, but negotiations fell through and the picture was never made. However, 1947 did see Gregory Peck cast in the definitive motion picture about anti-Semitism, *Gentlemen's Agreement,* which earned the Academy Award as Best Picture of the Year.

More newsworthy in 1947 than either her marriage or her partnership in Rampart Productions was an incident which took place between Miss Fontaine and her sister Olivia. The two sisters' personalities have often been described as distinctly opposite, but the "feud" as such, did not come to the fore until the presentation of the Academy Awards in March 1947, where Olivia was named Best Actress of the Year for her performance in *To Each His Own.* The basis of the feud, aside from the differences in their personalities, was allegedly Miss Fontaine's personal dislike of Olivia's husband — author Marcus Goodrich — who was regarded by Hollywood as Miss de Havilland's Svengali (and presumably responsible for Miss de Havilland turning down the role of Blanche DuBois in *A Streetcar Named Desire*). Olivia was quoted as saying, "Joan can be cutting with her wit and said some things which hurt." The night of the Oscar presentations found Miss Fontaine waiting backstage, hand extended, to congratulate her sister as she came off stage. Miss de Havilland had expressly asked her press agent not to have them meet backstage, but the press agent failed to follow instructions, probably hoping for a reconciliation. Upon seeing her sister, Miss de Havilland turned her back and walked away, exclaiming, "I don't know why she does that when she knows how I feel." The photographers caught this brush-off and it captured the next morning's headlines. Olivia later explained, in view of the discord that existed between them, she felt Miss Fontaine had chosen the wrong moment to attempt a reconciliation. Notwithstanding, the two sisters adamantly denied the existence of a feud.

Miss Fontaine had been quoted on one occasion as saying, "Being the little sister of a movie star does hurt. You discover that people are your friends only to reach your sister. People would rave to me that a certain performance of hers could never be matched. I served the cake at Livvie's parties. I drove her to the studio and waited outside. But there is no feud. That's just a publicity gag someone started. Why should there be a professional jealousy between us. We both have won Oscars and have reached what some people choose to call the top. And I didn't steal my sister's beau (Brian Aherne). Why Livvie was my bridesmaid when Brian and I were married."

Such comments did not however prevent the press from speculating and when the girls' mother was questioned by reporters, she said, "I don't know anything about the feud. But I do know that they are acting like children and not very intelligent children. Of course, Joan and Livvie quarreled when they were children. What sisters only fifteen months apart don't? But I wouldn't say they had conflicting personalities. Rather, they reached different stages of development at different times. However, Joan was always the more impetuous one, and she was the executive type, the organizer. Olivia was the student, the shy plugger. Both were thinkers, but Joan was always a more independent thinker. Olivia was more impressionable. But there is no reason for the girls to be jealous of each other. Both had successes and both are happily married." In the same speech to the press, Mrs. Fontaine went on to comment on the new "change" in Joan's personality, saying, "I credit it all to Bill, her husband. He was what she needed. When she married Bill, she married a man who is a faster thinker, who means security and who can dominate her."

That "change" in Miss Fontaine is better defined in the plural. Firstly, she had gone from the struggling young actress pursuing a career in the shadow of her supposedly more talented sister, to being the wife of an older English husband, Brian Aherne. During her marriage to Aherne, Miss Fontaine had been accused of being inhibitingly ladylike and stuffy. Then, immediately after her divorce, she was accused of swinging the pendulum and becoming temperamental and neurotic, driving press agents and directors mad with her unpredictable moods. In 1943, she had been named the most unco-operative actress by the Hollywood Women's Press Club. Her behaviour was attributed to frustration over the divorce, her financial problems with Selznick, and a feeling of insecurity about remaining on top of her career. She dropped her stuffy image and began using four-letter words to shock, causing her sense of humour to be tagged as evocative of that of Carole Lombard. (Miss Lombard was well-known for her proficiency with profanity.) And once, midway through a dinner party, she stalked out, exclaiming, "This party bores me."

For whatever reasons, the termination of her contract with Selznick and her marriage to Dozier, brought forth a new and co-operative Joan Fontaine.

During 1948, three pictures starring Miss Fontaine were released, two of which were produced by her husband. *Kiss the Blood Off My Hands,* cast her as a young nurse who falls in love with war veteran-murderer, Burt Lancaster, and was most noteworthy for what film historian, John Carlyle, called the "most gruesome title of 1948."*Letter From an Unknown Woman* was adapted from a story by Stefan Zweig, directed by Max Ophuls, and produced by her husband, William Dozier, for Rampart Productions. For Miss Fontaine's co-star, they negotiated with David Selznick, for the loan of the screen's newest romantic star, Louis Jourdan. Selznick had brought Jourdan from France and cast him in *The Paradine Case* (1947) and agreed to his being borrowed by Rampart Productions only if they released their picture after *The Paradine Case.* The Doziers consented to Selznick's terms and Miss Fontaine excitedly described the handsome, young actor for the press, "He combines the appeal of Valentino, Charles Boyer and Tyrone Power. He has a hot, firey look in his eyes." *Letter From an Unknown Woman* contains one of Miss Fontaine's best performances. She played a young girl who pursues a life-long but hopeless love for a philandering

With Louis Jourdan in *Letter From an Unknown Woman* (1948).

musician played by Jourdan. One critic called it a beautiful piece of kitsch, while another wrote, "Miss Fontaine is Hollywood's most accomplished mistress of sadness."

The third project which Miss Fontaine and her husband wished to do that year was a version of "Mayerling" with Miss Fontaine playing Marie Vetsera, the role that had made an international star of Danielle Darrieux. That project never materialised and in its place they chose the comedy, *You Gotta Stay Happy,* in which she played a runaway heiress opposite James Stewart. There were shades of *It Happened One Night* in the plot, but it turned out to only be mildly amusing and elicited but a few whole-hearted laughs.

While making this picture, Miss Fontaine became pregnant, and in November 1948, she gave birth to her only child, a daughter named Deborah Leslie. The following year, her personal and professional association with Dozier and Rampart Productions ended when, "He walked out of the house on August 4, 1949, and never came back. He told me that our marriage did not suit him." On one occasion she told the press that the roles of wife, mother and actress were too many and too exhausting a schedule. On another, she said, "I think Mr. Dozier is the nicest man in the world and the best friend I ever will have." Their divorce became final on January 25, 1951, but a bitter suit over custody of their daughter lasted until 1958, when the courts awarded custody of the child to Dozier.

Miss Fontaine's only screen venture in 1950 proved one of her worst. She played the husband-chasing gold-digger in *Born to Be Bad,* a project which Selznick had originally announced for her several years before, but under the direction of Nicholas Ray, it turned out to be just a bad soap-opera.

For the first time since she was a teenager, Miss Fontaine saw her father, when she had dinner with him in 1950. Walter de Havilland had come to the United States ten years earlier, pleading for money, after his Tokyo law practice had been ruined by the anti-British feeling in the Orient. He brought with him his Japanese wife and told reporters that he was planning to move to South America, where, on eighty dollars a month, "I am going to live and die, in poverty, but in peace." At that time, his ex-wife made a public statement regarding his sudden appearance. "The news of Mr. de Havilland's arrival comes as a complete surprise to me and my daughters because during the twenty-one years that have elapsed since our divorce (sic), my daughters and I have had only one contact with him. The girls and I came to America in 1919, where I brought them up." Olivia added to her mother's statement the following, "And that is all we possibly can say."

By 1950, de Havilland was seventy-eight years old, married for a third time, and living in Canada and at his birthday dinner, he urged Joan to end the feud with Olivia.

Despite the father's solicitations, the sisters did not reconcile until December 1956, and then there was a secondary motive. It seemed there had been not only misunderstandings between the two sisters, but also, since 1947, Olivia had not spoken to her mother, the cause of which was again attributed to family feelings about Olivia's marriage to Marcus Goodrich. (Olivia divorced Goodrich in 1953, charging he had made attempts on her life, and that she had not known until after they were married that he had been married four times before. In 1955, she married Pierre Galante, then editor of "Paris-Match" and took up residence in that capital city of France.) Finally, during Christmas of 1956, the mother and daughters held a family reunion in Olivia's home. After that occasion, any further questions from reporters about the "feud," were answered succinctly by Miss Fontaine, "I adore, respect and like my sister, but we don't seek out each other's company. We're such complete opposites." And Olivia's explanation was this, "We're both volatile and high strung, so perhaps it's not surprising we occasionally get offended at each other." While rarely photographed together, their joint presence in the lobby of the Lunt-Fontane Theatre in New York City on October 9, 1967, for the opening night of Marlene Dietrich's fabled one-woman show, created a stir amongst fellow first-nighters.

Shortly after her divorce from Dozier in 1951, Miss Fontaine traveled to South America for a film festival. While there, she visited Machu Picchu in the wilds of the Peruvian Andes and came upon a five-year-old Inca Indian child named Martita Valentina Pareja Calderon, living in poverty with her mother, several brothers and sisters and her father, who was a caretaker of the ruins of Machu Picchu. With the consent of the family, Miss Fontaine unravelled five days of legal red tape to arrange to adopt the child as her own and bring her back to the United States, the only stipulation being that she raise the child in the Catholic faith at her parents' request. After graduating from school at eighteen, Martita took up residence in Maine.

Joan Fontaine returned to picture-making by signing a three-picture deal with Paramount. The first assignment, *September Affair* (1951) was filmed in Europe, and was a respectable *Intermezzo*-like story of a pianist (Miss Fontaine) who has a brief love-affair with a married man (Joseph Cotten) in Italy. While making this picture, she and Cotten performed in unbilled bits in Orson Welles's *Othello*. Miss Fontaine played a page boy and Cotten was a senator. The picture was not released until 1955.

While in Europe, Miss Fontaine was on one occasion escorted by Prince Aly Khan to a party hosted by Elsa Maxwell. At the time Khan was in the middle of his legal imbroglio over divorce proceedings with Rita Hayworth, and when reporters and photographers kept bothering him and Miss Fontaine on the dance floor, he threatened to bump their heads together.

Miss Fontaine's second assignment for Paramount was *Darling, How Could You!* (1951) a mediocre version of J.M.Barrie's "Alice-Sit-By-the-Fire," in which Miss Fontaine was the giddy, childish mother. Her third, *Something to Live For* (1951), while essentially sentimental, was directed by George Stevens, fresh from his triumph with *A Place in the Sun* (1951), and Miss Fontaine was quite convincing as the young alcoholic actress who is reformed by an ex-alcoholic, Ray Milland. However, Paramount failed to promote the picture, and it got lost in the shuffle at the box-office.

She then had parts in two costume dramas, one of which she liked, and one she did not. She was a beautiful Rowena in *Ivanhoe* (1952) with Robert

With Joseph Cotten in *September Affair* (1951).

Taylor and Elizabeth Taylor, but thought the part "too straight up and down." However, she enjoyed playing the maid, the wife, the matron, and the widow in *Decameron Nights* (1953), a witty, four-part film based on the writings of Boccaccio and once again co-starring Louis Jourdan.

Miss Fontaine married her third husband, producer Collier Young, at the home of her mother and step-father in Saratoga, California, on November 12, 1951.

After starring with Jack Palance in *Flight to Tangier* (1953), a melodramtic work in which she was an FBI agent, Miss Fontaine appeared in *The Bigamist* (1953), a picture produced by Filmakers, a corporation formed by Collier Young when he had been married to Ida Lupino. Not only did the picture star Edmond O'Brien and Miss Fontaine, but also Miss Lupino and it was directed by Miss Lupino, and to make it even more of a "family" affair, Collier Young played a bit part as a barfly and Lillian Fontaine, Joan's mother, played Miss Lupino's landlady. It proved to be a moderately interesting story about a travelling salesman (O'Brien) who has two wives — a waitress (Miss Lupino) and a woman executive (Miss Fontaine.)

Released after this picture was *Casanova's Big Night* (1954), in which Miss Fontaine was merely a foil for some not-so-funny Bob Hope shenanigans; in actuality, this picture had been made before *Flight to Tangier*.

As the years went by, Miss Fontaine's film roles were becoming less than exciting and in June 1954, she took a two-year leave to make her Broadway debut, replacing Deborah Kerr in "Tea and Sympathy." She proved to be an excellent choice and Brooks Atkinson wrote, "Miss Fontaine gives a forceful and thoughtful performance that admirably preserves the sincerity and insight of the script. She is personally modest and professionally able, and her performance is a revealing piece of acting. This is one of the better lend-lease deals with Hollywood." Miss Fontaine took an apartment at 340 Park Avenue and signed to remain in the play until the following March. However, she was forced to leave the play a month earlier than planned when an attack of acute bursitis developed in one of her arms as the result of a sledding accident with her daughters.

Recalling her run in "Tea and Sympathy" Miss Fontaine told the author, "It was difficult because I had two children and I had to take care of them in an apartment in New York City. That is bad enough if you've got another parent, but with indifferent help, I would sometimes have to call home between acts to see how their fevers were and then rush home to them after. I loved the experience of the stage. Playing to a huge, full house, all whistling and cheering — that was a marvelous sensation. You can almost reach out and touch those rows of people and the response from them is a kind of energy that warms you. It's like the sun. Tony (Perkins — who had replaced John Kerr) was sweet. He was very naive, but sweet. He loved the children and he would come up and play with them. What was difficult for me was the eight a week. I just think it's a terrible disciplinary grind. When I do theatre, I turn off the phone at five o'clock, have a little tray, try to sleep, listen to the evening news and go quietly to the theatre. Then needlepoint back stage so we don't gossip or smoke, and then it's usually home by yourself and playing solitaire. And I just think that's a terrible life."

Her return to films was to have been opposite Van Johnson in Gottfried Reinhardt's *Rosalinda,* but that never materialised. Instead, she was the sophisticated patron of Mario Lanza with a "jewel-like bitchiness," in *Serenade* (1956), a role that had originally been offered to Tallulah Bankhead. After that picture, she played the virtuous wife of murderer Ray Milland, in Fritz Lang's second-rate thriller, *Beyond a Reasonable Doubt* (1956). This was followed by the film of Alec Waugh's controversial novel, *Island in the Sun* (1956), about miscegenation and revolt on a West Indian island. Its plot was muddied in its transference to the screen and Miss Fontaine was not to blame because her role of the neurotic society playgirl who falls in love with native labour leader (Harry Belafonte) was psychologically unbelievable. As a result of this performance, Miss Fontaine received many letters of protest for having accepted the part. Today the picture appears simply pretentious and in no way precedent-setting.

Miss Fontaine's next assignment finally gave her a first-class role and proved once again when the script is good the lady herself could be very good. *Until They Sail* (1957) was one of those little pictures with a cast of talented performers — Jean Simmons, Paul Newman, Piper Laurie. Robert Anderson's screenplay was based on a story by James Michener about four New Zealand sisters and their war-time romances. Miss Fontaine was the eldest sister, whose soldier-lover, Charles Drake, is killed, after which she bears his illegitimate child and is brought to the United States by his parents.

Good parts do not always come in pairs, and

With Charles Drake in *Until They Sail* (1957).

Miss Fontaine was back once again, playing the enobled wife, this time enduring the dalliance of husband, Rossano Brazzi, with his teenage flirtation (Christine Carere) in *A Certain Smile* (1958), a bit of boring fluff by Francoise Sagan. The only relief from tedium was the scenic photography of the Riviera.

Following this picture, Miss Fontaine was hospitalised with hepatitis, undulant fever and mononucleosis at the UCLA Medical Center, after which she recuperated at Lake Arrowhead in the San Bernadino mountains, and at her home in Maine. By this time, she and husband, Collier Young, "had been going our own ways." (They officially separated in 1960, and divorced in January, 1961. She charged mental cruelty and said he drank too much and was awarded one dollar monthly token alimony.) Miss Fontaine spent her recuperation in solitude and said later, "Getting sick was quite an eye-opener for me. I lay up there at Lake Arrowhead without phone calls, without letters, without anybody coming to see me. I thought of all the parties I had given, all the people I had entertained. Where were they now? I was too ill to kill myself, but if I had had the strength, I would have."

When she recovered, she performed in a summer stock stint in "Hillary" (1959) and attended the Colombian Film Festival in South America the same year. While there, Miss Fontaine supposedly chose not to curtsey to the Empress of Iran to whom she was presented in a reception line. When questioned about this by reporters, Miss Fontaine was quoted as saying, "Why should I? I didn't even curtsey when I met Joan Crawford!" When questioned about this by the author, Miss Fontaine replied, "No, I didn't say it, but I'm glad. I like it!"

The following summer she returned to stock, appearing in a production of "Susan and God."

After a three-year absence from the screen, Miss Fontaine was subjected to an overdose of radiation and subsequently devoured by a shark in the science-fiction film, *Voyage to the Bottom of the Sea* (1961), after which she was faultlessly cast as the spoiled, unscrupulous Chicago heiress in *Tender Is the Night* (1961). However, only the ambience of that exquisitely photographed and costumed picture evoked F. Scott Fitzgerald's version of the 1920's. Miss Fontaine's part was not written as a integral part of the script and her character was largely one-dimensional. Jennifer

In *Tender Is the Night* (1961).

Jones could have been an effective Nicole, but she lacked proper direction by Henry King and appeared merely neurotic. It was a such a waste of talent and material that it made movie audiences regret that David Selznick had sold it as a package to 20th Century-Fox, rather than personally producing it as he had once planned.

It was this picture that made Miss Fontaine decide to never again play in a supporting role. She said, ''I shall never forget doing that picture with Jennifer Jones, whom I adore. We are good friends. I remember them saying, 'Miss Jones is ready, bring on the *girl*.' That was me. And Miss Jones had the big dressing room and I had a smaller one, and I thought that was ridiculous. We started at the same time and this didn't make sense at all. So since then, I realized that you must never play supporting roles, you must never play mothers; not if you want to maintain your stardom.''

Miss Fontaine had leased her home in the Santa Monica mountains in 1960 and made New York her permanent residence. Her explanation is, ''When my agent called me and asked me to play Elvis Presley's mother, that is when I moved to New York.'' Her California home, its furnishings, and her possessions were destroyed in the 1961 Bel-Air Brentwood forest fire. Miss Fontaine told reporters, ''It all went up in smoke. Everything! My whole past. Pictures of my three husbands. Pictures of my daughters. Copies of my three interlocutory divorces. My scrapbooks, letters, paintings. Everything! I was born again — free!'' A year later, her apartment at 36 Central Park South was robbed of some $50,000 in jewels and furs.

Except for occasional appearances on television in such dramatic shows as ''Four Star Playhouse,'' ''The Loretta Young Show,'' ''G-E Theatre,'' ''Desilu Playhouse,'' and ''Four Star Time,'' Miss Fontaine remained inactive until 1964 when ''tired of loafing,'' she accepted the lead in a sophisticated marital comedy, ''A Severed Head,'' a play by Iris Murdoch. Four members of the cast, including Miss Fontaine, left the play out of town. It arrived on Broadway on October 38th with Jessica Walters in the lead and closed after twenty-nine performances. Miss Fontaine says, ''It was a terrible thing. Four of us were asked to leave the cast and we did so gladly. It was not American fodder and we didn't know what the hell they wanted us to do.''

For a time in 1962, Miss Fontaine had been seen on several occasions being escorted by United Nations Ambassador Adlai Stevenson. Despite Miss Fontaine's comment that she had known Stevenson for ten years, the columnists had a field day. Hedda Hopper said, ''Adlai has a new girlfriend and I won't make you guess who. It's Joan Fontaine;'' and ''Life'' magazine carried a two-page photograph of the couple showing Stevenson laughing at something said by Miss Fontaine. They elected to stop seeing each other because of the comments by the press and Miss Fontaine spoke to the press about her three marriages. She was quoted as saying she had married Brian Aherne to get away from her mother and her sister, William Dozier to have children, and Collier Young for companionship. ''The next time, I'm going to get married for myself. I think a diplomat is the sort of man I could be happy with. A diplomat needs a successful and pleasant woman to give parties and be a good hostess. There's nothing competitive about their career. This makes for a good relationship.''

However, the man she chose to be her fourth husband was not a diplomat. Alfred Wright, Jr. was the senior editor of ''Sports Illustrated.'' They were married on January 27, 1964, and two years later, she obtained a ''friendly divorce.''

After the divorce, she was quoted by Radie Harris of ''The Hollywood Reporter'' as saying, ''All I want now is to grow up and become an imperious, demanding old bag who will be just as rude to young people as old people were to me when I was young.'' When asked by the author if she had really made this statement, Miss Fontaine replied with a smile, ''Now you don't *really* believe everything Radie Harris says, do you?'' She also added, ''I would prefer not to marry again, but I would like a lifetime mate. I don't think you have to marry them and I'm not sure a relationship wouldn't endure more if both of you had your own digs, as it were, rather than come home every night and talk about taxes.''

After her divorce, she obtained the motion-picture rights to *The Devil's Own* (1966), a novel by Peter Curtis about an English headmistress who is involved in voo-doo by one of her pupils. Filmed in England, it was a taut little thriller, but more appropriate for television consumption than world-wide distribution.

Since that outing, she has appeared in no more feature films and has accepted very little television work. There was a play called ''Relatively Speaking'' that failed to reach Broadway in 1970, and the same year she dropped out of an Italian-produced picture entitled *A Girl Named Jules* when her salary was not paid weekly in advance as she had stipulated. Two years later, in Johannesburg, South Africa, she left a theatre production of "Dial M For Murder," which she had played in stock in the United States, when there was a contractual dispute over what traveling luxuries and living expenses she was to be given.

She herself has limited the amount of work available to her by refusing to play mothers or character roles. Always ambivalent about her dedication as an actress, she once said, "There is nothing in the world so satisfying as acting in something you love." More succinct and probably closer to the truth was the following, "Pictures are hard work. I take them seriously and try to live each character I play. But I don't pretend my ambition is to give a deathless performance before I die. I make pictures because I like to be able to get a good table when I go to a nightclub, and because I like to travel. There are two ways I know to be able to do such things. One is to be a movie star, and the other is to be a millionaire. I am not a millionaire."

Miss Fontaine now lives in an apartment which occupies an entire floor of an apartment house in New York City's East Seventies. The apartment is beautifully furnished in antiques and appointed with paintings by Chagall, Utrillo, Derain, and some she has painted herself. She likes poetry, is a Cordon-Bleu chef, and circulates in the best of New York's social and theatrical circles. She supports numerous charities and philanthrophies, including Waterloo Village, the restored, pre-Revolutionary War village in New Jersey. For her charitable endeavours, she was awarded the Eleanor Roosevelt Memorial Award in 1966. She is an avid world traveller and says, "I love to travel. I've been to almost sixty countries and played golf in twenty-three. I think that travel is one's education."

Of the social life in the Hollywood of the past, she recalls, "There was a tremendous caste system there. You were allowed to invite a producer or director to your home but one never invited a cameraman. You could possibly invite your own agent, that is, if you were very rich. But otherwise, he was taboo. It was very peculiar but that's the way it was. Here in New York, anything goes, and it probably does out there now. I can invite anybody here I choose and be glad to see them. But you couldn't do that then. You only invited stars. You hardly ever invited character actors, unless they were venerable like Dame May Whitty or Ethel Barrymore."

In 1973, Miss Fontaine began making radio and television commercials for Arnold's Bread, which she continues to do, and put together a lecture called "Life In a Love," which she plans to take on a tour of colleges. The lecture consists of the letters and poems of Robert Browning contrapuntally with those of Elizabeth Barrett. She has written the lecture herself and says if successful, she wishes to do the same with the works of the Rossettis. She explains, "I like language and the use of words. I think that we are lacking in language today. I think that the young people have such a limited vocabulary today that it is really my desire to restore language." She performed the lecture at the East Hampton Playhouse in August 1973 and at New York's Town Hall in July 1974.

While she does not feel that the movies are dead, she does feel it is a director's medium today and not the stars'. "I'm not sure that Watergate won't give this country an entirely new point of view about honesty. In that case, we'd have no more violence and none of the crudity that we have today. We might just swing back to decency and honour and those nice things that are so lacking." She eschews any further political comments, saying, "I'm a naturalised citizen and I had my passport taken from me during the McCarthy era. Had it not been for the fact that I knew a lot of people in Washington, it would not have been fixed instantly. But I was only given a six-month extension and I hate being on proviso: that be-a-good girl kind of thing. So I resolved then and there *never* to realise that I was anything but a guest in the country, especially when I think of Charlie Chaplin. I'm a registered Republican, but I have voted either way."

She does not see herself as part of acting today, and maintains that with all the insecurities of being an actor today, she fails to see how many can really pursue acting as much more than an avocation. "The smell of the greasepaint means nothing to me. My drive has been to earn my own living. And I love beautiful things and I love to travel. I like to dress well. I like all these books you see here. I like to go to the theatre and the opera. I like to live in a certain way which I'm lucky, to say, that I could do as an actress where I couldn't do it anywhere else. Also I could be asked everywhere and be presented to kings and queens, which is pretty marvelous. I'm very grateful to my career and especially to David for really starting it all.''

There are no particular roles that she covets or really regrets not having played. She did, however, tell the author, ''I would have played Alexandra in *Nicholas and Alexandra*. That is, until I saw it. But had I been offered the script to play her, I might have taken it. But then, Alexandra was a *star*, wasn't she? A czarina and a star!'' Shortly thereafter, Miss Fontaine was signed by Dico Dimitrov to play Alexandra in his production of *The Escape of Nicholas and Alexandra*. Based on twenty-five years of research by the producer, the story maintains that the royal family did escape from Russia in 1918. Rossano Brazzi was signed to play Nicholas, and Victor Mature to play the American government offical who helps them escape. However the production has failed to materialize. In the meantime Miss Fontaine has become one of the most popular attractions in dinner theatre tours and spent the first six months of 1974 performing in ''Forty Carats'' to sold-out audiences, and during the same period in 1975, she continued this new success by starring in ''Cactus Flower.''

The Feature Film Appearances of Joan Fontaine

No More Ladies (M-G-M, 1935). Screenplay by Donald Ogden Stewart and Horace Jackson from a play by A.E. Thomas. Directed by Edward H. Griffith. *Cast:* Joan Crawford, Robert Montgomery, Charles Ruggles, Franchot Tone, Edna May Oliver, Gail Patrick, Reginald Denny, Vivienne Osborne, Joan Burfield (Joan Fontaine), Arthur Treacher, David Horsley, Jean Chatburn, William Wagner, Charles Coleman, Isabelle La Mal, Frank Dawson, Walter Walker, E.J. Babiel, Ed Hart, Tommy Tomlinson, Charles O-Malley, Lew Harvey, David Thursby, Sherry Hall, Clem Beauchamp, Veda Buckland, Mabel Calcord.

Quality Street (RKO, 1937). Screenplay by Mortimer Offner and Allan Scott from the play by Sir James M. Barrie. Directed by George Stevens. *Cast:* Katharine Hepburn, Franchot Tone, Fay Bainter, Eric Blore, Cora Witherspoon, Estelle Winwood, Florence Lake, Helena Grant, Bonita Granville, Clifford Severn, Sherwood Bailey, Roland Varno, Joan Fontaine, William Bakewell, York Sherwood, Carmencita Johnson.

The Man Who Found Himself. (RKO, 1937). Screenplay by J. Robert Bren, Edmund L. Hartmann, G.V. Atwater and Thomas Lennon from the story ''Wings of Mercy'' by Alice F. Curtis. Directed by Lew Landers. *Cast:* John Beal, Joan Fontaine, Philip Huston, Jane Walsh, George Irving, James Conlin, Frank M. Thomas, Diana Gibson, Dwight Fryle, Billy Gilbert.

You Can't Beat Love (RKO, 1937). Screenplay by David Silverman and Maxwell Shane from the story ''Quintuplets To You'' by Olga Moore. Directed by Christy Cabanne. *Cast:* Joan Fontaine, Preston Foster, Herbert Mundon, William Brisbane, Alan Bruce, Paul Hurst, Bradley Page, Berton Churchill, Frank M. Thomas, Harold Huber, Paul Guilfoyle, Barbara Pepper.

Music For Madame (RKO, 1937). Screenplay by Gertrude Purcell and Robert Harari from a story by Robert Harari. Directed by John Blystone. *Cast:* Joan Fontaine, Nino Martini, Alan Mowbray, Billy Gilbert, Alan Hale, Lee Patrick, Frank Conroy, Bradley Page, Ada Leonard, Alan Bruce, Romo Vincent, Barbara Pepper, Edward H. Robins, George Shelley, Jack Carson, Grant Mitchell, Erik Rhodes, Ralph Lewis, Mary Carr, Ben Hendricks, William Corson, Ben Hall, Jack Mulhall, Larry Steers, Harold Miller, Ralph Brooks, Grace Hayle, Mira McKinney, George Meeker, Stanley Blystone, Pat O'Malley, Robert Homans, Milburn Stone, Harry Tenbrook, James Donlan, Russ Powell, Ward Bond, Sam Hayes, Jac George.

A Damsel in Distress (RKO, 1937) Screenplay by P.G. Wodehouse, Ernest Pagano and S.K. Lauren from a story by P.G. Wodehouse. Directed by George Stevens. *Cast:* Fred Astaire, Joan Fontaine, George Burns, Gracie Allen, Reginald Gardiner, Constance Collier, Montagu Love, Harry Watson, Jan Duggan, Pearl Amatore, Betty Rone, Mary Dean, Jac George, Joe Numeyer, Bill O'Brien, Mary Gordon, Ralph Brooks, Fred Kelsey, Major Sam Harris.

A Million to One (Puritan, 1938). Screenplay by John T. Neville. Directed by Lynn Shores. *Cast:* Herman Brix (Bruce Bennett), Joan Fontaine, Reed Howes, Monte Blue, Kenneth Harlan, Suzanne Kaaren, Joe O'Brien, Joe Healy, Ed Piel, Ben Hall, Dick Simmons.

Maid's Night Out (RKO, 1938). Screenplay by Bert Granet from a story by Willoughby Speyers. Directed by Ben Holmes. *Cast:* Joan Fontaine, Allan Lane, Hedda Hopper, George Irving, William Brisbane, Billy Gilbert, Cecil Kellaway, Vicki Lester, Hilda Vaughn, Eddie Gribbon, Frank M. Thomas, Solly Ward.

Blond Cheat (RKO, 1938). Screenplay by Charles Kaufman, Paul Yantz, Viola Brothers Shore, and Harry Segall from a story by Aladar Laszlo. Directed by Joseph Santley. *Cast:* Joan Fontaine, Derrick de Marney, Cecil Kellaway, Cecil Cunningham, Lillian Bond, Robert Coate, Olaf Hytten, John Sutton, Gerald Hamer.

Sky Giant (RKO, 1938) Screenplay by Lionel Hauser. Directed by Lew Landers. *Cast:* Joan Fontaine, Richard Dix, Chester Morris, Harry Carey, Paul Guilfoyle, Vicki Lester, William Corson, James Bush, Edwin Marr, Harry Campbell, Robert Strange, Max Hoffman Jr.

The Duke of West Point (United Artists, 1938). Screenplay by George Bruce. Directed by Alfred E. Green. *Cast:* Joan Fontaine, Louis Hayward, Tom Brown, Richard Carlson, Alan Curtis, Donald Barry, Gaylord Pendleton, Charles D. Brown, Jed Prouty, Marjorie Gateson, Emma Dunn, George McKay, James Flavin, Nick Lukats, Kenneth Harlan, Jonathan Hale, William Bakewell, Art Raymond, Anthony Nace, Mary MacLaren, Edward Earle, Alan Connor.

Gunga Din (RKO, (1939). Screenplay by Joel Sayre and Fred Guiol from a story by Ben Hecht and Charles MacArthur based on a poem by Rudyard Kipling. Directed by George Stevens. *Cast:* Cary Grant, Victor McLaglen, Douglas Fairbanks Jr., Sam Jaffe, Eduardo Ciannelli, Joan Fontaine, Montagu Love, Robert Coote, Abner Biberman, Lumsden Hare, Cecil Kellaway, Reginald Sheffield, Ann Evers, Audrey Manners, Fay McKenzie, Charles Bennett, Les Sketchley, Frank Levya, Olin Francis, Geoge Ducount, Jamiel Hasson, George Regas, Bryant Fryer, Lal Chard Mehra, Roland Varno, Olive Morgan.

Man of Conquest (Republic 1939). Screenplay by Wells Root, E.E. Paramore Jr., and Jan Fortune from a story by Harold Shumate and Wells Root. Directed by George Nichols Jr. *Cast:* Joan Fontaine, Richard Dix, Gail Patrick, Edward Ellis, Victor Jory, Robert Barrat, Geoge Hayes, Ralph Morgan, Robert Armstrong, C. Henry Gordon, Janet Beecher, Pedro De Cordoba, Max Terhune, Ferris Taylor, Kathleen Lockhart, Leon Ames, Charles Stevens, Lane Chandler, Sarah Padden.

The Women (M-G-M, 1939). Screenplay by Anita Loos and Jane Murfin from the play by Clare Boothe. Directed by George Cukor. *Cast:* Norma Shearer, Joan Crawford, Rosalind Russell, Mary Boland, Paulette Goddard, Phyllis Povah, Joan Fontaine, Virginia Weidler, Lucile Watson, Florence Nash, Muriel Hutchinson, Esther Dale, Ann Morris, Ruth Hussey, Dennie Moore, Mary Cecil, Mary Beth Hughes, Virginia Grey, Marjorie Main, Cora Witherspoon, Hedda Hopper, Aileen Pringle, Judith Allen, Margaret Dumont, Mildred Shay, Priscilla Lawson, Estelle Etterre, Ann Morriss, Marjorie Wood, Theresa Harris, Virginia Howell, Barbara Jo Allen (Vera Vague), Mariska Aldrich, Veda Buckland, Charlotte Treadway, May Beatty, May Hale, Ruth Findlay, Charlotte Wynters, Florecne Shirley, Florence O'Brien, Hilda Plowright, Leila McIntyre, Dot Farley, Flora Finch, Dorothy Sebastian, Renie Riano, Grace Goodall, Lilian Bond, Winifred Harris, Gertrude Astor, Nell Craig, Grace Hayle, Maude Allen, Natalie Moorhead, Jo Ann Sayers, Betty Blythe, Dorothy Adams, Barbara Pepper, Peggy Shannon, Carol Hughes, Virginia Pine.

Rebecca. (Selznick International - United Artists, 1940). Screenplay by Robert E. Sherwood and Joan Harrison from an adaptation by Philip MacDonald and Michael Hogan of the novel by Daphne de Maurier. Directed by Alfred Hitchcook. *Cast:* Laurence Olivier, Joan Fontaine, George Sanders, Judith Anderson, Nigel Bruce, Reginald Denny, C. Aubrey Smith, Gladys Cooper, Florence Bates, Melville Cooper, Leo G. Carroll, Leonard Carey, Lumsden Hare, Edward Fielding, Philip Winter, Forrester Harvey.

Suspicion (RKO, 1941). Screenplay by Samson Raphaelson, Joan Harrison and Alma Reville, from the novel, "Before the Fact," by Francis Illes. Directed by Alfred Hitchcock. *Cast:* Cary Grant, Joan Fontaine, Sir Cedric Hardwicke, Nigel Bruce, Dame May Whitty, Isabel Jeans, Heather Angel, Auriol Lee, Reginald Sheffield, Leo G. Carroll, Maureen Roden-Ryan, Constance Worth, Violet Shelton, Carol Curtis-Brown, Faith Brook, Pax Walker, Leonard Carey, Clyde Cook, Kenneth Hunter, Gertrude Hoffman, Dorothy Lloyd, Elsie Weller, Aubrey Mather, Rex Evans, Edward Fielding, Hilda Plowright, Ben Webster, Gavin Gordon, Nondas Metcalf, Lumsden Hare, Vernon Downing, Clara Reid, Billy Bevan, Alec Craig.

This Above All (20th Century-Fox, 1942). Screenplay by R.C. Sherriff from a story by Eric Knight. Directed by Anatole Litvak. *Cast:* Joan Fontaine, Tyrone Power, Thomas Mitchell, Henry Stephenson, Nigel Bruce, Gladys Cooper, Sara Allgood, Alexander Knox, Queenie Leonard, Melville Cooper, Jill Esmond, Miles Mander, Rhys Williams, Arthur Shields, Dennis Hoey, John Abbott, Carol Curtis-Brown, Mary Field, Lilyan Irene, Holmes Herbert, Denis Green, Thomas Louden, Mary Forbes, Forrester Harvey, Harold de Becker, Jessica Newcombe, Billy Bevan, Brenda Forbes, Doris Lloyd, Alan Edmiston, Morton Lowry, Olaf Hytten, Aubrey Mather, Heather Thatcher, Jean Prescott, Rita Page, Clare Verdera, Joyce Wynn, Valerie Cole, Stephanie Insall, Dorothy Daniels de Becker, Virginia McDowell, Wyndham Standing, Alec Craig, Anita Bolster, May Beatty, Cyril Thornton, Leonard Carey, Val Stanton.

The Constant Nymph (Warner Brothers, 1943). Screenplay by Kathryn Scola from the novel by Margaret Kennedy and Basil Dean. Directed by Edmund Goulding. *Cast:* Charles Boyer, Joan Fontaine, Alexis Smith, Brenda Marshall, Charles Coburn, Dame May Whitty, Peter Lorre, Joyce Reynolds, Jean Muir, Montagu Love, Eduardo Ciannelli, Jeanine Crispin, Doris Lloyd, Joan Blair, Andre Charlot, Richard Ryen, Crauford Kent, Marcel Dalio, Clemence Groves, Louise Brien, Geoffrey Steele, George Kirby, Charles Irwin, Donald Stuart, Jean Ransome, Brandon Hurst, Max Rabinowitsh, David Clyde, Mildred Brook, Eric Mayne.

Jane Eyre (20th Century-Fox, 1944). Screenplay by Robert Stevenson and John Houseman from the novel by Charlotte Bronte. Directed by Robert Stevenson. *Cast:* Orson Welles, Joan Fontaine, Margaret O'Brien, Peggy Ann Garner, John Sutton, Sara Allgood, Henry Daniell, Agnes Moorehead, Aubrey Mather, Edith Barrett, Barbara Everest, Hillary Brooke, Ethel Griffies, Mae Marsh, Yorke Sherwood, John Abbott, Ronald Harris, Elizabeth Taylor, Elly Malyon, Mary Forbes, Thomas Louden, Charles Irwin, Ivan Simpson, Erskine Sanford, Gwendolen Logan, Moyna Macgill, Gerald Oliver Smith, Jean Fenwick, Bud Lawler, John Meredith, Leslie Vincent, Roseanne Murray, Marion Rosamond, Dan Wallace, Billie Seward, Ruthe Brady, Adele Jergens, Colin Campbell, Eustace Wyatt, Billy Bevan, Tempe Pigott, Harry Allen, David Clyde, Charles Coleman, Alec Craig, Federick Worlock, George Kirby, Arthur Gould-Porter, Alan Edmiston, Barry Macollum, Brandon Hurst, Nancy June Robinson.

Frenchman's Creek (Paramount, 1945). Screenplay by Talbot Jennings from the novel by Daphne de Maurier. Directed by Mitchell Leisen. *Cast:* Joan Fontaine, Arturo de Cordova, Basil Rathbone, Nigel Bruce, Cecil Kellaway, Ralph Forbes, Harald Ramond, Billy Daniels, Moyna MacGill, Patricia Barker, David James, Mary Field, David Clyde, Charles Coleman, Paul Oman, Arthur Gould-Porter, Evan Thomas, Leslie Denison, Denis Green, George Kirby, Fred Kohler Jr., Charles Irwin, Constance Worth, Phyllis Barry, David Thursby, Lauri Beatty, Ronnie Rondell, George Barton, Victor Romito, Bob Clark, Allen Pinson, Patrick Desmond, Jimmy Dine, Harvey Easton, Henry Escalante, Art Foster, Vincent Gironda, Jacques Karre, John Latito, Rube Schaffer, Sammy Stein, Armand Tanny, John Roy, Neal Clisby, Noble Blake, Edward Cooper, Bob Stevenson, Alfred George Ferguson, Frank Hagney, Keith Hitchcock, Leyland Hodgson, Kenneth Hunter, Boyd Irwin, Gordon Richards.

The Affairs of Susan (Paramount, 1945). Screenplay by Thomas Monroe, Laszlo Gorog and Richard Flournoy from a story by Thomas Monroe and Laszlo Gorog. Directed by William A. Seiter. *Cast:* Joan Fontaine, George Brent, Dennis O'Keefe, Walter Abel, Don DeFore, Rita Johnson, Mary Field, Byron Barr, Francis Pierlot, Lewis Russell, Vera Marshe, Frank Faylen, James Millican, Robert Sully, John Whitney, Jerry James, Crane Whitley, Bill Meader, Warren Hymer, Ralph Brooks, Natalie Draper, Alice Fleming, Almeda Fowler, Eddie Laughton, Milton Kibbee, Howard Mitchell, Kitty O'Neil, Gordon Richards, Cyril Ring, Ruth Roman, Eddy C. Waller. Mira McKinney, Douglas Carter, Teala Loring, Joel Friend, Renee Dupuis, Grace Gillern, Stan Johnson, Beverly Thompson, Audrey Westphall, Audrey Young, Wallace Earl, Brooke Evans, June Harris, Lucy Knoch, Mavis Murray, Adelaide Norris, Marjorie Silk, Jane Starr.

From This Day Forward (RKO, 1946). Screenplay by Hugo Butler, adapted by Garson Kanin from the novel, "All Brides Are Beautiful" by Thomas Bell. Directed by John Berry. *Cast:* Joan Fontaine, Mark Stevens, Rosemary De Camp, Henry Morgan, Wally Brown, Arline Judge, Bobby Driscoll, Mary Treen, Doreen McCann, Erskine Sanford, Renny McEvoy, Queenie Smith, Polly Bailey, Alan Ward, Sam Lufkin, Virginia Engels, Ellen Corby, George Magrill, Leota Lorraine, Amelia Romano, Jack Gargan, Patricia Prest, Pat Hennigan, Tim Hawkins, Bobby Barber, Tom Noonan, Moroni Olsen, Guy Beach, Ralph Dunn, Joey Ray, Ida Moore, Alf Haugen, Nan Leslie, Charles Wagenheim, Milton Kebbee, Manny Harmon, Sally Gordon, Doria Caron, Theodore Newton.

Ivy (Universal-International, 1947). Screenplay by Charles Bennett from the novel, "The Story of Ivy" by Marie Belloc Lowndes. Directed by Sam Wood. *Cast:* Joan Fontaine, Patric Knowles, Herbert Marshall, Richard Ney, Sir Cedric Hardwicke, Lucile Watson, Sara Allgood, Rosalind Ivan, Lillian Fontaine, Molly Lamont, Una O'Connor, Isobel Elsom, Alan Napier, Paul Cavanaugh, Sir Charles Mendl, Gavin Muir, Mary Forbes, Henry Stephenson, Norma Varden, Lumsden Hare, Matthew Boulton, Lydia Bilbrook, Alan Edmiston, Harry Hays Morgan, Holmes Herbert, C. Montague Shaw, Claire Du Brey, Gerald Hamer, Colin Campbell, Leon Lenoir, David Cavendish, Jean Fenwick, David Ralston, Ella Ethridge, Renee Evans, Judith Woodbury, Dave Thursby, Art Foster, Lois Austin, Herbert Clifton, James Logan, Eric Wilton, Charles Knight, Herbert Evans, Manuel Paris, Wyndham Standing, Clive Morgan, Elsa Peterson, Bess Flowers, James Fairfax.

The Emperor Waltz (Paramount, 1947). Screenplay by Charles Brackett and Billy Wilder. Directed by Billy Wilder. *Cast:* Bing Crosby, Joan Fontaine, Roland Culver, Lucile Watson, Richard Haydn, Harold Vermilyea, Sig Ruman, Julia Dean, Bert Prival, Alma Macrorie, Roberta Jonay, John Goldsworthy, Doris Dowling, James Vincent, Harry Allen, Eleanor Tennant, Vesey O'Davoren, Norbert Schiller, Frank Elliott, Paul de Corday, Jack Gargan, Cyril Delevanti, Frank Mayo, Franco Corsaro, Len Hendry, Hans Moebus, Albert Petit, Count Stefenelli, Renee Randall, Jean Marshall, Kathy Young, Jerry James, William Meader, Gene Ashley, John "Skins" Miller, Jac Fisher, Leo Lynn, Bob Stephenson, James Logan.

Kiss the Blood Off My Hands. (Universal-International, 1948). Screenplay by Leonard Bercovici, adapted by Ben Maddow and Walter Bernstein, from the novel by Gerald Butler. Directed by Norman Foster. *Cast:* Joan Fontaine, Burt Lancaster, Robert Newton, Jay Novello, Colin Keith-Johnson, Reginald Sheffield, Campbell Copelin, Leland Hodgson, Peter Hobbes, Leslie L. Russell, Amita Dyne, Gryelda Hervey.

Letter From an Unknown Woman (Universal- International, 1948). Screenplay by Howard Koch from "Brief einer Unbekannten" by Stefan Zweig. Directed by Max Ophuls. *Cast:* Joan Fontaine, Louis Jourdan, Mady Christians, Marcel Journet, Art Smith, Carol Yorke, Howard Freeman, John Good, Leo B. Pessin, Erskine Sanford, Otto Waldis, Sonja Bryden, Audrey Young, William Trenk, Fred Nurney, Torben Meyer, Hermine

Sterler, C. Ramsey Hill, Will Lee, William Hall, Lotte Stein, Ilka Greening, Paul E. Burns, Roland Varno, Leo Mostovoy, Shimen Ruskin, Celia Lovsky, Lester Sharpe, Michael Mark, Lois Austin, Lisa Golm, Rex Lease, Edmund Cobb, Betty Blythe, Diane Lee Stewart, Vera Stokes, Doretta Johnson, Lorraine Gale, Cy Stevens, Doug Carter, Jack Gargan, Authur Lovejoy, Guy L. Shaw, June Wood, Jean Ransome, Judith Woodbury, Manuel Paris, John McCallum, Robert W. Brown.

You Gotta Stay Happy (Universal-International, 1948). Screenplay by Karl Tunberg from a story by Robert Carson. Directed by H.C. Potter. *Cast:* James Stewart, Joan Fontaine, Eddie Albert, Roland Young, Willard Parker, Percy Kilbride, Porter Hall, Marcy McGuire, William Bakewell, Arthur Walsh, Paul Cavanaugh, Halliwell Hobbes, Stanley Prager, Mary Forbes, Edith Evanson, Peter Roman, Houseley Stevenson, Emory Parnell, Don Kohler, Hal K. Dawson, Vera Marshe, Jimmie Dodd, Robert Rockwell, Mary Forbes, Bert Conway, Bill Clauson, Eddie Ehrhart, Joe Cook Jr., Don Garner, Hal Melone, Frank White, Beatrice Roberts, Fritz Feld, Arthur Hohl, Frank Jenks, Frank Darien, Edward Gargan, Don Shelton, George Carleton, Chief Yowlachie, Isabel Withers, Al Murphy, Myron Healey, Harland Tucker, David Sharpe, Donald Dewar, Tiny Jones, William H. O'Brien.

Born To Be Bad (RKO, 1950). Screenplay by Edith Sommer, adapted by Charles Schnee from the novel, "All Kneeling" by Anne Parrish, with additional dialogue by Robert Soderberg and George Oppenheimer. Directed by Nicholas Ray. *Cast:* Joan Fontaine, Robert Ryan, Zachary Scott, Joan Leslie, Mel Ferrer, Harold Vermilyea, Virginia Farmer, Kathleen Howard, Dick Ryan, Bess Flowers, Jay Hallward, Hazel Boyne, Irving Bacon, Gordon Oliver, Sam Lufkin, Helen Crozier, Bobby Johnson, Tim Taylor, Peggy Leon, Ray Johnson, John Mitchum, Evelyn Underwood, Barry Brooks, Al Murphy, Homer Dickinson, Georgianna Wulff, Ann Burr, Frank Arnold, Don Dillaway, Avery Graves.

September Affair (Paramount, 1951) Screenplay by Robert Thoeron and Fritz Rotter. Directed by William Dieterle. *Cast:* Joan Fontaine, Joseph Cotten, Francoise Rosay, Jessica Tandy, Robert Arthur, Jimmy Lydon, Fortunio Bonanova, Grazia Narcise, Anna Demetrio, Lou Steele, Frank Yaconelli, Charles Evans, Jimmy Frasco, Michael Frasco, Charles La Torre, Gilda Oliva, Saverio Lomedico, George Nardelli, Nick Borgani, Georgia Clancy, Dick Elliott, Rudy Rama, Franz F. Roehm, George Humbert, Harry Cheshire, Iphigenie Castiglioni, Inez Palange, Zacharias Yaconelli, Victor Desny, James R. Scott, Stan Johnson, Douglas Grange, Larry Arnold, Walter Merrill.

Darling, How Could You! (Paramount, 1951) Screenplay by Dodie Smith and Lesser Samuels from the play, "Alice-Sit-By-the-Fire" by Sir James M. Barrie. Directed by Mitchell Leisen. *Cast:* Joan Fontaine, John Lund, Mona Freeman, Peter Hanson, David Stollery, Virginia Farmer, Angela Clarke, Billie Bird, Lowell Gilmore, Robert Barrat, Gertrude Michael, Mary Murphy, Frank Elliott, Willard Waterman, Gordon Arnold, John Bryant, Robin Hughes, David Eden, Allan Douglas, Dave Willock, Mary Ann Reimer, Maureen Lynn Reimer, Patsy O'Bryne, Gloria Winters, Maria J. Tavares, Fred Zendar, William Meader, Houseley Stevenson, Jimmie Dundee, Allan Douglas, Charles Sherlock, Mickey Little, Rudy Lee, Kathryn Towne, Dolores Hall, Percy Helton, Robert E. Burns.

Something To Live For (Paramount, 1951). Screenplay by Dwight Taylor. Directed by George Stevens. *Cast:* Joan Fontaine, Ray Milland, Teresa Wright, Richard Derr, Harry Bellaver, Douglas Dick, Herbert Heyes, Paul Valentine, Frank Orth, Bob Cornwaithe, Helen Spring, Rudy Lee, Patric Mitchell, Richard Barron, Paul Newlan, John Indrisano, Jessie Proctor, Lillian Clayes, Genivieve Bell, Patsy O'Byrne, Helen Dickson, Cora Shannon, Arthur Tovery, Joseph J. Greene, Mari Blanchard, James E. Moss, Lee Aaker, Douglas Spencer, Mary Field, Judith Allen, Kerry Vaughn, Paul Maxey, Slim Gaut, Anne M. Kunde, Raymond Bond, Peter Hanson, Laura Elliot, Charles Dayton, Sherry Jackson, Gerald Courtemarche, Susan Freeman, Helen Brown, Rolfe Sedan, Marcel De La Brosse, Charles Andre, Jeanne Lafayette, Harold Miller, Dulce Daye, Korla Pandit, King Donovan, Al Kunde, George M. Lynn, Don Dillaway, Gloria Dea, Josette Deegan, Lavonne Battle, Bob St. Angelo, Erville Alderson, Maurice Cass, Eric Alden, Ida Moore, Jody Gilbert.

Ivanhoe (M-G-M, 1951). Screenplay by Noel Langley from the novel by Sir Walter Scott. Directed by Richard Thorpe. *Cast:* Robert Taylor, Joan Fontaine, Elizabeth Taylor, George Sanders, Emlyn Williams, Robert Douglas, Finlay Currie, Felix Aylmer, Francis De Wolfe, Norman Wooland, Basil Sydney, Harold Warrender, Patrick Holt, Roderick Lovell, Sebastian Cabot, John Ruddock, Michael Brennan, Megs Jenkins, Valentine Dysell, Lionel Harris, Earl Haffe, Guy Rolfe, Patrick Lovell.

Decameron Nights (RKO, 1953). Screenplay by George Oppenheimer from the works of Boccacio. Directed by Hugo Fregonese. *Cast:* Joan Fontaine, Louis Jourdan, Godfrey Tearle, Joan Collins, Binnie Barnes, Mara Lane, Stella Riley, Melissa Stribling, Elliott Makeham, Meinhart Maur, George Bernard, Bert Bernard, Ban Boclen, Gordon Bell, Noel Purcell, Hugh Morton, Marjorie Rhodes.

Flight To Tangier (Paramount, 1953). Screenplay by Charles Marquis Warren. Directed by Charles Marquis Warren. *Cast:* Joan Fontaine, Jack Palance, Corinne Calvet, Robert Douglas, Marcel Dalio, Murray Matheson, Jeff Morrow, Richard Shannon, John Pickard, John Doucette, James Anderson, Don Dunning, Eric Alden, Bob Templeton, Peter Coe, Madeleine Holmes, John Wengraf, Otto Waldis, Jerry Paris, Rene Chatenay, Albert D'Arno, Anthony De Mario, Karin Vengay, Pilar Del Rey, Josette Deegan, Rodric Redwing, Mark Hanna.

The Bigamist (Filmakers, 1953) Screenplay by Collier Young. Directed by Ida Lupino. *Cast:* Joan Fontaine, Edmond O'Brien, Ida Lupino, Edmund Gwenn, Jane Darwell, Kenneth Tobey, Peggy Maley, John Maxwell, Lillian Fontaine, Collier Young, Mack Williams, James Todd, James Young, John Brown, Matt Dennis, Jerry Hausner, Kim Dibbs, Kenneth Drake, Mac McKim, George Lee.

Casanova's Big Night (Paramount, 1954). Screenplay by Hal Kanter and Edmund Hartmann from a story by Aubrey Wisberg. Directed by Norman Z. McLeod. *Cast:* Bob Hope, Joan Fontaine, Vincent Price, Basil Rathbone, Audrey Dalton, Hugh Marlowe, Arnold Moss, John Carradine, John Hoyt, Hope Emerson, Robert Hutton, Lon Chaney Jr., Raymond Burr, Frieda Inescort, Primo Carnera, Frank Puglia, Paul Cavanaugh, Romo Vincent, Henry Brandon, Natalie Schafer, Lucien Littlefield, Douglas Fowley, Nestor Paiva, Barbara Freking, Joan Shawlee, Oliver Blake, Kathryn Grant, Marla English, Joseph Vitale, John Alderson, Richard Karlan, Fritz Feld, Walter Kingsford, Paul 'Tiny' Newlan, Shelton Knaggs, Eric Alden, Keith Richards, Charley Cooley, Bess Flowers, Dick Sands, Charles Hicks, Arline Hunter, Rexene Stevens.

Othello (Mercury-United Artists, 1955). Screenplay by Orson Welles from the play by William Shakespeare. Directed by Orson Welles. *Cast:* Orson Welles, Michael MacLiammóir, Suzanne Cloutier, Robert Coote, Milton Edwards, Michael Lawrence, Fay Compton, Nicholas Bruce, Jean Davis, Doris Dowling, Joan Fontaine, Joseph Cotten.

Serenade (Warner Brothers, 1956) Screenplay by Ivan Goff, Ben Roberts and John Mann. Directed by Anthony Mann. *Cast:* Mario Lanza, Joan Fontaine, Sarita Montiel, Vincent Price, Joseph Calleia, Vincent Edwards, Harry Ballaver, Silvio Minciotti, Frank Puglia, Licia Albanese, Jean Fenn, Edward Platt, Frank Yaconelli, Mario Siletti, Maria Serrango, Edwards Noriega, Joseph Vitale, Victor Romito, Norma Zimmer, Francis Barnes, Lilian Molieri, Laura Mason, Richard Cable, Richard Lert, Jose Govea, Antonio Triano, Leo Mostovoy, Nick Mora, Joe De Angelo, William Fox, Jack Santora, Mickey Golden, Elizabeth Flournoy, Creighton Hale, Stephen Bekassy, Martin Garralaga, Don Turner, Perk Lazelle, April Stride, Diane Gump, Jose Torvay, Martha Acker, Vincent Padula.

Beyond a Reasonable Doubt (RKO, 1956) Screenplay by Douglas Morrow. Directed by Fritz Lang. *Cast:* Joan Fontaine, Dana Andrews, Sidney Blackmer, Philip Bourneuf, Shepperd Strudwick, Arthur Franz, Edward Binns, Robin Raymond, Barbara Nicols, William Leicester, Dan Seymour, Rusty Lane, Joyce Taylor, Carleton Young, Trudy Wroe, Joe Kirk, Charles Evans, Wendell Niles, Dorothy Ford, Joey Ray, Larry Barton, Frank Mitchell, Emma Blucher, Billy Reed, Carl Sklover, Phil Barnes, Baynes Barron, Jeffrey Sayre, Bob Whitney, Hal Taggart, Dorothy Gordon, Bill Boyett, Jol Mondeaux, Eric Wilton, Dave Wiechman, Tony De Mario, Harry Strang, Benny Burt, Myron Cook, Ralph Volkie, Franklyn Farnum.

Island In the Sun (20th Century-Fox, 1957). Screenplay by Alfred Hayes from the novel by Alec Waugh. Directed by Robert Rossen. *Cast:* James Mason, Joan Fontaine, Dorothy Dandridge, Joan Collins, Harry Belafonte, Michael Rennie, Patricia Owens, Stephen Boyd, John Justin, Diana Wynyard, Basil Sydney, John Williams, Ronald Squire, Hartley Power.

Until They Sail (M-G-M, 1957). Screenplay by Robert Anderson from a story by James A. Michener. Directed by Robert Wise. *Cast:* Jean Simmons, Joan Fontaine, Paul Newman, Piper Laurie, Charles Drake, Sandra Dee, Wally Cassell, Alan Napier, Ralph Votrain, John Wilder, Tige Andrews, Adam Kennedy, Mickey Shaughnessy, Patrick Macnee, Ben Wright, Kendrick Huxham, James Todd, David Thursby, Hilda Plowright, Nicky Blair, Morgan Jones, Pat Waltz, William Boyett, Jimmy Hayes, Jay Douglas, Pat Colby, Dan Eitner, Tom Mayton, Roger McGee, John Rosser, Jim Cox, Dean Jones, Robert Keys, Ann Wakefield, Alma Lauton, Dee Humphrey, Dorris Riter, Pamela Light, Phyllis Douglas, Vesey O'Davoren, Pat O'Hara, Stanley Fraser.

A Certain Smile (20th Century-Fox, 1958) Screenplay by Frances Goodrich and Albert Hackett based on the novel by Francoise Sagan. Directed by Jean Negulesco. *Cast:* Joan Fontaine, Rossano Brazzi, Bradford Dillman, Christine Carere, Katherine Givney, Steven Geray, Eduard Franz, Trude Wyler, Sandy Livingston, Renate Hoy, Muzaffer Tema, Katherine Locke, Carol Van Dyke, Gabrille Del Valle, Feridun Colgecan, Edit Angold, David Hoffman.

Voyage to the Bottom of the Sea (20th Century-Fox, 1961). Screenplay by Irwin Allen and Charles Bennett from a story by Irwin Allen. Directed by Irwin Allen. *Cast:* Walter Pidgeon, Joan Fontaine, Barbara Eden, Peter Lorre, Robert Sterling, Michael Ansara, Frankie Avalon, Regis Toomey, John Litel, Howard McNear, Henry Daniell, Mark Slade, Charles Tannen, Delbert Monroe, Anthony Monaco, Robert Easton, Jonathan Gilmore, Larry Gray, George Diestel, David McLean, Robert Buckingham, Dr. John Giovanni, Kendrick Huxham, Art Baker.

Tender Is the Night (20th Century-Fox, 1961) Screenplay by Ivan Moffatt from the novel by F. Scott Fitzgerald. Directed by Henry King. *Cast:* Jennifer Jones, Jason Robards Jr., Joan Fontaine, Tom Ewell, Cesare Danova, Jill St. John, Paul Lukas, Bea Benedaret, Charles Fredericks, Sanford Meisner, Albert Carrier, Mac McWhorter, Carole Mathews, Maurice Dallimore, Carol Veazie, Arlette Clark, Leslie Farrell, Michael Crisalli, Alan Napier, John Richardson, Maggi Brown, Linda Hutchins, Orrin Tucker, Nora Evans, Bruno Della Santana, Tom Hernandez, Jacques Gallo, Art Salter, Eric Feldarg.

The Devil's Own (Seven Arts-Hammer Productions,

1966). Screenplay by Nigel Kneale based on the novel by Peter Curtis. Directed by Cyril Frankel. *Cast:* Joan Fontaine, Kay Walsh, Alec McCowen, Ann Bell, Ingrid Brett, John Collin, Michele Dotrice, Gwen Ffrangcon-Davies, Martin Stephens, Duncan Lamont, Leonard Rossiter, Carmel McSharry, Viola Keats, Shelagh Fraser, Bryan Marshall.

Accepting her Oscar for *The Song of Bernadette* (1943) with Paul Lukas, Katina Paxinou and Charles Coburn.

6

JENNIFER JONES

One of the oddest careers in Hollywood history unquestionably belongs to Jennifer Jones. A tall sloe-eyed, dark haired beauty, her heart-shaped face projected a vulnerability and sensitivity which had the capacity to elicit audience empathy. She rose to stardom under the aegis of David O. Selznick, one of filmdom's most meticulous producers. Through his carefully planned tutelage and exploitation, her career equalled those of her more talented rivals among The Selznick Players, i.e., Ingrid Bergman, Joan Fontaine, Vivien Leigh. Cognizant of Selznick's promotional acumen and his influence upon her career, she once observed, "He knows what to do for women on the screen. Look what he did for Ingrid Bergman and Joan Fontaine. The talent was always there, this you cannot give an actress. But you need management, the right thing for you. I didn't think I would ever photograph well. I'm not the greatest beauty in the world. And I wouldn't have photographed well if David hadn't taken every minute care from the very beginning."

She first came to the attention of the public by playing Saint Bernadette in *The Song of Bernadette* in 1943, and for this, what was regarded as her motion-picture debut (although she had already appeared in two minor pictures), she captured the Academy Award as Best Actress of the Year.

Subsequently she captured the heart of her mentor and as his consort, ascended to the enviable position of having an inordinate amount of his professional attention lavished upon her career. While obviously helpful in perpetuating her career, there are those who maintain that this attention was more detrimental than advantageous. That in fact, less careful handling of her career by Selznick would have made her a more credible screen performer for a longer time. Many of the projects assigned her by Selznick either miscast her or found her playing characters for which she was not, by her own admission, ready to play.

Further complicating her accomplishments as an actress, were the eccentricities brought about by the emotional crises in her personal life. Her lack of confidence in her own ability was the most self-defeating aspect of all her screen portrayals and in later years, her huge, huge image on the wide screen cruelly revealed her inner neuroses. As a producer, Selznick was aware of these insecurities and once remarked by memo to one of her directors, "I think you would be well advised to always let her play the scene for you first as she sees it, of course then feeling free to re-direct it as you see fit; but since she is so completely disciplined as an actress, if you direct her before getting her conception, I am fearful that you will lose the benefits of the intense and very lengthy study she always gives to her roles."

However, as in *Portrait of Jennie* and *Love Letters,* when the character allowed her to incorporate her mystical ethereal qualities in her interpretation, she became a moving and credible and even memorable actress.

She was born Phyllis Isley on March 2, 1919, in Tulsa, Oklahoma, the only child of Philip R. and Flora Mae Suber Isley. The Isleys owned, managed and starred in the Isley Stock Company, a tent show which toured the Midwest charging ten cents admission to see such plays as "The Old Homestead" and "East Lynne."

Between acts of these plays, Philip Isley would recite such vaudeville shtick as "The Face on the Barroom Floor" and "The Shooting of Dan McGrew" and on occasion would lecture to the audience on the evils of New York City's Chinatown, aided by lantern slides and his wife's piano accompaniment. Although he had never been to New York, he did not allow that small inaccuracy to deter him from moralising to his rural audiences.

At about the age of ten, Phyllis became a part of her parents' troupe playing the juvenile leads and also helped out by selling candy and taking tickets. Between engagements, she attended the Edgemer Public School in Oklahoma City, where she continued her interest in the theatre by appearing in class plays. She was very popular with her fellow students and they elected her May Queen and the senior class president.

After her graduation, the Isleys, who were fairly well-to-do, sent their daughter to Monte Cassino Junior College, a Benedictine Sisters school in Tulsa, where she again took part in class plays. For one dramatic exercise, she played all the roles in Lulu Vollmer's playlet, "Sun-Up." On another occasion, she received honorary mention in a statewide radio contest sponsored by the University of Oklahoma for a play called "Voice," by Harriet Flexner.

During the summer months she returned to appear with the Isley Stock Company and while trying to decide how best to pursue her theatrical aspirations, she wrote a letter to her idol, Katharine Cornell, to ask her whether she should continue her college education or attend a New York drama school. Miss Cornell answered by saying a "cultural background" provided by formal education was more important than classes in drama. Still, Phyllis yearned to study in New York, but her father, who by this time was operating a chain of motion-picture theatres out of Dallas, tried to discourage her interest in the stage, because he felt there was more money to be made in motion pictures.

The world of Hollywood, however, seemed very remote to Phyllis, and after graduating from college, Phyllis spent the summer touring with three different stock companies — The Mansfield Players, The Ted North Players and The Harley Sadler Company — after which she enrolled as a drama major at Chicago's Northwestern University. After one semester, she overcame her father's objections and enrolled in the American Academy of Dramatic Art in New York City in the spring of 1938.

In the same class with her at the AADA was seventeen-year-old Diana Barrymore, and a lanky, boyishly handsome young actor from Salt Lake City named Robert Walker. Walker, also nineteen years old, was one of four sons of parents who had divorced when he was still a child. His mother had raised her four boys in her parents' home in Ogden, Utah. Walker was an energetic, mischievous loner from childhood and found his way only after he had been taken in hand by a benevolent aunt, Hortense McQuarrie Odlum. Mrs. Odlum was divorced from financier Floyd B. Odlum, who had been among other things, president of Bonwit Teller from 1934 to 1938.

Mrs. Odlum enrolled Walker in the San Diego Army and Naval Academy in Carlsbad-by-the-sea, California, where, after playing the lead in a class play, he won the best actor award in a statewide contest held at the Pasadena Playhouse performing in one-act plays. His achievement as an amateur actor inspired Mrs. Odlum to present her nephew with one year's tuition to the American Academy of Dramatic Art, and he arrived in New York in January, 1938.

At the Academy, Phyllis and young Walker were cast in a production of "The Barretts of Wimpole Street." While performing in this play, a romance blossomed between the two aspiring actors. The relatively penniless young lovers conducted their courtship during long walks around Manhattan, sightseeing bus rides, and jaunts on the Staten Island Ferry.

After a few short months, they became engaged and in an effort to save enough money to marry, Phyllis returned to summer stock, and Walker took a job on a freighter which toured Central American ports. They both returned to the AADA that fall and made the rounds of the casting offices without success. They managed to land small parts at Paul Gilmore's Cherry Lane Theatre in Greenwich Village where they earned fifty cents for each performance in such plays as "Springtime for Henry," "The Bishop's Courage," and "The Family Upstairs."

During this time the Isleys came to visit their daughter, and after seeing the plight of Phyllis and her fiancé, they returned home and arranged secretly for Phyllis to be offered a contract by station KOME in Tulsa, to play in radio dramas for thirteen weeks at $25 a week. When Phyllis accepted the job, she recommended Walker as a male lead, and he, too, was signed. They moved to Tulsa where they were married on January 2, 1939, one year from the day they had met. The Isleys presented the newlyweds with a blue convertible and a letter of introduction to Hollywood agent Leo Morrison, whereupon they set out for a honeymoon in Hollywood to seek their fortune in the movies.

Success in Hollywood was almost as evasive as it had been in New York. Phyllis did, however, manage to be cast, under her real name, Phyllis Isley, in two B-pictures at the Republic Studio. The first was a low-budget western, *New Frontier* (1939), starring John Wayne, and the second was *Dick Tracy's G-Men* (1939), a Republic serial. Walker landed bit parts in three pictures — *Winter Carnival* (1939) at Warner Brothers, and *These Glamour Girls* (1939) and *Dancing Co-Ed* (1939) at M-G-M. After playing these small parts, the couple screen-tested at Paramount Pictures in a scene where Phyllis played Walker's mother. The test was a failure, and they decided to sell their blue convertible and purchase train tickets for New York.

Arriving in New York, they rented a two-room, cold-water flat on Twelfth Street near Ninth Avenue. Phyllis found a job modeling millinery for the John Powers Agency, and after discovering she was pregnant, worked up until the time of the birth of Robert Walker Jr. on April 15, 1940.

Walker supported his family by writing radio scripts and reading manuscripts for a literary agent and earning twenty dollars a performance as an actor on radio's "Yesterday's Children" series. He soon began to obtain more acting parts in radio and appeared in such series as "Great Plays," "John's Other Wife," and "Against the Storm." In the summer of 1940, he was cast as a regular on "Myrt and Marge," a popular CBS series in which he played Ted Smith.

Three months after the birth of her first son, Phyllis became pregnant again. A second son, Michael, was born on March 13, 1941. With Walker's radio success, the growing family was now able to move from their "two dingy rooms on the fringe of Hell's Kitchen to six sunlit rooms in Garden City, Long Island." Although Phyllis had interrupted her theatrical ambitions to have a family, she nevertheless kept in touch with the Broadway scene.

The stories of how she met David O. Selznick vary in the telling over the years, as most Hollywood "discovery" stories do. However, the accepted version is that early in 1941, Phyllis and Walker attended a Broadway performance of "Claudia" starring Dorothy McGuire. Phyllis learned from her agent that Selznick owned the motion-picture rights to "Claudia," and although there had been a two-year hiatus in her acting career, she steadfastly maintained she was right for the part of Claudia. She walked into Selznick's New York office and declared to his Eastern Representative Kay Brown, "I want to play Claudia. I know I can play Claudia better then anyone!"

Impressed by her aggressiveness. Miss Brown arranged for her to read the part on July 22, 1941. Later, as Jennifer Jones, Phyllis recalled that incident. "They let me read the part and I was very, very bad." She in fact felt she was so bad, she burst into tears and fled from the office, whereupon Selznick happened to walk in on this display of histrionics and told his secretary to make an appointment for Phyllis to see him the next day. As Miss Jones explained, "I thought they were just trying to comfort me when they told me to come back tomorrow and see Mr. Selznick. I was busy with my children the next day when the phone rang and Selznick's office wanted to know where I was."

Elated to think that Selznick was serious, and with her hair still wet from just having washed it, she impetuously jumped into a cab for an extravagant ten dollar ride to Manhattan, drying her hair by hanging her head out the window.

The meeting with Selznick was a success and she was signed to a long-term contract. In one of his memos to Kay Brown, he referred to his new find as Phyllis Walker, "the big-eyed girl who had two children," and soon began considering her for two of his projected properties — *Claudia* and *The Keys of the Kingdom*.

The new Selznick contractee begged her boss to put her to work, and he acquiesed by casting her opposite Harry Bratsburg (later Harry Morgan) in William Saroyan's one-act play, "Hello, Out There." The production was presented at the Lobero Theatre in Santa Barbara, California, in

1941, under the direction of John Houseman and Alfred de Liagre Jr. De Liagre recalls that when Selznick proposed this stage production as a means of promoting new stars, he asked de Liagre to view five screen tests of young actresses. De Liagre looked at the tests and said, "I'll take that girl," meaning Jennifer Jones. He says he recalls that the test revealed "great personality and charm." Selznick was not involved in this production and de Liagre and Houseman were left on their own. After opening night, which Selznick attended, and good reviews, despite Miss Jones's lack of experience, Selznick was convinced that she was destined for stardom. To gain experience and confidence, Selznick demanded that she return to New York and study under Sanford Meisner of the Group Theatre. For the next year, she carefully studied drama, voice, posture, diction, etc. In the meantime, Selznick asked Kay Brown and Whitney Bolton, then his Advertising and Publicity director, to come up with a new name for Phyllis. When they failed to do so by January, 1942, he wrote them saying, "Where the hell is that new name for Phyllis Walker?" He then suggested the name Jennifer and advised them to at least propose a one syllable last name that had "rhythm" and added that "the best synthetic name in pictures that has been recently created is Veronica Lake." Before the end of January, Miss Brown suggested that Phyllis Walker become Jennifer Jones!

Walker, in a joint interview with his newly-named wife, said, "You know how she got that name? Mr. Selznick always said if he had a little girl he'd name her Jennifer. But like us, he never got anything better than a couple of boys."

Selznick's plans for a screen version of *Claudia* ran into several delays. He had wanted Cary Grant for the male lead, but Grant's salary demands were too high. More importantly, Rose Franken, the play's author, voiced her preference for Dorothy McGuire over the unknown Jennifer Jones. Selznick later sold *Claudia,* with Dorothy McGuire as its star, to 20th Century-Fox.

Selznick then introduced his new star to the press in February, 1942, as the candidate for the feminine lead in *The Keys of the Kingdom*. From the beginning, he avoided publicly mentioning her marriage, her two children, or her appearances in those two low-budget pictures at Republic in 1939.

Like *Claudia,* Selznick never formalised his plans for *The Keys of the Kingdom*, and that, too, was sold to 20th Century-Fox.

Except for her brief appearance in "Hello, Out There," Miss Jones had not acted in nearly three years, and Selznick still had no vehicle in which to launch his new discovery. When he learned that 20th Century-Fox was searching for the lead in *The Song of Bernadette* he knew instinctively that Miss Jones would be perfect as Bernadette Soubirous. The story was based on the novel by Franz Werfel, and in his book, Werfel had described Bernadette: "The round face is quite child-like, while the slight body already betrays the early maturity of this Southern race." Director Henry King agreed with Selznick about Miss Jones, but 20th Century-Fox stalled saying that they had promised to test their own contractee, Anne Baxter.

Selznick told the executives at 20th Century Fox, "Test everybody you like, but you'll come back to Jennifer." His insight proved correct and in December, 1942, 20th Century-Fox announced that Jennifer Jones had been cast. Selznick worked out a financial agreement whereby 20th Century-Fox would share Miss Jones' contract and would hold a six-year option for her services for one picture a year with star billing.

During the year-and-a-half that Selznick had been grooming Miss Jones for stardom, he had toyed with the idea of also putting her husband, Robert Walker, under contract. When he failed to find a place for Walker under the Selznick aegis, where actresses seemed to fare far better than actors, Hollywood assumed that it was Selznick's influence which gained Walker his contract with M-G-M, headed by Selznick's father in-law, Louis B. Mayer. Soon after, Walker was starred as the young sailor in *Bataan* (1943).

After it had been announced that Jennifer Jones would be starring in *The Song of Bernadette,* Miss Jones granted a press interview in which she discussed the turn of events for the Walker family. "They tested me in New York. I've only been out here for six weeks. Most of that time we've spent getting settled, and trying to get meat, milk and eggs. We get milk for the babies but getting food for us is like it is for everyone here: grab-as-one-can. My husband has been signed by M-G-M so we're very happy. It all seems too wonderful to be true. He is getting his big chance, too, in a top role in *Bataan Patrol* (sic.) We have rented a house in Westwood and right now my parents are with us on a visit. No, I'm not much of a cook, but mother is. We have a nurse for the babies." She said she remembered reading Werfel's "The Song of Ber-

With Anne Revere in *The Song of Bernadette* (1943).

nadette'' five times while at Monte Cassino Junior College, and added, ''It is a most wonderful opportunity — that's my miracle — but a responsibility too. Much more so than any ordinary role would be. I'm praying that I make good.''

At about this time, Louella Parsons, the doyenne of Hollywood columnists, met Miss Jones and observed her to be a 'strange, restrained, shy girl' and cattily noted that during an earlier meeting, Miss Jones ''either forgot or had been warned not to mention her marriage or her children.''

The Song of Bernadette was launched with what has been called one of Hollywood's most ''pious'' publicity campaigns. The publicity grist churned out such platitudes as ''a motion picture so powerful...so majestic...so deep in its understanding...that for one immortal moment you touch the eternal truth..the final fulfillment...of everything you are...or ever hope to be.'' That banality not withstanding, the picture when released, stood on its own merits as a beautiful tapestry of the events surrounding Bernadette Soubrirous' belief that she had seen ''the beautiful Lady'' in 1858. It documented the subsequent efforts by the Roman Catholic church and the state to discredit her and showed her eventual canonisation.

Critics for the first and only time in Miss Jones' career were unanimous in their praise of her performance. ''Variety'' said, ''It is an inspirationally sensitive and arresting performance that sets her solid as a screen personality.'' And the equitable James Agee stated at more than usual length, ''I have seldom seen so tender and exact an attention to mood, to over-all tone, to radiance, in terms of the image and the sound, more than the character, the story, the line, the music. Jennifer Jones especially, as Bernadette, whether through Henry King's direction or her own ability, impossibly combines the waxen circumspections of a convent school with abrupt salients of emotion of which Dostoyevsky himself need not have been ashamed.'' He added, ''As Bernadette, newcomer Jennifer Jones (real name: Phyllis Isley) makes one of the most impressive screen debuts (sic) in many years. It remains to be seen whether or not cinemactress Jones can do in other roles the delicately dynamitic things she achieves as this peasant saint. If she can, Hollywood should watch and guard Miss Jones as sedulously as the Church watched over Bernadette.''

On her twenty-fifth birthday, nervously biting her lip, Jennifer Jones accepted the Academy Award as Best Actress of the Year, saying, ''I am thrilled. I am grateful.''

Later that same evening she told her friend and fellow Selznick Player, Ingrid Bergman, ''You should have won it for *For Whom the Bell Tolls*.''

The following day she announced her intention to divorce her husband, Robert Walker, from whom she had now been separated since the previous November. At the time of the separation, she stated, ''We remain friends, but we have found it impossible to effect a reconciliation.'' The mutual personal insecurites of both Miss Jones and Robert Walker, in addition to Walker's drinking problem, had been eroding the couple's marriage for some time.

Despite their marital separation, Selznick, now fully convinced that Jennifer Jones was a star who should henceforth appear in only important vehicles, cast both Miss Jones and her estranged husband in *Since You Went Away* (1944) — his first personally produced motion picture since *Rebecca* (1940). The all-star cast headed by Claudette Colbert, included Joseph Cotton, Shirley Temple, Monty Woolley, and Agnes Moorehead, and the picture was a sharply-produced, idealistic view of the American home front during World War II, with Miss Jones and Walker playing the young lovers.

Selznick's personal interest in Jennifer Jones

became evident during this production and Miss Jones was visibly distraught on several occasions from the constant daily confrontations with her co-star-estranged husband and her producer-amour. Several times she ran to her dressing room in tears, whereupon Selznick would follow her, and soon after she would return to finish her scene, then run to the refuge of her dressing room again.

In the meantime, Selznick kept re-writing the script and as he did so, Miss Jones' part became larger and larger, but when the picture was released, it was Claudette Colbert who was nominated in the Best Actress category, and Miss Jones, surprisingly, in the Best Supporting Actress category for her unexpectedly sweet portrayal of the well-bred American daughter in the first blossom of womanhood and love.

The picture, touted as "the four most important words since *Gone With the Wind*" was not the critical success that Selznick had hoped it would be, and the damage to his ego was only slightly allayed by the healthy box-office receipts.

As part of her grooming for stardom, Miss Jones had been put under the tutelage of Selznick's Feminine Director, former model, Anita Colby. The chic Miss Colby advised Selznick's actresses on how to pose for photographs, how to dress, and how to present their best image to the movie-going public through her keen sense for publicity, a trait she shared with her equally astute boss. Of Miss Jones, she noted, "Her clothes need the dressmaker, rather than the tailored look. I'd rather have them pretty than terribly chic." She supposedly also taught the shy actress how to look people directly in the eye rather than avert their glances. Miss Jones protested by saying, "But I don't know what to say to people when they start telling me what a great actress I am!" to which Miss Colby replied, "Listen, darling, just raise your eyebrows the next next time that happens and say, 'Well, how have *you* been?"

Following *Since You Went Away,* Selznick loaned Miss Jones and Joseph Cotten to Paramount as the stars of *Love Letters* (1945), an implausible psychological fantasy scripted by Ayn Rand from Chris Massie's popular novel. Miss Jones played an amnesia victim whose romantic illusions are shattered when she discovers that her love letters were written by an ex-GI and not her husband. This moody picture was beautifully photographed and Miss Jones looked enchanting, partly thanks to Anita Colby. While the photography was the result of the work of the talented Lee Garmes, it was Miss Colby who, knowing that Miss Jones did not always photograph well, stopped production several times, to the chagrin of producer Hal Wallis, until she felt that Miss Jones was being properly protected by the camera. *Love Letters* was popular with wartime audiences and while many critics called her performance "fatuous," and took note for the first time of the intense and neurotic mannerisms which would characterise much of her future acting, Jennifer Jones was again nominated for an Academy Award.

In June, 1945, she obtained her divorce from Robert Walker, who, according to all the Hollywood columnists, was carrying the biggest torch in Hollywood. One friend of the unhappy couple stated, "It was terribly unfair but many people who didn't know them blamed Jennifer for the breakup. Actually, she had put off the divorce as long as she could. Have you any idea how difficult it is to live with a man who has been convinced most of his life that no one can really love him? I am sure Jennifer did her best to reassure him, but it was an impossible situation." Later, Walker told Hedda Hopper, "Our breakup gave me an excuse for amplifying my troubles. When I had a few drinks, I got to thinking about Poor Me and the broken home and all the et ceteras."

In *Love Letters* (1945).

During these wartime years, when not working on a picture, Miss Jones volunteered as a Nurse's Aid for which she was honored by the Red Cross. Also during the war, on October 16, 1944, she appeared on Lux Radio Theatre opposite Van Johnson in "Seventh Heaven."

Selznick's next project for Jennifer Jones was his much publicised, expensive ($5,255,000) production of *Duel in the Sun* (1946), an opulent, unrelentingly brutal, grandiose Western that took over a year and a half to make and which has been called by some a Wagnerian horse opera and a *Liebestod* among the cactus. Like *Since You Went Away,* it was another exercise in Selznick's obsession with surpassing *Gone With the Wind,* and he cast his prize actress-amour as Pearl Chavez, the tempestuous half-breed who comes between two brothers (Joseph Cotten and Gregory Peck). The plot included prostitution, rape, suicide, attempted fratricide, and ended with a protracted gun duel between Pearl and the outlaw brother (Peck) in which both are killed. *Duel in the Sun* earned both Miss Jones and supporting actress Lillian Gish nominations for Academy Awards, and $11,300,000 at the box-office, despite its critical lambasting. Today it receives some of the critical attention it failed to garner at the time of its release when its merits were overshadowed by opposition to its violent content.

The picture's director, King Vidor, observed that if he could talk Miss Jones into the mood of the part each day and keep her in that frame of mind all day long, the proper emotional reactions he needed in her performance registered clearly on her face. However, he was aware of her insecurities as an actress which at times caused her to do "strange tricks with her mouth."

Cluny Brown (1946), which was directed by Ernst Lubitsch and made immediately after *Duel in the Sun,* was released before that epic Western could be properly edited and scored. It was Miss Jones' first comedy and contains her favourite performance. She played a plumber's fey niece who meets a Czech refugee, Charles Boyer, in London during World War II. While it was not Lubitsch's best picture, it was a delightfully light satire of upper-class British society.

For her performance in that picture and *Duel in the Sun*, she was voted "Look" magazine's Best Actress of the Year award, and the same year, was named the Most Unco-operative Actress by the Hollywood Women's Press Association. Louella Parsons, who often chided Miss Jones for her loathing of interviews, said, "Self-assurance should be part of a successful actress' stock-in-trade." Once many years later, Miss Jones asked a reporter, "Are you going to ask me any horrible questions?" The reporter queried back, "What is a horrible question?" She responded, "*Any* question is a horrible question. I just don't have any answers."

With Lillian Gish and Walter Huston in *Duel in the Sun* (1946).

Miss Jones had no new picture released in 1947, but *Portrait of Jennie,* which was released in 1948, is the most popular picture among Jennifer Jones fans. Selznick had read the book by Robert Nathan several years before, but found that M-G-M had an option for the motion-picture rights. When he was informed on his birthday that M-G-M had dropped its option to the story, he felt the coincidence fortuitous and purchased it as a vehicle for Jennifer Jones. *Portrait of Jennie* was a fragile, romantic story about an artist who is inspired to paint his greatest work by the memory of a girl who has died years before. Miss Jones played the ghost of the girl who encounters the artist five times during the picture. While the part was relatively small, it took advantage of the ethereal aspect of Miss Jones' personality and is probably her most convincing performance.

Selznick personally produced the picture and as could be expected, it was overblown, over-romanticised and over-scored (by Dimitri Tiomkin in his use of Debussy's "Afternoon of a Faun"). Selznick released the picture to poor reviews, tried to salvage it by pulling it and adding to the end a storm sequence which used "Cycloramic" wide screen and stereophonic sound. These enormously expensive last-ditch efforts were to

With Charles Boyer and Richard Haydn in *Cluny Brown* (1946).

In *Portrait of Jennie* (1948).

no avail, and it was Miss Jones' first flop at the box-office.

A second box-office failure followed. *We Were Strangers* (1949) was directed by John Huston and was an off-beat melodrama about a Cuban girl who loves a revolutionary played by John Garfield.

Madame Bovary (1949) which followed is not without interest, but both Selznick and Miss Jones knew she was not ready for the part. Atmospherically directed by Vincente Minnelli, and co-starring Van Heflin and Louis Jourdan, Miss Jones' acting technique was not mature enough to reveal the intricacies of Emma Bovary's complex character.

For Miss Jones, the years between 1944 and 1949 were emotionally-scarred ones. Some felt that she had never recovered from the breakup of her marriage to Robert Walker and since their divorce agreement allowed him custody of their two sons for three months of each year, Walker's continued irrational alcoholic behaviour was constantly confronting her. One of his drunken escapades ended with a suspended jail sentence of one hundred and eighty days and a fine of $500 following a hit-and-run accident. On July 8, 1948, he had married Barbara Ford, the daughter of director, John Ford, but that marriage ended in divorce after six weeks. Arrested again on a drunk driving charge, photographers caught him in an uncompromisingly belligerent mood and when he saw the photographs, he realized he needed professional help. Dore Schary, then head of M-G-M, arranged his admittance to the Menninger Clinic in Topeka, Kansas, and there, after good behavior, they granted him privileges which permitted him to go into town alone. However, he became drunk and this time smashed his fist through a plate-glass window and took a swing at a policeman. He was returned to the clinic where he remained an additional eleven months. Upon his release, the newspapers reported that he had recovered from a nervous breakdown.

Selznick's personal life was similarly far from tranquil during this time. His wife, Irene, had been cognizant for some time of his romantic attachment to Miss Jones, and on the evening of April 29, 1945, their sixteenth wedding anniversary, he came home to find his suitcases in the foyer of their Beverly Hills house with his wife declaring that she could no longer live with him. These marital insecurities sent both Miss Jones and Selznick to psychiatrists.

In November, 1948, after completion of *Madame Bovary,* Selznick announced that Miss Jones' future plans included two British films on loan — *Gone to Earth* and *Tess of the D'Urbervilles*. He also announced that she would appear in a play for the American Theatre Guild, preferably "Romeo and Juliet."

Selznick's divorce decree from Irene became final in January, 1949, and it was assumed by everyone in Hollywood and by Selznick himself, that he and Miss Jones would marry. Miss Jones was not convinced that marriage to Selznick would be right for her. There was the obvious physical attachment and Selznick's overwhelming control of her personal and professional life, but Miss Jones was wary of the adjustments of a second marriage. On the verge of an emotional collapse, she sailed for Europe in March, 1949, with travelling companion Anita Colby. Upon her departure, Selznick released the following statement to the press, "I don't know exactly when or where we will be married, but it will be some time before the end of the summer when we can get a breather from our work." While on their tour, Miss Colby tried to persuade Miss Jones to put off marrying Selznick until she was in a more stable emotional state.

Selznick arrived in Europe several months later, and accompanied Miss Jones to the Riviera, where he chartered the thirty-three ton yacht, the "Manona" and invited Mr. and Mrs. Louis Jourdan and Mr. and Mrs. Leland Hayward as his guests. He finally, with the aide of his guests, persuaded Miss Jones to say yes to his marriage proposal, and at eight-thirty on the morning of July 13, 1949, they were married aboard the yacht off the coast of Genoa by the British captain, with the Jourdans and the Haywards as witnesses. To affirm the legality of the marriage, a second ceremony was performed at the Genoa city hall; this was followed by a wedding reception hosted by Italian millionaire, Rudi Crespi.

Shortly after the marriage, Miss Jones began work on the film version of *Gone to Earth* based on Mary Webb's novel. It was the story of a superstitious gypsy girl torn between the love of the spirit (Cyril Cusack) and the flesh (David Farrar). Selznick was not involved in this production but did own the American release rights. When he found the final print to be inept and so poorly received in England, he held its American release until he could re-shoot many scenes. Re-named *The Wild Heart*, it was released in the United States in 1952, through RKO, but it remained an unsalvageable picture. After completion of this picture, in December, 1950, Jennifer Jones suffered a miscarriage.

Selznick's second British film project for Miss Jones, *Tess of the D'Urbervilles* never materialized, nor did the theatre production of "Romeo and Juliet." In August, 1951, Miss Jones was informed of the death of her ex-husband, Robert Walker.

He had died on the night of August 28th, from "respiratory failure" after being administered seven and a half grains of sodium amytal. Walker had called his psychiatrist saying, "I feel terrible, Doc, do something quick." Suspecting that he had been drinking, the doctor called an associate who administered the drug which Walker had received several times in the past. However, this time a fatal reaction caused him to turn blue and stop breathing. His death occurred in his home in Pacific Palisades, where his two sons had been living with him, but who, that evening, had been visiting friends. When the boys' mother arrived from Europe, she chose not to have them attend their father's funeral, on August 30th in Ogden, Utah, reasoning, "I want them to remember him as he was." She also did not attend.

Miss Jones' next picture assignment was *Carrie* (1952) on loan to Paramount. Based on Theodore Dreiser's novel "Sister Carrie," it was an inadequately adapted version and unevenly directed by William Wyler, and Miss Jones "thoughtless and light-hearted" Carrie did not hold up well vis-a-vis Laurence Olivier's excellent Hurstwood.

She admitted in 1965, that like *Madame Bovary,* she had not been ready to play Carrie and said, "I wish I could have another crack at them now."

Again on loanout, this time to 20th Century-Fox, she was cast as another sensual temptress in *Ruby Gentry* (1952) playing a vixen from the wrong side of the tracks who eventually destroys the lives of her tycoon husband (Karl Malden) and her lover (Charlton Heston). Directed again by King Vidor, the picture had none of the majesty of his earlier *Duel in the Sun*. During shooting of one scene, Miss Jones was required to slap Heston, and in doing so, broke her hand. For her injury, the insurance company paid her $55,768.

Two theatre productions starring Jennifer Jones were announced in 1952 — "Saint Joan" in Chicago and Desdemona to Orson Welles' "Othello." When neither of these materialised, she toured, without ballyhoo, for the USO in Korea, visiting over 4,000 wounded soldiers.

With Laurence Olivier in *Carrie* (1952).

After this stint, she returned to Europe to work on two new picture assignments. The first of these was *Indiscretion of an American Wife* (1954) starring Montgomery Clift and directed by Vittorio de Sica. Selznick had wanted to work with de Sica for some time and they decided an appropriate vehicle for collaboration would be "Terminal Station." It was the story of two lovers — a married American woman and young Italian — saying goodbye in a train station. The production was plagued by the language barrier and the disparate work habits of Selznick and de Sica, and the script was worked on by a succession of writers which included Truman Capote, Carson McCullers, Alberto Moravia, and Paul Jarrico. Endless feet of film were shot which Selznick finally edited to sixty-three minutes, added a saccharine song sung by Patti Page, and released it under the inane title *Indiscretion of an American Wife*. Needless to say, it was a bomb.

The second European venture was *Beat the Devil* (1954). It was scripted by Truman Capote and directed by John Huston, and starred Humphrey Bogart, Miss Jones, Gina Lollobrigida, Robert Morley and Peter Lorre. It was particularly noteworthy as it was one of the screen's first attempts at black comedy. Filmed in an improvisa-

With Montgomery Clift in *Indiscretion of an American Wife* (1954).

tional style, with Capote reading the script to the cast each morning, it was a screwball satire of international thrillers, the story of a ring of uranium swindlers in which a blonde-wigged Jennifer Jones was a delightful comedic surprise, playing the compulsive liar. When released, the audiences were baffled and it was a flop. Bogart, unfamiliar to this kind of filmmaking, said, "Only the phonies think it's funny. It's a mess." However, today, it is a film buff's delight and much more appreciated. Pauline Kael maintains it is one of the two Jennifer Jones performances she can watch, the other being the earlier satire, *Cluny Brown*.

On August 12, 1954, Miss Jones gave birth to a daughter, Mary Jennifer, and Selznick said it was one of the proudest moments of his life. Thereafter he referred to his two Jennifers as Jennifer the First and Jennifer the Second.

Throughout her professional association with Selznick, there had been periodic announcements of her plans to appear in several stage productions, and Miss Jones occasionally verbalised her regret that she had not pursued her early desire to be a stage actress. She finally got her chance to return to the stage and make her Broadway debut in a dramatisation of Henry James' "Portrait of a Lady" directed by Jose Quintero. She had seen Quintero's production of Tennessee Williams' "Summer and Smoke" and admired his work, and after discussions with her husband, he suggested the James vehicle would be a fitting debut. In conjunction with that announcement, Selznick expressed his desire to do a screen version starring Miss Jones at a later date.

The play opened at the ANTA Theatre on December 21, 1954, and while critics found her beautiful and charming as Isabel, they also thought her

With Humphrey Bogart in *Beat the Devil* (1954).

With William Holden in *Love Is A Many-Splendored Thing* (1955).

technically immature and felt the emotional scenes beyond her grasp. The production quickly closed and plans for a screen version were forgotten, whereupon Miss Jones signed with 20th Century-Fox for three pictures.

The first of these commitments was the blatantly sentimental and very popular *Love Is a Many-Splendored Thing* (1955) which re-established her as a box-office star and earned her a fifth nomination for an Academy Award for her portrayal of the Eurasian doctor who was in love with war-correspondent, William Holden. The New York "Herald-Tribune" called it "the most embarrassing phenomenon of the movie year," but audiences ignored such criticism and she was voted the Audie, a movie audience award as best actress of the year. When Miss Jones heard her name called at the awards presentation ceremony, she turned to her husband and said, "You accept for me." Selznick however, refused to do so, insisting she accept the award herself, and when she got on stage she accepted it by saying it meant more to her than the Oscar, because it had been voted by the audience and not the industry.

Also sentimental, but in a less specious way, was *Good Morning, Miss Dove* (1955), the endearing story of a spinster school teacher in New England. For this Miss Jones received good critical notices.

Both the audience and the critics were less pleased with her performance as the wife of Madison Avenue businessman Gregory Peck in *The Man in the Grey Flannel Suit* (1956), a performance which most felt was adversely affected by her nervous mannerisms. Following that picture, she went to England to star in *The Barretts of Wimpole Street* (1957) in which she was more appropriately cast than Norma Shearer had been in the 1934 version, but in which her performance suffered in contrast to the splendid one given by John Gielgud as her domineering father.

Her next film project, *A Farewell to Arms* (1957), was the last picture David O. Selznick would produce and proved to be perhaps the biggest mistake in both his and his wife's careers. Not only was Jennifer Jones miscast as Hemingway's heroine, Catherine Barkley, she was simply too old to play the part. Selznick again saw this as a successor to *Gone With the Wind* and consequently imbued it with all his technical prowess. John Huston was signed to direct but from the beginning he and Selznick clashed over interpretation of the script. Huston wished to keep the script as close to Hemingway's original story as possible, but Selznick kept re-writing it. Another bone of contention was over Miss Jones' portrayal of Catherine. The picture was shot in Italy, and in March, 1957, the differences between the two strong-headed men reached an impasse and Huston left the picture to be replaced by Charles Vidor. *A Farewell to Arms* premiered on December 18, 1957, allowing it to qualify for both the New York Film Critics Awards and the Academy Awards. The critical reception was devastatingly negative and such a blow to Selznick's ego that he never produced another picture.

With Rock Hudson in *A Farewell to Arms* (1957).

Critics agreed that Miss Jones had been miscast and were offended by her mannerisms. The "Saturday Review" stated, "Miss Jones has a good deal of skill as an actress but she's a fairly mature woman now, the mother of children, and that big movie screen has a gruesome way of revealing a disparity between what might be termed screen age and actual age." And Henry Hart, in "Films in Review," said, "What you think of Jennifer Jones will largely determine your reactions to *A Farewell to Arms*. I think little of her screen personality nowadays, and hence did not have too good a time during the 155 minutes of the first film David O. Selznick has produced in nine years. Indeed, I was constantly irritated that so great a cinematic talent as Selznick's should be squandered upon so mediocre an actress as his present wife. In the all important role of Catherine Barkley, Miss Jones seems quite neurotic, which is fatally wrong, for Hemingway's heroine was certainly not neurotic. She was profoundly realistic and out-going, so much so, in fact, she was almost a romantic (as true realists often seem to be). In some of the lovemaking close-ups Miss Jones looked as though she was about to bite poor Rock Hudson, in a snarling, not an amorous way. Her face, which no longer photographs well from certain angles, was often strained in unsuitable grimaces, and many of her movements were sudden, truncated, and otherwise uneasy. Her voice was also inexplicably variegated, and usually harsh. She lacked, in every possible way, the warmth that was the essence of Hemingway's heroine."

Of these awkward scenes, Miss Jones later said, "I wasn't aware that I was doing it. But that can happen to an actress in Hollywood. You start relying on old tricks and you get carried away with them." While still in Europe during the making of *A Farewell to Arms*, Selznick announced that Miss Jones and her co-star, Rock Hudson, would appear in *The Devine Sarah,* a filmed version of the life of Sarah Bernhardt, but as a result of the disappointment with *A Farewell to Arms,* Jennifer Jones withdrew from acting for four years.

Except for the occasion when she substituted for Elizabeth Taylor as a presenter of the Academy Award for the Best Short Subjects in March, 1958, (Michael Todd's death preventing Miss Taylor's appearance), she remained out of the public eye.

In preparation for her return to the screen four years later she began studying with Lee Strasberg of the Actors Studio to regain her self-confidence. The vehicle chosen for her comeback was F. Scott Fitzgerald's *Tender Is the Night* (1961), another one of her husband's favorite planned projects.

Selznick eschewed producing the picture himself however, because he could not risk another disaster like *A Farewell to Arms*. Therefore he sold the project to 20th Century-Fox with Miss Jones cast as Nicole, but not until he had worked on the script himself in conjunction with screen writer Ivan Moffatt. There were provisions in the contract stating that the script was not to be altered without Selznick's approval and that he would also have casting approval. However, 20th Century-Fox ignored Selznick's suggestions and the resultant film was a lushly photographed, sporadically-interesting picture with wooden characters who barely resembled those of Fitzgerald. Miss Jones was sleekly costumed and coiffured and more glamorous than she had ever been on the screen, and for some of the critics, her neurotic screen behaviourisms were not incompatible with the character of Nicole. Despite its defects it remains a curious if disappointing film.

With Jason Robards, Jr., in *Tender Is the Night* (1961).

During production of *Tender Is the Night,* with a newly-found confidence, she told the press that she thought the picture was a turning point in her career and that for her next project she would like to try a sophisticated comedy. However, after the picture was completed, she said, "As far as I'm concerned, *Tender Is the Night* was never made. The original script was good, but by the time the gremlins got it, it wasn't. Every film is a gamble and it's a miracle when one good moment comes out." Once again shattered by the notices, Miss Jones disappeared from the screen for five years.

In the summer of 1964, she was to have appeared at the Bucks County Playhouse in Eleanor Perry's "Any Decent Woman" at $1,000 week. However, this plan collapsed when Miss Jones' husband and Miss Perry's husband, director Frank Perry, had artistic differences. Instead, Miss Jones signed to star in "Goddess on the Couch" by Patricia Joudry, which opened in December, 1964, in Miami and Palm Beach under the title, "The Man With the Perfect Wife." The play did not make it and plans to bring it to Broadway were forgotten.

In 1965, Selznick announced another film for his

wife, another of his favourite ambitions and this time he was to produce. The film was a life of evangalist Aimee Semple McPherson, but that and other projects were destroyed when, on June 22, 1965, Selznick suddenly died of a coronary occlusion. He had been stricken in his lawyer's offfice in Beverly Hills and was rushed to the intensive care unit of the Mount Sinai Hospital. Miss Jones stood sobbing outside the intensive care unit as her husband was pronounced dead.

In his will, Selznick left his widow an undisclosed but presumably considerable amount of money, their Malibu beach house, and their thirty-room Bel Air mansion, once owned by John Gilbert, which was built on the shoulder of a mountain providing a breath-taking view of Beverly Hills.

Several months after being widowed, Miss Jones, to the public's surprise, returned to the screen in *The Idol* (1966). The screen rights to that picture had been optioned by Carlo Ponti first and at that time he had asked Miss Jones to star in it and she had refused. When the rights were acquired by Joseph E. Levine, he cast Kim Stanley in the lead, and when illness prevented Miss Stanley's appearance, he offered it to Miss Jones. Filmed in London, it was an ugly, pretentious story of a domineering American woman who seduces her son's best friend.

During the production of this picture, one reporter asked her if she had any plans for retirement, to which she responded, "How can one talk of retiring when one has been an actress since the age of six."

In the same interview she said, that acting was like riding a bicycle, you never forget how, then qualified that remark by adding, "I realized afterwards I had made it all too glib and easy. The truth is that with me it doesnt't matter if the gap is three months or three years, I'm always taut with nerves for the first few days. The only thing that's true about the bicycle bit is that you know you've done it before so you *must* be able to do it again."

With a desire to keep working, she signed to appear in the New York City Center revival of "The Country Girl" in 1966. Her co-stars were to have been Rip Torn and Franchot Tone, but already the illness that would kill him two years later had begun to take its toll on the suave Mr. Tone and he was replaced by Joseph Anthony. The limited engagement opened on September 30, 1966 to excellent reviews and of Miss Jones's performance the New York "Times" said, while "muted and reserved" at the beginning, she "gradually took on power as the evening progressed." Franchot Tone attended that evening's performance as did Miss Jones' son, Robert Walker Jr.*

After her opening night performance in "The Country Girl," Miss Jones left City Center by the stage door, alone, signed no autographs for the less than a dozen fans who waited for her, and walked home alone.

She returned to her obsessively private life after that play and did not appear in the public eye until November 9, 1967, when the tabloids headlined her reported suicide attempt. As reporters and police put together the story, it appeared that one hour after hearing of the death of veteran character actor, Charles Bickford (her close friend since he had appeared with her in the *Song of Bernadette* and *Duel in the Sun),* she drove her sports car to a Malibu motel, where she registered under the name of Phyllis Walker, took several seconals with champagne, and telephoned her physician, Dr. William Molley, telling him she had taken the pills, and intended to take some more. He persuaded Miss Jones to tell him where she was and called the police. They discovered her automobile on the highway, its lights ablaze, and found her body lying in the surf on the beach at the bottom of a 400-foot cliff. Policemen revived her by mouth to mouth resuscitation after which she was rushed to Mount Sinai Hospital in Hollywood. In three days she had recovered, but her only explanation for her action was, "It was an accident, it was just a foolish accident. Now I want to live!"

There are those who, having known her during her years in Hollywood, allege that it was not an accident, but simply a fake attempt to take her life. These same observers add that any depression stemmed from the fact that the money left by her husband's will was arranged to provide her with a set yearly annuity and that she found this prevented her from continuing the opulent life-style she had come to enjoy when Selznick was alive,

*Miss Jones' two sons by her first marriage, Robert Jr., and Michael, have both intermittently pursued acting careers. Robert Jr., has been the more successful of the two and because of the strong resemblance to his father, there are the inevitable comparisons. He says, "It's a compliment to me if I remind people of my father. He was a fine, marvellous actor who did some great things even at an early stage in his career." Of his mother, he says, "I don't see her much, but I think she's pleased about my becoming an actor. I even think she's pleased about becoming a grandmother." Miss Jones' daughter, Mary Jennifer Selznick, has studied with Lee Strasberg and wishes to be an actress, but is presently studying film and culture at the University of Grenoble in France.

and that after selling the beautiful Bel Air home they had shared, she was not happy with living in her beach house in Malibu.

Shortly after this incident a fan magazine quoted several unnamed friends who gave reasons for the attempted suicide. One commented, "She has been living like a recluse for years. She was always a loner, but far more so since the death of her husband, David Selznick, two-and-a-half years ago. It was a terrible blow." Another explained, "She has been very upset and sometimes melancholy since David died. After all, they'd been married for sixteen years. But I think the root goes back much farther that that. Jennifer is a very gentle, sensitive woman and she still has a sense of guilt about her first marriage to Robert Walker, and its unhappy aftermath."

She renewed her reclusive life style after her recuperation until four years later, when she again appeared on the screen, this time in the ridiculous, sexually overt *Angel, Angel, Down We Go* (1971), which was filmed in Britain and which co-starred Jordan Christopher. She played the ex-star of stag films in this patently disgusting film and the nadir of her career occurred with the lines, "I've made thirty-eight stag films and I never once faked an orgasm."

However, early in 1971, her personal life once again came to the public's attention when she became the wife of multi-millionaire industrialist and art collector, Norton Simon. After knowing each other for only three-and-a-half weeks, they were married by a Unitarian minister on May 30, 1971, aboard a yacht off the English coast.

Simon, who made his first million dollars before he was twenty-nine, has earned his estimated $200,000,000 through Hunt Foods and Industries, a conglomerate which includes Wesson Oil, Canada Dry, Ohio Match Company, "McCall's" and "Saturday Review" magazines, and Halston couture. He is also one of the world's largest collectors of impressionist and post-impressionist paintings and purchased the Duveen Gallery in 1964. The following year, he paid $2,234,400 for Rembrandt's portrait of his son, Titus. In 1973, as head of the Norton Simon, Inc. Museum Collection and the Norton Simon Foundation Collection, he auctioned forty-seven of his collected works at the Sotheby-Park Bernet for $6,782,000. Simon had divorced his wife, Lucille Ellis, in 1970, after thirty-seven years of marriage, shortly after their younger son, Robert, who had been ill for some time, committed suicide. His older son, Donald, is an investment banker in Paris. Simon's meeting with Miss Jones occured on May 5, 1971, when he arrived at a party to learn that Miss Jones, also an invited guest, was late. "I'll go pick her up," he said, and in the course of the evening they discovered mutual interests, most important of which was Miss Jones' involvement, for over the past year, with the Manhattan Project, a set of Salvation Army residential treatment facilities on the West Coast for young people strung out on narcotics this side of heroin. Miss Jones had been supporting this organisation with her time and her money and would frequently have as many as fifteen of the youngsters in her home for weekends.

Simon was quoted as saying, "She happened to be going to Paris (to visit the head of the Manhattan Project who was on vacation in that city) and I happened to be going to the Caribbean and decided not to. Then we made up our minds on the spur of the moment to go together to Paris. Maybe it sounds rather unusual for our respective ages, but..." (Simon is twelve years older than Miss Jones).

Once in Paris, they found themselves falling in love and on the way home via London, they decided to marry. Since that time, Miss Jones has appeared at numerous social functions, many of them involving Republican political functions with her husband, as a new, smiling Jennifer Jones. When they returned to the United States after their marriage, they flew directly to Salt Lake City, where Miss Jones helped open a new center for the Manhattan Project. Of that evening, Simon said, "I'll tell you, Jennifer Jones was fabulously good in talking with the people in Salt Lake on the solution of their problems, and I was proud of her to be Jennifer Jones Simon that night."

Early in 1974, with a newly found confidence from her third marriage, Miss Jones signed for one of the cameo roles in Irwin Allen's *The Towering Inferno,* an all-star production released by Warner Brothers and 20th Century-Fox. The picture stars Steve McQueen, Paul Newman, Faye Dunaway, Fred Astaire, Richard Chamberlain, Robert Wagner, and Miss Jones' favourite co-star, William Holden. Miss Jones earned favorable notices in the sympathic role of the wealthy widow to whom Fred Astaire tries to sell phoney bonds.

While Jennifer Jones' professional career has been only intermittently satisfactory and her personal life fraught with emotional vicissitudes, today she seems to have found her desired life style. Possibly one of the more cogent observations of the enigmatic Miss Jones was made by her long time friend and fellow Selznick Player, Joan Fontaine — "I don't think she liked acting. I think she wanted to be a star, but when I worked with her (*Tender Is the Night*, 1961), I've never seen anybody except Orson Welles, who would do anything rather than be on the set, any excuse not to have that closeup. And she had with her always, her drama coach, even when we were in Zurich together. But Jennifer was always very doubting about herself. If we gave a party together, which we did one time, she would ask what to wear, where to go, whom to ask, whom to seat next to each other. It was a tremendous problem to her. And when Selznick did all that for her, she would come to dinner rather than the cocktail hour in her own home. Then she would disappear shortly after dinner. I think she is probably a dedicated loner. I met them (Miss Jones and Norton Simon) the other night in Princeton, and he seems quite a realist and probably is the kind of mentor that David was. And she needs somebody like that, I think."

The Feature Film Appearances of Jennifer Jones

New Frontier (Republic, 1939). Screenplay by Betty Burbridge and Luci Ward. Directed by George Sherman. *Cast:* John Wayne, Ray Corrigan, Raymond Hatton, Phillis Isley (Jennifer Jones), Eddy Walker, Sammy McKim, Leroy Mason, Harrison Greene, Dave O'Brien, Jack Ingram, Bud Osborne.

Dick Tracy's G-Men (Republic, 1939). Screenplay by Barry Shipman, Franklyn Adreon, Rex Taylor, Ronald Davidson and Sol Shor based on the cartoon strips of Chester Gould. Directed by William Witney and John English. *Cast:* Ralph Brrd, Irving Pichel, Phyllis Isley (Jennifer Jones).

The Song of Bernadette (20th Century-Fox, 1943). Screenplay by George Seaton from the novel by Franz Werfel. Directed by Henry King. *Cast:* Jennifer Jones, William Eythe, Charles Bickford, Vincent Price, Lee J. Cobb, Gladys Cooper, Anne Revere, Roman Bohnen, Mary Anderson, Patricia Morison, Aubrey Mather, Charles Dingle, Edith Barrett, Sig Ruman, Blanche Yurka, Ermadean Walters, Marcel Dalio, Pedro de Cordoba, Jerome Cown, Charles Waldron, Moroni Olsen, Nana Bryant, Manart Kippen, Merrill Rodin, Nino Pipitone, Jr., John Maxwell Hayes, Jean Del Val, Tala Birell, Eula Morgan, Frank Reicher, Charles La Torre, Linda Darnell, Mae Marsh, Dickie Moore, Dorothy Shearer, Andre Charlot, Alan Napier, Fritz Leiber, Arthur Hohl, Edward Van Sloan.

Since You Went Away (Selznick International-United Artists, 1944) Screenplay by David O. Selznick from the novel by Margaret Buell Wilder. Directed by John Cromwell. *Cast:* Claudette Colbert, Jennifer Jones, Joseph Cotten, Shirley Temple, Monty Woolley, Lionel Barrymore, Robert Walker, Hattie McDaniel, Agnes Moorehead, Guy Madison, Craig Stevens, Keenan Wynn, Albert Basserman, Nazimova, Lloyd Corrigan, Jackie Moran, Gordon Oliver, Jane Devlin, Ann Gillis, Dorothy (Cindy) Garner, Andrew McLaglen, Jill Warren, Helen Koford (Terry Moore), Robert Johnson, Dorothy Dandridge, Johnny Bond, Irving Bacon, George Chandler, Addison Richards, Barbara Pepper, Byron Foulger, Edwin Maxwell, Florence Bates, Theodor Von Eltz, Adeline de Walt Reynolds, Doodles Weaver, Warren Hymer, Jonathan Hale, Eilene Janssen, William B. Davidson, Ruth Roman, Rhonda Fleming.

Love Letters (Paramount, 1945). Screenplay by Ayn Rand from the novel by Chris Massie. Directed by William Dieterle. *Cast:* Jennifer Jones, Joseph Cotton, Ann Richards, Anita Louise, Cecil Kellaway, Gladys Cooper, Byron Barr, Robert Sully, Reginald Denny, Ernest Cossart, James Millican, Lumsden Hare, Winifred Harris, Ethel May Halls, Matthew Boulton, David Clyde, Ian Wolfe, Alec Craig, Arthur Hohl, Conrad Binyon, Nina Borget, Mary Field, George Humbert, Constance Purdy, Ottola Nesmith, Harry Allen, Anthony Marsh, Louise Curries, Catherine Craig.

Cluny Brown (20th Century-Fox, 1946). Screenplay by Samuel Hoffenstein and Elizabeth Reinhardt from the novel by Margery Sharp. Directed by Ernest Lubitsch. *Cast:* Jennifer Jones, Charles Boyer, Peter Lawford, Helen Walker, Reginald Gardiner, C. Aubrey Smith, Richard Haydn, Margaret Bannerman, Sara Allgood, Ernest Cossart, Florence Bates, Una O'Connor, Queenie Leonard, Billy Bevan, Michael Dyne, Christopher Severn, Rex Evans, Ottola Nesmith, Harold de Becker, Jean Prescott, Al Winters, Olive Morgan, Charles Coleman, George Kirby, Whit Bissell, Betty Rae Brown, Mira McKinney, Philip Morris, Betty Fairfax, Norman Ainsley, Buster Slaven.

Duel in the Sun (Selznick Releasing Organization. 1946). Screenplay by David O. Selznick from an adaptation by Oliver H.P. Garrett of the novel by Niven Busch. Directed by King Vidor. *Cast:* Jennifer Jones, Joseph Cotten, Gregory Peck, Lionel Barrymore, Lillian Gish, Walter Huston, Herbert Marshall, Charles Bickford, Joan Tetzel, Harry Carey, Otto Kruger, Sidney Blackmer, Tilly Losch, Scott McKay, Butterfly McQueen, Francis MacDonald, Victor Kilian, Griff Barnett, Frank Cordell, Dan White, Steve Dunhill, Lane Chandler, Lloyd Shaw, Thomas Dillon, Robert McKenzie, Charles Dingle, Kermit Maynard, Hank Bell, Johnny Bond, Bert Roach, Si Jenks, Hank Worden, Rose Plummer, Guy Wilkerson, Lee Phelps. *Narrated by Orson Welles.*

Portrait of Jennie (Selznick Releasing Organization, 1948) Screenplay by Paul Osborn and Peter Berneis from the novel by Robert Nathan. Directed by William Dieterle. *Cast:* Jennifer Jones, Joseph Cotten, Ethel Barrymore, Cecil Kellaway, David Wayne, Albert Sharpe, Florence Bates, Lillian Gish, Henry Hull, Esther Somers, Maude Simmons, Felix Bressart, John Farrell, Clem Bevans, Robert Dudley.

We Were Strangers (Columbia, 1949). Screenplay by Peter Viertel and John Huston based on an episode in the novel "Rough Sketch" by Robert Sylvester. Directed by John Huston. *Cast:* Jennifer Jones, John Garfield, Pedro Armendariz, Gilbert Roland, Jose Perez, Morris Ankrum, Tito Renaldo, Paul Monte, Leonard Strong, Robert Tafur.

Madame Bovary (M-G-M 1949). Screenplay by Robert Ardrey from the novel by Gustave Flaubert. Directed by Vincente Minnelli. *Cast:* Jennifer Jones, Van Heflin, James Mason, Louis Jourdan, Christopher Kent, Gene Lockhart, Gladys Cooper, John Abbott, George Zucco, Ellen Corby, Eduard Franz, Henry Morgan, Frank Allenby.

Carrie (Paramount, 1951). Screenplay by Ruth and Augustus Goetz from the novel, "Sister Carrie," by Theodore Dreiser. Directed by William Wyler. *Cast:* Laurence Olivier, Jennifer Jones, Miriam Hopkins, Eddie Albert, Basil Ruysdael, Ray Teal, Barry Kelley, Sara Berner, William Reynolds, Mary Murphy, Jacqueline DeWitt, Harry Hayden, Walter Baldwin, Dorothy Adams, Royal Dano, James Flavin, Harlan Briggs, Melinda Plowman, Margaret Field, Jasper D. Weldon, Irene Winston, Charles Halton, Leon Taylor, George Melford, John Alvin, Don Beddoe, Judith Adams, Julius Tannen, Snub Pollard, Franklyn Farnum, Stuart Holmes, Kid Guard, Francis Morris.

The Wild Heart (Selznick-RKO, 1952). Screenplay by Michael Powell and Emeric Pressburger from the novel, "Gone To Earth," by Mary Webb. Directed by Michael Powell and Emeric Pressburger. *Cast:* Jennifer Jones, Cyril Cusack, David Farrar, Esmond Knight, Sybil Thorndyke, Hugh Griffith, George Cole, Beatrice Varley, Francis Clare, Raymond Rollett, Gerald Lawson. *Narrated by Joseph Cotten.*

Ruby Gentry (20th Century-Fox, 1952). Screenplay by Sylvia Richards from a story by Arthur Fitz-Richard. Directed by King Vidor. *Cast:* Jennifer Jones, Charlton Heston, Karl Malden, Tom Tully, Bernard Phillips, James Anderson, Josephine Hutchinson, Phyllis Avery, Herbert Heyes, Myra Marsh, Charles Cane, Sam Flint, Frank Wilcox.

Indiscretion of an American Wife (Selznick-Columbia, 1954) Screenplay by Cesare Zavattini, Luigi Chiarini and Georgia Presperi from a story by Cesare Zavattini and dialogue by Truman Capote. Directed by Vittorio De Sica. *Cast:* Jennifer Jones, Montgomery Clift, Gino Cervi, Dick Beymer.

Beat the Devil (United Artists, 1954). Screenplay by John Huston and Truman Capote from the novel by James Helvick. Directed by John Huston *Cast:* Humphrey Bogart, Jennifer Jones, Gina Lollobrigida, Robert Morley, Peter Lorre, Edward Underdown, Ivor Barnard, Bernard Lee, Marco Tulli, Marrio Perroni, Alex Pochet, Aldo Silvani.

Love Is a Many-Splendored Thing (20th Century-Fox, 1955) Screenplay by John Patrick from the story, "A Many Splendored Thing," by Han Suyin. Directed by Henry King. *Cast:* William Holden, Jennifer Jones, Torin Thatcher, Isobel Elsom, Murray Matheson, Virginia Gregg, Richard Loo, Soo Yong, Philip Ahn, Jorja Curtright, Donna Martell, Candace Lee, Kam Tong, James Hong, Herbert Heyes, Angela Loo, Marie Tsien, Ashley Cowan, Jean Wong, Joseph Kim, Marc Krah, Salvador Baguez, Edward Colmans, Leonard Strong, Howard Soo Hoo, Walter Soo Hoo, Keye Luke, Lee Tung Foo.

Good Morning, Miss Dove (20th Century-Fox, 1955). Screenplay by Eleanor Griffin from the novel by Frances Gray Patton. Directed by Henry Koster, *Cast:* Jennifer Jones, Robert Stack, Kipp Hamilton, Robert Douglas, Peggy Knudsen, Marshall Thompson, Chuck Connors, Biff Elliot, Jerry Paris, Leslie Bradley, Edward Firestone, Richard Deacon, Mary Wickes, Ted Marc, Dick Stewart, Than Wyenn, Martha Wentworth, Alfred Caiazza, John Hensley, Gary Pagett.

The Man in the Gray Flannel Suit (20th Century-Fox, 1956). Screenplay by Nunnally Johnson from the novel by Sloan Wilson. Directed by Nunnally Johnson. *Cast:* Gregory Peck, Jennifer Jones, Fredric March, Marisa Pavan, Ann Harding, Lee J. Cobb, Keenan Wynn, Gene Lockhart, Gigi Perreau, Portland Mason, Arthur O'Connell, Henry Daniell, Connie Gilchrist, Joseph Sweeney, Sandy Descher, Michey Maga, Kenneth Tobey, Ruth Clifford, Geraldine Wall, Alex Campbell, Jerry Hall, Jack Mather, Frank Wilcox, Nan Martin, Tris Coffin, William Philips, Leon Alton, Phyllis Graffeo, Dorothy Adams, Dorothy Phillips, Mary Benoit, King Lockwood, Lomax Study, John Breen, Renato Vanni, Mario Siletti, Lee Graham, Michael Jeffries, Roy Glenn.

The Barretts of Wimpole Street (M-G-M, 1957) Screenplay by John Dighton from the play by Rudolf Beisier. Directed by Sidney Franklin. *Cast:* Jennifer Jones, John Gielgud, Bill Travers, Virginia McKenna, Susan Stephen, Vernon Gray, Jean Anderson, Maxine Audley, Leslie Phillips, Laurence Naismith, Moultrie Kelsall, Michael Brill, Kenneth Fortescue.

A Farewell to Arms (Selznick-20th Century-Fox, 1957). Screenplay by Ben Hecht from the novel by Ernest Hemingway. Directed by Charles Vidor. *Cast:* Jennifer Jones, Rock Hudson, Vittorio De Sica, Albert Sordi, Kurt Kasznar, Mercedes McCambridge, Oscar Homolka, Elaine Stritch, Leopoldo Trieste, Franco Interlenghi, Jose Bieto, Georges Brehat, Memmo Carotenuto, Guido Martufi, Umberto Spadaro, Umberto Sacripanti, Victor Francen, Joan Shawlee, Alberto D'Amario.

Tender Is the Night (20th Century-Fox, 1961) Screenplay by Ivan Moffatt from the novel by F. Scott Fitzgerald. Directed by Henry King. *Cast:* Jennifer Jones, Jason Robards Jr., Joan Fontaine, Tom Ewell, Cesare Danova, Jill St. John, Paul Lukas, Bea Benedaret, Charles Fredericks, Sanford Meisner, Albert Carrier, Mac McWhorter, Carole Mathews, Maurice Dallimore, Carol Veazie, Arlette Clark, Leslie Farrell, Michael Crisalli, Alan Napier, John Richardson, Maggi Brown, Linda Hutchins, Orrin Tucker, Nora Evans, Bruno Della Santana, Tom Hernandez, Jacques Gallo, Art Salter, Eric Feldary.

The Idol (Embassy, 1966)Screenplay by Millard Lampell from a story by Ugo Liberatore. Directed by Daniel Petrie. *Cast:* Jennifer Jones, Michael Parks, John Leyton, Jennifer Hilary, Guy Doleman, Natasha Pyne, Caroline Blakiston, Jeremy Bulloch, Fanny Carby, Vernon Dobtcheff, Micahel Gordon, Gordon Gostelow, Ken Haward, Renee Houston, Priscilla Morgan, Edna Morris, Peter Porteous, Terry Richards, Derek Ware, Jack Watson, Rita Webb, Tina Williams.

Angel, Angel, Down We Go (American International, 1971). Screenplay by Robert Thom. Directed by Robert Thom. *Cast:* Jennifer Jones, Jordan Christopher, Roddy McDowall, Holly Lear, Lou Rawls, Charles Aidman, Davey Davison, Marty Brill, Hiroko Watanabe, Carol Costello, Sandrine Gobet, Rudy Battaglia, Ron Allen, Danielle Aubry, Joan Calhoun, George Ostos, Romo Vincent.

The Towering Inferno (Warner Brothers-20th Century-Fox, 1974). Screenplay by Stirling Silliphant from the novels, "The Tower," by Richard Martin Stern and "The Glass Inferno," by Thomas N. Scortia and Frank M. Robinson. Directed by John Guillermin and Irwin Allen. *Cast:* Steve McQueen, Paul Newman, William Holden, Faye Dunaway, Fred Astaire, Susan Blakely, Richard Chamberlain, Jennifer Jones, O.J. Simpson, Robert Vaughn, Robert Wagner, Susan Flannery, Jack Collins, Sheila Mathews, Norman Burton, Carol McEvoy, Michael Lookinland, Carlena Gower, Olan Soule, LCDR Norman Hicks, LTJG Thomas Karnahan.

With Robert Young in *Claudia* (1943).

7

DOROTHY McGUIRE

Dorothy McGuire "is an actress who can best be described as different. She doesn't fit into the usual category of a leading lady or a glamour actress, yet she gets important roles in important pictures and is considered a definite asset to any movie she's in." So said Sidney Skolsky in trying to assess the appeal of one of our most refined and successful actresses.

Although she never achieved super stardom like so many of Selznick's Players, Dorothy McGuire exhibited an *élan vitale* which enabled her to sustain and develop those remarkable qualities which she revealed in her first motion picture — *Claudia* (1943).

A five-foot, six inch, ash-blonde parcel of American wholesomeness, she projects the synthesis of those characteristics and virtues which we hold a part of our pioneering heritage. Not beautiful, not glamourous, yet she possessed a low-key sexuality and innate attractiveness which made us believe in her and her characterisations. This appeal and her personal charm made her the perfect American wife and mother, a role she played on screen and off.

Not unlike many actresses who even in childhood nurtured theatrical aspirations,Dorothy McGuire moved from Omaha, Nebraska, to New York City in an effort to become a "hit in a hit." Again, not unlike many other actresses, she spent three years ambitiously struggling toward that goal. When she achieved this, as star of the Broadway production of "Claudia" in 1941, her success brought her to Hollywood under the sponsorship of producer, David O. Selznick.

Although theatre seemed to be her whole life, the motion pictures intrigued her, and once she became a star in that medium, it was there she would spend most of the remainder of her career. However, simultaneously with this new success, she married, and with a wisdom and foresight unique among Hollywood leading ladies, she wisely and unwaveringly decided never to become a slave to her screen image and made her marriage and family the focal point of her life.

From that time, her career was secondary and because of this perspective, she was perhaps better able to cull the good from the bad scripts she was offered. Even on those rare occasions when the picture was less than adequate, Dorothy McGuire brought to each portrayal a realism which won unfailing critical acclaim.

Today, a veteran of thirty years in motion pictures and thirty years of marriage, she proves that *ars gratia artis* need not be the mainstay of an actress's career.

Dorothy Hackett McGuire was born on June 14, 1918, in Omaha, Nebraska, the only child of Thomas Johnson McGuire, a well-to-do attorney, and Isabelle Flaherty McGuire. As a child in Omaha's public schools, Miss McGuire wrote, directed, and acted in her own theatrical productions. Because of this early preoccupation with theatre, her school principal suggested that her parents permit her to join the Omaha Community Playhouse, and there in 1930, at age twelve, she made her stage debut in Sarah Crewe's "The Little Princess." The following year she had the lead in the Playhouse's production of James M. Barrie's "A Kiss for Cinderella." Her co-star in this play was a fellow native of Omaha, Henry Fonda, fresh from his first theatrical success on Broadway.

Her performance in "A Kiss for Cinderella" exhibited an ability and confidence that belied her years and the play's director, Bernard Szold, said, "She seems to have a natural instinct for the stage, a skill that is more than a childish aptitude." Performing in Omaha at this time with a visiting theatre company, was actress Violet Heming. After seeing Miss McGuire's amazing performance, she commented, "The girl is a born actress. She reads lines with natural intuition, not as a child who's been coached. She is like a breath of spring. I hope her parents will let her continue her training and go on the professional stage."

Miss McGuire's parents did encourage her devotion to the theatre until their divorce, when Miss McGuire went to live with her father. Shortly after her fourteenth birthday, her father died by his own hand, at which time she went to live with her mother who had married Harry Burkley, an Omaha businessman. Mrs. Burkley enrolled her daughter in the Ladywood Convent School in Indianapolis, Indiana, where, a vivacious and effervescent youngster, she excelled in her academic studies and appeared in the school theatricals, once playing the Virgin Mary. She later enrolled in Pine Manor Junior College at Wellesley, Massachusetts, and after graduation, spent the summer of 1937 with the Deertrees Summer Theatre in Harrison, Maine.

That season with the Deertrees Summer Theatre whetted her appetite for bigger things. While she admitted, "All children play act and I guess I just never grew up," she set her sights on New York and a chance at Broadway. "Acting had been just play and I don't know exactly why it suddenly became serious. But it did, and from then on I wanted more than anything to be a hit in a hit. (I knew I had something to offer as an actress)." It was this attitude which would be the driving force in her life during the next few years.

With enough money from her father's estate to live on, she moved to New York where she lived at 9 East 55th Street. In the winter of 1937, she replaced Haila Stoddard as Sue Evans in a five-day-a-week CBS soap opera called "Big Sister." "There were excellent players in that company and I learned a lot from them. It was a wonderful experience." She was hired to understudy the ingenue in "Stop-Over," a play by Matt Taylor and Sam Taylor, which starred Sidney Blackmer and opened at the Lyceum Theatre on January 11, 1938. Although the play was a flop and closed immediately, she was quickly cast as the ingenue in "Bachelor Born" by Ian Hunter. As the only American in a British cast, Miss McGuire's co-players felt her "Nebraska twang" a liability, and she was fired before the play opened at the Morosco Theatre on January 25, 1938.

Not discouraged, she then went to read for producer, Jed Harris, who hired her to replace Martha Scott in Thornton Wilder's "Our Town." Miss Scott left that play in July 1938, seven months after it had opened on February 4th, and Miss McGuire assumed the role successfully for the remainder of its Broadway run and its subsequent six-month tour. Her performance as Wilder's poignant heroine, Emily, earned excellent notices. Wilder himself played the stage manager, and aspiring actress, Teresa Wright, was Miss McGuire's understudy for this role.

After "Our Town" Miss McGuire signed for the role of Portia, one of the daughters of a celebrated actor-rogue played by John Barrymore in "My Dear Children" by Catherine Turney and Jerry Horwin. She was with that play for eight months on its cross-country tour and left the show in Chicago, at which time she was quoted as saying, "I'd come blissful and starry-eyed from 'Our Town' into this roughhouse. I really and truly was shocked." She was referring to the seeming lack of discipline in the company largely the result of the dissipated Barrymore's bouts with heart ailments and alcohol. Later, however, she recalled that Barrymore was very kind to her and "we were all very proud of him and protective. On my final night he departed from the script and spoke an improvised and sympathetic farewell; saying, 'You are like a pear tree in the spring rain.' "

Immediately upon leaving "My Dear Children," she was hired as Helena in "Swingin' The Dream," a musical-variety version of "A Midsummer Night's Dream" by Gilbert Seldes and Erik Charell with lyrics by Eddie de Lange and music by Jimmy Van Heusen. The play went to extremes in its unorthodox adaptation of Shakespeare and one critic stated, "From time to time, the original plot turns up and you will find an attractive Helena in the person of Dorothy McGuire." But for the most part, she was lost amid the musical and comedic antics of Benny Goodman, Louis Armstrong, and Butterfly McQueen. The play opened at the Center Theatre on November 29, 1939, but closed quickly enough for Miss McGuire to spend the Christmas holidays with her family.

Another failure followed in the form of "The Medicine Show." This was part of the Living Newspaper project, an offspring of the Federal Theatre, and was a hard-hitting survey of the medical profession written by Oscar Saul (pseudonym for Oscar Halpern) and Hoffman R. Hays. The play starred Martin Gabel and opened on April 12, 1940 at the New Yorker Theatre. Miss McGuire was reviewed as "attractive" in the role of Dora.

About this time, Miss McGuire heard that the Theatre Guild was planning to produce Philip Barry's "Liberty Jones" and she went to the Guild confident she was right for the part. However, her hopes were premature as "Liberty Jones" was only in the planning stages. The Guild instead offered her the role of understudy to Julie Hayden in a touring company of William Saroyan's "The Time of Your Life." Hoping she would not be taking a step backwards, she accepted the part, though her sights were still set on the lead in "Liberty Jones." While on tour with "The Time of Your Life" she was informed that her coveted role had been given to Nancy Coleman. Hurt and angry, Miss McGuire quit the show and accepted the role of Ada, the epileptic in Edward Chodorov's "Kind Lady." The play starred Gladys George and opened in New York at the Playhouse Theatre on September 3, 1940. It closed before the end of the year and Miss McGuire's reviews were mixed though they conceded that she was convincing.

At what appeared to be the low point in the young actress's career, luck and her unflagged ambition suddenly blossomed into success. In making the rounds of the theatre world, she heard that John Golden was testing numerous actresses for the role of Claudia Naughton in "Claudia," the impulsive, frivolous young child-bride who matures only after learning her mother has but a short time to live in Rose Franken's part-comedy, part-drama morality play. Golden had very definite opinions of the kind of actress who should play Claudia. He said, "To put 'Claudia' on Broadway it will be necessary to find an actress in her early twenties, who can look nineteen, who has about twenty-five years experience in show business, who is up to her knees in sawdust. She must be able to play one of the longest parts ever written to my knowledge and play the hell out of it. The odds are a thousand to one that there is no such actress." Golden had already tested 209 actresses for the part when Miss McGuire walked into audition, wearing an oversize sweater, a tweed skirt, saddle shoes and a beaver coat. Rose Franken, the author of the play which had been adapted from her "Redbook" stories, noticed the sweater and recalled that Dorothy McGuire looked unlike any actress she had ever seen. Miss McGuire says, "I just wanted a simple loose sweater that any country girl would wear to keep warm in, not the kind that keeps the audience warm." Aside from the sweater, Miss Franken noticed the young girl "had a fresh, windblown quality and an impressive, though subdued personality." Miss McGuire recalls, "Miss Franken marched around me, looking at me as though I were a *thing*! I then had no idea what she was thinking. I read her play to her and I read it again for Mr. Golden. Miss Franken said to him: 'Here is Claudia!' and he responded by saying 'She stands like a winner, and that made me feel like a filly."

Dorothy McGuire was given the role and the play opened to excellent reviews on February 12, 1941, at the Booth Theatre. Miss McGuire was on stage for all but five minutes of the play and Broadway was captivated by the genuine, fresh, enchanting, simple and unmannered actress. John O'Hara writing in "Newsweek," said, "I expect that the name of Dorothy McGuire will be quite well known, and this will be to her like 'The Warrior's Husband' was to Katherine Hepburn." In the New York "Times," Brooks Atkinson said, "She gives a splendid performance of a part that would be irritating if it were played by a dull actress. She is personally genuine; the charm she radiates across the play is not merely a theatre mannerism. In her acting, Claudia becomes the first real portent of spring in this reluctant latitude." Miss McGuire recalls taking her first solo curtain call, "It was out of this world. It was so wonderful. I couldn't see a person, the lights were so bright and so hazy at the same time. I was really beside myself. Nothing like that can ever happen again."

After nearly four years of trial and error, she had found herself a "hit in a hit," but her humility allowed her to keep this new-found success in perspective. "It's funny. You knock around for months, years, sometimes, and all of a sudden you wind up in a hit and everybody makes a fuss over you. You keep reminding yourself that maybe next year you'll have to start all over again, or perhaps get into a flop or two. That's what keeps you balanced."

Miss McGuire appeared in "Claudia" for one year on Broadway and another year on tour for a total of 722 performances and was named Best Dramatic Actress of the Year by the Drama League of New York. During the run of the play, its screen rights were purchased by David O. Selznick and Selznick sent director George Cukor to New York to screen test Miss McGuire. Cukor recalls that she was "lovely and charming," and Selznick approved the test and signed her to a seven-year contract.

At first, "Claudia" was to be personally produced by Selznick at a date when Miss McGuire, who was still performing in the play, would be available. At this same time Selznick had acquired another actress named Jennifer Jones who very much wanted to play the same part. Selznick then began thinking of using Miss Jones in *Claudia* and having Dorothy McGuire make her screen debut as Nora in *The Keys of the Kingdom,* another project he owned. Finally, it became obvious that Miss Jones would be making her starring debut in *The Song of Bernadette* and that the role of Claudia would be Miss McGuire's.

Selznick elected not to produce *Claudia* and sold the property and half of Miss McGuire's contract to 20th Century-Fox. The cast included Robert Young and Ina Claire and the picture was directed by Edmund Goulding. After seeing some of the first rushes from 20th Century-Fox, Selznick wrote a memo to the studio executives stating that no effort should be made to glamourise the new star, that instead every effort should be made to retain the naturalness that had been so appealing on the stage. He pointed out that he felt Miss McGuire's values were 1) an extra-ordinary talent, 2) a pixie kind of personality that has never been seen on the stage with the exception of Maude Adams, 3) cute mannerisms: "she is gay and bouyant, youthful and natural."

While working at 20th Century-Fox, Miss McGuire was given Loretta Young's former dressing room. The room was an opulent satin-padded affair which left Miss McGuire unimpressed and reminded her of a coffin.

After *Claudia's* release, Dorothy McGuire became an overnight star with the motion-picture public who ironically were unaware of the years of dedication which had brought her to this point. The picture was a tremendously popular success, and she received excellent reviews. The New York "Times" said, "In the film's earlier scenes her tomboyish gaucheries sometimes are a little too flamboyant and like a precocious youngster trying to show off, but in the latter scenes, her tortured transition is entirely believeable and touching."

Despite this sudden rise to stardom, Miss McGuire remained level-headed and undeluded by the role of the "movie star." In an interview after *Claudia's* opening, she stated, "People's careers have phases. For an actor in the theatre there's that beginning period when you are stage-struck, you are overwhelmed with that burning desire to act. You work terribly hard at what you can get. You think it's tough but in some ways it is so much easier than the next period, when you begin to have choices. It's hard to decide what to do next and you've got to make decisions fast while you're hot. You are still devoted to the theatre, it means a lot to you, but motion pictures are interesting, too. You suddenly realize it's a business and there are plenty of traps to fall into. You begin to worry about age, time passing and dough. Everything is awfully complicated. Some of the angles are hard to understand. You worry and try to figure it all out. And there are a whole lot of other things in life that interest me besides my career."

It was this objective philosophy which pervaded all aspects of Dorothy McGuire's career beyond *Claudia*. Had she chosen to exert all her energies and interest in motion pictures, she probably would have become one of the screen's most prominent actresses and "stars." But she chose to divide her life into two parts — that of an actress and that of a very privately married lady, and as the years progressed, her private life took precedent and her acting became an avocation.

Near the end of Miss McGuire's run in the stage production of *Claudia*, she had been introduced to photographer, John Swope, when Helen Morgan of "Life" magazine brought him backstage. Swope was the son of Gerard Swope, the president of General Electric. A romance blossomed and Swope continued to court her after she had moved to Hollywood. On July 18, 1943, they were married at the home of Miss McGuire's agent, Leland Hayward, with Frances Starr as matron of honour and James Stewart, Swope's best friend, as best man. They honeymooned in Mexico and went to live in Scottsdale, Arizona, where Swope was a civilian flying instructor at the nearby Thunderbird Field.

Selznick's next offer to Miss McGuire was a sequel to *Claudia*, but she refused at the time, saying, "I was grateful for all *Claudia* had done for me, but I wanted to get away from her ingenue flutter." Today she says she does not recall using the phrase "ingenue flutter" but "if I did it was wicked of me."

Selznick personally supervised a ten-minute documentary entitled, *Reward Unlimited*, which was made for the United States Public Health Service, and which cast Miss McGuire as a cadet nurse. The cast included Aline MacMahon and James Brown and would be the only picture that Selznick would ever personally produce for her, making Dorothy McGuire the only Selznick Player never to appear in one of his feature productions. The reason was simply that her rise to stardom coincided with that of Jennifer Jones and Selznick gave the career of the latter preference.

For her second feature she was offered the role of Katie Nolan in 20th Century-Fox's *A Tree Grows in Brooklyn*, after Gene Tierney's pregnancy prevented her from accepting it. The picture is a wonderful piece of Americana and Miss McGuire gave a beautiful performance as the wife of James Dunn, the waiter who drinks too much. Her noble Katie Nolan was the mainstay of the poverty-stricken family in the middle of the big city. The picture earned Dunn an Academy Award as Best Actor in a Supporting Role, and Joan Blondell, as the live-and-let-live Aunt Cissy, gave the best performance of her career.

Selznick then loaned Miss McGuire to RKO for

With Lloyd Nolan, Joan Blondell, Ted Donaldson, James Dunn and Peggy Ann Garner in *A Tree Grows in Brooklyn* (1945).

The Enchanted Cottage (1945), an off-beat love story based on the play by Sir Arthur Wing Pinero. A silent film version had been made in 1924 starring Richard Barthelmess and May McAvoy. Miss McGuire played an ugly duckling who finds happiness, moral courage and spiritual beauty after marrying a disfigured war veteran, Robert Young. While hardly the ingredients for a commercial love story, its timing proved propitious and it was widely accepted by the public. Miss McGuire was felt by some to be too pretty to play a homely girl but her sincere and poignant portrayal minimised this objection.

In the spring of 1945, Miss McGuire starred in an overseas USO production of "Dear Ruth;" and after the end of the war, she and her husband moved from Arizona to a carriage house in New York City.

In the meantime, Selznick had acquired the rights to *The Spiral Staircase* and had Ingrid Bergman as his first choice as the star. The story was based on Mel Dinelli's novel, "Some Must Watch," and had been adapted from a Theatre Guild radio production starring Helen Hayes. Selznick assigned Robert Siodmak to direct and when Miss Bergman elected not to star in the picture, he cast Dorothy McGuire in the lead and sold the package to RKO. In *The Spiral Staircase* (1946) Miss McGuire played the mute who had not spoken a word since witnessing the fire that had destroyed her childhood home and killed her parents. Working as a domestic in a New England home ruled by invalid matriarch, Ethel Barrymore, Miss McGuire discovers that one of Miss Barrymore's two sons is a psychopath who feels he must kill any young women who are physically deformed. In a lucid performance in pantomime, she conveyed the nuances of her fear-ridden character by the use of her facial expressions and her luminous eyes. The New York "Times" said, "Her characterization of one who senses a dread shadow over her but is incapable of communicating her fears is restrained and effectively pathetic."

In *The Spiral Staircase* (1946).

With Robert Young in *The Enchanted Cottage* (1945).

For her next picture, Miss McGuire asked Selznick to allow her to star in *Till the End of Time* (1946). Selznick thought her miscast for the part and acquiesced only when she agreed to do a sequel to *Claudia*, which she had refused to do earlier. *Claudia and David* (1946) was released in May and to Miss McGuire's surprise was a success despite that old saw about sequels being instant death at the box-office. The picture reunited Miss McGuire and Robert Young and portrayed her as a matured married woman who suspects her husband is having an affair with a widow, Mary Astor. It was all romance, but successful. *Till the End of Time*, released in July, was a wartime romance which cast Miss McGuire as a war widow who is sought after by three service men: Guy Madison, Robert Mitchum, and Bill Williams. Miss McGuire was given the glamour treatment

With Guy Madison in *Till the End of Time* (1946).

for the first time and proved an unbelievable sex symbol. However, the picture had built-in commercial appeal with Guy Madison, the bobbysoxer's new rage, as the troubled veteran who loves Miss McGuire, and a popular title song derived from a Chopin *Polonaise*. When Selznick's prediction that the part was not right for her proved true, she said, "I've fought for things and sometimes I have been right. I fought the hardest for this role and it was my least successful part."

Miss McGuire has great respect for David O. Selznick as a man and as a producer and recalls her working relationship with him as very pleasant. She says, "When I first arrived in Hollywood the word everyone seemed to be using was *quality*. Well, I soon found that it was David who was at the apex of the producers of quality. He went to great extremes with time, money and casting to try and get the best for the properties in which he believed. Both he and 20th Century-Fox guided me during those years and I suppose at times he thought me whimsical in my turning down certain parts or wanting others. I know I read the galleys of *The King and I* and turned it down because I wanted at that time to play women my own age. And the same was true of the sequel to *Claudia* and besides, I had played that part. And I asked to do *Till the End of Time* because she was a character my own age and she was different even though the part was not a developed one. I have never seen *Till the End of Time* so I don't know what that movie is like, but I did of course do Claudia Number 2 and it was a huge success. So he may have thought me whimsical at times but we liked each other. I suppose in looking back that I may not have had all that defined an idea of what my career should be, but as it turned out, it was a pretty good career."

Miss McGuire recalls that while Selznick was certainly a man with an ego, he was "extremely open, generous and concerned about his stars."

He was not on an ego trip as we say today. He lived his whole life like that. I remember going to my first party at his home when he was married to Irene and it was like walking onto a motion-picture set. I don't mean synthetic, but elegant; and I remember Kay Francis was there." When the author asked Miss McGuire if she had remembered Miss Francis being there because of any awe at meeting motion-picture stars, she replied, "No. I can't remember who else was there and I probably didn't know who half of them were at the time. No, I have enough of my own theatrical ego not to be in awe of other actors."

The American wholesomeness which Dorothy McGuire so easily projects came to the fore in her performance as the socialite who discovers she is not as free of bigotry and anti-Semitism as she had believed, when she falls in love with journalist Gregory Peck, who is posing as a Jew to write a magazine article about anti-Semitism. The picture was *Gentlemen's Agreement* (1947). Based on Laura Z. Hobson's novel, it was considered a trail-blazer in liberalism at the time of its release, as had been the novel when it was published. While today it fails to impress as little more than a contrived view of anti-Semitism in a very small segment of society, the upper-middle class, the script by Moss Hart succeeded in sharpening the focus of Miss Hobson's restricted observations. Peck and Miss McGuire were a marvelously sympathetic screen couple although they never had the opportunity to appear together again on the screen, and each of them was nominated for an Academy Award. Miss McGuire lost the award to

With Gregory Peck, John Garfield and Celeste Holm in *Gentlemen's Agreement* (1947).

Loretta Young for her performance in *The Farmer's Daughter*. The remaining competition included Joan Crawford for *Possessed*, Susan Hayward for *Smash-Up: The Story of a Woman*, and Rosalind Russell for *Mourning Becomes Electra*.

During production of *Gentlemen's Agreement*, Miss McGuire and Peck, who had both trained in the theatre, came up with the idea of forming a theatre stock company in which movie actors could appear for limited engagements between pictures. They enlisted the help of their employer, David Selznick, and formed the Actors Company at the La Jolla Playhouse — a group which included Joseph Cotten, Mel Ferrer, and on occasion, Jennifer Jones. The company's first production was "Night Must Fall," starring Dame May Whitty in 1947. That same year Miss McGuire starred in Nöel Coward's "Tonight at 8:30." She subsequently became one of the company's most frequent performers appearing in "The Importance of Being Earnest," "I Am a Camera," "The Winslow Boy," "Still Life," and "The Astounded Heart." In 1951, her husband, John Swope, signed on as producer for this organisation which now had become simply La Jolla Players, and when her schedule permitted, Miss McGuire acted as stage supervisor or director.

During this renewed activity with stage performing, Miss McGuire's contract with Selznick expired and shortly thereafter, Selznick discontinued his production company. Two projects he had in mind for Miss McGuire never materialised: a re-make of *Little Women* (three months of shooting had taken place before Selznick shelved it), and a screen version of Ibsen's "A Doll's House" to have been filmed in Scandinavia. Miss McGuire had starred in "A Doll's House" on radio, a medium in which she also read "Hamlet" and "Claudia." Miss McGuire recalls that *Little Women* was vaguely talked about but that she was never actually involved in shooting any scenes.

Free of any contractual associations, she and her husband spent nearly a year travelling in Europe, and shortly after their return, Miss McGuire gave birth to her first child, Mary Hackett, on February 14, 1949. A cover photograph of the newly born infant taken by her father decorated "Life" magazine.

That same year Dorothy McGuire signed a five-year, non-exclusive contract with 20th Century-Fox calling for one picture a year. Upon signing she said, "This contract permits me to work for other studios and that's exactly what I intend to do.'' That statement implies more ambition than is actually displayed in her film output during the next decade. Until this time she had achieved stardom via seven carefully-chosen parts in first class productions, but between 1950 and 1961, she appeared in one or two pictures a year that, for the most part, simply capitalized on her guileless womanly appeal. Her private life and her occasional appearances on stage seemed more important to her than did her motion-picture roles.

Her first committment for 20th Century-Fox was a mildly amusing marital comedy, *Mother Didn't Tell Me* (1950), which cast her as the wife of a physician, William Lundigan. Miss McGuire was required to be baffled by the vicissitudes of an unorganised life-style as a doctor's wife and the role hardly advanced her career. June Havoc, as the wife of the obstetrician, stole the picture. *Mister 880* (1950) was much more fun and cast her as the United Nations interpreter who spends a counterfeit dollar manufactured by an endearingly dishonest Edmund Gwenn. She was appropriately convincing as a career girl and it was to her credit that the sentimental ending proved palatable. Also in 1950, she returned to the La Jolla Playhouse to star in a production of Tennessee Williams' ''Summer and Smoke'' with John Ireland, Una Merkel and Michele Farmer (Gloria Swanson's daughter). After touring with that play briefly, she signed with M-G-M to star in *Callaway Went Thataway* (1951), a satire on television cowboys in which she and Fred MacMurray were a pair of zany advertising agents who create western stars and sell them to television.

Samuel Goldwyn cast her as the bright and sensible wife of a Second World War veteran, Dana Andrews, who is recalled to Korea in *I Want You* (1951), but despite its topical subject, it was a poorly written and directed film that was quickly forgotten. It is memorable only for the scene where Mildred Dunnock, playing Andrews' mother, tears the World War I trophies of her dead husband off the wall and denounces him as a fake hero. Miss Dunnock was emotionally brilliant.

Callaway Went Thataway had been part of a two-picture deal with M-G-M, arranged by her agent, Leland Hayward, and for her second committment, she was cast opposite Van Johnson in a soap-opera called *Invitation* (1951). Its much-used plot had her as a dying heiress who learns her husband (Johnson) has been bribed into marrying her. One critic found her convincing as a woman ''who has had almost all the blood drained out of her veins and is living on pulse beats of love for her husband,'' but it was a synthetic, one-dimensional part which could only have been saved by a Margaret Sullavan.

Late in 1951, she signed to star on Broadway in Jean Anouilh's ''Legend of Lovers.'' The play was a modern version of Orpheus and Eurydice with Miss McGuire as the actress and Richard Burton as the ne'er-do-well musician: a pair of star-crossed lovers. The play opened on December 26, 1951, but closed after twenty-two performances. Brooks Atkinson said, ''She is too tangible for speculative hocus-pocus.''

She was inactive until after the birth of her second child, a son named Mark, born May 14, 1953, but during her pregnancy she designed a group of maternity clothes which were sold by Saks Fifth Avenue and Neiman-Marcus.

After the birth of her son, she played the newspaper editor who is terrorised by her homicidal ex-husband in *Make Haste to Live* (1953), a deft suspense story produced by second-rate Republic Pictures.

She appeared in one of her most popular and successful pictures in 1954, as the mature, loyal and patient secretary of eccentric novelist, Clifton Webb, in *Three Coins in the Fountain*. Its romantic plot, title song, and Cinema Scope Technicolor travelogue of Rome made it a box-office bonanza, despite its being an updated re-make of the Thirties hackneyed plot about gold-diggers abroad.

She was lauded for several very good television performances during the Fifties: ''Garden in the Sea'' on U.S. Steel Hour, ''The Philadelphia

With Clifton Webb in *Three Coins in the Fountain* (1954).

Story,'' and ''To Each His Own'' on Lux Video Theatre. The latter was televised in 1954, and that same year she turned down an invitation to star in a comedy series on television.

She was miscast as the secretary to defense lawyer Glenn Ford, who had once been a Communist in *Trial* (1955). This confused picture was an attack on McCarthyism which had a Mexican youth indicted for the murder of a white girl who had suffered a heart attack in his presence. The McGuire character was aware that the boy was a martyr for the Communist party.

She was much better cast in two theatre productions in 1955 — ''Joan at the Stake'' and ''The Country Girl.'' ''Joan at the Stake'' was Paul Honnegger's oratorio in which Ingrid Bergman had appeared throughout Europe and which had been put on film by Miss Bergman's husband, Roberto Rossellini. Miss McGuire appeared in this play in the San Francisco Opera House, the Shrine Auditorium in Los Angeles and in appearances with the San Diego and Salt Lake City symphony orchestras. ''The Country Girl'' was produced at her ''alma mater,'' the Omaha Community Playhouse, and cast her opposite Henry Fonda, who had starred with her in ''A Kiss for Cinderella.'' It was a benefit production to raise funds for the theatre and a third native Nebraskan, Marlon Brando, was to have played the director, but motion-picture commitments prevented his appearance. Fonda's daughter, Jane, made her stage debut in this play.

Dorothy McGuire's next picture was the one in which she gave her best performance and for which she was named the Best Actress of the Year by the National Board of Review. *Friendly Persuasion* (1956) is one of the best pictures directed by William Wyler and a memorable bit of Americana. Miss McGuire played the implacable Quaker preacher in Indiana who was against husband Gary Cooper and son Anthony Perkins being involved in the Civil War. Miss McGuire admired Wyler greatly and said, ''Wyler is a wonderful director. The humor he gets into a serious story is simply great. Out in Hollywood they are saying that he has the Lubitsch touch, whatever that means. But the Wyler touch cannot be beaten by any director.''

In talking to the author about Wyler, Miss McGuire said, ''It took me a whole picture to figure him out, but I would love to work with him again today. He is difficult and enigmatic. I remember for one whole day he had me kneading bread and I thought, 'Why?' But he wanted me to be very familiar with the set. It may have been frivolous to have spent a whole day kneading bread. I am sure I would have felt just as at home without spending all that time, but I learned what he was driving at. He was not articulate about giving you direction. I had to poke around and explain the character for myself and he would simply wait. Then he would add something here and there and wait some more. When you don't know what the director wants explicitly, you go on your own, you just go. And afterwards he would come up to you and give you a bouquet, verbally. He loved humor and loved the family, loved the grain that makes a family. And that grain takes in all — the ridiculous, the sentiment, the humor and the explosions, all of it, and that is his great contribution.''

Her experience with the picture pleased Miss McGuire, and she was not concerned about playing the mother of a teenaged son although she was only thirty-nine years old. With a realism few actresses possess at that crucial age, she said, ''I decided to keep right on playing woman who were my age.'' On another occasion she said, ''I've been fortunate to play mothers with dimensions. They haven't been just symbols of motherhood.'' It was this sense of reality and her admirable performance in *Friendly Persuasion* which cast the die for all her motion-picture appearances that were to follow. She had gained her reputation and stardom by skillfully depicting the wholesome qualities of the young bride and later of the mature wife, and without any pretence, she willingly accepted her fate as a screen mother, continuing to bring to those portrayals the same virtues her young women had possessed.

Following *Friendly Persuasion,* Walt Disney chose her for the role of Katie Oates, the sympathetic rancher's wife and pioneer mother in *Old Yeller*(1957), set in Texas in the 1860's. This role was similar to the one she had played in *Friendly Persuasion,* although the picture was more of a good dog story than a depiction of Americana. Disney used her on two other occasions and again, both were motherly roles: *Swiss Family Robinson* (1960) cast her as the mother of a brood who is marooned on an island after being shipwrecked, and *Summer Magic* (1963) cast her as the rural widow-mother of three children who is both gentle and genteel despite the family's impoverished hard times. The latter was a vehicle for English child star, Hayley Mills, and was a re-make of

With Anthony Perkins and Gary Cooper in *Friendly Persuasion* (1956).

Mother Carey's Chickens (1938), which had starred Ruby Keeler. All three of these assignments for Disney were record-breaking money-makers.

Dorothy McGuire did not appear on the screen in 1958 but chose to return to Broadway as Eliabeth Willard, the heart disease-ridden mother in Sherwood Anderson's "Winesburg, Ohio." The play opened on February 8, 1958, but was too dreary and verbose to enjoy a respectable run. Critics, however, did praise her ability to suggest the emotional force of a woman who is physically debilitated, once again giving credence to this lady's ability to inject a sense of reality in all her work.

She returned to the screen in 1959, as the benign wife of Clifton Webb, in *The Remarkable Mr. Pennypacker,* a typically Hollywood casting ploy which capitalised on her skillful ability to project tolerance. She was the wife of a bigamist by whom she had nine children and discovers he has a second wife with eight more children. It was an amusing and profitable bit of fluff.

Her second picture in 1959, *This Earth Is Mine,* was one of the most unusual bits of casting in her career. She played the embittered and vindictive daughter of winery patriarch, Claude Rains, who, after Rain's health prevents him from ruling his dynasty, is determined she will be the surrogate head of the family. This part had originally been offered to Barbara Stanwyck who turned it down, but Miss McGuire's sleek witchery proved impressive and her low-key sexuality even more so.

A Summer Place (1960) was a banal soap-opera commercially devised to exploit two of Hollywood's least likely candidates for lasting stardom: Troy Donahue and Sandra Dee. In a New England setting, Miss McGuire was the unloved wife of Arthur Kennedy and the mother of Donahue who found herself renewing her relationship with the man she had always loved, Richard Egan. Complicating the plot, Donahue falls in love with Egan's daughter, Miss Dee. The scriptwriters failed to polish their product and the picture lacked the gloss of the then-popular Ross Hunter soap-operas. "Variety" said, "With the single exception of Dorothy McGuire, who comes through with a radiant performance and is lovely to look at, the cast does an average job."

William Inges's *The Dark at the Top of the Stairs* (1960) provided Dorothy McGuire with a much more believable role as the long-suffering and frigid wife of Robert Preston. A typical Inge drama about middle-class American neuroticism, Miss McGuire and Preston played the dissatisfied couple whose marriage is complicated by money problems, infidelity and two introverted children. Her subtle performance was extraordinarily touching, but she was upstaged by the flashy theatrics of two of Hollywood's grossly underrated scene stealers, Angela Lansbury and Eve Arden.

Susan Slade (1961) was a continuation of Dorothy McGuire's unfortunate preoccupation with the soap-opera genre of the early sixties. This was another attempt to solidify Troy Donahue in the hearts of America's teenagers. This time his co-star was that blonde concoction of half saccharine—half soda fizz—Connie Stevens. Another improbable script had Miss McGuire play the mother who passes her daughter's illegitimate child off as her own. It did not come off!

She was away from the screen for two years, when she returned to play the mother in Disney's *Summer Magic* (1963) and the following year was a visual beauty in the cameo role of the Virgin Mary in George Stevens's *The Greatest Story Ever Told* (1964).

The Swopes live in the Mediterrean-style house in Holmby Hills that once belonged to silent screen star, Corinne Griffith, where Dorothy McGuire chose to spend the next seven years cultivating her life as wife and mother. The Swope's daughter, Mary Hackett, using her nickname, Topo, made her motion-picture debut in 1971 in *Glory Boy*.

In 1972, Miss McGuire returned once again to the screen playing the archetypal Irish grandmother in *Flight of the Doves*, the Disney-like adventure of two youngsters who run away from their cruel step-father in Liverpool to search for the kindly grandmother. This picture is her last to date.

In January, 1972, she played the head of an uneasy household haunted by the ghost of a dead girl in a television feature, "She Waits." The following October 2nd, on the Public Broadcasting System she gave a wonderful performance as Lavinia, the sensitive and religious wife and mother who is driven to insanity by her tyrannical husband in Lillian Hellman's "Another Part of the Forest."

In 1973, plans were announced in the New York "Times" to reunite her with her favourite and most popular co-star, Robert Young, in a remake of *The Enchanted Cottage*. According to Young, "This time the setting will not be World War II, of course, and Dorothy and I will not be playing the leads. We'll play the parts of the housekeeper and the blind pianist, done by Mildred Natwick and Herbert Marshall in the original."

Miss McGuire explains why this project never materialised. "Robert Young did invite me to his home to see a screening of *The Enchanted Cottage* with the idea of making it today, but after watching it I felt it belonged to another period and I don't wish to step backward. The story is just not right for today and today young people judge other people from the interior, which is far more important." Then she added emphatically, "But my career is not over. I have not stopped. My husband and I travel a great deal but I fully plan to return to the theatre."

In the meantime she starred as the brusque but kindly kennel owner in "The Runaways," a television family movie aired by CBS on April 1, 1975.

Eschewing the social life of a typical Hollywood actress, Dorothy McGuire remains an obsessively private person. Her modest off-stage demeanour stands her in good stead with Hollywood's old guard and her personal fulfillment via an incredibly happy marriage, protects her from the mistake made by many of her acting comtemporaries who over-expose themselves in less than flattering roles.

The Feature Film Appearances of Dorothy McGuire

Claudia (20th Century-Fox, 1943). Screenplay by Morrie Ryskind from the play by Rose Franken. Directed by Edmund Goulding. *Cast:* Dorothy McGuire, Robert Young, Ina Claire, Reginald Gardiner, Olga Baclanova, Jean Howard, Frank Tweddell, Elsa Janssen, John Royce.

A Tree Grows In Brooklyn (20th Century-Fox, 1945). Screenplay by Tess Slesinger and Frank Davis from the novel by Betty Smith. Directed by Elia Kazan. *Cast:* Dorothy McGuire, Joan Blondell, James Dunn, Lloyd Nolan, Peggy Ann Garner, Ted Donaldson, James Gleason, Ruth Nelson, John Alexander, B.S. Pulley, Ferike Boros, Charles Halton, Patricia McFadden, Robert Strange, Robert Tait, Teddy Infuhr, Mickey Kuhn, Constance Purdy, J. Farrell Mac Donald, Adeline Dewalt Reynolds, George Melford, Mae Marsh, Edna Jackson, Vincent Graeff, Susan Lester, Johnnie Berkes, Lillian Bronson, Alec Craig, Al Bridge, Joseph L. Greene, Virginia Brissac, Harry Harvey Jr., Robert Anderson, Art Smith, Erskine Sanford, Martha Wentworth, Francis Pierlot, Al Eben, Harry Seymour.

The Enchanted Cottage (RKO, 1945). Screenplay by DeWitt Bodeen and Herman J. Mankiewicz from the play by Sir Arthur Wing Pinero. Directed by John Cromwell. *Cast:* Dorothy McGuire, Robert Young, Herbert Marshall, Mildred Natwick, Spring Byington, Hilary Brooke, Richard Gaines, Alec Englander, Mary Worth, Josephine Whittell.

The Spiral Staircase (RKO, 1946). Screenplay by Mel Dinelli from the novel, "Some Must Watch," by Ethel Lina White. Directed by Robert Siodmak. *Cast:* Dorothy McGuire, Ethel Barrymore, George Brent, Kent Smith, Rhonda Fleming, Gordon Oliver, Elsa Lanchester, Sara Allgood, Rhys Williams, James Bell.

Claudia and David (20th Century-Fox, 1946). Screenplay by Rose Franken and William Brown Meloney. Directed by Walter Lang. *Cast:* Dorothy McGuire, Robert Young, John Sutton, Mary Astor, Gail Patrick, Rose Hobart, Harry Davenport, Florence Bates, Jerome Cowan, Elsa Janssen, Frank Tweddell, Anthony Sydes, Pierre Watkin, Henry Mowbray, Clara Blandick, Betty Compson, Eva Noval, Eric Wilton, Frank Darien.

Till The End of Time (RKO, 1946). Screenplay by Allen Rivkin from the novel, "They Dreamed of Home," by Niven Busch. Directed by Edward Dmytryk. *Cast:* Dorothy McGuire, Guy Madison, Robert Mitchum, Bill Williams, Jean Porter, Tom Tully, Loren Tindall, Johnny Sands, Ruth Nelson, Selena Royle, Harry Von Zell, Richard Bennett.

Gentlemen's Agreement (20th Century-Fox, 1947). Screenplay by Moss Hart from the novel by Laura Z. Hobson. Directed by Elia Kazan. *Cast:* Gregory Peck, Dorothy McGuire, John Garfield, Celeste Holm, Anne Revere, June Havoc, Albert Dekker, Jane Wyatt, Dean Stockwell, Nicholas Joy, Sam Jaffe, Harold Vermilyea, Ransom M. Sherman, Roy Roberts, Kathleen Lockhart, Curt Conway, John Newland, Robert Warwick, Robert Karnes, Gene Nelson, Marion Marshall, Louise Lorimer, Howard Negley, Victor Kilian, Frank Wilcox, Marilyn Monk, Wilton Graff, Morgan Farley, Mauritz Hugo, Olive Deering, Jane Green, Virginia Gregg, Jesse White.

Mother Didn't Tell Me. (20th Century-Fox, 1950). Screenplay by Claude Binyon from "The Doctor Wears Three Faces," by Mary Bard. Directed by Claude Binyon. *Cast:* Dorothy McGuire, William Lundigan, June Haver, Gary Merrill, Jessie Royce Landis, Leif Erickson, Joyce MacKenzie, Reiko Sato, Georgia Backus.

Mister 880 (20th Century-Fox. 1950). Screenplay by Robert Riskin from articles in "The New Yorker" by St. Clair McKelway. Directed by Edmund Goulding. *Cast:* Dorothy McGuire, Burt Lancaster, Edmund Gwenn, Millard Mitchell, Minor Watson, Howard St. John, Hugh Sanders, James Millican, Howland Chamberlain, Larry Keating, Kathleen Hughes, Geraldine Wall.

Callaway Went Thataway (M-G-M, 1951). Screenplay by Norman Panama and Melvin Frank, Directed by Norman Panama and Melvin Frank. *Cast:* Fred MacMurray, Dorothy McGuire, Howard Keel, Jesse White, Fay Roope, Natalie Schafer, Douglas Kennedy, Elizabeth Frazer, Stan Freburg, Don Haggerty, and guests: Clark Gable, Elizabeth Taylor, Esther Williams.

I Want You (Goldwyn-RKO, 1951). Screenplay by Irwin Shaw from the stories of Edward Newhouse. Directed by Mark Robson. *Cast:* Dorothy McGuire, Dana Andrews, Farley Granger, Peggy Dow, Robert Keith, Mildred Dunnock, Ray Collins, Martin Milner, Jim Backus, Marjorie Crossland, Walter Baldwin, Walter Sande, Peggy Maley, Jerrilyn Flanney, Erik Nielsen.

Invitation (M-G-M, 1951). Screenplay by Paul Osborn from a story by Jerome Weidman. Direct by Gottfried Reinhardt. *Cast:* Dorothy McGuire, Van Johnson, Ruth Roman, Louis Calhern, Ray Collins, Michael Chekhov, Lisa Golm, Diane Cassidy, Stapleton Kent, Barbara Ruick, Norma Field, Matt Moore, Patrick Conway, Alex Gerry, Lucile Curtis.

Make Haste To Live (Republic, 1953). Screenplay by Warren Duff. Directed by William A. Seiter, *Cast:* Dorothy McGuire, Stephen McNally, Mary Murphy, Edgar Buchanan, John Howard, Ron Hagerthy, Carolyn Jones, Pepe Herr.

Three Coins In The Fountain (20th Century-Fox. 1954). Screenplay by John Patrick from the novel by John H. Secondari. Directed by Jean Negulesco. *Cast:* Clifton Webb, Dorothy McGuire, Jean Peters, Louis Jourdan, Maggie McNamara, Rossano Brazzi, Howard St. John,

Kathry Givney, Cathleen Nesbitt, Vincent Padula, Mario Siletti, Alberto Morin, Dino Bolognese, Tony De Mario, Jack Mattis, Willard Walterman, Zachary Yaconelli, Celia Lovsky, Larry Arnold, Renata Vanni, Grazia Narcisso, Gino Corrado, Iphigenie Castiglioni, Norma Varden, Merry Anders, Charles La Torre.

Trial (M-G-M, 1955). Screenplay Don M. Mankiewicz from his novel. Directed by Mark Robson. *Cast:* Glenn Ford, Dorothy McGuire, Arthur Kennedy, John Hodiak, Katy Jurado, Rafael Campos, Juano Hernandez, Robert Middleton, John Hoyt, Paul Guilfoyle, Elisha Cook Jr., Ann Lee, Whit Bissell, Richard Gaines, Barry Kelley, Frank Cady, Charles Tannen, David Leonard, John Rosser, James Todd, Sheb Wooley, Charlotte Lawrence, Percy Helton, Dorothy Green, Everett Glass, Grandon Rhodes, Charles Evans, Frank Wilcox. Wilson Wood, Robert Bice, John Maxwell, Michael Dugan, Vince Townsend, Frank Ferguson, Robert Forrest, Mort Mills, Rodney Bell, Richard Tyler, Mitchell Lewis.

Friendly Persuasion (Allied Artists, 1956). Screenplay by Michael Wilson from the stories of Jessamyn West. Directed by William Wyler. *Cast:* Gary Cooper, Dorothy McGuire, Marjorie Main, Anthony Perkins, Richard Eyer, Robert Middleton, Phyllis Love, Mark Richman, Walter Catlett, Richard Hale, Joel Fluellen, Theodore Newton, John Smith, Edna Skinner, Marjorie Durant, Frances Farwell, Russell Simpson, Charles Halton, Everett Glass, Frank Jenks, Joe Turkel, James Anderson, Jean Inness, Nelson Leigh, Helen Kleeb, Mary Carr, Diane Jergens, John Craven, Harry Hines, Henry Rowland, Ivan Rasputin, Donald Kerr, Steve Warren, Earle Hodgins, Tom London, John Pickard, Richard Garland, Norman Leavitt, Don Kennedy.
Note: The screenwriter, Michael Wilson, is not given credit in most references nor was he eligible for his nomination for the Academy Award as he was among those writers who were blacklisted.

Old Yeller (Disney-Buena Vista, 1957). Screenplay by Fred Gipson and William Tunberg from the novel by Fred Gipson. Directed by Robert Stevenson. *Cast:* Dorothy McGuire, Fess Parker, Tommy Kirk, Kevin Corcoran. Jeff York, Chuck Connors, Beverly Washburn.

The Remarkable Mr. Pennypacker (20th Century-Fox, 1959). Screenplay by Walter Reisch from the play by Liam O'Brien. Directed by Henry Levin. *Cast:* Dorothy McGuire, Clifton Webb, Charles Coburn, Jill St. John, Ron Ely, Ray Stricklyn, David Nelson, Dorothy Stickney, Larry Gates, Richard Deacon, Mary Jayne Saunders. Mimi Gibson, Donald Losby, Chris Van Scoyk, Jon Van Scoyk, Terry Rangno, Nora O'Mahoney, Doro Merande, Harvey B. Dunn, Ralph Sanford, Joan Freeman, Donald Harrison, David Harrison, Pamela Baird, Nancy Ann DeCarl, Anna Marie Nanasi, Diane Mountford, Ray Ferrell.

This Earth Is Mine (Universal, 1959). Screenplay by Casey Robinson from the novel, "The Cup and the Sword," by Alice Tisdale Hobart. Directed by Henry King. *Cast:* Rock Hudson, Jean Simmons, Dorothy McGuire, Claude Rains, Kent Smith, Anna Lee, Ken Scott, Cindy Robbins, Augusta Merighi, Frances Bethencourt, Stacy Graham, Peter Chong.

A Summer Place (Warner Brothers, 1959). Screenplay by Delmer Daves from the novel by Sloan Wilson. Directed by Delmer Daves. *Cast:* Dorothy McGuire, Richard Egan, Sandra Dee, Arthur Kennedy, Troy Donahue, Constance Ford, Beulah Bondi, Jack Richardson, Martin Eric, Peter Constanti, Junius Matthews, Gertrude Flynn, Marshall Bradford, Phil Chambers, Robert Griffin, Arthur Space, George Taylor, Roberta Shore, Ann Doran, Dale J. Nicholson, Lewis Martin, Helen Wallace, Everett Glass, Eleanor Audley, Richard Deacon, Howard Hoffman, Nancy Matthews, Susan Odin, Cheryl Holdridge, Bonnie Franklin.

The Dark at the Top of the Stairs (Warner Brothers, 1960). Screenplay by Harriet Frank Jr., and Irving Ravetch from the play by William Inge. Directed by Delbert Mann. *Cast:* Robert Preston, Dorothy McGuire, Eve Arden, Angela Lansbury, Shirley Knight, Frank Overton, Lee Kinsolving, Robert Eyer, Penney Parker, Dennis Whitcomb, Ken Lynch, Nelson Leigh, Emerson Treacy, Ben Erway, Helen Brown, Jean Paul King, Helen Wallace, Peg La Centra, Paul Birch, Mary Patton, Paul Comi, Addison Richards, Robin Warga, Charles Seel, Stoddard Kirby.

Swiss Family Robinson (Disney-Buena Vista, 1960). Screenplay by Lowell S. Hawley from the novel by Johann Wyss. Directed by Ken Annakin. *Cast:* John Mills, Dorothy McGuire, James MacArthur, Tommy Kirk, Kevin Corcoran, Cecil Parker, Janet Munro, Sessue Hayakawa.

Susan Slade (Warner Brothers, 1961). Screenplay by Delmer Daves from the novel by Doris Hume. Directed by Delmer Daves. *Cast:* Troy Donahue, Connie Stevens, Dorothy McGuire, Lloyd Nolan, Brian Aherne, Grant Williams, Natalie Schafer, Kent Smith, Bert Convy, Guy Wilkerson.

Summer Magic (Disney-Buena Vista, 1963). Screenplay by Sally Benson from the story by Kate Douglas Wiggin. Directed by James Nelson. *Cast:* Hayley Mills, Burl Ives, Dorothy McGuire, Deborah Walley, Eddie Hodges, Kimmy Mathers, Michael Pollard, Wendy Turner, Una Merkel, Peter Brown, Jim Stacy, O.Z. Whitehead.

The Greatest Story Ever Told (United Artists, 1965). Screenplay by James Lee Barrett in Creative Association with Carl Sandburg. Directed by George Stevens. *Cast:* Max Von Sydow, Dorothy McGuire, Robert Loggia, Charlton Heston, Michael Anderson Jr., Robert Blake, Burt Brinckeroff, John Considine, Jamie Farr, David Hedison, Peter Mann, David McCallum, Roddy McDowall, Gary Raymond, Tom Reese, David Sheiner, Ina Balin, Janet Margolin, Michael Tolan, Sidney Poitier, Joanna Dunham, Carroll Baker, Pat

Boone, Van Heflin, Sal Mineo, Shelley Winters, Ed Wynn, John Wayne, Telly Savalas, Angela Lansbury, Johnny Seven, Paul Stewart, Harold J. Stone, Martin Landau, Nehemiah Persoff, Joseph Schildkraut, Victor Buono, Robert Busch, John Crawford, John Lupton, Rodolfo Acosta, Michael Ansara, Philip Coolidge, Dal Jenkins, Joe Perry, Marian Seldes, Donald Pleasance, Richard Conte, Frank De Kova, Joseph Sirola, Cyril Delevanti, Mark Lenard, Frank Silvera, Members of the Inbal Dance Theatre of Israel.

Flight of the Doves (Columbia, 1972). Screenplay by Frank Gabrielson and Ralph Nelson from the novel by Walter Macken. Directed by Ralph Nelson. *Cast:* Ron Moody, Jack Wild, Dotothy McGuire, Stanley Holloway, Helen Raye, William Rushton, Dana, John Molloy, Barry Keegan, Brendan O'Reilly, Emmett Bergin, Noel Purcell, Nial O'Brien, Ronnie Walsh, Thomas Hickey, Brendan Cauldwell, Clara Mullen, Des Keogh, Joe Cahill, Tom Irwin.

In *Since You Went Away* (1944).

8

JOSEPH COTTEN

At the relatively mature age of thirty-six, Joseph Cotten made his auspicious film debut in *Citizen Kane* (1941), after being invited to do so by his Mercury Theatre colleague, Orson Welles. No other actor can look back at his first film and know it has become what is considered to be America's finest, in which he gave a remarkable performance. With this propitious beginning, one would have expected this burgeoning actor to achieve super stardom. Yet Cotten, while talented and ambitious, never fully realised this acclaim.

His association with Welles, one of Hollywood's most unorthodox figures, ended after two more pictures, whereupon, Joseph Cotten, the elegant, urbane gentleman, was offered a contract by Hollywood's most celebrated independent producer, David O. Selznick. Selznick astutely recognised that Cotten's dignified appeal was a rare commodity in Hollywood at the time because World War II had greatly reduced the number of eligible leading men on the screen. Selznick's incomparable instinct for promotion enabled him to catapult this relatively unknown, albeit distinguished, actor into one of the top romantic leading men of the war years. He did so by carefully casting Cotten opposite some of the screen's most famous leading ladies — Ingrid Bergman, Deanna Durbin, Claudette Colbert, Loretta Young — and most notably, his own wife, Jennifer Jones.

The public readily accepted this American version of Charles Boyer and also found Cotten equally attractive when he used his innate charm to convincingly depict villainy, as in *Shadow of a Doubt* (1943).

Ironically, the same combination of circumstances which were responsible for Cotten's meteoric rise to fame, later on were responsible for his inability to attain motion picture greatness. Whereas his rise was the result of timeliness and careful management, so was his decline. When Selznick disbanded his group of players in 1949 and the motion-picture industry was beginning to feel the first twinges of competition from that monster medium — television — Cotten's career began to ebb.

Cotten acquiesced to these inevitable circumstances, and the remainder of his career has been that of a respectable working actor dutifully doing his job — always giving his best — regardless of the merit of the project. And unlike many of his colleagues, Cotten has fought no battle for that gold statuette.

Cotten is a personable, polished man with a droll sense of humour and an unpretentious modesty which has earned him the enduring respect of both his colleagues and his public. He has never made any attempt to justify the fluctuations of his career. Without apology, he says, "Movies and the theatre aren't life. They're only part of it. We make a living out of acting and pray we don't get associated with too much junk."

Joseph Chesire Cotten was born in Petersburg, Virginia, on May 15, 1905, where his father, Joseph Chesire Cotten Sr., was the assistant superintendent of mails. His heritage was that of a proper Southern country gentlemen. His grandfather, John Whittiker Cotten had been a Brigadier-General in the North Carolina militia. The family of his mother, the former Sally Willson, owned two plantations, one of which, Mayfield, is still standing in Dinwiddie, Virginia, just outside Petersburg.

Cotten attended the local Petersburg public schools and enterprisingly worked after school delivering special delivery packages for the postal service by bicycle. "I had the best pair of legs in the world. I'll bet anybody on it. I pedalled a million miles if I pedalled a yard." He got his first whiff of grease paint while performing in school plays. This was enough to make him feel he was destined to become an actor. Whereas his parents would have preferred he study engineering at the University of Virginia, they did not try to discourage his theatrical aspirations. His brother Whittiker, however, did study engineering, and his other brother, Samuel, became a research officer for the postal service.

After high school, Cotten rejected further academic studies, and armed with a small subsidy from his family, he moved to Washington, D.C., where he enrolled in the Robert Nugent Hickman School of Expression. "Washington wasn't Petersburg in a financial way," he soon discovered, and when his money ran out, he changed his studies to night classes and took a daytime job selling vacuum cleaners. When that job proved less lucrative than he had wished, he put his "best pair of legs in the world" to use on the professional football field as a member of the Department of Interior football team. That increased his bank account faster than vacuum cleaners but it also awarded him "a handsome sock in the puss" during one game. The result of this mishap is a bridge on one side of his mouth containing teeth "that were never there before."

Now bent upon pursuing a serious career in the theatre, Cotten left Washington for the more alluring promises of New York. He spent a desultory year knocking fruitlessly on agents' doors. For two years he paid his rent by selling paint and while doing so met an "impecunious African diamond merchant" who had "cornered the market on a trick gadget for saving gasoline." The "merchant" offered Cotten the chance to join him in business in St. Petersburg, Florida. The discouraged Cotten accepted the offer, and on his way south, stopped to visit his family in Virginia, where an unlucky poker game left him without the fare to continue to Florida. A benevolent friend, variously described as a "policeman and a mail carrier," offered him one half of an excursion ticket to Miami on the condition the other half be given to the man's daughter so she could come home.

Once Cotten landed in Miami he liked the city so much, and still being without funds, he decided not to follow his spurious merchant to St. Petersburg. Instead he went to work for the Miami "Herald" as an advertising salesman and earned $35 a week. His salary hardly covered his monthly rent of $150, but undaunted he picked up a few extra bucks writing occasional drama criticism for the same newpaper and by bartering. "In the morning you'd pick up an old wreck of a typewriter; sell it by afternoon for fifteen bucks profit."

The 1929 stock market crash found Cotten still living in Miami and while he had precious little money to lose, he said for everybody else it was "Boom! Bust and blow! When it was all over the place was a paradise. Rents had gone down to nothing; merchants clamored for the opportunity of providing provisions on a lend lease basis." Not unrealistically, Cotten opted for the "slow life" of a beachcomber. His advertising job took him only a few hours each week and left him time for beach and sun. Still maintaining his interest in the theatre, he often worked in the evenings with the University Players of the Miami Civic Players. He subsequently became secretary-treasurer of that organisation and also acted in its stage productions. In one production, "Paris Bound," he was required to play the piano, and not being a musician, the music was dubbed backstage by a young divorcee, Lenore Kipp Lamont. Lenore, the mother of a young daughter, Judith, took an immediate interest in the aspiring young actor, and encouraged him to try New York again. At the time, nothing looked better to Cotten than Miami, but he wisely accepted Lenore's advice, and they set out for New York together in the summer of 1930.

A mutual friend had provided Cotten with a letter of introduction to critic Burns Mantle who introduced the young Southerner to theatrical impresario David Belasco. One version of Cotten's biography maintains that he never used the letter, but simply walked into Belasco's office where Belasco mistook him for someone else, and quickly ushered him into the 44th Street Theatre where rehearsal for one of his plays was taking place, saying, "Why, Mr. Cotten, it's a pleasure. You come right with me. I'm going down to rehearsal." Once inside the theatre, Cotten sat in the auditorium beside Belasco, who turned and said, "Now those costumes of the girls, Mr. Cotten; don't you think they would be better in yellow instead of red?" "Yes, sir," replied Cotten. "Pete," Belasco cried, "I have an excellent suggestion here from Mr. Cotten. He thinks the costumes should be yellow instead of red. Don't you think Mr. Cotten is right?" Pete agreed and Belasco turned to Cotten beaming.

Cotten told the author that the story, while amusing, was certainly apocryphal and what actually happened was that he had asked Burns Mantle to provide him with letters of introduction to the only Broadway producers whose names he knew — David Belasco and John Golden. Cotten went to see Belasco first and says, "Belasco saw me because he had to see me. What else could one do under the circumstances? Luckily he liked me enough to hire me. I still have the letter to John Golden which I never used."

Belasco hired Cotten as an assistant stage manager and understudy, first in August, 1930, as understudy to Lynne Overman in "Dancing Partner," and later in November, as understudy to Melvyn Douglas in "Tonight or Never." Cotten never had to go on for either of these healthy gentlemen and recalls it was just as well because, "I couldn't learn the lines. I don't know why it was, but I never did get them straight."

Belasco's death in 1931 terminated Cotten's New York job, and during a visit with Lenore's Boston relatives, he accepted a job as an actor with the Copley Square Theatre. That group specialised in suspense dramas and Cotten always seemed to play either the reporter or the insurance man who solves the crime. During the year-and-a half he spent with that group, he and Lenore were married in October, 1931. His last production with the company was in "The Gray Shadow," which he recalls had been "written by the stagehand who for years had scribbled in a notebook the most effective gags and situations and finally put them all in one play."

Following his tenure with the Copley Square Theatre group, Cotten hit the road in summer stock. One stint took him to Richmond in his native Virginia, where he appeared in "White Collars." The second took him to Bar Harbor, Maine, where he appeared in "Murray Hill," "Private Lives" and "The Importance of Being Earnest."

But again, New York was really the place to pursue a full-time acting career and Cotten and his wife once again returned to that city. He was lucky enough to be cast as Larry, the social *bon vivant* in "Absent Father," by Francis DeWitt. That play opened at the Vanderbilt Theatre on October 17, 1932, and was panned as a dull comedy of manners about the sanctity of divorce. Cotten was not singled out in the reviews. When theatre work was not available, he appeared in industrial films, did bits in radio, and modeled for photographers. "I was the Mr. After in those Before and After collar and suit ads. You know, the guy who goes out and gets the job because he's wearing the right collar and the right suit."

On December 19, 1933, Cotten opened at the Ethel Barrymore Theatre playing the part of Dick Ashley in "Jezebel," which starred Miriam Hopkins. While again not singled out for reviews, the play lasted on the strength of Miss Hopkins' performance. It was not until he opened in "Loose Moments" by Courtney Savage and Bertram Hobbs on February 2, 1935, that critics began to take notice of him. In a Southern aristocratic setting, Cotten played the self-centered grocery clerk who was the object of the passion of three Southern ladies. The play was bad and "Variety" said he was miscast, but as least they singled him out as a new young actor with a "pleasant stage presence."

Encouraged by this small success, Cotten was convinced that New York was the place for him. His wife, always supportive of his ambitions, became an associate editor with "Harper's Bazaar," and they moved to a house on Washington Square. In May, 1935, Cotten obtained his best role to date when he replaced Theodore Reynolds as Dickie Reynolds in "Accent on Youth," by Samuel Raphaelson at the Plymouth Theatre. The following year he played the policeman in James M. Cain's "The Postman Always Ring Twice," which opened at the Lyceum Theatre on February 25, 1936. The star of that play was the silent movie heart-throb, Richard Barthelmess, but the ensemble performers and not the star, walked off with the good reviews.

While performing in this play, Cotten was cast in a radio show along with an arrogant young dynamo named Orson Welles. The show was an educational programme about Greece and culture and when one of the actors fluffed his line, Cotten, recognising the *double entendre*, giggled out loud. Welles, who was standing beside him, joined in the laughter. This unprofessional behaviour got them both fired. They continued laughing over a cup of coffee; this *faux pas* became the basis of a long-standing friendship. Welles, who was working with the Federal Theatre, asked Cotten to join this innovative troupe.

In his memoirs, *Run-through*, John Houseman, famous theatrical producer-director, writes, "The Federal Theatre of the Works Progress Administration, which, within two years, was to be described by a leading critic as 'the chief producer of works of art in the American theatre' and which came to play such a vital part in so many of our lives, was not primarily a cultural activity. It was a relief measure conceived in a time of national misery and despair. The only artistic policy it ever had was the assumption that thousands of indigent theatre people were eager to work and that millions of Americans would enjoy the results of this work if it could be offered at a price they could afford to pay. Within a year of its formation, the Federal Theatre had more than fifteen thousand men and women on its payroll at an average wage of approximately twenty dollars a week. During the four years of its existence its productions played to more than thirty million people in more than two hundred theatres as well as portable stages, school auditoriums and public parks the country over."

Orson Welles had become involved with the Federal Theatre in 1936, when he directed his all-black version of "Macbeth" at the Lafayette Theatre in Harlem. Welles' second project for the Federal Theatre was a play called "Horse Eats Hat," which he and poet-critic Edwin Denby adapted from "Un chapeau de paille d'Italie," "The Italian Straw Hat" by Eugene Labiche. The plot of this amusing farce, according to Houseman, was "that a horse eats a hat and the owner of the horse, a bridegroom on the way to his wedding, must find the hat's owner a similar hat immediately because she, the hat's owner, cannot go home to her husband without it." The cast included Welles as the "bride's ferocious father," Virginia Welles as "the shy bride," Paula Lawrence as "The unfaithful wife," Arlene Francis as "the glamorous modiste," and Joseph Cotten, as the "harried bridegroom." The play opened at the Maxine Elliott Theatre in New York on September 26, 1936, to mixed reviews and according to Houseman, "It had for its finale one of the most extravagent accumulations of farcical horror ever assembled behind the proscenium arch of a respectable American theatre—not excluding 'Hellzapoppin.' I can still see Joe Cotten, wearing his bright yellow leather gloves, with the coveted straw hat grasped firmly between his teeth, caught between the Countess' indignant guests and the vengeful pursuit of the wedding party, leaping from sofa to table to piano top to chandelier which, at that instant, started to rise like a great golden bird, carrying him upward at the seat of his pants and Cotten himself, clinging to the rising chandelier with one hand and grasping a siphon in the other, squirted streams of soda water over the madly whirling crowd below. As he rose, scenery moved erratically up and down, props, seized with a sudden life of their own, were seen to fly off suddenly in various directions and a huge Paris-by-night backdrop came crashing down onto the stage floor, narrowly missing a platoon of stagehands — one of them in red flannel underwear — who had chosen this moment to carry a thirty-two foot ladder slowly, horizontally and imperturbably across the stage."

While not listed in the cast, Cotten worked in Welles' next production for the Federal Theatre, "The Tragical History of Doctor Faustus." It opened at the Maxine Elliott Theatre on January 9, 1937, and ran until the following May 9th. The fourth and final Welles project was "The Cradle Will Rock," by Marc Blitzstein, which opened at the Windsor Theatre on January 3, 1938. It had been scheduled for the summer of 1937, but when an Equity ruling involving WPA subsidies and non-Equity actors postponed it, Welles, with Houseman and Cotten, left to form their own theatre group which they called The Mercury Theatre. Houseman was named president and Welles, vice-president. The company found a home in the Comedy Theatre at 110 West 41st Street, which they renamed the Mercury. There, for the next two years, they presented some of the most revolutionary theatre ever seen on the American stage.

Their first production was a modern-dress "Julius Caesar" starring Welles. Cotten played Plubius and the play and the acting ensemble earned excellent reviews. For their next production they chose an uproariously funny and undisciplined bit of Elizabethan mirth, "The Shoemaker's Holiday," by Thomas Dekker. Cotten played Rowland Lacy, a juvenile romantic lover, and the cast included George Coulouris, John Hoysradt (Hoyt), and Vincent Price; all won raves from the critics.

Cotten did not appear in Welles' production of George Bernard Shaw's "Heartbreak House" but was cast in Welles' version of William Gillette's "Too Much Johnson." Welles envisioned this comedy as a sort of Mack Sennett caprice and planned to include in the production two filmed interludes consisting of chase scenes in the Keystone Kops genre. Houseman recalls one of these scenes: "Orson Welles, seated high astride the peaked roof of the Washington Market, urging Joe Cotten to greater efforts as he swung from eave to eave while a raging cucold threatened him from above and the Keystone Kops, all twelve of them, including myself, in sugar-loaf helmets, waited for him on the cobblestones thirty feet below." Money unfortunately ran out on this production and the filming was stopped, but they did manage to present the play without the filmed sequences at the Stony Creek Summer Theatre in Stony Creek, Connecticut. It flopped, but one member of the audience was so impressed with Cotten's performance that she remembered him nine months later when she was preparing a play for Broadway. The lady was Katharine Hepburn and the play was "The Philadelphia Story."

During that nine-month interlude, Cotten performed his last role for the Mercury Theatre playing Barrere in *Danton's Death,* Geoffrey Dunlop's play about the French Revolution, which opened November 2, 1938.

Of working with Orson Welles, Cotten told the author, "We were all blessed to have worked with such a man as Welles, to have had the opportunity to appear as an ensemble was a rare and wonderful experience and it gave us the chance to develop a precise style of acting. I have always been grateful for that opportunity."

In the meantime, Katharine Hepburn had taken a less than self-imposed hiatus from the screen after being named box-office poison by the motion picture exhibitors. Miss Hepburn felt that the best way to regain her reputation was to captivate Broadway with a good play and her intuition proved correct. The play she selected was Philip Barry's "The Philadelphia Story" and Miss Hepburn joined the author, the Theatre Guild, and a silent fourth partner, Howard Hughes, in backing the play. It opened at the Shubert Theatre on March 28, 1939, with a cast that included Van Heflin, Shirley Booth and an adolescent Anne Baxter. The reviews were unanimously enthusiastic, and the play settled in for a run of 415 performances after which it toured for 254 more. Cotten played C.K. Dexter Haven, the well-bred imbibing ex-husband of Tracy Lord, a stuffy Philadelphia blue-blood played by Miss Hepburn. Critics finally had the proper chance to evaluate Cotten as an actor and found him perfect as Barry's urbane and suave character who skillfully brought charm and insight to his performance. One critic admired his "easy stage presence and unaffected graciousness of manner" and said "he makes the character human."

During the play's run, Cotten also appeared in a radio soap-opera with Martha Scott called "The Story of Alice Blair." Cotten's radio work right up until the Fifties was prolific and included the "Columbia Workshop" and "Mercury Theatre on the Air" (both with Orson Welles), a series in 1944-45 with Constance Moore called "Ceiling Unlimited," "Screen Guild Theatre" and the "Philco Radio Playhouse" in 1953. He also appeared several times on the "Lux Radio Theatre" — "The Great Man's Lady" with Barbara Stanwyck (June 28, 1943), "Penny Serenade" with Irene Dunne (May 8, 1944).

It was on this series that he allegedly made a blunder which has been quoted ever since. As the star on one week's programme, he was to announce the star for the following week. TV Guide's version maintains that "Just before air time, there was a sudden change in plans for the latter production. Sonny Tufts was substituted for the actor whose name Cotten had read at rehearsal. The change was made in the script, but Cotten had not been informed. As was customary, the upcoming star was introduced with great fanfare and a description befitting one of the Barrymores. On the air, when Cotten reached the end of a string of high-flown adjectives and unexpectedly came upon the name of Sonny Tufts, he read it — disbelievingly, incredulously — as "Sonny *Tufts*?"

However, Cotten told the author that this incident actually occured on a segment of the show, "Suspense" directed by Bill Spears. The guest star he was to have introduced was Cary Grant. Cotten was not informed of the casting change and says, "How else could you have read it?" He added that over the years many actors have taken credit for this famous *faux pas*.

When Katharine Hepburn began to peddle the screen rights to "The Philadelphia Story" as her "comeback" vehicle, she elected not to co-star with either Cotten or Van Heflin, both unproven commodities on the motion-picture screen, and instead hand-picked box-office insurance in Cary Grant and James Stewart.

While the role of C.K. Dexter Haven would have been a plum as a motion-picture debut, Cotten had other fish to fry and was therefore not displeased over the rejection. By the end of the play's tour, Orson Welles asked Cotten and others from his Mercury Theatre days to join him in Hollywood, thereby providing Cotten with a motion-picture debut in the greatest American film classic — *Citizen Kane*.

Cotten was Jedediah Leland, the boyhood friend-reporter, who becomes the "conscience and gadfly" of Charles Foster Kane in this controversial masterpiece. While all the players in the cast were overshadowed by the brilliant and egocentric Welles himself, they were all praised for their excellent interpretations and the ensemble playing was reminiscent of their earlier success with the Mercury Theatre. Otis Ferguson, writing in the "New Republic," said, "Joseph Cotten had a part that was possibly short on savor because when he was with the great man he had to be something of a chump and when he was talking of him afterwards he had to be something of a Mr. Chips, with a twinkle and lip-smacking." Of this first experience in feature filmmaking, Cotten later explained, "I'd never made a movie before and I was scared to death of the machinery, the technical things. I didn't know if I could handle it. But Orson made it easy. He was prepared. He had done his homework for two years in Hollywood. He turned out to be an instinctive master of the camera, in the same category as Carol Reed and Hitchcock."

With Orson Welles in *Citizen Kane* (1941).

After *Citizen Kane*, British producer Alexander Korda cast Cotten as one of the many suitors of Merle Oberon (then Korda's Wife) in *Lydia* (1941). Cotten played the doctor who loved her the best. Welles then cast him in one of his best roles, that of Eugene Morgan in *The Magnificent Ambersons* (1942), Welles' picturesque though somewhat lackadaisical depiction of the decline of a minor American aristocratic family. While the roles played by Agnes Moorehead, Tim Holt and Anne Baxter (whom Cotten had remembered from "The Philadelphia Story" and suggested to Welles for the part) were more energetically compelling, Cotten's ability to express the verities of gentlemanliness — i.e. kindness, tolerance, steadfastness — made his characterisation effective.

Welles used Cotten and the Mercury Players once again in *Journey Into Fear* (1942). Cotten and Welles prepared this script together and of this endeavour, Cotten said, "With Orson you write for hours, then discuss for hours, and then write for hours. Sometimes you don't even get home for weeks." The direction of this picture was assigned by RKO to Norman Foster with Welles being only the co-author and producer. The result was heavyhanded, rather than the light parody of innocents abroad as was intended, in which Cotten played an armament expert.

While at RKO with the Mercury Players, Cotten appeared in a short subject, *How To Be a Star* (1942). The players included Arlene Francis, Anne Baxter, Chester Morris, Milton Berle and Leif Erickson. Cotten and Miss Baxter were seen having their portraits sketched at the Brown Derby.

Welles' unorthodox and expensive production habits and the ensuing controversy which followed *Citizen Kane's* release made it impossible for him to maintain his Mercury Players as a motion-picture ensemble. The group was forced to split up, and its actors left to seek jobs at other studios. Cotten had the good fortune to sign a seven-year contract with David O. Selznick in 1942. Part of *Citizen Kane* had been shot on the

With Anne Baxter in *The Magnificent Ambersons* (1941).

Pathé lot in Culver City where Selznick International was housed. Cotten says, "I had come to have a how-do-you-do friendship with Selznick. It was simply a matter of geography and when RKO and the Mercury Theatre ended their association, I was invited by Selznick to join his company." Selznick cast him in several of his personally produced motion pictures and loaned him out to other studios as the romantic lead in first-rate pictures opposite some of the screen's most popular feminine stars.

His first assignment was in Alfred Hitchcock's *Shadow of a Doubt* (1943), where he played a silken villain, the murderer of wealthy widows, and who in the end is killed by a train. This picture is Hitchcock's favorite, and the New York "Times" said of Cotten, "As the progressively less charming Uncle Charles, Joseph Cotten plays with smooth, insinuating ease while injecting a harsh and bitter quality which nicely becomes villainy. He has obviously kept an eye on Orson Welles."

Selznick then loaned him to Universal in the thankless role of the daring young Flying Tiger in *Hers To Hold* (1943) opposite a now grown-up, and still extremely popular, Deanna Durbin. Neither critics nor audiences were offended by this bit of patriotic musical nonsense, and it helped introduce Cotten to the ladies in the audience. During the making of this picture, Hedda Hopper had ridiculously linked Cotten and Miss Durbin as a romantic duo in her gossip column. Cotten warned Miss Hopper, saying it was very embarrassing to both him and his wife and told her what he would do if she persisted. As always, the persistent Miss Hopper persisted and one evening Cot-

With Teresa Wright in *Shadow of a Doubt* (1943).

ten met her at a party, walked over and planted a kick of his foot on her posterior, as he had threatened he would. Miss Hopper did not mention Cotten in that light again.

Once again on loan-out, this time to M-G-M, Cotten was cast as the Scotland Yard detective who discovers that Charles Boyer, a suave murderer, is endeavouring to drive his young wife, Ingrid Bergman, insane. The picture was *Gaslight* (1944). Based on Patrick Hamilton's play, "Angel Street," it was deftly directed by the cultivated George Cukor and earned Miss Bergman the first of her two Academy Awards. While Cotten was his usual, smoothly restrained self, film historian, Gary Carey said, "Joseph Cotten has the unhappy chore of playing the completely revamped character of the detective who helps the wife out of her plight. In the play, he is a roly-poly eccentric; in the film he becomes a bland second lead whose function is to provide Miss Bergman with a happily-ever-after ending." When Selznick heard that the script had been changed to implicate a romance between the characters played by Miss Bergman and Cotten, he wrote his objections to M-G-M executives saying, "I'm sorry to say this, but I think the attempt to indicate a love story with the Cotten character is impossible. I don't believe it, and there is no reason why I should believe it. I'd like to believe it, because I'd like to see Cotten's very weak part become as important as possible, but in the final analysis, it is the picture that is important, and the better the picture, the more even Cotten will benefit." The implications remained in the script despite Selznick's objections, and while there is no doubt that Selznick was a powerhouse at promotion and advertising with his eye on the dollar, it was this kind of insight concerning the integrity of each aspect of a particular film which set him apart from the ordinary dollar-grabbing producer.

Gaslight was certainly timely and beneficial to Cotten's career. But it was Selznick's astute handling of this gentleman star that was more beneficial. Their professional alliance came at a time when most of Hollywood's leading men were off the screen serving in the military. Cotten's age (thirty-nine) and a football injury prevented his induction. This left him in the enviable position as one of the few mature, romantic leads on the screen. While Spencer Tracy was active at M-G-M, he did not have the same romantic appeal, and Clark Gable, James Stewart, Robert Montgomery, Erroll Flynn, et. al. were all in the military; while the younger leads — Van Johnson, Gregory Peck — were not yet strong competition for Cotten in the eyes of the American female movie-going audience.

Selznick shrewdly cast Cotten as the Naval Lieutenant-suitor of Claudette Colbert in *Since You Went Away* (1944), Selznick's personally produced idealistic view of the American home front. James Agee cleverly poked fun at Cotten's role by saying, "As the forever rejected bachelor suitor, who, clouding the screen with discreetly alarming threats of adulterous desire, forever comes back to Miss Colbert for more." Selznick's casting paid off and in a Gallup Poll for "Photoplay" magazine, Joseph Cotten was named one of the year's top ten stars.

Cotten, who was working on *Gaslight* and *Since You Went Away* simultaneously, had always been fond of practical jokes. In a bit of frivolity he enlisted *Gaslight* co-star, Ingrid Bergman, to play a masterful prank on Selznick. They dressed up as maid and butler, and successfully passed themselves off as domestics for the evening's dinner party at Selznick's home. After an hour of not being recognised, Miss Bergman leaned over and whispered in Selznick's ear, "As long as Joe and I are your slaves, we figured we might as well serve your guests."

By now Joseph Cotten was firmly established as a leading member in the Selznick Players. Selznick announced that he would be the star of "The House of Dr. Edwards" to be directed by Alfred Hitchcock and of *Double Indemnity,* to co-star Joan Fontaine. However, per usual, Selznick's packaging plans never quite materialised and

With Ginger Rogers in *I'll Be Seeing You* (1944).

neither of these pictures starred Cotten. "The House of Dr. Edwards" was re-titled *Spellbound* and starred Gregory Peck and Ingrid Bergman, both fellow Selznick Players, and Paramount acquired the rights to *Double Indemnity* and cast Fred MacMurray and a Dietrichesque Barbara Stanwyck in the leading roles. Instead, Selznick assigned Cotten the role of the shell-shocked soldier who is rehabilitated by ex-convict Ginger Rogers in *I'll Be Seeing You* (1944), produced by Dore Schary.

When Schary first suggested the story to Selznick, Selznick wanted no part of the off-beat script and refused to lend him the services of Cotten, saying, "You won't be able to get an important star to play either part." Schary bet Selznick $100 he could and came back a short time later saying Miss Rogers had accepted the part. Selznick gave Schary the one hundred dollars and Cotten's services. Surprisingly, this depressing picture met with audience approval and Cotten, as the soldier, and Miss Rogers, as the prison parolee, who meet at Christmas time without knowing of each other's embarrassments, were both excellent. The New York "Times" said, "Cotten plays the shell-shocked veteran with a supreme restraint and with a calm and determined independence that beautifully reveals his pain and pride." The New York "Herald-Tribune" said, "The scene with him alone in his hotel room suffering an attack of battle fatigue with his racing heart thumping on the sound track is as hair-raising a sequence as has ever been filmed."

This series of box-office successes convinced Selznick to entrust Cotten to co-star with Jennifer Jones in *Love Letters* (1945), a position Selznick thought any actor should consider the *ne plus ultre,* for by now Miss Jones occupied the foremost positon in Selznick's career and private life. *Love Letters* was a bit of wartime fantasy in which Cotten played the G-I who wrote letters to Miss Jones, who believed them to be from her husband, who, unbeknownst to her was dead. This bit of fluff delighted the harried wartime public and was one of the most popular pictures of the year. Spurred with enthusiasm and confidence in Cotten, Selznick cast him in another co-starring role with Miss Jones in *Duel in the Sun* (1946), Cotten played the good brother who rivals his outlaw brother, Gregory Peck, for the affections of half-caste Jennifer Jones. Although a top money-making picture, most ctitics found this over-blown western too exaggerated and violent and felt Cotten merely looked "mournful."

Cotten's next role, and one of his most popular, was the romantic consort of Loretta Young in *The Farmer's Daughter* (1947). Produced by Dore Schary, this picture cast him as the senator-son of political patriarch Ethel Barrymore, into whose home comes a Swedish domestic, Loretta Young, whose abilities included not only cooking, skating and the art of the *masseuse,* but also political aspirations as an incorruptible lady of Congress. Although super stardom continued to elude him, Cotten scored another resounding box-office triumph.

What turned out to be Cotten's last film under the Selznick aegis is ironically one of his best remembered. This was *Portrait of Jennie* (1948) and for a third time co-starred him with Jennifer Jones. Cotten had the role of the painter who uses as his inspiration the ghost of a girl who had been dead for many years. At the time of its release, it was considered an overly-produced fantasy that was a box-office flop. However, Europeans, including director, Luis Buñuel liked the picture, and Cotten received the Best Actor Award at the Venice Film Festival. In retrospect, this has be-

With Jennifer Jones in *Love Letters* (1945).

With Jennifer Jones in *Duel in the Sun* (1946).

With Loretta Young in *The Farmer's Daughter* (1947.)

With Jennifer Jones in *Portrait of Jennie* (1948).

With Michael Wilding and Ingrid Bergman in *Under Capricorn* (1949).

come a very popular cult picture with film buffs, partially erasing its initial critical disregard.

In 1948, David O. Selznick Productions, Incorporated was in the process of liquidation after years of financial erosion. A veteran of twenty-five years of producing, Selznick said he was tired and sold the contracts of his players to Warner Brothers. The remainder of Cotten's contract was included in this transaction and although he objected, he resignedly accepted his fate and remained Selznick's close friend until his death in 1965.

Cotten has great admiration for Selznick and says, "In my opinion, it was David's extraordinary ability and taste in conducting and presenting his stable of talent that gave it its unique aura, and set it off as an elite group of stars." Cotten goes on to say, "I only received two memos from David in my life. One was while I was in London and the bellboy in my hotel arrived at my room with it. I said, "Slip it under the door." And he said, "I don't think I can get it *through* the door even after you open it."

The two assignments given to Cotten by Warner Brothers were enough to make any actor balk. The first was *Under Capricorn* (1949), a costume drama-thriller directed by Alfred Hitchcock. The story revolved around Ingrid Bergman, an English lady who falls in love with a stable groom and ex-convict, Joseph Cotten. It was slowly-paced and not the usual Hitchcock fodder and a flop at the box office which only French audiences accepted. Hitchcock, who likes the story even today, says it was simply a matter of Cotten being miscast. He was too much the gentleman for the role of the groom, but Hitchcock was unable to acquire Burt Lancaster whom he had originally wanted.

The second Warner Brothers assignment was even a bigger disaster, notorious for its inducing Bette Davis to sever her seventeen-year association with that studio. The picture was *Beyond the Forest* (1949), in which Warner Brothers again miscast Cotten as the unsuspecting earnest Wisconsin country doctor whose wife, Rosa Moline (Bette Davis doubly miscast), is having an affair with a Chicago industrialist (David Brian) and who berates her husband for not being able to afford the money for her much-needed "vacation" in Chicago. The advertisements blazened, "A twelve o'clock girl in a nine o'clock town," but it all simply spelled BOMB! Today, Miss Davis has two succinct comments to make when recalling

With Bette Davis in *Beyond the Forest* (1949).

this picture. One is "Now, *really*, do you think anything could have stopped me from getting to Chicago if I wanted to get there?" Secondly, "Why would any wife in her right mind want to leave a man as charming as Joseph Cotten. They should have cast Eugene Pallette!"

After these two flops, Cotten was free of his commitments to Warner Brothers, and curiously it was Selznick who rescued him. Selznick had entered into a co-production deal in Great Britain with Sir Alexander Korda and Sir Carol Reed and offered Cotten the lead in *The Third Man* (1950), one of the screen's most celebrated suspense films. Cotten played the American who blunders upon the mystery of a friend's dubious death in the streets of Vienna and has a romance with a beautiful refugee, Alida Valli. This tautly-written, directed and musically scored film comes to a

In *The Third Man* (1950).

nerve-wracking *denouement* when, after travelling the streets of Vienna learning what he can about his missing friend, he discovers him to be alive, but by that time has learned so much about this evil character (Harry Lime as played by Orson Welles) that he kills him.

Before this picture was made, Cotten and Valli had appeared at RKO in a similarly enigmatic but less compelling thriller, *Walk Softly, Stranger* (1950). Here Cotten played a mysterious man who works in an Ohio shoe factory and courts the boss's crippled daughter, but he turns out to be an ex-criminal. This B-thriller was held from release until after *The Third Man* and gained box-office mileage as a result.

Also as part of Selznick's English productions, Cotten narrated the revised American version of *The Wild Heart* (1952), which Jennifer Jones had made abroad in 1950, but which Selznick had reworked and held for release in the United States.

At the age of forty-five, Cotten found parts in first-rate pictures harder to obtain, and therefore signed a short-term, non-exclusive contract with 20th Century-Fox. During the next three years, he appeared in a series of B-pictures with star billing, most of which, because of the success of *The Third Man,* were second-rate thrillers.

20th Century-Fox first cast him in the western, *Two Flags West* (1950). It co-starred Linda Darnell and Jeff Chandler, and Cotten played a chivalrous Southern colonel. Two undistinguished romances followed — *September Affair* (1951) at Paramount with Joan Fontaine and *Half Angel* (1951) at 20th Century-Fox with Loretta Young. Paramount then cast him in *Peking Express* (1951) at M-G-M co-starring Barbara Stanwyck and he vied with Scott Brady for the affections of waitress Shelley Winters, in Universal's *Untamed Frontier* (1952).

Returning to 20th Century-Fox, he starred in three suspense-dramas. He was the bank embezzler in *The Steel Trap* (1952), and the brother-in-law who discovers Jean Peters to be guilty of murder in *Blueprint for Murder* (1953), but his best picture during these three years was *Niagara* (1953). This was the film that catapulted Marilyn Monroe to stardom via a skin-tight red dress and one of the longest on-screen walks — 116 feet of film — showing Miss Monroe's undulating body. Cotten played her psychotic Korean veteran husband whose explanation of his love for her was, "I guess it was the way she slopped beer on the tables." Cotten discovers that Miss Monroe and her lover, Richard Allan, plan to kill him, but he kills Allan first, and in a dramatic scene in the Carillon Belfry, he strangles Miss Monroe and in a boat plunges over Niagara Falls to his death.

Not finding this string of B-pictures to his liking, Cotten withdrew from the screen for two years and appeared on Broadway in "Sabrina Fair" opposite Margaret Sullavan. The play opened in November 1953, and ran until the following July. While Miss Sullavan was definitely the star of the play, Cotten received outstanding notices as Linus Larrabee Jr., the strong, sporting, laconic, pipe-smoking Don Juan, a role he had played in the late Forties at the La Jolla Playhouse in California.

During his absence from the motion-picture screen, he explored another professional avenue — television. He debuted in Evelyn Waugh's "The Green Wall" on October 3, 1954, and on November 16, 1954, he and Margaret Sullavan starred in a television production of "State of the Union." Since that time he has appeared continually as a guest on most of television's dramatic shows, including being host-narrator-star on "The 20th Century-Fox Hour" (1955), and "The Joseph Cotten Theatre" (1959). One of his most important appearances was as the star of "Breakdown" (November 13, 1955), the first television show to be directed by Alfred Hiltchcock on "Alfred Hitchcock Presents."

Returning to motion pictures in 1955, he continued to draw only B roles. In the German-made *Special Delivery* (1955) he was an embassy *charge d' affairs* in a Soviet satellite country, and in *The Bottom of the Bottle* (1956) he was a rich rancher. In *The Killer Is Loose* (1956) he was the detective on whom Wendell Corey seeks vengeance, in *The Halliday Brand* (1957) he was a cotton baron, and in *From Earth to the Moon* (1958), he was a munitions manufacturer. During this time Orson Welles released two films in which Cotten made guest appearances. In *Othello* (1955) he played a Roman senator (the picture was actually made in 1951) and in *Touch of Evil* (1958), he was the sheriff.

This string of mediocre film fare convinced a fifty-three-year-old Cotten that his position in Hollywood had, with the advent of television, diminished to the point where he could no longer command first-rate vehicles. Yet, a ham at heart, with an ever-present desire to keep working, he once again left screen for stage. This time he starred in "Once More, With Feeling" which opened at the National Theatre on October 21, 1958. He played Victor Fabian, an egomaniacal orchestra

With Marilyn Monroe in *Niagara* (1953).

conductor who renews his love affair with his ex-wife and harpist, Arlene Francis. As always, Cotten was praised for his deft attractiveness, but some critics felt he was not ruthless enough as the musical egoist.

While television continued to offer him starring roles, he returned to motion pictures now accepting supporting roles with star billing. He supported Dirk Bogarde and Ava Gardner in *The Angel Wore Red* (1960), as the cynical, one-eyed American journalist during the Spanish Civil War. While *The Angel Wore Red* was being filmed on location in Italy, his wife of twenty-nine years died of leukemia in a Rome clinic on January 7, 1960. She had been ailing for months but neither she nor her husband had realised how seriously ill she really was. Their storybook marriage and gracious life-style had made the Cottens one of Hollywood's most admired couples and had earned them a reputation for being among the elite of Hollywood's social arbiters. In her autobiography, "The Lonely Life," Bette Davis wrote of Hollywood's social life and its hostesses — "Hollywood's social whirl is for the most part, pretentious and politic. There were a few who gathered fascinating people together at a well-appointed board groaning under excellent food and wine. Certainly Basil Rathbone's wife, Ouida, was a magnificent hostess as was Joseph Cotten's wife, Lenore. The David Selznicks and the Jules Steins also entertained brilliantly. But most of Hollywood who decorated their homes like Scottish shooting boxes and sent the ladies off to the powder room while the gentlemen stayed at the table sipping brandy didn't know a cadenza from an arpeggio."

Cotten, who rarely discussed his personal life for the press, said on one occasion, "In 1931, I met a beautiful girl. She was called Lenore Kipp. She wasn't an actress, and she didn't come to me for any autograph. Lenore and I met by chance and we decided to marry. Well, here today we are still married. We haven't had any trouble, no separations, no divorces." (Cotten's step-daughter-Judith, married television director James P. Young in 1950, by whom she has a daughter.)

Shortly after his wife's sudden death, friends invited Cotten to dinner and present on that occasion was actress Patricia Medina whom Cotten had met many years before when she was married to English actor, Richard Green. Miss Medina was born in London on July 19, 1923. She made her debut in motion pictures in England in 1942, and four years later came to the United States where she appeared in supporting roles in *The Secret Heart* (1946), *Moss Rose* (1947), *The Foxes of Harrow* (1947) and *The Three Musketeers* (1948). Her career in motion pictures never really got off the ground, but during the Fifties she appeared in starring roles in B films, the most important of which was Orson Welles' *Mr. Arkadin* (1955). In 1969, she played the prostitute in *The Killing of Sister George*. She had married Green in 1941 and divorced him eleven years later.

Cotten quietly courted Miss Medina for several months, and on October 20, 1960, they were married in the Tower Drive Bel Air home of David Selznick and his wife, Jennifer Jones, Cotten's former co-star. Selznick gave the bride away.

Another supporting role which gave Cotten star billing was in *The Last Sunset* (1961) starring Rock Hudson, Kirk Douglas and Dorothy Malone, after which he left the screen yet another time, this time for four years. He appeared on television and starred in two theatre productions with Patricia Medina. The first of these was a coast-to-coast tour from January to May, 1962, in a minor mystery play called "Prescription: Murder" by William Link and Richard Levinson with a cast that included Agnes Moorehead and Thomas Mitchell. That fall, on October 31, the couple opened on Broadway in "Calculated Risk" a slightly better mystery play written by Joseph Hayes and directed by Robert Montgomery. The play earned very good reviews and ran for 222 performances. Of this experience Cotten said, "I'm enjoying 'Calculated Risk.' I've enjoyed this experience particularly because of the pleasure I've had in working with Bob Montgomery. He is quite a gentleman, has enormous finesse and a fine background in the theatre."

In 1963, Cotten signed as narrator of the NBC television series entitled "Hollywood and the Stars," an immensely popular nostalgia series which presented retrospective views of celebrities such as Bette Davis. Cotten says, "I've had more comment on that than anything I've done on television. Stars of the Thirties and Forties had so much more glamour than we have today."

The following year Cotten and his wife toured for three months in a new play "The Seven Ways of Love," an episodic digest of romantic tales from Ovid to Norman Mailer (Norman *Mailer*!) devised by Paul Gregory, Thomas Clapp and George Eels.

Cotten's return to the screen in 1965, after a four-year interlude, was part of the pubescent nostalgia revival when he played the evil doctor in *Hush...Hush, Sweet Charlotte* which cast him opposite two veterans of those glamorous thirties — Bette Davis and Joan Crawford. This picture was planned as a sequel to *What Ever Happened to Baby Jane?* (1964) which had so brilliantly used the diverse talents of Misses Davis and Crawford. However, Miss Crawford got pneumonia and when the production could be delayed no longer,

With Bette Davis and Olivia de Havilland in *Hush...Hush, Sweet Charlotte* (1965).

she was replaced by Miss Davis' friend and former co-star, Olivia de Havilland. Director Robert Aldrich's first choice for a replacement was Katharine Hepburn who was not available. His second choice was Vivien Leigh whom Miss Davis felt would be miscast. Other candidates included Loretta Young, but it was Miss Davis who whole-heartedly endorsed Miss de Havilland.

Cotten defended Miss Crawford by saying, "I've never been able to understand this business about the show must go on. It's absolute nonsense. People in other lines of work are allowed to be sick now and then. Why shouldn't actors? If we owe anything to the theatre — and I've never been convinced of that — it is to get well so we can give a good performance." Of his two veteran co-stars, Cotten said, "Olivia is charming and intelligent. She never ruffles. Unlike a lot of actresses, she works with you, not against you." And he called Miss Davis "the most direct person in the world. She works harder to achieve perfection than anyone I know."

At sixty, Cotten, a twenty-four-year veteran of films, witnessed more major changes in the motion-picture industry than at any other time in his career. With the decline of Hollywood and the rise of television as the major entertainment medium, the motion-picture industry experienced growing pains which now emphasised youth, and a taste for what was often exaggerated "realism."

Actors of Cotten's age were a little better off than actresses of the same age. Although the roles now offered him were not always first-rate parts in first-rate pictures, he was fortunate enough to still be a marketable commodity in that mercurial profession. Whether the roles were supporting ones in major productions or starring parts in low-budget European products, Cotten accepted each philosophically and brought to each the professional elan that had become his trademark. During the past decade Cotten has continued to be one of the most-employed veteran actors in both motion pictures and television and insists the ham in him will never allow him to retire. He steadfastly maintains that "one must today read a script with benign eyes." That same realism allowed him to appear in a television commercial promoting Bufferin, of which he said, "The money was just too good; it would have been disrespectful to turn it down."

In 1966, he played the film producer in *The Oscar* and patterned his portrayal after David O. Selznick. In the final release however, several of his scenes were cut out because they were so identifiably Selznick, and Selznick had died the summer before. Cotten had said of his former employer, "He's a lot like David Belasco in his mania for accuracy and his absolute insistance on personally checking every detail, from script to screen. Selznick's a terrific worker. I think he's the nearest thing to a real genius in Hollywood and Hollywood is full of geniuses."

Despite the dearth of good roles, once in a while a plum part comes along as with the role of Richard Chamberlain's father in *Petulia* (1968), where Cotten was at his professional best. Considerably less of a plum, but curious for its casting, was *Latitude Zero* (1970) the Japanese produced science fiction in which Cotten's wife, Patricia Medina, stabbed him to death.

In another co-Japanese production, that same year, he played Henry Stimson, Secretary of War in *Tora! Tora! Tora!,* a lavishly-produced extravaganza. Fun and the money enticed him to join Vincent Price, a friend from the Mercury Theatre days, for a blood-thirsty romp in *The Abominable Dr. Phibes* (1971), where he played a doctor. The following year he appeared in another horror flick, *Baron Blood,* an Italian production which cast him as the reincarnation of a sadistic nobleman. In 1973, he appeared in *Soylent Green,* the science-fiction film set in New York City in the year 2022.

Although Cotten managed to land a few choice roles during these lean Hollywood years, he was for the most part only marking time to keep his name before the public in between these occasional good roles. Unquestionably his best film during this decade was *A Delicate Balance* (1973) based on Edward Albee's play. It co-starred Katharine Hepburn, Paul Scofield, Lee Remick, Kate Reid and Betsy Blair and was directed by Tony Richardson. Cotten and Miss Blair played the terrified and unwanted neighbors in Albee's claustrophobic melodrama.

Many of the pictures Cotten has appeared in since 1965 were made in Europe and many of these have never been released either because they were never completed due to lack of financing or have yet to be dubbed into English. The most noteworthy of these is *The Scientific Cardplayer* made in Italy in 1972, in which Cotten's co-star for the third time was Bette Davis. Some of his better performances in recent years have been in films made expressly for television, the best of which was "The Screaming Woman" (1972) which co-starred Olivia de Havilland and Walter Pidgeon.

Since his first success in motion pictures, Cotten has always maintained a luxurious life-style, which for years centered around Villa Tramonto, an imposing Mediterranean-style house in Pacific Palisades. Sumptuous almost beyond description, it boasted both outdoor and indoor swimming pools and a tennis court.

When much of his work began to take him to Europe for many months each year, he sold this home and bought a penthouse in the Los Angeles Shoreham Towers. Always fastidiously groomed, he keeps in shape playing tennis. He owns a collection of *commedia dell'arte* figures which would be the pride of any museum, and one of his greatest pleasures it to travel cross-country in his Rolls-Royce.

Cotten makes no pretence about the "art" of acting. He says, "Directors don't like 'thinking actors'—actors who discuss their work too much. They want you to do it, not talk about it. Well, I don't analyze my own talent. One director told me, 'When you come on, bring *something* with you.' What is the something? It may be superconfidence, the thing that makes many people dislike actors personally. But you need the confidence. Imagine a grown man getting up in the morning and saying, 'Well, I'm going to play cowboys today.' You have to make people believe you. You have to spin this thread of reality." It is this pragmatic stance which has been the mainstay of Cotten's career.

Although he prefers not to discuss his own opinions of acting in depth, nevertheless he has great respect for his fellow players and is quick to compliment them. Marilyn Monroe: "She was a shy, lovely creature who had an extraordinary sense of humor when it came to looking at herself." Ava Gardner: "A very accomplished actress, more so than most people realize." Katharine Hepburn: "I respected her and adored her. She's one of those actresses with a sure instinct for theatre, and as a human being her principles and values are completely sound." Ingrid Bergman: "She has extraordinary talent and a luminous quality. She has lived a lot of life." Orson Welles: "Orson is the best director in the world. He is unerringly perceptive about what an actor can and can't do." Margaret Sullavan: "She had a rare and wonderful talent." Marlene Dietrich (Cotten did a magic act with her and Welles for the USO during World War II): "She's a cozy person to be with, and a great giggler. She giggles a lot. She's simple and direct." Jennifer Jones: "My favorite leading lady. But then she was the boss's wife." And finally, of himself, he simply states, "I'm never completely satisfied with anything I do. I always think my best is the one I'm going to do next."

The Feature Film Appearances of Joseph Cotten

Citizen Kane (RKO, 1941) Screenplay by Herman J. Mankiewicz and Orson Welles. Directed by Orson Welles. *Cast:* Orson Welles, Dorothy Comingore, Joseph Cotten, Everett Sloane, George Coulouris, Ray Collins, Ruth Warrick, Erskine Sanford, William Alland, Agnes Moorehead, Richard Baer, Paul Stewart, Fortunio Bonanova, Joan Blair, Buddy Swan, Harry Shannon, Georgia Backus, Al Eben, Charles Bennett, Philip Van Zandt, Milt Kibbee, Tom Curran, Sonny Bupp, Irving Mitchell, Edith Evanson, Arthur Kay, Tudor Williams, Herbert Corthell, Alan Ladd, Louise Currie, Eddie Cole, Walter Sande, Arthur O'Connell, Richard Wilson, Katherine Trosper, Benny Rubin, Edmund Cobb, Frances Neal, Robert Dudley, Ellen Lowe, Gus Schilling, Gino Corrado.

Lydia (Korda-United Artists, 1941) Screenplay by Ben Hecht and Samuel Hoffenstein from a story by Julien Duvivier and L. Bus-Fekete. Directed by Julien Duvivier. *Cast:* Merle Oberon, Joseph Cotten, Edna May Oliver, Alan Marshall, Hans Yaray, George Reeves, John Halliday, Sara Allgood, Billy Roy, Frank Conlan.

The Magnificent Ambersons (RKO, 1942). Screenplay by Orson Welles from the novel by Booth Tarkington. Directed by Orson Welles. *Cast:* Joseph Cotten, Dolores Costello, Anne Baxter, Tim Holt, Agnes Moorehead, Ray Collins, Richard Bennett, Erskine Sanford, Don Dillaway, J. Louis Johnson, Charles Phipps, Dorothy Vaughan, Elmer Jerome, Olive Ball, Nina Guilbert, John Elliott, Anne O'Neal, Kathryn Sheldon, Georgia Backus, Henry Roquemore, Hilda Plowright, Mel Ford, Bob Pittard, Lillian Nicholson, Billy Elmer, New Kelly, Maynard Holmes, Gus Schilling, Bobby Cooper, Drew Roddy, Jack Baxley, Heenan Elliott, Nancy Gates, John Maguire, Ed Howard, William Blees, James Westerfield, Philip Morris, Jack Santoro, Louis Hayward; *Narration of Credits:* Orson Welles.

Journey Into Fear (RKO, 1942). Screenplay by Orson Welles and Joseph Cotten from the novel by Eric Ambler. Directed by Norman Foster. *Cast:* Orson Welles, Joseph Cotten, Dolores Del Rio, Ruth Warrick, Agnes Moorehead, Everett Sloane, Jack Moss, Richard Bennett, Jack Durant, Eustace Wyatt, Frank Readick, Stefan Schnabel, Hans Conreid, Robert Meltzer.

Shadow of a Doubt (Universal, 1943). Screenplay by Thornton Wilder, Alma Reville and Sally Benson from a story by Gordon McDonell. Directed by Alfred Hitchcock. *Cast:* Joseph Cotten, Teresa Wright, MacDonald Carey, Henry Travers, Patricia Collinge, Hume Cronyn, Wallace Ford, Charles Bates, Edna May Wonacott, Irving Bacon, Clarence Muse, Janet Shaw, Estelle Jewell.

Hers To Hold (Universal, 1943). Screenplay by Lewis R. Foster from a story by John D. Klorer. Directed by Frank Ryan. *Cast:* Deanna Durbin, Joseph Cotten, Charles Winninger, Nella Walker, Gus Schilling, Ludwig Stossel, Irving Bacon, Nydia Westman, Murray Alper, Samuel S. Hinds, Iris Adrian, Fay Helm, Douglas Wood, Minna Phillips. Evelyn Ankers. Eddie Acuff, Eddie Dunn, Harry Holman, Henry Roquemore, Brooks Benedict, William B. Davidson, Billy Nelson, Billy Wayne, George O'Hanlon, Leon Belasco, Ruth Lee, Jody Gilbert, Eddie Borden, Ernie S. Adams, George Chandler, Alice Talton, Marie Harmon, Virginia Sale, James Bush, Evelyn Wahle, Spec O'Donnell, Teddy Infuhr, Jennifer Holt.

Gaslight (M-G-M, 1944). Screenplay by John Van Druten, Walter Reisch and John L. Balderston from the play "Angel Street" by Patrick Hamilton. Directed by George Cukor. *Cast:* Charles Boyer, Ingrid Bergman, Joseph Cotton, Dame May Whitty, Angela Lansbury, Barbara Everest, Emil Rameau, Edmund Brean, Halliwell Hobbes, Tom Stevenson, Heather Thatcher, Lawrence Naismith, John Gimpel.

Since You Went Away (Selznick International - United Artists, 1944). by David O. Selznick from the novel by Margaret Buell Wilder. Directed by John Cromwell. *Cast:* Claudette Colbert, Jennifer Jones, Joseph Cotten, Shirley Temple, Monty Woolley, Lionel Barrymore, Robert Walker, Hattie McDaniel, Agnes Moorehead, Guy Madison, Craig Stevens, Keenan Wynn, Albert Basserman, Nazimova, Lloyd Corrigan, Jackie Moran, Gordon Oliver, Jane Devlin, Ann Gillis, Dorothy (Cindy) Garner, Andrew McLaglen, Jill Warren, Helen Koford (Terry Moore), Robert Johsnon, Dorothy Dandridge, Johnny Bond, Irving Bacon, George Chandler, Addison Richards, Barabra Pepper, Byron Foulger, Edwin Maxwell, Florences Bates, Theodor Von Eltz, Adeline de Walt Reynold, Doodles Weaver, Warren Hymer, Jonathan Hale, Eilene Janssen, Willima B. Davidson, Ruth Roman, Rhonda Fleming.

I'll Be Seeing You (United Artists, 1944). Screenplay by Marion Parsonnet from a story by Charles Martin. Directed by William Dieterle. *Cast:* Ginger Rogers, Joseph Cotten, Shirley Temple, Spring Byington, Tom Tully, Chill Wills, Dare Harris (John Derek), Kenny Bowers.

Love Letters (Paramount, 1945). Screenplay by Ayn Rand from the novel by Chris Massie, Directed by William Dieterle. *Cast:* Jennifer Jones, Joseph Cotten, Ann Richards, Anita Louise, Cecil Kellaway, Gladys Cooper, Byron Barr, Robert Sully, Reginald Denny, Ernest Cossart, James Millican, Lumsden Hare, Winifred Harris, Ethel May Halls, Matthew Boulton, David Clyde, Ian Wolfe, Alec Craig, Arthur Hohl, Conrad Binyon, Nina Borget, Mary Field, George Humbert, Constance Purdy, Ottola Nesmith, Harry Allen, Anthony Marsh, Louise Curries, Catherine Craig.

Duel in the Sun (Selznick Releasing Organization, 1946). Screenplay by David O. Selznick from an adaptation by Oliver H.P. Garrett of the novel by Niven Busch. Directed by King Vidor. *Cast:* Jennifer Jones, Joseph Cotten, Gregory Peck, Lionel Barrymore, Lillian Gish, Walter Huston, Herbert Marshall, Charles Bickford, Joan Tetzel, Harry Carey, Otto Kruger, Sidney Blackmer, Tilly Losch, Scott McKay, Butterfly McQueen, Francis MacDonald, Victor Kilian, Griff Barnett, Frank Cordell, Dan White, Steve Dunhill, Lane Chandler, Lloyd Shaw, Thomas Dillon, Robert McKenzie, Charles Dingle, Kermit Maynard, Hank Bell, Johnny Bond, Bert Roach, Si Jenks, Hank Worden, Rose Plummer, Guy Wilkerson, Lee Phelps. *Narrated by Orson Welles.*

The Farmer's Daughter (RKO, 1947). Screenplay by Allen Rivkin and Laura Kerr from the play, "Juurakon Hulda" by Juhani Tervapaa (pseudonym for Hella Wuolijok). Directed by H.C. Potter. *Cast:* Loretta Young, Joseph Cotten, Ethel Barrymore, Charles Bickford, Rose Hobart, Rhys Williams, Harry Davenport, Tom Powers, William Harrigan, Lex Barker, Harry Shannon, Keith Andes, Thurston Hall, Art Baker, Don Beddoe, James Aurness (Arness), Anna Q. Nilsson, Sven Hugo Borg, John Gallaudet, William B. Davidson, Charles McGraw, Jason Robards, Cy Kendall, Frank Ferguson, William Bakewell, Charles Lane, Douglas Evans, Robert Clarke, Bess Flowers.

Portrait of Jennie (Selznick Releasing Organization, 1948). Screenplay by Paul Osborn and Peter Berneis from the novel by Robert Nathan. Directed by William Dieterle. *Cast:* Jennifer Jones, Joseph Cotten, Ethel Barrymore, Cecil Kellaway, David Wayne, Albert Sharpe, Florence Bates, Lillian Gish, Henry Hull, Esther Somers, Maude Simmons, Felix Bressart, John Farrell, Clem Bevans, Robert Dudley.

Under Capricorn (Warner Brothers, 1949). Screenplay by James Bridie from Hume Cronyn's adaptation of the play by John Colton and Margaret Linden and the novel by Helen Simpson. Directed by Alfred Hitchcock. *Cast:* Ingrid Bergman, Joseph Cotten, Michael Wilding, Margaret Leighton, Cecil Parker, Denis O'Dea, Jack Watling, Harcourt Williams, John Ruddock, Bill Shine, Victor Lucas, Ronald Adam, Francis de Wolff, G.H. Mulcaster, Olive Sloane, Maureen Delaney, Julia Lang, Betty McDermott, Roderick Lovell.

Beyond the Forest (Warner Brothers, 1949). Screenplay by Lenore Coffee from the novel by Stuart Engstrand. Directed by King Vidor. *Cast:* Bette Davis, Joseph Cotten, David Brian, Ruth Roman, Minor Watson, Dona Drake, Regis Toomey, Sarah Selby, Mary Servoss, Frances Charles, Harry Tyler, Ralph Littlefield, Creighton Hale, Joel Allen, Ann Doran.

The Third Man (Selznick Releasing Organization, 1950) Screenplay by Graham Greene from his own story. Directed by Carol Reed. *Cast:* Joseph Cotten, Trevor Howard, Alida Valli, Orson Welles, Bernard Lee, Ernest Deutsch, Erich Ponto, Siegfried Breuer, Wilfrid Hyde-White, Paul Hoerbiger, Hedwig Bleitreu, Frederick Schehcher, Herbert Mabik, Jenny Wermer, Nelly Amo, Alexis Chesnakov, Leo Rieber.

Walk Softly, Stranger (RKO, 1950). Screenplay by Frank Fenton from a story by Manny Seff and Paul Yawitz. Directed by Robert Stevenson, *Cast:* Joseph Cotten, Alida Valli, Spring Byington, Paul Stewart, Jack Paar, Jeff Donnell, John McIntire, Howard Petrie, Frank Puglia, Esther Dale, Marlo Dwyer, Robert Ellis.

Two Flags West (20th Century-Fox, 1950). Screenplay by Casey Robinson from a story by Frank Nugent and Curtis Kenyon. Directed by Robert Wise. *Cast:* Joseph Cotten, Linda Darnell, Jeff Chandler, Cornel Wilde, Dale Robertson, Jay C. Flippen, Noah Beery, Harry Von Zell, John Sands, Arthur Hunnicutt, Jack Lee, Robert Adler, Harry Carter, Ferris Taylor, Sally Corner, Everett Glass, Marjorie Bennett, Roy Gordon, Lee MacGregor, Aurora Castillo, Stanley Andrews, Don Garner.

September Affair (Paramount, 1951). Screenplay by Robert Thoren and Fritz Rotter. Directed by William Dieterle. *Cast:* Joan Fontaine, Joseph Cotten, Francoise Rosay, Jessica Tandy, Robert Arthur, Jimmy Lydon, Fortunio Bonanova, Grazia Narciso, Anna Demetrio, Lou Steele, Frank Yacanelli, Charles Evans, Jimmy Frasco, Michael Frasco, Charles La Torre, Gilda Oliva, Saverio Lomedico, George Nardelli, Nick Borgani, Georgia Clancy, Dick Elliott, Rudy Rama, Franz F. Roehm, George Humbert, Harry Cheshire, Iphigenie Castiglioni, Inez Palange, Zacharias Yaconelli, Victory Desny, James R. Scott, Stan Johnson, Douglas Grange, Larry Arnold, Walter Merrill.

Half Angel (20th Century-Fox, 1951). Screenplay by Robert Riskin from a story by George Carleton Brown. Directed by Richard Sale. *Cast:* Joseph Cotten, Loretta Young, Cecil Kellaway, Basil Ruysdael, Jim Backus, Irene Ryan, John Ridgely, Theresa Lynn, Mary George, Gayle Pace, Mary Tarcai, Steve Fritko, Art Smith, Edwin Max, Herbert Vigran, Harris Brown, George Eldridge, Anthony Jochim, Grace Field, Bob Adler, Cecil Weston, Jack Davidson, Freeman Lusk, William Johnstone, Roger Laswell, Lou Nova, Harris Brown, Herbert Vigran, Luther Crockett, Tunius Matthews.

Peking Express (Paramount, 1951) Screenplay by James Meredyth Lucas from an adaptation by Jules Furthman of a story by Harry Hervey. Directed by Willliam Dieterle. *Cast:* Joseph Cotten, Corinne Calvet, Edmund Gwenn, Marvin Miles, Benson Fong, Soo Yong, Victor Sen Yung, Gregory Gay, Robert W. Lee, Peter Chong, Harold Fong, Eddie E. Lee, Beal Wong, Leon M. Lontok, Lane Nakand, George T. Lee, Wing Foo, Alfred Santos, Wei Fan Msuch, James Leong, Jury Lim, Rollin Monjama, Walker Ng, Silam Chen, Gregory Merius, William Yip, Mong Wing Gim, Vanga Dimitrova, Walter Levy.

The Man With a Cloak (M-G-M, 1951). Screenplay by Frank Fenton from a story by John Dickson Carr. Directed by Fletcher Markle. *Cast:* Joseph Cotten, Barbara Stanwyck, Louis Calhern, Leslie Caron, Margaret Wycherly, Joe De Santis, Jim Backus, Roy Roberts, Nicholas Joy, Richard Hale, Mitchell Lewis.

The Wild Heart (Selznick-RKO, 1952). Screenplay by Michael Powell and Emeric Pressburger from the novel "Gone To Earth," by Mary Webb. Directed by Michael Powell and Emeric Pressburger. *Cast:* Jennifer Jones, Cyril Cusack, David Farrar, Esmond Knight, Sybil Thorndyke, Hugh Griffith, George Cole, Beatrice Varley, Francis Clare, Raymond Rollett, Gerald Lawson. *Narrated by Joseph Cotten.*

Untamed Frontier (Universal, 1952). Screenplay by Drayson Adams and John and Gwen Bagni. Directed by Hugo Fregonese. *Cast:* Joseph Cotten, Shelley Winters, Scott Brady, Minor Watson, Suzan Ball, Katherine Emery, Lee Van Cleef, Antonio Moreno. Douglas Spencer, John Alexander, Richard Garland, Robert Anderson, Fess Parker.

The Steel Trap (20th Century-Fox, 1952). Screenplay by Andrew Stone. Directed by Andrew Stone. *Cast:* Joseph Cotten, Teresa Wright, Eddie Marr, Aline Towne, Bill Hudson, Benny Burt, Joey Ray, Sam Flint, Charlie Collins, Kurt Martell, Jonathan Hale, Stephanie King, Carleton Young, Katherine Warren, Walter Sunde, Tom Powers.

Niagara (20th Century-Fox, 1953). Screenplay by Charles Brackett, Walter Reisch and Richard Breen. Directed by Henry Hathaway. *Cast:* Marilyn Monroe, Joseph Cotten, Jean Peters, Casey Adams, Denis O'Dea, Richard Allan, Don Wilson, Lurene Tuttle, Russell Collins, Will Wright, Lester Matthews, Carleton Young, Sean McClory, Minerva Urecal, Nina Varela, Tom Reynolds, Winfield Hoeny, Neil Fitzgerald, Norman McKay, Gene (Baxter) Wesson, George Ives, Patrick O'Moore, Arch Johnson, Henry Beckman, Willard Sage, Bill Foster, Robert Ellis, Harry Carey Jr., Gloria Gordon.

Blueprint For Murder (20th Century-Fox, 1953). Screenplay by Andrew Stone. Directed by Andrew Stone. *Cast:* Joseph Cotten, Jean Peters, Gary Merrill, Catherine McLeod, Jack Kruschen, Barney Phillips, Fred Ridgeway, Joyce McCluskey, Mae Marsh, Harry Carter, Jonathan Hale, Walter Sande, Tyler McVey, Teddy Mangean, Aline Towne, Ray Hike, Charles Collins, Eugene Bordea, Caleton Young, Orandem Rhodes, Herb Butterfield, George Melford.

Othello (United Artists, 1955). Screenplay by Orson Welles from the play by William Shakespeare. Directed by Orson Welles. *Cast:* Orson Welles, Michael Mac Liammóir, Suzanne Cloutier, Robert Coote, Milton Edwards, Michael Lawrence, Fay Compton, Nicholas Bruce, Jean Davis, Doris Dowling, Joan Fontaine, Joseph Cotten.

Special Delivery (Columbia, 1955). Screenplay by Phil Reisman and Dwight Taylor based on an idea by Geva Radvanyi. Directed by John Brahm. *Cast:* Joseph Cotten, Eva Bartok, Niall MacGinnis, Rene Deetgen, Robert Cunningham, Bruni Loebel, Don Hanmer, Gert Froebe, Lexford Richards, Ursula Herking.

The Bottom of the Bottle (20th Century-Fox, 1956). Screenplay by Sydney Boehm from the novel by Georges Simenon. Directed by Henry Hathaway. *Cast:* Joseph Cotten, Van Johnson, Ruth Roman, Jack Carson, Margaret Hayes, Nancy Gates, Bruce Bennett, Brad Dexter, Peggy Knudsen, Jim Davis, Margaret Lindsay, Gonzales-Gonzales, Henry Morgan, Sandy Descher, Kim Charney, Mimi Gibson, Joane Jordan.

The Killer Is Loose (United Artists, 1956). Screenplay by Harold Medford from the story by John and Ward Hawkins. Directed by Budd Boetticher. *Cast:* Joseph Cotten, Rhonda Fleming, Wendell Corey, Alan Hale, Michael Pate, Virginia Christine, John Larch, John Beradino, Paul Bryan, Dee J. Thompson.

The Halliday Brand (United Artists, 1957). Screenplay by George W. George and George S. Slavin. Directed by Joseph H. Lewis. *Cast:* Joseph Cotten, Viveca Lindfors, Ward Bond, Betsy Blair, Bill Williams, Jay C. Flippen. Christopher Dark, Jeanette Nolan, Glen Strange, John Dierkes, Stanford Jolley, John Ayres, Robin Short, Jay Lawrence, George Lynn, John Halloran, Michael Hinn.

Touch of Evil (Universal, 1958). Screenplay by Orson Welles from the novel "Badge of Evil" by Whit Masterson. Directed by Orson Welles. *Cast:* Orson Welles, Charlton Heston, Janet Leigh, Joseph Calleia, Akim Tamiroff, Joanna Moore, Ray Collins, Dennis Weaver, Valentin De Vargas, Mort Mills, Victor Milan, Lalo Rios, Michael Sargent, and Guests: Marlene Dietrich, Zsa Zsa Gabor, Mercedes McCambridge, Joseph Cotten.

From the Earth to the Moon (Warner Brothers, 1958). Screenplay by Robert Blees and James Leicester. Directed by Byron Haskin. *Cast:* Joseph Cotten, George Sanders, Debra Paget, Don Dubbins, Patric Knowles, Carl Esmond, Henry Daniell, Melville Cooper, Ludwig Stossel, Morris Ankrum.

The Angel Wore Red (M-G-M, 1960). Screenplay by Nunnally Johnson. Directed by Nunnally Johnson. *Cast:* Ava Gardner, Dirk Bogarde, Joseph Cotten, Vittorio De Sica, Aldo Fabrize, Arnoldo Foa, Finlay Currie, Rossano Rory, Enrico Maria Salerno, Robert Bright, Franco Castellani, Bob Cunningham, Gustavo De Nardo, Nino Castelnuevo, Aldo Pini.

The Last Sunset (Universal, 1961). Screenplay by Dalton Trumbo from the novel, "Sundown at Crazy Horse," by Howard Rigsby. Directed by Robert Aldrich. *Cast:* Rock Hudson, Kirk Douglas, Dorothy Malone, Joseph Cotten. Carol Lynley, Neville Brand, Regis Toomey, Rad Fulton, Adam Williams, Jack Elam, John Shay, Margarito De Luna, Jose Torvay.

Hush...Hush, Sweet Charlotte (20th Century-Fox, 1965). Screenplay by Henry Farrell and Lukas Heller from a story by Henry Farrell. Directed by Robert Aldrich. *Cast:* Bette Davis, Olivia de Havilland, Joseph Cotten, Agnes Moorehead, Cecil Kellaway, Victor Buono, Mary Astor, William Campbell, Wesley Addy, Bruce Dern, George Kennedy, Dave Willock, John Megna, Ellen Corby, Helen Kleeb, Marianne Stewart, Frank Ferguson, Mary Henderson, Lillian Randolph, Geraldine West, William Walker, Idell James. Teddy Buckner and His All-Stars.

The Great Sioux Massacre (Columbia, 1965). Screenplay by Fred C. Dobbs from a story by Sidney Salkow and Marvin Gluck. Directed by Sidney Salkow. *Cast:* Joseph Cotten, Darren McGavin, Philip Carey, Julie Sommers, Nancy Kovack, John Mathews, Michael Pate, Don Haggerty, Iron Eyes Cody, House Peters Jr., John Napier, William Tannen, Blair Davies, Louise Serpa.

The Money Trap (M-G-M, 1966). Screenplay by Walter Bernstein from the novel by Lionel White. Directed by Burt Kennedy. *Cast:* Glenn Ford, Elke Sommer, Rita Hayworth, Joseph Cotten, Ricardo Montalban, Tom Reese, James Mitchum, Argentine Brunetti, Fred Essler, Eugene Iglesias, Teri Lynn Sandoval.

The Oscar (Embassy, 1966). Screenplay by Harlan Ellison, Russell Rouse and Clarence Greene from the novel by Richard Sale. Directed by Russell Rouse. *Cast:* Stephen Boyd, Elke Sommer, Milton Berle, Eleanor Parker, Joseph Cotten, Jill St. John, Tony Bennett, Jean Hale, Ed Begley, Walter Brennan, Broderick Crawford, James Dunn, Peter Lawford, Jack Soo, and as themselves: Bob Hope, Edith Head, Hedda Hopper, Merle Oberon, Frank Sinatra, Nancy Sinatra.

The Tramplers (Embassy, 1966). Screenplay by Albert Band and Ugo Liberatore from the novel, "Guns of North Texas" by Will Cook. Directed by Albert Band. *Cast:* Joseph Cotten, Gordon Scott, James Mitchum, Ilaria Occhini, Franco Nero, Emma Vannoni, George Lycan, Muriel Franklin, Aldo Cecconi, Franco Balducci, Claudio Gora, Romano Puppo, Dario Michaels, Ivan Scatuglia, Carla Calo, Nino Desmond, Silla Bettina, Edith Peters.

Brighty of the Grand Canyon (Feature Film Corporation of America, 1967). Screenplay by Norman Foster from the book by Marguerite Henry. Directed by Norman Foster. *Cast:* Joseph Cotten, Pat Conway, Dick Foran, Karl Swenson, Dandy Curran.

Jack of Diamonds (M-G-M, 1967). Screenplay by Jack DeWitt and Sandy Howard with additional dialogue by Robert L. Joseph. Directed by Don Taylor. *Cast:* George Hamilton, Joseph Cotten, Marie Laforet, Maurice Evans, Wolfgang Preiss, Karl Lieffen, Eduard Linkers. Alexander Hegarth, with appearances by Carroll Baker, Zsa Zsa Gabor, Lilli Palmer.

Some May Live (RKO, 1967). Directed by Vernon Sewell. *Cast:* Joseph Cotten, Peter Cushing, Martha Hyer, John Rondance.

The Hellbenders (Embassy, 1968). Screenplay by Albert Band and Ugo Liberatore from a story by Virgil C. Gerlach with additional dialogue by Louis Garfinkle. Directed by Sergio Corbucci. *Cast:* Joseph Cotten, Norma Bengell, Julian Mateos, Gino Pernice, Angel Arando, Maria Martin, Al Mulock, Aldo Sambrell, Enio Girolani, Jose Nieto, Claudio Gora, Alvaro De Luna, Ivan Scatruglia, Julio Pena, Rafael Vaquero, Simon Arriaga. Claudio Scarchilli.

Petulia (Warner Brothers-Seven Arts, 1968).

Screenplay by Lawrence B. Marcus from an adaptation by Barbara Turner of the novel, "Me and the Arch Kook Petulia," by John Haase. Directed by Richard Lester. *Cast:* Julie Christie, George C. Scott, Richard Chamberlain, Arthur Hill, Shirley Knight, Pippa Scott, Kathleen Widdoes, Joseph Cotten, Roger Bowen, Richard Dysart, Ruth Kobart, Ellen Geer, Lou Gilbert, Nat Esformes, Maria Val, Vincent Arias, Eric Weiss, Kevin Cooper, Austin Pendleton, Barbara Colby, Rene Auberjonois, Josephine Nichols, De Ann Mears, The Grateful Dead, Big Brother and the Holding Company, Members of the Committee, Members of the American Conservatory Theatre.

White Commanche (RKO, 1969). Screenplay by Frank Gruber and Robert Holt. Directed by Gilbert Lee Kay. *Cast:* Joseph Cotten, William Shatner, Nick Adams. Made in 1967, this was released on television in 1969.

The Grasshopper (National General Pictures, 1970). Screenplay by Jerry Belson and Garry Marshall from the novel, "The Passing of Evil," by Mark McShane. Directed by Jerry Paris. *Cast:* Jacqueline Bissett, Jim Brown, Joseph Cotten, Corbett Monica, Ramon Bieri, Christopher Stone, Roger Garrett, Stanley Adams, Dick Richards, Tim O'Kelly, Stephanianna Christopherson.

Latitude Zero (National General Pictures, 1970). Screenplay by Ted Sherdeman from his stories. Directed by Ishiro Honda. *Cast:* Joseph Cotten, Cesar Romero, Richard Jaeckel, Patricia Medina, Linda Haynes, Akira Takarada, Masumi Okada, Hikaru Kuroki.

Tora! Tora! Tora! (20th Century-Fox, 1970) Screenplay by Larry Forrester, Hideo Cguni and Ryuzo Kikushima from the novel by Gordon W. Prange and "The Broken Seal" by Ladislas Farago. Directed by Richard Fleischer, with Japanese sequences directed by Toshio Masuda and Kinji Fukasaku. *Cast:* Martin Balsam, Jason Robards Jr., Soh Yamamura, Joseph Cotten, Tatsuya Mihashi, E.G. Marshall, Takahiro Tamura, James Whitmore, Eijiro Tono, Wesley Addy, Shogo Shimoda, Koreya Senda, Leon Ames, Kazuo Kitamura, Keith Andes, Edward Andrews, Neville Brand, Leora Dana, Asao Uchida, George Macready, Jeff Donnell, Richard Erdman, Shunicki Nakamura, Misao Toake.

The Abominable Dr. Phibes (American-International, 1970). Screenplay by James Whiton and William Goldstein. Directed by Robert Fuest. *Cast:* Vincent Price, Joseph Cotten, Hugh Griffith, Terry-Thomas, Virginia North, Augrey Woods, Susan Travers, Alex Scott, Edward Burnham, Peter Gilmore, Peter Jeffrey, Maurice Kaufman, Norman Jones, John Cater, Derek Godfrey, Sean Bury, Walter Horsbrugh, Barbara Keogh, David Hutcheson, Caroline Munro, Dallas Adams, Alan Zipson, Alister Williamson, Thomas Heathcote, Ian Marter, Julian Grant.

Baron Blood (American International, 1972). Screenplay by Vincent Forte and William A. Bairn. Directed by Mario Bava. *Cast:* Joseph Cotten, Elke Sommer, Massimo Girotti, Antonio Cantafora, Alan Collines, Nicoletta Elmi, Rada Rassimov, Dieter Tressler, Humi Raho.

Lady Frankenstein (New World Pictures, 1972). Screenplay by Edward di Lorenzo and Edward Reed. Directed by Mel Wells. *Cast:* Joseph Cotten, Sarah Bay, Mickey Hargitay, Paul Muller, Andrew Ray.

Doomsday Voyage (Futurama International, 1972). Screenplay by John Vidette. Directed by John Vidette. *Cast:* Joseph Cotten, John Gabriel, Ann Randall.

Soylent Green (M-G-M, 1973). Screenplay by Stanley R. Greenberg from the novel by Harry Harrison. Directed by Richard Fleischer *Cast:* Charlton Heston, Leigh Taylor-Young, Chuck Connors, Joseph Cotten, Brock Peters, Paula Kelly, Edward G. Robinson, Stephen Young, Mike Henry, Lincoln Kilpatrick, Roy Jenson, Leonard Stone, Whit Bissell, Celia Lovsky, Dick Van Patten, Margan Farley, John Barclay, Belle Mitchell, Curil Delevanti, Forrest Wood, Faith Quabius, Jane Dulo, Tim Herbert, John Dennis, Jan Bradley, Carlos Romero, Pat Houtchens, Joyce Williams, Erica Hagen, Beverly Gill, Suesie Eejima, Cheri Howell, Kathy Silva, Jennifer King, Marion Charles.

A Delicate Balance (American Film Theatre, 1973). Screenplay by Edward Albee from his play. Directed by Tony Richardson. *Cast:* Katharine Hepburn, Paul Scofield, Lee Remick, Kate Reid, Joseph Cotten, Betsy Blair.

Accepting his Oscar for *To Kill a Mockingbird* (1962) from Sophia Loren.

9

GREGORY PECK

America's immensely popular motion-picture hero, Gregory Peck, came to the screen possessing all the necessary physical attributes which that larger-than-life medium requires for stardom. He is a lanky, six-foot-three, dark-haired man with a superbly photogenic angular face reflecting solidarity, the very essence of the American hero. These characteristics immediately qualified him as a romantic hero for the ladies in the audience, and conversely, his masculine humility won him the respect of the male members of the audience, who, without feeling threatened, could identify with his roles. Perhaps Peck's most subtly distinctive feature is his resonant speaking voice which he had learned to use to the ultimate advantage during his apprenticeship on the stage.

This Lincolnesque image propelled Peck to instant screen stardom, but he intelligently realised that if he were to become a star of enduring stature, he had to do more. While he wisely capitilised on these physical traits, he at once set about learning and perfecting his new craft. Peck learned his lessons well and has become one of America's finest character actors, one who can believably project pathos, strong vulnerability and courageous heroism as witnessed in *The Keys of the Kingdom, Twelve O'Clock High,* and *To Kill a Mockingbird*.

There are those, however, who dismiss Peck, saying he is simply playing himself on the screen, or more strongly, that he is one of the screen's most lacklustre actors. One drama coach stated, "Peck's performances are exactly like Peck — honest and workmanlike, humorless and uninspired."

These criticisms can hardly be said to be perceptive analyses of this dedicated man's talent. If one looks more deeply at Peck's performances, they reveal thoughtful and painstakingly-detailed interpretations.

Producer-director-writer Nunnally Johnson, thinks Peck "works harder than practically any other actor in the world." And his wife, Veronique, further explains, "He gets so far into a role that they (the critics) don't realize he is acting. Their criticism is really a compliment."

This is not to imply that Peck is one of Hollywood's most versatile actors. During his first years in Hollywood, his agent, Leland Hayward, counselled Peck, "I think you were wonderful in *The Keys of the Kingdom,* but I don't think you'll ever develop the facility to play just anything. You will always have to have the right material."

And Peck himself objectively concurs, "When I'm wrongly cast, or in a poor script, I sink with the ship. I don't believe in spontaneity. I don't believe anything can be done well without thought."

This objectivity has been the force behind Peck's thirty years of success in Hollywood as an actor and later as a producer. Throughout these years, Peck has been an active off-screen citizen in Hollywood's and the nation's political scene. In

1947, he voluntarily appeared before the California State Un-American Activities Committee and named every organization to which he had ever sent a cheque and said he would do so again because they had been worthy causes. This candour earned him a citation from the Committee proclaiming him innocent of pro-Communism. The following year he made a speech at the Gilmore Stadium in Los Angeles in support of Harry S. Truman's campaign against Thomas E. Dewey. Peck later supported Adlai Stevenson, John F. Kennedy, Lyndon B. Johnson, and California's Governor Pat Brown. While campaigning for Brown, newspapers hinted that Peck was interested in running for public office. Peck's response was, "That all started when Brown was defeated by Reagan, and I think Pat Brown said it rather wryly. I never said I was interested in public office, but I am interested in public service."

The only child of Irish-Catholic parents — Gregory and Bernice Ayres Peck — Eldred Gregory Peck was born on April 5, 1916 in La Jolla, California. Peck's mother had decided to name him Eldred after seeing the name in the telephone book. As Peck was not fond of this name, he dropped it as soon as he graduated from college.

Peck's father, who had always dreamed of being a doctor, had become a pharmacist when that profession proved economically impossible. He opened La Jolla's first drug store. Unfortunately, Peck was such a warm-hearted man that he failed to send bills to his regular customers and was eventually forced to sell the pharmacy and take a job as a night-time druggist in San Diego.

The Pecks separated in 1918, because Peck's mother felt their disparate ages (nine years) and their money problems caused irreconcilable differences, and after two reconciliation attempts, they divorced when Peck was six years old.

During the time his parents were separated, Peck lived with his mother and maternal grandmother. Following the divorce, his mother took him to St. Louis where she worked for the telephone company. They lived in a boarding house and the young Peck sold newspapers. When her attempt at independence in St. Louis failed, Mrs. Peck moved to San Francisco where her brother was a streetcar motorman. Eventually Mrs. Peck and her son moved back to La Jolla where she opened a tea shop and sent her son to St. Johns Military Academy near San Diego.

In 1927, Bernice Peck married a gregarious Italian by the name of Joseph Maysuch. Peck readily adjusted to this new situation and saw both his father and his step-father during this time. He enjoyed the security of life at the military academy where he became involved in numerous school activities. He edited the school paper, was elected a cadet captain, won a gold medal for his religious studies and learned to love the theatricality of the Catholic Mass.

Upon leaving St. Johns, he went to live with his father who had remarried seven years before, and he now attended the San Diego High School. His father's fondest dream was for his son to become the doctor he had never been able to be, and he urged the adolescent to attend the University of Southern California. Peck's high school scholastic achievements were not outstanding and prevented him from enrolling at the University. Instead he entered the less prestigious San Diego State College.

Peck's Italian step-father loved the theatre and had once told his step-son he should be an actor. Peck, however, was disinterested in acting until he had recited a portion of Eugene O'Neill's "Emperor Jones" for his public speaking class, not only speaking the lines of each character, but actually acting out each part.

A girl friend at the State College tutored him in his studies to enable him to make grades good enough to enroll him in the University of Southern California. He passed the entrance examinations but could not afford the tuition. To remedy this situation, he quit school for a time and took a job as a night watchman and utility delivery man for the Union Oil Company. A year-and-a-half later, he enrolled at USC.

Remembering his experience with O'Neill he rekindled his interest in theatre and became a member of the dramatic club. The Berkeley drama club was looking for a tall student to play opposite a short, fat Captain Ahab in its production of "Moby Dick." The novice Peck, more for his height than his ability, landed the part. After gleaning more experience by playing Matt Burke in O'Neill's "Anna Christie," Peck became convinced that he wanted to be an actor. Of this introduction to college drama, Peck later said, "I got rid of Gregory Peck, the guy who was so unsure of himself, and became, to myself, a veritable wonderman." Although his mother and step-father were pleased with his choice of vocation, his father crustily told him he would be "broke at thirty-five."

The tall, handsome Peck finally graduated from

college in 1939, and promptly boarded a train for New York City. His first job was as the barker for the Meteor Speedway concession at the 1939 World's Fair which paid him $25 a week. When the concession closed, he became a $40-a-week tour guide at Rockefeller Center and shortly thereafter he auditioned for and was awarded a two-year scholarship to the Neighborhood Playhouse and School of Dramatics which paid him $50 a month. He supplemented this income by working as a photographer's model. Among the alumni of that theatrical group are Jo Van Fleet, Richard Conte, Eli Wallach, Edmond O'Brien, Tony Randall, Efrem Zimbalist Jr. and Betty Garrett. During one strenuous lesson at the school in physical training, Peck threw his back out, an injury which required him to wear a brace for six years and prevented his induction into the military.

With fellow-student, Evelyn Fargo, he won an award endowed by Dorothy Stickney, wife of playwright Howard Lindsay, which entitled him to work for a summer at the Barter Theatre in Abingdon, Virginia. He continued his studies at the Playhouse and during the summer of 1941, he appeared with Diana Barrymore at the White Plains Theatre in "Captain Jinks of the Horse Marines" a play in which Miss Barrymore's aunt Ethel had appeared many times. Maynard Morris, an agent for the Leland Hayward office, saw Peck in this appearance and offered to represent him. Later, when Peck would negotiate for terms in Hollywood, the Hayward office proved a most valuable asset.

Peck returned to the Neighborhood Playhouse in the fall of 1941, where Guthrie McClintic and his wife, Katharine Cornell, saw him and offered him a seven-line part as Mr. Denby in their touring production of Shaw's "The Doctor's Dilemma." This experience was the turning point for Peck and he recalls it and the McClintics fondly, "Miss Cornell made all the difference for me. She gave me the chance to find out whether or not I belonged on the same stage with distinguished professionals." After 'The Doctor's Dilemma,' she and McClintic put me in 'Rose Burke,' the play by Henri Bernstein with Miss Cornell which closed out of town in 1942. I understudied Philip Merivale (and Jean-Pierre Aumont) and rehearsed this role opposite Miss Cornell. It was the best training I could have had. I never went on, but I was ready to. The fact that Miss Cornell had confidence in me gave me confidence." He adds, "I also learned to my surprise that though Miss Cornell was the first lady of the American theatre, she was shy, and had never fully conquered stage fright. I used to see her backstage, before her entrances, keyed up and trembling, and then sweep on stage and take command, projecting self-assurance, grace, nobility. Since then I have observed many great actors constantly struggle with stage fright, even after years of success. It seems true that courage is not so much the absence of fear as the ability to overcome it, and to do what has to be done. Courage, intelligence, and personal detachment are the qualities I most admire in an actor."

After a summer stock stint at the Cape Playhouse in Dennis, Massachusetts, McClintic cast Peck as Cliff Parrilow, the juvenile lead in Emlyn William's "Morning Star." The play opened on September 14, 1942, at the Plymouth Theatre and was about a middle-class English family who represented the backbone of that nation during wartime London. Peck played the sensitive young doctor who has a breakdown, discontinues his medical studies, and takes up with a prostitute. Emlyn Williams had played the role himself in the British version. The play had been a success in England where it ran for a year, but American audiences did not take to it. The New York version starred Gladys Cooper, Jill Esmond, Rhys Williams, and Wendy Barrie, in her stage debut. George Freedley of the New York "Morning-Telegraph" said of Peck, "After a nervous first act, Gregory Peck settled down to prove himself the most likely leading-man material we have seen on the stage recently. Looking rather like Gary Cooper, he has a pleasing manner, a good voice, and an inner clarity which made the surgeon believable even when the author was straining credulity to the utmost." And the venerable John Mason Brown wrote, "Gregory Peck is a remarkable young actor, sensitive, intelligent, expert and an uncommon type, who by the playing of the war-shocked and regenerate doctor, promises to go far."

"Morning Star" closed in one month, but not before Peck married Greta Konen on October 4th. Of Finnish ancestry, Miss Konen was hair-dresser and cosmetician to Katharine Cornell and Peck had first been introduced to her on the station platform in Philadelphia where the theatre company of "The Doctor's Dilemma" was waiting for a train. Peck recalls, "When I first met her she was making more money than I was and when she married me I was making no money at all." The young marrieds took a fifth-floor walk-up apartment in Manhattan where they shared a kitchen with another couple.

After "Morning Star" closed, Peck was cast in the dual role of a doctor and his son in John Patrick's "The Willow and I" which opened at the Windsor Theatre on December 10, 1942. This melodrama of unrequited love portrayed two sisters (played by Barbara O'Neil and Martha Scott) in love with the same man. Critic Burns Mantle said, "Mr. Peck confirms the fine impression made as another young doctor in "Morning Star" and is by way of becoming, I strongly believe, one of our most popular leading men, both here and on the coast. He has poise, good looks, a splendid voice, and a compelling sympathy." Robert Coleman called him "New York's new matinee idol."

Following "The Willow and I," Peck starred in a touring production of "Punch and Juliette" with Jane Cowl, Arthur Margetson and Frances Heflin. He returned to the Broadway stage playing the imagined son of Geraldine Fitzgerald in Irwin Shaw's anti-war play, "Sons and Soldiers." The play was directed by Max Reinhardt and also starred Karl Malden and Stella Adler, and opened at the Morosco Theatre on May 4, 1943. Peck recalls an incident with Reinhardt about his direction of a scene in which Peck was required to prolong a laugh. "Five-foot-three, seventy-three year old Reinhardt, who just about reached my chest, came up to me and grinned, and said very softly, so only I could hear: 'You know this is just a game, and you and I can go right on playing games forever because we're in the theatre. But the people in the audience — they had to stop when they were twelve. Come on now, you can do it!' And Peck says he did. Critics regarded his portrayal as "immensely human."

Peck's reputation as a Broadway matinee idol had brought him several offers from Hollywood. On one occasion, his agent, Maynard Morris, convinced Kay Brown, Eastern Representative for David O. Selznick that Peck was screen material. Miss Brown agreed, arranged a screen-test in New York and had it shipped to her boss in California. Selznick's reply was, "Where did you pick up Abe Lincoln?" Despite her pleading, Miss Brown said he was not interested in signing Peck and adds, "I fought, bled and died over that."

Up until that time, Peck had given a cinema career short shrift, but when screenwriter-producer Casey Robinson offered him the starring part in *Days of Glory* (1944), Peck decided to give Hollywood a try.

With Tamara Toumanova in *Days of Glory* (1944).

Leland Hayward, probably the most astute talent agent in the business except for Myron Selznick, saw a chance for Peck to enter motion pictures under very profitable circumstances. The United States was in the middle of World War II, and the ranks of Hollywood leading men were depleted by military inductions. Clark Gable, James Stewart, Henry Fonda, Tyrone Power, *et.al.* were absent from the screen. Hayward realised that Peck, disqualified from military service, would be making his screen debut at a most propitious time. Furthermore, Hayward advised Peck not to accept *any* long-term contracts. Peck listened to Hayward and signed a non-exclusive contract with Robinson and RKO to star in *Days of Glory,* which allowed him to simultaneously sign other non-exclusive deals with 20th Century-Fox, Metro-Goldwyn-Mayer (a three-picture deal) and David O. Selznick, who by this time was convinced of Peck's potential as a screen actor.

The screenplay for *Days of Glory* had been written by Casey Robinson from a story by Melchior Lengyel, as a vehicle to introduce to the screen, Robinson's *fiancée,* ballerina Tamara Toumanova. Miss Toumanova and Peck played Russian guerrillas fighting for their country and the Allies during

World War II. The picture was a critical and commercial failure, notable only as Peck's motion-picture debut. The director of the picture was Jacques Tourneur and Peck told an interviewer later, "I had been used to projecting from a stage and Tourneur had to keep reminding me that I had only to project as far as the people I was playing with. Eventually, I hope, I caught on. Vocal virtuosity is of little interest to an audience. What they want to see in a film actor is how he thinks and reacts."

Despite the failure of that picture, Darryl F. Zanuck of 20th Century-Fox liked Peck's performance well enough to offer him a multiple picture deal which first cast the young actor as the selfless missionary-priest in *The Keys of the Kingdom* (1945) based on the novel by A.J. Cronin. The part called for Peck to age from eighteen to eighty, not an easy feat for even a veteran screen actor let alone one with a single picture to his credit. However, Peck handled the transition with finesse and staggering realism and earned his first nomination for an Academy Award. Cronin was impressed with Peck's performance because he had captured "the clumsiness and beauty of Father Chrisholm's character;" and the New York "Times" said, "Gregory Peck, a tall and spare newcomer, gives a quiet and forceful performance in the role of the priest and conveys a fine impression of godly devotion and dignity." Of this performance, Peck said later, "That's one of those films I would love to do over because it was such a wonderful part and I was so green that I really couldn't do it justice. All I could do was invest all the sincerity that I could in it, which I did. That's *all* I was able to do, because I simply wasn't skillful enough to do more. I could do it much better now, but all the same, it was the *kind* of film that I like best and probably that I do best in."

In *The Keys of the Kingdom* (1945).

That performance was the one which prompted M-G-M's Louis B. Mayer to make Peck an offer of a long-term contract. Peck recalls when Mayer tried to tantalise him with the rewards of a seven-year contract, Mayer gave one of his emotionally-charged, pleading performances which ended with the usual tears flowing down his cheeks. Of Mayer's excessive display, Peck says, "I never saw anything like that before and I never have since." When Mayer's ploy failed to entice Peck, the two men agreed upon a three-picture deal: *The Valley of Decision* (1945) for which Peck was paid $45,000; *The Yearling* (1946) where his salary was $55,000; and *The Great Sinner* (1949) for which he received $65,000.

The first of these M-G-M commitments, *The Valley of Decision,* was a vehicle for Greer Garson, then reigning queen of the M-G-M lot. It cast Peck as the quietly-commanding, wealthy son of a Pittsburgh steel magnate (Donald Crisp) who falls in love with the family maid (Garson) while bethrothed to social snob, Jessica Tandy. While the picture was indeed Miss Garson's, the supporting cast was made up of polished veterans including Crisp, Lionel Barrymore, as Miss Garson's father, and Gladys Cooper as Peck's aristocratic mother. However, director Tay Garnett made sure to protect Peck from this loveable group of scene-stealers. Peck's most important scene was the speech in which he refused to merge his family's company with a steel monopoly because he preferred to remain close to his faithful employees. Garnett showcased this scene and Peck came off like a veteran.

The Keys of the Kingdom and *The Valley of Decision* had convinced David O. Selznick that Peck would be an important screen actor. Knowing of Peck's refusal to commit himself to one studio, Selznick agreed to hire Peck on a non-exclusive basis.

Peck's first assignment for Selznick was *Spellbound* (1945), the psychological thriller directed by Alfred Hitchcock and starring Selznick's most important star, Ingrid Bergman. Peck played an ex-Army doctor and head of an asylum who is an amnesiac and was suspected of being a murderer. Miss Bergman played the psychiatrist who cured him and proved his innocence. Peck did not like the script but acknowledged that his career was boosted *vis-a-vis* Hitchcock and Miss Bergman. Of Peck, Miss

With Ingrid Bergman in *Spellbound* (1945).

With Claude Jarman, Jr., and Jane Wyman in *The Yearling* (1946).

Bergman says, "He is never pleased with a scene and always wants to do it over."

M-G-M's second assignment for Peck was *The Yearling* (1946), a project which earlier had been slated as a vehicle for Spencer Tracy. Peck played the gentle homesteader in Florida scrub country who gives his son, Claude Jarman Jr., a pet fawn and later has to kill the animal when it becomes destructive. This portrayal earned Peck his second Academy Award nomination, and director Clarence Brown, says, "Peck is an inspiration, an actor of quiet strength." In retrospect, Peck says, "I would have liked *The Yearling* better had its Walt Disney aspects been pushed into the background. It was too lushly done, and, the boy cried too much."

Peck's second picture for Selznick changed his audience image, by casting him as Lewt McCanles, the lecherous, rascal brother of Joseph Cotten in *Duel in theSun* (1946). The film's violent climax had him fight a gruesome death duel with Jennifer Jones. Peck was not considered appropriately cast by most critics, but in viewing the picture today his realistic performance is one of the most vibrant and sensual of his career. The picture was a top money-maker in addition to earning Peck "Look" Magazine's actor of the year award for this portrayal and his work in *The Yearling*.

With Joan Bennett in *The Macomber Affair* (1947).

With Jennifer Jones in *Duel in the Sun* (1946).

Casey Robinson then cast Peck as Robert Wilson, the cynical hunter who adjusts his morals to suit those whose whiskey he drinks, in Robinsons's screen adaptation of Ernest Hemingway's "The Short Happy Life of Francis Macomber." Re-titled for the screen, *The Macomber Affair* (1947), it is one of the best screen versions of a Hemingway work despite the ending which indicated that Macomber's selfish wife, Joan Bennett, had *accidentally* shot him. Peck exhibited Hemingway's masculine independence toward both women and cowards, but there were those who felt he would have been better cast as the unmanly husband, played by Robert Preston. Peck owned ten percent of *The Macomber Affair,* the first of many such participatory financial deals. (The year before, the financially astute Peck had invested in the successful Broadway production of "A Bell for Adano," based on John Hershey's Pulitzer prize winning novel.)

During 1946-47, producer Samuel Goldwyn had

planned to bring to the screen, *Earth and High Heaven,* a story of a Jew married to a Gentile. He wanted Peck and Joan Fontaine, another Selznick Player, for the leading roles. That production never materialised, but when 20th Century-Fox decided to produce a screen version of Laura Hobson's popular novel, *Gentlemen's Agreement* (1947), they cast Peck as the widowed father who passes as a Jew to write a series of magazine articles about anti-Semitism. Dorothy McGuire, also a Selznick Player, played the wealthy publisher's divorced daughter, who after falling in love with Peck, finds she is not without prejudice. The picture was directed by Elia Kazan and at the time revolutionised Hollywood subject-matter. Today Kazan feels the picture looks like an "illustration for "Redbook" and "Cosmopolitan" magazines, but at the time it struck new ground in adult filmmaking. The picture earned Academy Award nominations for Peck, Miss McGuire, and received Oscars for Best Picture of the Year, Best Director (Kazan), and Best Actress in a Supportilng Role (Celeste Holm). Peck recalls he did not like Kazan's direction because he tried to pursuade him "to punch the wall in frustration *a la* Brando and Newman," but Peck felt strongly about the film's message and still feels it was a milestone at that time.

While his career was now dominated by filmmaking, he nevertheless held the theatre in great esteem. During the summer of 1946, he had appeared briefly in a production of John Millington Synge's "The Playboy of the Western World" at the Cape Playhouse in Dennis, Massachusetts. During the production of *Gentlemen's Agreement,* he and Dorothy McGuire, who had begun her career on the stage, decided to apply their experience and establish a stock company of film actors who would perform in stage productions when their motion-picture schedules permitted. They enlisted the help of David O. Selznick and members of the Selznick Players — Jennifer Jones and Joseph Cotten. The company was known as the Selznick Actors Group and they set up their repertory theatre in La Jolla, Peck's home town. In 1949, Peck appeared there in a production of "Angel Street" with Laraine Day and when time permitted acted as managing producer for several years.

The two motion pictures in which Peck appeared next — *The Paradine Case* and *Yellow Sky* — did little to elevate his career. *The Paradine Case* was written and produced by David O. Selznick and co-starred Ann Todd, Charles Laughton, Charles Coburn, Ethel Barrymore, Louis Jourdan and Alida Valli. Directed by Alfred Hitchcock, Peck called it "a rather minor Old Bailey trial movie, with a magnificent cast." He played a married barrister who defends and falls in love with nymphomaniac murderess, Alida Valli. *Yellow Sky,* for 20th Century-Fox, was a minor post-Civil War western in which Peck opposes fellow bank robber, Richard Widmark, and ends up returning the money they had stolen.

In *The Paradine Case* (1947).

Selznick's liquidation of his production company in 1948 ended his association with Peck after only three films, although Peck had frequently been professionally associated with other Selznick Players. He and Selznick remained good friends throughout their professional relationship and beyond; Peck says he was never harrassed by the seemingly endless bombardment of Selznick memos. He says, "David did a great deal for me by casting me in *Duel in the Sun.* It gave me a chance of playing a likeable no-good right after my portrayal of Father Chrisholm in *The Keys of the Kingdom.* Also, he cast me opposite Ingrid Bergman just when she was at the top of the ladder, with the result that in a sense, I got a free ride — an exposure to her wide audience. He finally had to stop producing because he had a fixation he had to do everything as big as *Gone With the Wind,* or more heart-breaking, to top *Gone With the Wind.* He made picture after picture — *Since You Went Away,* my own *The Paradine Case* — with tremendous all-star casts and TV-type stories that were inappropriate, and sometimes no good. And David would unnerve directors, even ones as skilled as Hitch, to say nothing of the actors, by rewriting the dialogue the night before it was to be shot. The only reason I didn't do more pictures for him is because he went out of production. He was a good friend."

Peck's third and final commitment with M-G-M was *The Great Sinner* (1949), an adaptation of Dostoievsky's "The Gambler." Peck was the writer who becomes a compulsive gambler after being introduced to that diversion by a Russian beauty, Ava Gardner. Except for two excellent supporting performances by Agnes Moorehead as the pawnshop crone and Ethel Barrymore as the Russian matriarch, it was a distinct flop.

Twelve O'Clock High, released by 20th Century-Fox the same year, probably contains Peck's best performance. In this picture he played General Savage, who, in 1942, reorganised a lax bombing group based in England, after which he suffers a nervous breakdown. Of this performance, The New York "Times" stated, "He passes with ease and conviction through the various phases of reluctance to take the job, humor at the base's reaction to his sudden authority, worry about the success or failure of his task, and finally collapses after the job is done." The picture

With Agnes Moorehead in *The Great Sinner* (1949).

In *Twelve O'Clock High* (1949).

earned him the New York Film Critics Award and his fourth nomination for an Academy Award.

Peck followed this portrayal with another good one, this time as the killer in an unpretentious western entitled *The Gunfighter* (1950), directed by Henry King for 20th Century-Fox. Not long after this picture was released, producer Stanley Kramer sent Peck the script to *High Noon.* Peck explains, "I suppose I still, at that time, was nursing along the idea that I shouldn't repeat myself, or try not to at any rate. I recognized it as a good script, but I said no, which was a very foolish thing to have done. However, it worked out fine, because Gary Cooper was ideal, perfect, for it; and Kramer was probably wrong in offering it to me in the first place. All the same, I would like to have done it because it's a classic film, and really, that's one ambition that we all have: to be in a film, or two, or three, that'll be regarded as of lasting quality, and they don't come often. There's just a handful of those kind of films, and *High Noon* is one of them."

Peck's next four pictures were hardly classics. *Captain Horatio Hornblower* (1951) cast him as a British sea captain during the Napoleonic Wars opposite Virginia Mayo. *Only the Valiant* (1951) was a third-rate western in which he played a cavalry officer. *David and Bathsheba* (1951) had him embarrassingly miscast; and *The World in His Arms* (1952) was another seafaring yarn with Ann Blyth as his co-star.

In the early Fifties, Peck appeared to be in professional limbo as an independent actor who, without the protection of a studio, was beginning to feel the bite of that omniverous, one-eyed

With Torin Thatcher and Ava Gardner in *The Snows of Kilimanjaro* (1951).

With Audrey Hepburn in *Roman Holiday* (1953).

monster — television. Furthermore, while young enough to remain a romantic lead, he had not yet come into his own as a resonant character actor, except for his portrayal in *Twelve O'Clock High*.

Ironically it was Casey Robinson, his original mentor, who extricated him from his professional morass by urging 20th Century-Fox to cast him as the autobiographical Ernest Hemingway-writer-hunter in *The Snows of Kilimanjaro* (1952). Robinson had become Hollywood's authority on translating Hemingway for the screen and had also written this screenplay. 20th Century-Fox complied, and Peck was perfectly cast as the introspective writer who remembers the women of his past — Ava Gardner, Susan Hayward, Hildegarde Neff. Of working with Miss Gardner, Peck says, "It was the second of the three pictures I made with Ava Gardner. As a person she has always been a close friend, and as an actress she is my favorite leading lady."

Peck's next assignment, *Roman Holiday* (1953), also provided him with box-office security. Beautifully directed by William Wyler, Peck was the journalist who cavorts with a princess, Audrey Hepburn, in what is now a classic comedy and an all-time favourite with television audiences. While not always at ease in comedies, Peck enjoys performing in them, but says he is only offered a comedy script "after Cary Grant has turned it down." Of *Roman Holiday* he says, "It was fun right from the start. There was so much affection and goodwill among the cast. We all knew Audrey Hepburn would become a star the day after the opening." Miss Hepburn received the Academy Award for her glowing performance.

Peck's wife, Greta, and their three sons — Jonathan Gregory, Stephen, and Carey Paul — joined Peck in Europe during the production of *Roman Holiday*. Greta and the children returned from Europe without Peck and on January 13, 1953, announced a separation. In the meantime, Peck had met a young journalist in Paris named Veronique Passani, of French, Italian and Russian heritage. She had interviewed Peck for the Paris "Presse" and Peck later asked her to dinner. As reports of a romance made the newspapers, Peck stated, "She's just a girl I met in Paris. Nothing serious. I see her once in a while just like any old friend."

On the July 4th weekend of 1954, the Pecks announced their plan for a divorce. Greta Peck stated, "He stayed away from home nights and wouldn't tell me what he was doing." Peck stated simply, "We had become indifferent toward each other. I may have been intolerant, she may have been at fault. I don't know the reason for our unhappiness." The interlocutory decree was granted on December 29, 1954 on grounds of "grievious mental suffering and embarrassment." The divorce provided Greta Peck with custody of the children, $750 monthly child support, their home at 1700 Remo Drive in Pacific Palisades, one half their community assets, and alimony in excess of $65,000 annually. The alimony clause was intricately based on Peck's earning power: 20% of the first $100,000, 12½% of the second $100,000, 10% of the third $100,000, 7½% of the fourth $100,000, and 5% thereafter, till 1965, at which time the alimony would simply be ten percent of his entire earnings until she remarried. Greta Peck has never remarried and she and Peck remain on friendly terms.

Peck married Veronique in Lompoc, California, on December 31, 1955, three days after his divorce became final. They now have two children — Anthony (October 24, 1956) and Cecilia Alexandre (May 1, 1959).

In 1953, Peck signed a lucrative, non-exclusive contract with 20th Century-Fox, but the films provided him with few good roles. *Night People* (1954) was only a moderately good spy story. *The Man in the Gray Flannel Suit* (1956) in which Peck

With Jennifer Jones in *The Man in the Gray Flannel Suit* (1956).

played a nine-to-five commuter battling life and integrity in the business world, was an unsuccessful parody of Madison Avenue. *The Bravados* (1958) was a boring off-beat western; and *Beloved Infidel* (1959), his last commitment with Fox, was not any better, but gained a box-office notoriety for being the story of Sheilah Graham's love affair with F. Scott Fitzgerald. Of this picture Peck said, "Both Deborah Kerr and I owed 20th Century-Fox a picture and so we did *Infidel*. The schizophrenic quality of the script spoiled it. They didn't know whether they wanted it to be the last episode in the life of an American writer, which I would have liked, or a Cinderella yarn about Little Nell from Cockney London."

Peck's pictures for other studios during this time were equally un-noteworthy. *Man With a Million* (1954) was a British version of Mark Twain's "The Million Pound Bank Note" in which Peck was the penniless American. *The Purple Plain* (1955) cast him as a reckless, neurotic pilot in World War II Burma, and *Designing Woman* (1957), was a less-than-amusing comedy which cast him as a gruffly charming sports writer in love with fashion designer, Lauren Bacall.

The one picture Peck made during this time which he claims was his career's turning point and which he claims was responsible for his "loss of innocence" was *Moby Dick* (1956). Peck explains it, "When John Huston, who produced and directed *Moby Dick* (1956), talked to me about it, I thought he wanted me for Starbuck, for which I am suited. Later I learned he needed me to finance the production. Which is what I meant when I said *Moby Dick* was the end of my innocence. Anyway, John, who has too much Irish charm, wove his spell and convinced me I'd be the ticket as Ahab. And though I'd always thought Ahab a damned old fool, I tried to portray him." Peck owned ten percent of the picture, which was a $5,000,000 flop, and he earned no profits from it. Two earlier versions of Herman Melville's tale were made with John Barrymore—*The Sea Beast* (1926) and *Moby Dick* (1930). Of Peck's attempt to portray Ahab, film critic and historian, Henry Hart, wrote in "Films in Review," "Melville's Ahab was lashed and lacerated ceaselessly by monomania. His ever fewer contacts with reality consisted of irrational and fanatical attempts to get others to accept as real his unreal delusions. Such welter of the soul is beyond Peck's capacity. Peck can project an implacable inner strength that is conquering and unconquerable because it is cognizant of the outside world and of the purposes of the people who live in it — reasonable, tolerant, forgiving, but nevertheless sure to prevail. None of this has anything to do with Ahab. How Barrymore could have played Ahab for Huston!"

With Lauren Bacall in *Designing Woman* (1957).

Even though Peck knew he was miscast and obviously had been chosen as the star of the picture to insure it as a bankable project, he nonetheless tried to inject some of Melville's mystique into his Ahab, albeit unsuccessfully. Not all the blame was his. Of Huston's direction, Peck says, "I remember one scene on which all he said was: 'Feel the camera on your face.' Which merely confused me. And in the important scene in which I had a long speech beginning 'If there is a God there must be a malevolent God,' I was told: 'Kid, if you ever deliver the goods this has got to be the time.' Is that direction?"

After this devastating financial and personal disaster, Peck decided to pick up the reins of his career and became co-producer, with director William Wyler of *The Big Country* (1958), which they released through United Artists. Their production company was called Anthony World Wide Productions after Peck's youngest son, and the picture was a grandiose western not unlike Selznick's *Duel in the Sun*. Peck portrayed a retired seaman from Baltimore who comes West to marry Carroll Baker, the daughter of rancher Charles Bickford, but ends up marrying ranch-owner, Jean Simmons. Peck, who had enjoyed working with Wyler on *Roman Holiday,* discovered Wyler was shooting too much footage at great expense and this brought an end to their amicable relationship. Peck says, "We've since made it up and I have great affection for him and admiration for his talent. He offers actors what they need most: a one-man audience demanding nothing less than their best."

At the time he had entered into co-production with Wyler, Peck said, "I get a regular salary plus part of the profits on deferrment, which means if there are no profits I get nothing but salary. The backers, in this case United Artists, take a relatively small slice of the profits, and Willie and I, as producers, take big slices. The question is whether the time you put in is worthwhile, whether we'll strike it rich over the years. You have to be a businessman as well as an actor nowadays to keep any money at all. As an actor on salary, I can't make money after $200,000 a year."

Also in 1958, Peck narrated a documentary about insect life called *The Small World,* written by Robert Snyder and C. Sonnabend.

His next picture, *Pork Chop Hill* (1959), was also co-produced, this time with Sy Bartlett who had worked on the screenplay of *The Big Country,* and this picture was also released through United Artists. Based on the real-life story of Korean War hero, Joseph Clemens, Peck played the title role and endeavoured to make it a *human* war drama. Director Lewis Milestone objected to Peck's view for editing the picture saying that the whole aspect of the Koreans fighting the Chinese was lost. Milestone said, "I did have the Chinese side adequately shown at the beginning, but not for long. Gregory Peck took it out at the urging of his wife. 'You know, darling,' she said, 'nothing happens until you come on the screen, so why don't you just lop it off?' He thought it was a great idea and lopped it off." Once again the fledgling producer did not "strike it rich." Three years later he stated that while he believed independent producers have "saved the industry," he nevertheless, spent "two profitless years" producing *The Big Country* and *Pork Chop Hill.* He added with levity that the former picture grossed $8,000,000 and the latter $3,400,000, but "as yet none of this pleasant money has rubbed off on the producer. The banks have taken a small, and I hope, well-distributed loss. On the other hand, the distributor has taken thirty-five cents of every dollar from the first to last, as per agreement. Exhibitors have shared in the take on two pictures that would not have been made except at the instigation of this 'shoemaker.' Hollywood actors, technicians and teamsters were not unhappy with the work created for them or with their well-earned paychecks. Who then was the real loser? Why, yours truly, who spent two highly educational but profitless years learning that turning out motion pictures of quality can be lovely for everyone but the producer."

Simultaneously with the release of Peck's *Pork Chop Hill,* Stanley Kramer, now as producer and director, offered Peck *On the Beach* (1959). While no *High Noon*, it was a gruesomely realistic story of radioactive fallout. Peck played the submarine commander who temporarily becomes infatuated with Ava Gardner, while refusing to believe that his wife and children are dead of an atomic blast. Peck and Gardner once more made an attractive on-screen love duo.

Despite Peck's two unprofitable undertakings as producer, he still felt he could make a financial killing producing his own pictures, given the right script at the right time. This kind of tenacity paid off with *The Guns of Navarone* (1961). This exciting story of commandoes who blow up a formidable German gun emplacement was an immediate box-office grosser. Peck followed this with the respectable but less financially rewarding *Cape Fear* (1962), a suspenseful melodrama in which lawyer Peck has the lives of his wife (Polly Bergen) and child (Lori Martin) threatened by an escaped rapist (Robert Mitchum).

By far Peck's most artistically rewarding venture as a producer was *To Kill a Mockingbird* (1962). Based on Harper Lee's prize-winning novel about racial discrimination, Peck's portrayal of Atticus Finch, the small town Southern attorney who defends a Negro accused of rape, was the synthesis of his Lincolnesque screen image. Of this picture, Peck says, "Well, of course, the subject matter is something I feel strongly about, you know, the racial question. I thought it was of some value to portray a fair-minded Southerner for a change — a white Southern lawyer who *would* risk and incur enmity, a loss of his standing in the town, by defending a Negro on an unpopular charge like that. There *are* such Southerners, so I was glad, for a change, to be able to portray one on the screen. And the relationship between the father and the children was something I could identify with. And that small-town life is familiar to me, because I was a kid in La Jolla, California." This superb film earned Peck the Academy Award as Best Actor of the Year, and would probably have won him a second New York Film Critics Award had the New York newspaper strike not prevented that body of critics from bestowing awards that year. Upon winning the Oscar, Peck stated, "Having won it makes you feel at home with yourself."

Peck was one of the huge cast of stars in *How the West Was Won* (1963), playing the gambler whom Debbie Reynolds loves. After which he produced both an artistic and financial flop in

In *To Kill a Mockingbird* (1962).

In *How the West Was Won* (1963).

Behold a Pale Horse (1964). Here he was miscast as a Spanish loyalist and even the excellent director, Fred Zinnemann, could not get the script off the ground.

In the middle Sixties, Peck's career had reached a point where most of his starring roles were little more than attempts to trade on the Peck image. Although he personally liked his role as the compassionate psychiatrist in *Captain Newman, M.D.* (1964), most of his roles since that time have been perfunctory. In *Mirage* (1965) he was a physiochemist who suffers from amnesia, and in *Arabesque* (1966) he and Sophia Loren spoofed the spy *genre*. Concurrently, Peck, a friend of the New Frontier, was chosen to narrate the documentary, *John F. Kennedy: Years of Lightning, Day of Drums* (1966), produced by the U.S. Information Agency.

No pictures starring Peck were released during 1967 and 1968. At this time however, he was named National Crusade Chairman of the American Cancer Society, in addition to being actively involved in establishing the American Film Institute, serving as a member of the National Council on the Arts, and being elected president of the Academy of Motion Picture Arts and Sciences (June 1967 to May 1969). In February, 1968, at the Academy's awards presentations for 1967, Rosalind Russell was chosen to present Peck with the Jean Hersholt Humanitarian Award. At the same ceremony, Peck, as the Academy's president, made an opening speech paying tribute to the late Martin Luther King: "Society has always been reflected in its art and one measure of Dr. King's influence on the society in which we live is that of the five films nominated for Best Picture of the Year, two (*Guess Who's Coming to Dinner?* and *In the Heat of the Night*) dealt with the subject of understanding between the races. It was his work and dedication that brought about the increasing awareness of all men that we must unite in compassion in order to survive. The lasting memorial that we of the motion-picture community can build to Dr. King is to continue making films which celebrate the dignity of man, whatever his race, or color or creed."

Peck's feature films since 1966 have been largely mediocre. *The Stalking Moon* (1969), originally to have been directed by George Stevens, was directed by Robert Mulligan, who had directed *To Kill a Mockingbird*, and was an unsatisfactory western in which Peck played a professional scout in Arizona in 1881. *Mackenna's Gold* (1969) reunited Peck with producer-writer Carl Foreman and director J. Lee Thompson of *The Guns of Navarone*, but again was another expensive, below-par western in which Peck played a U.S. marshall. *The Chairman* (1969) cast Peck as a Nobel Prize winning scientist but this too was a disappointing picture. *Marooned* (1970) was a timely drama about our Houston space centre with Peck as the head of the ground controls, but despite its timeliness, it failed to capture an audience. Two more routine westerns followed. *I Walk the Line* (1970) cast Peck as a sheriff obsessed with a moonshiner's daughter (Tuesday Weld), and *Shootout* (1971) had him as a hardened ex-convict seeking revenge after leaving prison.

While these pictures kept Peck's name in front of the audience, that audience preferred to watch the now popular made-for-television movies in the comfort of their homes rather than go to see their once popular hero in the movie houses. In 1972, Peck decided to produce a picture whose theme he believed in, but in which he refused to star. *The Trial of the Cantonsville Nine* was based on Father Daniel Berrigan's anti-war play. Peck, a practising Catholic, says, "I think the effect the play had on me when I first saw it in Los Angeles had something to do with my Catholicism, the Catholic Left: these are people who are willing to *live* their religion, not just recite it." The picture was a filmed version of the play as it had appeared on stage, except for a few connecting scenes as in the opening scene of the burning of the draft cards. It was filmed at the old Selznick studio in Culver City at the cost of $250,000. Its critical reception was respectful, but it did not gain any large audience.

In 1974, Peck returned to the screen as the star of *Billy Two Hats*, an Israeli-produced western, where a bushily bearded Peck was excellent in the character role of an outlaw.

After thirty years as one of Hollywood's top stars, Peck's considerable fortune allows him the luxury of devoting most of his time to producing. This financial stability enables him to turn down those embarrassing, mediocre roles which cropped up so often in his later years and to accept only an occasional starring role in a picture which interests him. For his own company, Atticus Corporation (named after the lawyer in *To Kill a Mockingbird*), Peck recently produced with David Wolper a four-part television series for ABC, called "Primal Man." His most recent project as producer is the screen version of *The Dove*, based on the book by Robin Lee Graham and Derek Gill, which tells the true story of Graham's solo, round-the-world cruise aboard a twenty-four-foot sloop.

Of his early years as a screen actor, Peck, in the Fifties, commented, "I was tied to five separate contracts. It took me seven years to work out all the deals I owed, with the exception of one upcoming picture *(Beloved Infidel)* sometime in the future for Fox. I don't have any regrets, though. I feel it wasn't a state of bondage, but a foundation for the career which now is a challenge. I wasn't particularly good in my early movie days. I know for sure, since I've looked at myself on television in *Spellbound* and *The Valley of Decision*."

While always an active citizen of Hollywood both socially and politically, he is an intensely private person who says, "I've worked with some of the top moguls — Goldwyn, Selznick, Zanuck — and they were interested only in whether or not I made money for them on the motion-picture screen. What I did with my private life did not concern them and they couldn't have cared less about how or how many times my name appeared in the columns of Louella Parsons and Hedda Hopper."

Peck likes acting and his colleagues and speaks out against Hollywood's denegrators, "My profession makes the most fascinating talk I know. I don't understand these people who say they want to get away from everything connected with their work when they're not acting. I love everything and almost everyone connected with my job."

The Feature Film Appearances of Gregory Peck

Days of Glory (RKO, 1944). Screenplay by Casey Robinson from a story by Melchior Lengyel. Directed by Jacques Tourneur. *Cast:* Gregory Peck, Tamara Toumanova, Alan Reed, Maria Palmer, Hugo Haas, Lowell Gilmore, Dena Penn, Glenn Vernon, Igor Dolgoruki, Edward L. Durst, Lou Crosby, William Challee, Joseph Vitale, Erford Gage, Ivan Tresatt, Maria Babikov, Edgar Licho, Gretl Dupont, Peter Helmers.

The Keys of the Kingdom (20th Century-Fox, 1945). Screenplay by Joseph L. Mankiewicz and Nunnally Johnson from the novel by A.J. Cronin. Directed by John M. Stahl. *Cast:* Gregory Peck, Thomas Mitchell, Vincent Price, Rose Stradner, Roddy McDowall, Edmund Gwenn, Sir Cedric Hardwicke, Peggy Ann Garner, Jane Ball, James Gleason, Anne Revere, Ruth Nelson, Benson Fong, Leonard Strong, Philip Ahn, Arthur Shields, Edith Barrett, Sara Allgood, Richard Loo, Ruth Ford, Kevin O'Shea, H.T. Tsiang, Si-Lan Chen, Eunice Soo Hoo, Dennis Hoey, Abner Biberman Jr., Anthony Hughes, George Nokes, Hayward Soo Hoo, James Leong, Moy Ming, Frank Eng, Oie Chan, Beal Wong, Eugene Louie, Ruth Clifford.

The Valley of Decision (M-G-M, 1945). Screenplay by John Meehan and Sonya Levien from the novel by Marcia Davenport. Directed by Tay Garnett. *Cast:* Greer Garson, Gregory Peck, Donald Crisp, Lionel Barrymore, Preston Foster, Gladys Cooper, Marsha Hunt, Reginald Owen, Dan Duryea, Jessica Tandy, Barbara Everest, Marshall Thompson, Mary Lord, John Warburton, Mary Currier, Arthur Shields, Russell Hicks, Geraldine Wall, Norman Ollstead, Evelyn Dockson, Connie Gilchrist, Willa Pearl Curtis, William O'Leary, Richard Abbott, Dean Stockwell, Joy Harrington, Lumsden Hare, Anna Q. Nilsson, Sherlee Collier, Mike Ryan.

Spellbound (Selznick International-United Artists, 1945). Screenplay by Ben Hecht from Angus MacPhail's adaptation of the novel "The House of Doctor Edwards" by Francis Beeding. Directed by Alfred Hitchcock. *Cast:* Ingrid Bergman, Gregory Peck, Michael Chekhov, Jean Acker, Donald Curtis , Rhonda Fleming, Leo G. Carroll. Norman Lloyd, John Emery, Paul Harvey, Steven Geray, Erskine Sanford, Janet Scott, Victor Kilian, Wallace Ford, Dave Willock, Bill Goodwin, George Meader, Matt Moore, Harry Brown, Art Baker, Regis Toomey, Joel Davis, Clarence Straight, Teddy Infuhr, Richard Bartell, Addison Richards, Edward Fielding.

The Yearling (M-G-M, 1946). Screenplay by Paul Osborn from the novel by Marjorie Kinnan Rawlings. Directed by Clarence Brown. *Cast:* Gregory Peck, Jane Wyman, Claude Jarman Jr.. Chill Wills, Clem Bevans, Margaret Wycherly, Henry Travers, Forrest Tucker, Donn Gift, Daniel White, Matt Willis, George Mann, Arthur Hohl, June Lockhart, Joan Wells, Jeff York, B.M. Chick York, Houseley Steveson, Jane Green, Victor Kilian, Robert Porterfield, Frank Eldredge.

Duel in the Sun (Selznick Releasing Organization, 1946). Screenplay by David O. Selznick from an adaptation by Oliver H.P. Garrett of the novel by Niven Busch. Directed by King Vidor. *Cast:* Jennifer Jones, Joseph Cotten, Gregory Peck, Lionel Barrymore, Lillian Gish, Walter Huston, Herbert Marshall, Charles Bickford, Joan Tetzel, Harry Carey, Otto Kruger, Sidney Blackner, Tilly Losch, Scott McKay, Butterfly McQueen, Francis MacDonald, Victor Kilian, Griff Barnett, Frank Cordell, Dan White, Steve Dunhill, Lane Chandler, Lloyd Shaw, Thomas Dillon, Robert McKenzie, Charles Dingle, Kermit Maynard, Hank Bell, Johnny Bond, Bert Roach, Si Jenks, Hank Worden, Rose Plummer, Guy Wilkerson, Lee Phelps. *Narrated by Orson Welles.*

The Macomber Affair (United Artists, 1947). Screenplay by Casey Robinson and Seymour Bennett from Bennett's adaptation of "The Short Happy Life of Francis Macomber, by Ernest Hemingway. Directed by Zoltan Korda. *Cast:* Gregory Peck, Joan Bennett, Robert Preston, Reginald Denny, Frederic Worlock, Carl Harboard, Jean Gille, Earl Smith, Vernon Downing.

Gentlemen's Agreement (20th Century-Fox 1947). Screenplay by Moss Hart from the novel by Laura Z. Hobson. Directed by Ella Kazan. *Cast:* Gregory Peck, Dorothy McGuire, John Garfield, Celeste Holm, Anne Revere, June Havoc, Albert Dekker, Jane Wyatt, Dean Stockwell, Nicholas Joy, Sam Jaffe, Harold Vermilyea, Ransom M. Sherman, Roy Roberts, Kathleen Lockhart, Curt Conway, John Newland, Robert Warwick, Robert Karnes, Gene Nelson, Marion Marshall, Louise Lorimer, Howard Negley, Victor Kilian, Frank Wilcox, Marilyn Monk, Wilton Graff, Morgan Farley, Mauritz Hugo, Olive Deering, Jane Green, Virginia Gregg, Jesse White.

The Paradine Case (Selznick Releasing Corporation, 1947) Screenplay by David O. Selznick from an adaptation by Alma Reville and James Bridie of the novel by Robert Hichens. Directed by Alfred Hitchcock. *Cast:* Gregory Peck, Charles Laughton, Charles Coburn, Ann Todd, Ethel Barrymore, Louis Jourdan, Alida Valli, Leo G. Carroll, Joan Tetzel, Isobel Elson, Lester Matthews, Pat Aherne, Colin Hunter, John Williams, John Goldsworthy.

Yellow Sky (20th Century-Fox, 1948). Screenplay by Lamar Trotti from the story by W.R. Burnett. Directed by William A. Wellman. *Cast:* Gregory Peck, Anne Baxter, Richard Widmark, Robert Arthur, John Russell, Henry Morgan, James Barton, Charles Kemper, Robert Adler, Victor Kilian, Paul Hurst, William Gould, Norman Leavitt, Chief Yowlachie, Eula Guy.

The Great Sinner (M-G-M, 1949). Screenplay by Ladislas Fodor and Christopher Isherwood from a story by Fodor and Rene Fueloep-Miller based on Dostoievsky's "The Gambler." Directed by Robert Siodmak. *Cast:* Gregory Peck, Ava Gardner, Melvyn Douglas, Walter Huston, Ethel Barrymore, Agnes Moorehead, Frank Morgan, Frederick Ledebur, Ludwig Donath, Curt Bois, Ludwig Stossel, Erno Verebes.

Twelve O'Clock High (20th Century-Fox, 1949). Screenplay by Sy Bartlett and Beirne Lay Jr., from their novel. Directed by Henry King. *Cast:* Gregory Peck, Hugh Marlowe, Garry Merrill, Millard Mitchell, Dean Jagger, Robert Arthur, Paul Stewart, John Kellogg, Robert Patton, Lee MacGregor, Sam Edwards, Roger Anderson, John Zilly, William Short, Richard Anderson, Lawrence Dobkin, Kenneth Tobey, John McKee, Campbell Copelin, Don Guadagno, Peter Ortiz, Steve Clark, Joyce MacKenzie, Don Hicks, Ray Hyke, Harry Lauter, Leslie Denison, Russ Conway.

The Gunfighter (20th Century-Fox, 1950). Screenplay by William Bowers and William Sellers from the story by Bowers and Andre de Toth. Directed by Henry King. *Cast:* Gregory Peck, Helen Westcott, Millard Mitchell, Jean Parker, Karl Malden, Skip Homeier, Anthony Ross, Verna Felton, Ellen Corby, Richard Jaeckel, Alan Hale Jr., David Clarke, John Pickard, D.G. Norman, Angela Clarke, Cliff Clark, Jean Inness, Eddie Ehrhart, Albert Morin, Kenneth Tobey, Michael Brandon, Eddie Parkes, Ferris Taylor, Hank Patterson, Mae Marsh, Credda Zajac, Ann Wiitfield.

Captain Horatio Hornblower (Warner Brothers, 1951). Screenplay by Ivan Goff, Ben Roberts and Aenas MacKenzie from an adaptation by C.S. Forester of his novel. Directed by Raoul Walsh. *Cast:* Gregory Peck, Virginia Mayo, James Robertson Justice, Robert Beatty, Dennis O'Dea, Ingeborg Wells, Alec Mango, Moultrie Kelsall, Terence Morgan, Richard Hearne, James Kenney.

Only the Valiant (Warner Brothers, 1951). Screenplay by Edmund H. North and Harry Brown from the novel by Charles Marquis Warren. Directed by Gordon Douglas. *Cast:* Gregory Peck, Ward Bond, Gig Young, Barbara Payton, Lon Chaney, Neville Brand, Jeff Corey, Warner Anderson, Steve Brodie, Dan Riss, Terry Kilburn, Herbert Heyes, Art Baker, Hugh Sanders, Michael Ansara, Nana Bryant.

David and Bathsheba (20th Century-Fox, 1951). Screenplay by Philip Dunne. Directed by Henry King. *Cast:* Gregory Peck, Susan Hayward, Raymond Massey, Kieron Moore, James Robertson Justice, Jayne Meadows, John Sutton, Dennis Hoey, Walter Talun, Paula Morgan, Francis X. Bushman, Teddy Infuhr, Leo Pessin, Gwyneth (Gwen) Verdon, Gilbert Barnett, John Burton, Lumsden Hare, George Zucco, Allan Stone, Paul Newlan, Holmes Herbert, Robert Stephenson, Harry Carter, Richard Michelson, Dick Winters, John Duncan, James Craven, Shepard Menken, John Dodsworth.

The World in His Arms (Universal, 1951). Screenplay by Borden Chase. Directed by Raoul Walsh. *Cast:* Gregory Peck, Ann Blyth, Anthony Quinn, John McIntyre, Andrea King, Carl Esmond, Eugenie Leontovitch, Sig Ruman. Hans Conreid, Bryan Forbes, Rhys Williams, Bill Radovich, Gregory Gay, Henry Kulky.

The Snows of Kilimanjaro (20th Century-Fox, 1952). Screenplay by Casey Robinson from the short story by Ernest Hemingway. Directed by Henry King. *Cast:* Gregory Peck, Susan Hayward, Ava Gardner, Hildegarde Neff, Leo G. Carroll, Torin Thatcher, Ava Norring, Helen Stanley, Marcel Dalio, Vincent Gomez, Richard Allen, Leonard Carey, Paul Thompson, Emmett Smith, Victor Wood, Bert Freed, Agnes Laury, Monique Chantal, Janine Grandel, John Dodsworth, Charles Bates, Lisa Ferraday, Maya Van Horn, Ivan Lebedeff, Martin Garralaga, George Davis, Julian Rivero, Edward Colmans, Ernest Brunner, Arthur Brunner.

Roman Holiday (Paramount, 1953). Screenplay by Ian McLellan Hunter, and John Dighton from the story by Hunter. Directed by William Wyler. *Cast:* Gregory Peck, Audrey Hepburn, Eddie Albert, Hartley Power, Laura Solari, Harcourt Williams, Margaret Rawlings, Tullio Carminati, Paola Carlini, Claudio Ermelli, Paola

Borboni, Heinz Hindrich, Gorella Gori, Alfredo Rizzo.

Night People (20th Century-Fox, 1954). Screenplay by Nunnally Johnson from a story by Jed Harris and Thomas Reed. Directed by Nunnally Johnson *Cast:* Gregory Peck, Broderick Crawford, Anita Bjork, Rita Gam, Walter Abel, Buddy Ebsen, Casey Adams, Jill Esmond, Peter Van Eyck, Marianne Koch, Ted Avery, Hugh McDerrott, Paul Carpenter, John Horseley, Lionel Burton.

Man With a Million (United Artists, 1954). Screenplay by Jill Cragie based on Mark Twain's story, "The Million Pound Bank Note." Directed by Ronald Neame. *Cast:* Gregory Peck, Jane Griffith, Ronald Squire, A.E. Matthews, Wilfred Hyde-White, Reginald Beckwith, Hartley Power, Brian Oulton, Wilbur Evans, Maurice Denham, Bryan Forbes, John Slater, Hugh Wakefield, Ronald Adam, Joan Hickson.

The Purple Plain (United Artists, 1955). Screenplay by Eric Ambler from the novel by H.E. Bates. Directed by Robert Parrish. *Cast:* Gregory Peck, Bernard Lee, Maurice Denham, Brenda De Banzie, Lyndon Brook, Win Min Than, Ram Gopal, Anthony Bushell, Jack McNaughton, Harold Siddons, Peter Arno, Mya Mya Spencer, Josephine Griffin.

The Man in the Gray Flannel Suit (20th Century-Fox, 1956). Screenplay by Nunnally Johnson from the novel by Sloan Wilson. Directed by Nunnally Johnson. *Cast:* Gregory Peck, Jennifer Jones, Fredric March, Marisa Pavan, Ann Harding, Lee J. Cobb. Keenan Wynn, Gene Lockhart, Gigi Perreau, Portland Mason, Arthur O'Connell, Henry Daniell, Connie Gilchrist, Joseph Sweeney, Sandy Descher, Mickey Maga, Kenneth Tobey, Ruth Clifford, Geraldine Wall, Alex Campbell, Jerry Hall, Jack Mather, Frank Wilcox. Nan Martin, Tris Coffin, William Philips. Leon Alton, Phyllis Graffeo, Dorothy Adams, Dorothy Phillips, Mary Benoit, King Lockwood, Lomax Study, John Breen, Renato Vanni, Mario Siletti, Lee Graham, Michael Jeffries, Roy Glenn.

Moby Dick (Warner Brothers, 1956). Screenplay by Ray Bradbury and John Huston from the novel by Herman Melville. Directed by John Huston. *Cast:* Gregory Peck, Richard Basehart, Leo Genn, Orson Welles, James Robertson Justice, Harry Andrews, Bernard Miles, Noel Purcell, Edric Connor, Mervyn Johns, Joseph Tomelty, Francis De Wolff, Philip Stainton, Royal Dano, Seamus Kelly, Friedrich Ledebur, Ted Howard, Tamba Allenery, Tom Clegg, Iris Tree.

Designing Woman (M-G-M, 1957). Screenplay by George Wells based on an idea by Helen Rose. Directed by Vincente Minnelli. *Cast:* Gregory Peck, Lauren Bacall, Dolores Gray, San Levene, Tom Hellmore, Mickey Shaughnessy, Jesse White, Chuck Connors, Edward Platt, Alvy Moore, Carol Veazie, Jack Cole.

The Bravados (20th Century-Fox, 1958). Screenplay by Philip Yordan. Direct by Henry King. *Cast:* Gregory Peck, Kathleen Gallant, Stephen Boyd, Joan Collins, Barry Coe, George Voskovec, Herbert Rudley, Lee Van Cleef, Andrew Duggan, Ken Scott, Gene Evans, Ninos Cantores De Morelia Choral Group, Jack Mather, Joe De Rita, Robert Adler, Jason Wingreen, Robert Griffin, Ada Carrasco, Juan Garcia, Jacqueline Evans, Alicia del Lago.

The Big Country (United Artists, 1958). Screenplay by James R. Webb, Sy Bartlett and Robert Wilder from an adaptation by Jessamyn West and Robert Wilder from the novel by Donald Hamilton. Directed by William Wyler. *Cast:* Gregory Peck, Jean Simmons, Carroll Baker, Charlton Heston, Burl Ives, Charles Bickford, Alfonso Bedoya, Chuck Connors, Chuck Hayward, Buff Brady, Jim Burk, Dorothy Adams, Chuck Robertson, Bob Morgan, John McKee, Jay Slim Talbot, Donald Kerr, Ralph Sanford, Harry V. Chesire, Dick Alexander, Jonathan Gregory Peck, Stephen Peck, Carey Paul Peck.

Pork Chop Hill (United Artists, 1959). Screenplay by James R. Webb from the book by S.L.A. Marshall. Directed by Lewis Milestone. *Cast:* Gregory Peck, Rip Torn, Harry Guardino, James Edwards, George Peppard, Woody Strode, George Shibata, Norman Fell, Biff Elliot, William Wellman Jr., Martin Landau, Bob Steele, Barry Atwater, Michael Garth.

Beloved Infidel (20th Century-Fox, 1959). Screenplay by Sy Bartlett based on the book by Sheilah Graham and Gerold Frank. Directed by Henry King. *Cast:* Gregory Peck, Deborah Kerr, Eddie Albert, Philip Ober, Herbert Rudley, John Sutton, Karin Booth, Ken Scott, Buck Class, A. Cameron Grant, Cindy Ames.

On the Beach (United Artist, 1959). Screenplay by John Paxton and James Lee Barrett from the novel by Nevil Shute. Directed by Stanley Kramer. *Cast:* Gregory Peck, Ava Gardner, Fred Astaire, Anthony Perkins, Donna Anderson, John Tate, Lola Brooks, Lou Vernon, Guy Doleman, Ken Wayne, John Meillon, Richard Meikle, Harp McGuire, Jim Barrett, Basil Buller Murphy, Keith Eden, John Royle, John Casson, Kevin Brennan, C. Harding Brown, Grant Taylor, Peter Williams, Harvey Adams, Stuart Finch, Joe McCormick, Audine Leith, Jerry Ian Seals, Carey Paul Peck, Katherine Hill.

The Guns of Navarone (Columbia, 1961). Screenplay by Carl Foreman from the novel by Alistair MacLean. Directed by J. Lee Thompson. *Cast:* Gregory Peck, David Niven, Anthony Quinn, Stanely Baker, Anthony Quayle, Irene Papas, Gia Scala, James Darren, James Robertson Justice, Richard Harris, Bryan Forbes, Allan Cuthbertson, Michael Trubshawe, Percy Herbert, George Mikell, Walter Gotell, Tutte Lemkow, Albert Lieven, Norman Wooland, Cleo Scouloudi, Nicholas Papakonstantantinou, Christopher Rhodes.

Cape Fear (Universal, 1962). Screenplay by James R. Webb from the novel, "The Executioners" by John D. MacDonald. Directed by J. Lee Thompson. *Cast:* Gregory Peck, Robert Mitchum, Polly Bergen, Lori Martin, Martin Balsam, Jack Kruschen, Telly Savalas, Barrie Chase, Paul Comi, Edward Platt, John McKee, Page Slattery, Ward Ramsey, Will Wright, Joan Staley, Mack Williams, Thomas Newman, Bunny Rhea, Carol Sydes, Norma Yost, Alan Reynolds, Herb Armstrong, Alan Wells, Allan Ray, Paul Levitt.

To Kill a Mockingbird (Universal, 1962). Screenplay by Horton Foote from the novel by Harper Lee. Directed by Robert Mulligan. *Cast:* Gregory Peck, Mary Badham, Philip Alford, John Megna, Frank Overton, Rosemary Murphy, Ruth White, Brock Peters, Estelle Evans, Paul Fix, Collin Wilcox, James Anderson, Alice Ghostley, Robert Duvall, William Windom, Crahan Condit, Bill Walker, Hugh Sanders, Pauline Lyers, Jester Hairston, Jamie Forster, Nancy Marshall, Kim Hamilton, Kelly Thorsden, Dan White, Tex Armstrong, Kim Hector, David Crawford, Barry Seltzer, Guy Wilkerson, Charles Fredericks, Jay Sullivan.

How the West Was Won (M-G-M-Cinerama, 1963). Screenplay by James R. Webb suggested by a series of articles in "Life" Magazine. Directed by John Ford, Henry Hathaway, George Marshall. *Cast:* Carroll Baker, Lee J. Cobb, Henry Fonda, Carolyn Jones, Karl Malden, Gregory Peck, George Peppard, Robert Preston, Debbie Reynolds, James Stewart, Eli Wallach, John Wayne, Richard Widmark, Brigid Bazlen, Walter Brennan, David Brian, Andy Devine, Raymond Massey, Agnes Moorehead, Henry (Harry) Morgan, Thelma Ritter, Mickey Shaughnessy, Russ Tamblyn, Spencer Tracy, Kim Charney, Bryan Russell, Tudor Owen, Barry Harvey, Jamie Ross, Mark Allen, Lee Van Cleef, Charles Briggs, Jay C. Flippen, Clinton Sundberg, James Griffith, Walter Burke, Joe Sawyer, John Larch, Jack Pennick, Craig Duncan, Claude Johnson, Rodolfo Acosta.

Captain Newman, M.D. (Universal, 1964). Screenplay by Richard L. Breen and Phoebe and Henry Ephron from the novel by Leo Rosten. Directed by David Miller. *Cast:* Gregory Peck, Tony Curtis, Angie Dickinson, Eddie Albert, Bobby Darin, James Gregory, Jane Withers, Bethel Leslie, Robert Duvall, Dick Sargent, Larry Storch, Robert F. Simon, Crahan Denton, Gregory Walcott, Martin West, Syl Lamont, Vito Scotti, Penny Santon, Amzie Strickland, Barry Atwater, Ann Doran, Joey Walsh, David Winters, Byron Morrow, David Landfield, Ron Brogan, Robert Strong, John Hart, Charles Briggs, Paul Carr, Sam Reese, Ted Bessell, Marc Cavell, Seamon Glass, Jack Grinnage.

Behold a Pale Horse (Columbia, 1964). Screenplay by J.P. Miller from the novel by Emeric Pressburger. Directed by Fred Zinnemann. *Cast:* Gregory Peck, Anthony Quinn, Omar Sharif, Raymond Pellegrin, Paola Stoppa, Mildred Dunnock, Daniela Rocca, Christian Marquand, Marietto Angeletti, Perette Pradier, Zia Mohyeddin, Rosalie Crutchley.

Mirage (Universal, 1965). Screenplay by Peter Stone based on a story by Walter Ericson. Directed by Edward Dmytryk. *Cast:* Gregory Peck, Diane Baker, Walter Matthau, Kevin McCarthy, Jack Weston, Leif Erickson, Walter Abel. George Kennedy, Robert H. Harris, Anne Seymour, House B. Jameson, Hari Rhodes, Syl Lamont, Eileen Baral, Neil Fitzgerald, Franklin E. Cover.

John F. Kennedy: Years of Lightning, Day of Drums (Embassy, 1966). Produced by George Stevens Jr., for the United States Information Agency. Directed, written and musically scored by Bruce Herschensohn. Gregory Peck narrated this documentary about the two years and ten months of John F. Kennedy's service as President of the United States, with all proceeds going to the John F. Kennedy Center for the Performing Arts in Washington, D.C.

Arabesque (Universal, 1966). Screenplay by Julian Mitchell, Stanley Price and Pierre Malton from the novel "The Cipher" by Gordon Cotler. Directed by Stanley Donen. *Cast:* Gregory Peck, Sophia Loren, Alan Badel, Kieron Moore, Carl Duering, John Merivale, Duncan Lamont, George Coulouris, Ernest Clark, Harold Kasket.

The Stalking Moon (National General, 1969). Screenplay by Alvin Sargent from the adaptation by Wendell Mayes of the novel by Theodore V. Ilsen. Directed by Robert Mulligan. *Cast:* Gregory Peck, Eva Marie Saint, Robert Forester, Noland Gray, Nathaniel Narcisco, Frank Silvera.

Mackenna's Gold (Columbia, 1969.) Screenplay by Carl Foreman from the novel by Will Henry. Directed by J. Lee Thompson. *Cast:* Gregory Peck, Omar Sharif, Telly Savalas, Camilla Sparv, Keenan Wynn, Julie Newmar, Red Cassidy, Lee J. Cobb, Raymond Massey, Burgess Meredith, Anthony Quayle, Edward G. Robinson, Eli Wallach, Eduardo Ciannelli, Dick Peabody, Rudy Diaz, Robert Phillips, Shelley Morrison, J. Robert Porter, John Garfield Jr., Pepe Callahan, Madeleine Taylor Holmes, Duke Hobbie, Victor Jory.

The Chairman (20th Century-Fox, 1969). Screenplay by Ben Maddox from the novel by Jay Richard Kennedy. Directed by J. Lee Thompson. *Cast:* Gregory Peck, Anne Heywood, Arthur Hill, Alan Dobie, Conrad Yama, Zienia Merton, Ori Levy, Eric Young, Keye Luke, Francisca Tu.

Marooned (Columbia, 1970). Screenplay by Mayo Simon. Directed by John Sturges. *Cast:* Gregory Peck, Richard Crenna, David Janssen, James Franciscus, Gene Hackman, Lee Grant, Nancy Kovack, Mariette Hartley, Scott Brady, Frank Marth, Craig Huebing, John Carter.

I Walk the Line (Columbia, 1970). Screenplay by Alvin Sargent from the novel, "The Exile," by Madison Jones. Directed by John Frankenheimer. *Cast:* Gregory Peck, Tuesday Weld, Estelle Parsons, Ralph Meeker, Lonny Chapman, Charles Durning.

Shootout (Universal, 1971). Screenplay by James Poe and Marguerite Roberts from the novel, "Lone Cowboy," by Will James. Directed by Henry Hathaway. *Cast:* Gregory Peck, Robert F. Lyons, Susan Tyrell, Dawn Lyn, John Chandler, Pepe Serna, Nicolas Bauvy, James Gregory, Jeff Corey.

The Trial of the Cantonsville Nine (Cinema 5, 1972). Screenplay by Father Daniel Berrigan and Saul Levitt from Berrigan's play. Directed by Gordon Davidson. *Cast:* Given Arner, Edward Flanders, Barton Heyman, Mary Jackson, Rick Jordan, Nancy Malone, Donald Moffatt, Davis Roberts, Leon Russom, William Shallert, David Spielberg, Peter Strauss, Douglas Watson. Produced by Gregory Peck.

Billy Two Hats (United Artists, 1974). Screenplay by Alan Sharp. Directed by Ted Kotcheff. *Cast:* Gregory Peck, Desi Arnaz Jr., Jack Warden, Sian Barbara Allen, David Huddleston, John Pearce, Dawn Littlesky, Vincent St. Cyr, Zev Berlinsky, Henry Medicine Hat, Antony Scott.

The Dove (Paramount, 1974). Screenplay by Peter Beagle and Adam Kennedy from the book by Robin Lee Graham and Derek Gill. *Cast:* Joseph Bottoms, Deborah Raffin, John McLiam, Dabney Coleman, John Anderson, Colby Chester, Ivor Barry, Setoki Ceinaturoga, Reverend Nikula, Apenisa Naigulevu, John Meillon, Gordon Glenwright, Garth Meade, Peter Gwynne, Cecily Polson, Anthony Fridjon, Dale Cutts, Jose Augusto de Lima Sampaio a Silva. Produced by Gregory Peck.

Accepting her Special "little" Oscar from Irvin S. Cobb on February 27, 1935.

10

SHIRLEY TEMPLE

Never before or since, in Hollywood or any other place for that matter, has there been a more famous child star than Shirley Temple—that dimpled, curly-headed, singin'-'n-dancin' dynamo who skipped into the hearts of an entire generation here and abroad. While the plots of most of her pictures were little more than the escapism demanded by the times, Shirley Temple was much more than simply a trained and tutored performer who learned her lines by rote. She had a spontaneity and a natural charm which could bequile even a W.C.Fields. More importantly, she was a child actress.

As the world's most famous child star, she reigned supreme for five years, during which time she made forty-two feature films which paid her an astronomical salary and which earned for 20th Century-Fox nearly $30,000,000. By the time she was eleven years old, her stellar fame began to dim. Ironically the same youngster who had been called an Ethel Barrymore at six, was unable to sustain the public's interest at eleven.

The years between the ages of eleven and fifteen found her playing to a less and less interested audience. Finally at fifteen, the burgeoning young woman made a transition into more mature roles under the sponsorship of David O. Selznick. Her first several pictures as a teenager were successful, but the transition between the frothy fantasies of the Thirties and the more mature roles of the Forties was never fully realised. This was largely because Shirley Temple's personal goals had changed. An early and rocky marriage at seventeen prevented her from devoting her full attention to the future of her career. When that marriage ended in divorce at the age of twenty-one, Shirley Temple discarded Hollywood and everything connected with motion pictures. This action was intended to be temporary until such time as the young woman could pull her life together.

Almost like the clichéd plots of her old movies, the sweet and confused young thing met her Prince Charming, and a second marriage provided her with, to date, a life-style which has only intermittently allowed her to return to acting.

The same incidents — early marriage, motherhood and divorce — have permanently flawed the personalities of many of her fellow child actors and actresses. Miss Temple, however, coped with these vicissitudes with a wisdom unique among those who have spent their adolescence in the public eye. Her obviously strong character coupled with a successful marriage has allowed her to adjust to a life far removed from "Shirley Temple," and enabled her to devote much of her energies to meaningful public service. This remarkable lady's life is a living testimonial to the verities of life.

Shirley Jane Temple was born on April 23, 1928, in Santa Monica, California, the daughter of George Francis and Gertrude Craiger Temple. She had two older brothers — John (1916) and George

(1920), and their father was a bank teller at the California Bank in Los Angeles. At the suggestion of one of Mr. Temple's banking customers, the Temples enrolled their shy, blonde daughter in dancing school at the age of three in an effort to make her more outgoing. The school was located eighteen miles from Santa Monica, and Mrs. Temple had to learn to drive an automobile so she could accompany her daughter to school. As Shirley recalls, "I remember the school very clearly. Especially the day the movie scout came in because that was how I started making movies. When Mom discovered they expected a movie scout who was looking for child talent, we left. She had the car started, ready to go home, when my teacher asked her if she would let the scout see me. I wanted her to come in with me, but she had to stay outside with the other mothers while thirty or forty of us paraded up and down. The next week another man came in to look us over. He was Charles Lamont of Education Pictures, looking for twenty-five children to play in a series they were going to make, and he picked me."

When Gertrude Temple informed her husband that their daughter had been chosen to make moving pictures, she said he blew his stack until he learned that she would be earning $10 a day. With her family's consent, Shirley Jane Temple made her debut in the one-reeler, *War Babies* (1932), and she vividly remembers the experience: "The Baby Burlesk Series were one-reel takeoffs on famous motion pictures, with tiny children playing all the parts. The phenomenal success of Hal Roach's *Our Gang* comedies had made child movies sure-fire at the box-office. Baby Burlesks were shot in four days. At $10 a day, I wasn't doing too badly for a four-year-old in the middle of the depression! I carried the leading lady roles which were heavily costumed but a little sketchy on dialogue. The first words I spoke on the screen, strange as it seems, were French. I said, *'Mais oui, mon cher,'* Naturally I didn't know what the funny sounds meant and my accent must have been something. All of us wore very elaborate costumes, authentic grown-up clothes from the waist up and diapers pinned with enormous safety pins. One of my roles was a take-off on Marlene Dietrich and I was billed as Morelegs Sweetrick. I wore lots of blue feathers and sequins, which I considered really dreamy. That's probably the most sirenish outfit I've ever worn on the screen."

During 1932, and part of 1934, Shirley Temple appeared in over a dozen of these short subjects; however, as her contract with Educational Pictures was not exclusive, Gertrude Temple seized the opportunity and took her budding young star from studio to studio trying to get her cast in feature films. Shirley had a bit part in Capital's *The Red-Haired Alibi* (1932), and was the daughter of Gail Patrick and Barton MacLane in the Paramount western, *To the Last Man* (1933). She had a walk-on in Universal's *Out All Night* (1933) and bit parts in Warner Brother's *Mandalay* (1934) starring Kay Francis and Fox's *Carolina* (1934) starring Janet Gaynor.

By the time Shirley was six, she had worked for just about every major studio in Hollywood. Curiously, most of the child stars in Hollywood at that time were boys and except for Mary Pickford, there had been few girls who had captured the hearts of America as the boys had, e.g. Jackie Coogan. For this reason, many studios were reluctant to invest time and energy in promoting girls.

At a preview of one of her Educational shorts, Fox assistant director, Lou Horick, introduced Shirley to songwriter, Jay Gorney, who told her mother he had written a song for a little girl to be sung in Fox's *Stand Up and Cheer* (1934). He convinced Mrs. Temple she should promote her daughter for the part. The by now ambitious Gertrude Temple accepted Gorney's advice and several weeks later the Fox studio telephoned her and asked her to bring Shirley in for a test. When they arrived at the studio, the co-producer of *Stand Up and Cheer* quickly scribbled the words to the song, "Baby, Take a Bow" on the back of an envelope and told Shirley to memorise the words. In a few minutes the youngster was seated on top of a grand piano and accompanied by a forty-piece orchestra sang the song to James Dunn who was to star in the picture. Gertrude Temple later recalled, "It was perfectly done. Even I was thrilled. Harold Lloyd was standing in the back of me. He was saying, 'My God! Another Jackie Coogan!' "

Fox's production head, Winfield Sheehan liked the little moppet and signed her to a one-picture deal at $150 per week and for publicity reasons subtracted a year from her age (Shirley was not told of that missing year until her twelfth birthday.) When *Stand Up and Cheer* was released at Radio City Music Hall on April 19, 1934, "Variety" proclaimed her the "unofficial star of this Fox musical." With her long blonde curls, those famous dimples, and a polka dot dress, she sang and danced to "Baby, Take a Bow" with the ease of a veteran. The New York "Herald-Tribune" said, "A charming and remarkably engaging baby of perhaps five years, this little Shirley Temple proves a winning and natural child, with genius qualities of personality."

Immediately after the completion of *Stand Up and Cheer,* Paramount cast her in *Little Miss Marker* (1934) based on a story by Damon Runyon, where she played the child adopted by race-track gambler Adolphe Menjou. The picture was a hit; Menjou recalled. "I've played with a lot of actresses and I've had to learn how to defend myself. But this child frightens me. She knows all the tricks. She backs me out of the camera, blankets me, grabs my laughs, she's making a stooge out of me. Why, if she were forty years old and on stage all her life, she wouldn't have had time to learn all she knows about acting. Don't ask me how she does it. You've heard of chess champions at eight and violin virtuosoes at ten. Well, she's an Ethel Barrymore at six."

The successful acceptance of *Stand Up and Cheer* had convinced Fox's Winfield Sheehan that he should immediately sign Shirley Temple to a seven-year contract, before Paramount realised what a box-office treasure they had. The girl's parents agreed to the terms of the contract and put most of her salary into a trust fund. Gertrude Temple was then retained as her daughter's mentor-coach at $1,000 per week. Fox quickly put Shirley into bit parts in *Now I'll Tell* (1934) and *Change of Heart* (1934) which were both released before Paramount's *Little Miss Marker*. Their first starring role for her was in a film called *Baby Take a Bow* (1934) starring James Dunn and Claire Trevor in which Shirley sang "On Accounta I Love You" and walked away with the picture.

With Adolphe Menjou in *Little Miss Marker* (1934).

Fox then loaned her to Paramount for *Now and Forever* (1934) in which she was the daughter who rehabilitates her swindler father, Gary Cooper. Fox brought their dynamic little six-year old back to her home lot and cast her in her ninth and last feature film of 1934 — *Bright Eyes*. Again her co-star was James Dunn, and Fox threw in another child performer, Jane Withers, as her nasty rival. It was Shirley's rendition of "On the Good Ship Lollipop" that convinced the public and Fox that Shirley Temple was not merely a performing elephant or a freak, but a truly remarkable and gifted child actress.

Suddenly, there was a *blitzkreig* of Shirley Temple-itis after only one year of really being in the public eye. She was named by the Motion Picture "Herald" as number eight in the top ten money-making stars of 1934; and the public was deluged by the profit making business of producing Shirley Temple dolls, Shirley Temple comic books, Shirley Temple colouring books, Shirley Temple clothing, ad *infinitum*. Shirley Temple was presented with a special *little* Oscar "in grateful recognition of her outstanding contribution to screen entertainment during the year of 1934." Shortly thereafter her footprints were imprinted in the courtyard of Grauman's Chinese Theatre. Shirley Temple had taken the industry and the hearts of the public by storm. Quite a coup for a seven-year old who had begun her career by simply taking dancing lessons because her parents thought she was too shy and introverted.

Unlike most parents of gifted children, the Temples wisely protected their daughter from the public spotlight as much as they could. Shirley recalls, "I think I had the best kind of childhood anyone could have. Don't you see, instead of having all the great stories of myth and fiction read to me, it was possible for me to actually live the parts."

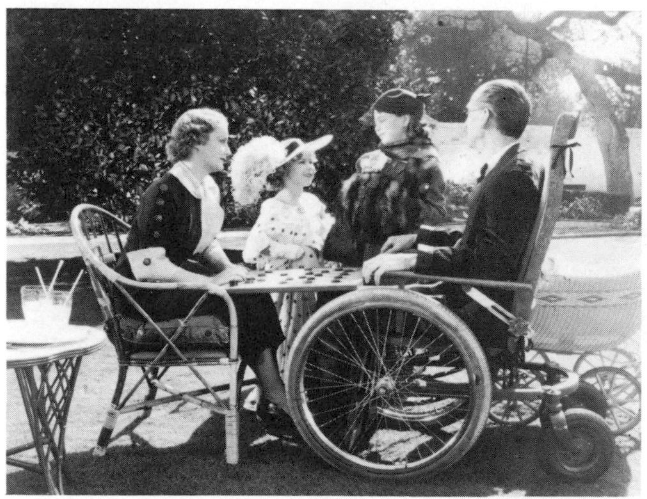

With Jane Withers in *Bright Eyes* (1934).

Two more successes followed *Bright Eyes* — *The Little Colonel* (1935) and *Our Little Girl* (1935), and production had begun on *Curly Top* (1935) when Fox merged with 20th Century. Winfield Sheehan was replaced as head of the studio by Darryl F. Zanuck, and the astute Zanuck realised Miss Temple was the studio's major commercial asset and continued to showcase her in carefully written and produced vehicles. Her first production under Zanuck's aegis was the popular *The Littlest Rebel* (1935) and for the next three years—1935-1938—she ranked number one at the box-office. The public flocked to see each of her pictures including —*Dimples* (1936), *Wee Willie Winkle* (1937), *Heidi* (1937) and *Rebecca of Sunnybrook Farm* (1938).

By 1936 she was receiving 3,500 fan letters a week and earning $307,014 annually. Each of her productions became more elaborate, but by 1939, the eleven-year-old's appeal had begun to wane. One production that most likely would have put her back on top was M-G-M's now classic *The Wizard of Oz* (1939). Louis B. Mayer, who owned the motion-picture rights to this story, coveted Miss Temple for the role of Dorothy and offered Zanuck the services of Clark Gable and Jean Harlow — two of M-G-M's biggest box-office draws — to star in Fox's *In Old Chicago* in exchange for Shirley Temple. Miss Harlow's premature death in 1937, put an end to that deal, and production of *The Wizard of Oz* was delayed until M-G-M decided to use the slightly older Judy Garland. Judy was already under contract to M-G-M and when she proved such a success in *The Broadway Melody of 1938* (released in 1937), Mayer and the picture's producer, Mervyn LeRoy, decided that, rather than become involved in an expensive loan-out deal, they would use their own property. This of course made Judy Garland a star.

By 1940, with the release of *Young People,* it became apparent that the public no longer showed a consuming interest in Shirley Temple. By this time Alice Faye had become 20th Century-Fox's number one draw at the box-office. Rather than shuttle Shirley from studio to studio, Gertrude Temple chose to settle her daughter's contract with 20th Century-Fox for $300,000 and enroll her in the exclusive Westlake School for Girls.

With Frank Morgan in *Dimples* (1936).

With Victor McLaglen in *Wee Willie Winkle* (1937).

Shirley Temple performed in a Lux Radio Theatre presentation of "The Littlest Rebel" on October 14, 1940, with Claude Rains, Bill Robinson, and Preston Foster, and the following February, it was announced that she would sign a contract with M-G-M at $2,500 per week and her mother would draw her usual $1,000. Various projects were announced for the young star but all failed to materialise. There were suggestions to team her with Mickey Rooney in the Andy Hardy series, to co-star her with Judy Garland, and to co-star her with Spencer Tracy in *National Velvet*. Nothing happened because Gertrude Temple and M-G-M could never come to a decision on any of these vehicles mainly because Mrs. Temple felt they did not showcase her daughter to the best advantage. And when the normally untemperamental Shirley refused to star in *Barnacle Bill* with Wallace Beery, an exasperated M-G-M put her into the now forgotten *Kathleen* (1941) starring Laraine Day and Herbert Marshall, and finally settled her contract with her mother. From M-G-M she went to United Artists where she made the moderately successful, *Little Annie Rooney* (1942), after which she was off the screen during 1943.

It was David O. Selznick who came to her rescue in 1943, and signed her to a long-term contract with his Selznick International Pictures with plans to promote her as a teenaged ingenue—a sweet, uncomplicated, unglamourised, and non-singing and dancing actress. Her mother negotiated the initial contractual agreement with Selznick, whereupon, unlike the typical stage mother, she told Shirley it was up to her to decide if she wished to continue acting. The fifteen-year-old Shirley, who had always loved performing and had never considered it work, only a great deal of fun, said she would like to continue.

Selznick cast her as the younger sister of Jennifer Jones in his wartime opus, *Since You Went Away* (1944), and even the sometimes cynical James Agee found her "enchanting." The same year, Selznick loaned her to his Vanguard Productions, a subsidiary headed by Dore Schary, to play the niece of Ginger Rogers, in *I'll Be Seeing You*. Again critics were kind to her and for a time she seemed to have regained her status and was re-

With Jennifer Jones and Claudette Colbert in *Since You Went Away* (1944).

ceiving more fan-mail than any of the other Selznick Players including Ingrid Bergman, Joseph Cotten and Jennifer Jones.

In 1945, Broadway producer George Abbott borrowed her from Selznick to star in his film version of the Broadway hit, *Kiss and Tell,* in which she played the irrepressibly scatter-brained teenager, Corliss Archer. She proved an adept comedienne and the New York "Times" said, "She's superb in the leading role, a compound of girlish innocence and female perversity."

During production of this picture, Miss Temple graduated from the Westlake School for Girls and at age seventeen announced her engagement to a young air-force sergeant named John George Agar Jr., who was seven years her senior.

Agar was born on January 31, 1921, the son of a well-to-do meat packing family in Chicago, Illinois. He had met Shirley at a party given by ZaSu Pitts in 1943. By that time he had already spent a $100,000 inheritance.

News of the engagement of the seventeen-year-old child star made national headlines, and the publicity-aware Gertrude Temple made a firm statement to the press saying, "Both Shirley and John have assured us they they have no intention of marrying for at least two years and possibly three." Enough for publicity, for less than four months later, on September 19, 1945, the teenage star became Mrs. John George Agar Jr. At first she had said, "I wanted an old-fashioned wedding, not a Hollywood circus." The wedding turned out to be one of Hollywood's most lavish in years with 500 guests, including Governor Earl Warren, and thousands of screaming fans outside the Wilshire Methodist Church.

The newly-weds honeymooned in Santa Barbara and took up living quarters in the doll's house that had been her dressing room on the 20th Century-Fox lot, and which was located behind the Temple estate.

Kiss and Tell was released as her "honeymoon" picture and in October, 1945, she published her autobiography, "My Young Life."

At the same time, her husband resumed his military service and Shirley was scheduled for Selznick's abortive production of *Little Women.* Selznick had gained the re-make rights to this picture from RKO in his famous loan-out deal for RKO's use of Ingrid Bergman in *The Bells of St. Mary's.* His cast included Jennifer Jones, Guy Madison, Miss Temple, Dorothy McGuire and Diana Lynn, but after three months of expensive delay and problems, he decided to drop the picture and sold the rights to M-G-M, which produced it in

With husband, John Agar.

With Cary Grant in *The Bachelor and the Bobby-Soxer* (1947).

1949, with June Allyson, Margaret O'Brien and Elizabeth Taylor. Selznick then loaned Miss Temple and Guy Madison to RKO for *Honeymoon* (1947) in which critics thought it was time "the buxom young lady" stopped acting like a kid.

Selznick loaned her again to RKO for *The Bachelor and the Bobby-soxer*(1947), a very popular comedy starring Cary Grant and Myrna Loy in which she played a teenager with a crush on a local artist-bon vivant, Cary Grant. This was her last box-office hit.

On still another loan-out, this time to Warner Brothers, she played the teenager who thinks she is the illegitimate daughter of her school teacher in *That Hagen Girl* (1947). This picture was a box-office flop and was criticised for its purported pro-communist outlook of American life. Its star was the future governor of California, Ronald Reagan. Curiously, in 1964, the politically-conservative Miss Temple stated, "I'm not too proud of the movies I made as a grownup except for *That Hagen Girl,* which nobody remembers, but which gave me a chance to act."

By this time her husband had been discharged from military service. Although she had shied away from publicity about the possibility of her handsome husband becoming a film star, Selznick grabbed the chance to create some publicity interest in her now floundering career and consequently signed Agar a to contract which shared his services with RKO. Agar's first picture was *Fort Apache* (1949), part of the John Ford trilogy which included *She Wore a Yellow Ribbon* (1949) and *Rio Grande* (1950). The picture starred John Wayne and Henry Fonda and cast Agar as the West Point graduate who is sent to a frontier post. His wife, Shirley Temple, was cast opposite him as the love interest playing the daughter of the military post's commander, Henry Fonda. Critics liked the picture but objected to the emphasis on the romantic scenes between Agar and Miss Temple, saying they slowed down the action. During production, the picture received a publicity dividend when it was learned Miss Temple was pregnant. She gave birth to a daughter named Linda Susan on January 30, 1948.

20th Century-Fox, the studio which Shirley Temple had almost built brick by brick, now paid Selznick $100,000 to borrow their former box-office bonanza to play oppisite Clifton Webb in *Mr. Belvedere Goes to College* (1949). As the young war widow, she came off second best to the sententious Webb.

Shirley and her husband were cast a second time as a romantic team in RKO's *Adventure in Baltimore* (1949) also starring Robert Young. Unfortunately she no longer exerted box-office pull and the New York "Times " complained, "As the supposedly strong, enlightened maiden, she seems a mildly precocious child whose moods are expressed either by pouting or by dimpling her chubby cheeks."

Concurrently Selznick had closed his independent production company and after two more loan-outs, Shirley Temple's career in motion pictures ended. Warner Brothers borrowed her for *The Story of Seabiscuit* (1949) and United Artists cast her in a sequel to the Corliss Archer character she had played in *Kiss and Tell,* entitled *A Kiss for Corliss* (1949).

One of the reasons given by the motion-picture exhibitors for her box-office decline was the bad press surrounding her now troubled marriage to Agar. To many, he was little more than a spoiled boy who was using his wife to gain a foothold in motion pictures. Miss Temple denied this, saying, she did not know until later that, before he had entered the military service, he had briefly been a singer with a band and had failed a Hollywood screen-test. While this deception by Agar may have caused part of their marital problems, the real problem was his alcoholism. On December 5, 1949, she testified in court she had suffered extreme mental cruelty during the marriage and had even contemplated suicide. She was granted a divorce and $100 monthly child support and Agar agreed never again to see their daughter.

Later, in "Look" magazine, she said, "One of the mistakes I made was always acting the happy wife in public. I felt the responsibility of being Shirley Temple. I thought of the hundreds of girls who had written me saying that they had persuaded their parents to let them marry young because I had done it. I thought about all the girls who had married in copies of my wedding dress, dreaming high hopes, as I did. You see, no publicity campaign or even a studio genius made me a star. The Public did it. I felt a responsibility to them."

Following the divorce, Agar continued to pursue a spotty career in B-pictures and continued to receive bad press. During 1950-51, there were several arrests for drunken driving and one five-month jail sentence. He served two months in the Los Angeles County Honor Farm and was released for good behaviour. In 1951, he married Loretta Barnett Combs, but the wedding had to be postponed for one hour when the county clerk said Agar had been drinking. In 1953, he served a second jail sentence of one hundred days and upon his release, said "I'm on the wagon for keeps. I've been going to Alcoholics Anonymous and won't be back here." His career continued to flounder and in 1959, he was arrested again for speeding.

Miss Temple's emotional state following her divorce was such that David Selznick suggested she go to Europe, study drama, and even change her name. However, she opted to spend a vacation with her daughter in Hawaii, where, at a dinner party, she met John Alden Black Jr. Black was the son of the former chairman of the board of Pacific Gas and Electric, had attended Hotchkiss, Harvard Business School and Stanford Business School, was a part of the San Francisco social establishment and was working in Hawaii as a radio-television executive. Of their meeting, he has said, "I wasn't interested in meeting Shirley Temple. I was living a very full life of my own and well, I just didn't care. I had never seen a Shirley Temple movie in my life."

Their courtship began during that vacation, and when Miss Temple returned to California, Black resigned his job and accepted one with KTTV in Los Angeles, "as I felt I couldn't compete for her hand 3,000 miles away."

They were quietly married at Black's family home in Monterey on December 16, 1950, and shortly thereafter, when Black, a naval reserve officer, was recalled to active duty at the Pentagon, the couple moved to Bethesda, Maryland, where, on April 28, 1952, Shirley gave birth to a son, Charles Jr. The birth was by caesarean section and "they had me get up the second day and walk and the stitches broke and I eviscerated. It wasn't discovered until my bandages were changed eight hours later." Further complicating this condition, she developed pleurisy and a blood clot in the right lung and lay near death for six weeks.

Discharged from his military service in 1953, Black moved his family to Los Angeles where he took a job as business manager for ABC television. Shortly thereafter, he became director of business operations for Stanford Research Institute and moved his family to Atherton, California, near Palo Alto. There on April 9, 1954, Miss Temple gave birth to a daughter, Lori.

Her contract with Selznick had long since expired, and she remained professionally inactive until 1958, when NBC hired her to host and occasionally act in a series, "The Shirley Temple Storybook," an hour-long show of children's classics. She was paid $100,000 plus twenty-five percent of the profits and the show ran from January 12, 1958, to December 21, 1958. The same network devised a similar series called "The Shirley Temple Show" which ran for another season.

In 1963, Black became an executive with Ampex, the electronics corporation, and the Blacks moved to the fashionable Woodside, California, near San Francisco. As Mrs. Shirley Temple Black she balks as being called part of San Francisco society, saying, "I don't think of the people around home as being society so much as people who accomplish something. We are just young families, although the real estate man calls us the 'new old fogies.' We just have a sense of community responsibility. Of course, being Shirley Temple is still an important part of my life. But I don't feel any conflicts. The big job is to keep a balance; my husband and my children come first."

She became civicly active in Woodside, and contributed nearly 300 hours each year to local charities. In 1965, she filmed a pilot for a television series called "Go Fight City Hall," which failed to find a sponsor. From 1964-66, she was Chairman of the Program Division of the San Francisco Film Festival, but resigned from that position when the board out-voted her when she argued against admitting the Swedish film, *Night Games,* as she found it pornographic. In resigning, she stated, "With the announcement of the programme today, my major job is done, and so am I. The issue is the inclusion in our Programme of a movie titled *Night Games,* directed by Mai Zetterling. In my opinion, the film has little to recommend it, either in pace, characterization, continuity or direction. It is not salvaged despite outbursts of lurid play-acting. In my view the film merely utilized pornography for profit. The members of the selection committee had every right to attend the film and may well disagree with my appraisal. I, too, have the right to my opinion. I cannot acquiesce in the committee's selection, and am disassociating myself. This resignation underscores my personal conviction that inclusion of *Night Games,* degrades the volunteer efforts of many others beside myself, and debases the professional ideal of the festival."

The following year, Shirley Temple Black entered the primary race for California's eleventh Congressional District (San Mateo County). Her main opponent was Republican Paul N. McCloskey. Mrs. Black, also a Republican, refused to debate her fellow candidate and ran a quiet race taking a hawkish view on the war in Vietnam and a stand against pornography, welfarism, crime and drugs. Polls gave her a fifty percent chance of defeating McCloskey on her name as a former movie star, but when the votes were cast, McCloskey won by a large margin (52,878 to 34,521). The newspapers headlined: "McCloskey Torpedoes Good Ship Lolli-pop!" In her conceding speech, Mrs. Black stated, "I am going to dedicate my life to public service."

She realised that ambition when President Nixon appointed her as a delegate to the United Nations in 1969, a position Clare Boothe Luce had refused. She moved into a suite in the Barclay Hotel in New York City and carried a pen to work to sign autographs for fellow delegates who liked the idea of having Shirley Temple as a member of their august body. Following that term, in 1972, she was sworn in as Special Assistant to the Chairman of the President's Council on Environmental Quality, and while serving in that capacity, she discovered she had a lump in her left breast. It was malignant, and she underwent a radical mastectomy. During her ordeal in the hospital, she received over 50,000 letters. After her recuperation, she bravely and with dignity told her story to "McCall's" magazine in an effort to help the thousands of other women with the same problem overcome their fears.

In that article she spoke of her recuperation and adjustments to the operation, "This whole healthy process is aided by support from a loving husband. His is a love without sham, a love that does not look aside. It is direct, constant and strong. How fortunate I am to mark among my blessings that sort of love from that sort of husband — love that faces fact and continues unaffected. The support from my family makes all the difference in the way I can appraise all the unexpected and traumatic experiences of the past several weeks. Leave the questions of beauty and vanity aside. In a well-balanced existence, these are unworthy virtues. Consider instead, as I do, the more fundamental virtues of enthusiasm, intellectual vigour and the unquenchable desire to serve others until the final bell rings. With or without a breast, I plan to keep doing precisely what I have been doing, only better!" Recovered from her operation, it was announced in May, 1974 that Shirley Temple Black had been elected to the board of directors of Walt Disney Productions. She is the first woman to hold this position. In the fall of 1974, Shirley Temple Black resumed her public service duties when she was appointed U.S. Ambassador to Ghana.

Few child stars have come through the ordeal of growing up in the public spotlight with this kind of well-balanced optimism. She understands well what being Shirley Temple has meant to her life, but she now regards that little, blonde, loveable moppet as a separate person. Of her life as a star, there are no regrets, "I have nothing to be sad about. I have enjoyed every instant of my life as Shirley Temple and in spite of all the adjustments I had to make, and still do, I wouldn't have changed it for anything."

The Feature Film Appearances of Shirley Temple

The Red-Haired Alibi (Capitol, 1932). Screenplay by Edward T. Lowe Jr., from the novel by Zane Grey. Directed by Christy Cabanne. *Cast*: Merna Kennedy, Theodor von Eltz, Grant Withers, Purnell Pratt, Huntley Gordon, Fred Kelsey, John Vosburgh, Shirley Temple.

To the Last Man (Paramount, 1933) Screenplay by Jack Cunningham from the novel by Zane Grey. Directed by Henry Hathaway. *Cast:* Randolph Scott, Esther Ralston, Noah Beery, Buster Crabbe, Jack LaRue, Gail Patrick, Barton MacLane, Egon Brecher, Fuzzy Knight, James C. Eagles, Eugenie Besserer, Harlan E. Knight, Harry Cording, James Burke, John Carradine, Jay Ward, Cullen Johnson, Rosita Butler, Shirley Temple, Russell Powell.

Out All Night (Universal, 1933). Screenplay by William Anthony McGuire from the story by Tim Whelan. Directed by Sam Taylor. *Cast:* Slim Summerville, Za Zu Pitts, Laura Hope Crews, Shirley Grey, Alexander Carr, Billy Barty, Shirley Jane Temple, Philip Purdy, Gene Lewis.

Carolina (Fox, 1934). Screenplay by Reginald Berkeley from the play, "The House of Connelly," by Paul Green. Directed by Henry King. *Cast:* Janet Gaynor, Lionel Barrymore, Henrietta Crosman, Robert Young, Mona Barrie, Almeda Fowler, Richard Cromwell, Russell Simpson, Alden Chase, Ronald Cosbey, John Cosbey, Stepin Fetchit, Anita Brown, James Ellison, Beulah Hall, Clinton Rosemond, Mary Forbes, Joe Young, Shirley Temple.

Mandalay (Warner Brothers, 1934). Screenplay by Austin Parker from the story by Paul Hervey Fox. Directed by Michael Curtiz. *Cast:* Kay Francis, Ricardo Cortez, Lyle Talbot, Warner Oland, Ruth Donnelly, Reginald Owen, David Torrence, Etienne Girardot, Rafaela Ottiano, Lucien Littlefield, Halliwell Hobbes, Bodil Ann Rosing, Lillian Harmer, Herman Bing, Harry C. Bradley, Torben Meyer, James Leong, Shirley Temple, Frank Baker, Desmond Roberts, Otto Frisco.

Stand Up and Cheer (Fox, 1934). Screenplay by Will Rogers. Directed by Hamilton McFadden. *Cast:* Warner Baxter, Madge Evans, Nigel Bruce, Stepin Fetchit, Frank Melton, Lila Lee, Ralph Morgan, Frank Mitchell, Jack Durant, James Dunn, Skins Miller, Theresa Gardella, Shirley Temple, Nick Foran, John Boles, Sylvia Froos, Jimmy Dallas, George K. Arthur, Edward Earle, Bess Flowers.

Now I'll Tell (Fox, 1934). Screenplay by Edwin Burke from the book by Mrs. Arnold Rothstein. Directed by Edwin Burke. *Cast:* Spencer Tracy, Helen Twelvetrees, Alice Faye, Robert Gleckler, Hobart Cavanaugh Henry O'Neill, G.P. Huntley Jr., Shirley Temple, Theodore Newton, Ray Cooke, Donald Haines. Selmer Jackson, Lane Chandler, Irving Bacon, Leon Ames, James Murray, Jack Norton, June Lang, Mary Forbes, Gertrude Astor, Mae Madison, Claude King.

Change of Heart (Fox, 1934). Screenplay by Sonya Levien, James Gleason and Samuel Hoffenstein from the novel by Kathleen Norris. Directed by John G. Blystone. *Cast:* Janet Gaynor, Charles Farrell, James Dunn, Ginger Rogers, Beryl Mercer, Gustav Von Seyfferitz, Shirley Temple. Irene Franklin.

Little Miss Marker (Paramount, 1934). Screenplay by William R. Lipman, Sam Hellman and Gladys Lehman from the story by Damon Runyon. Directed by Alexander Hall. *Cast:* Adolphe Menjou, Dorothy Dell, Charles Bickford, Shirley Temple, Lynne Overman, Frank McGlynn Sr., Jack Sheehan, Gary Owen, Willie Best, Peggy White, Tammany Young, Sam Hardy, Edward Earle, Warren Hymer, John Kelly, Frank Conroy, James Burke.

Baby Take a Bow (Fox, 1934). Screenplay by Philip Klein and E.E. Paramore Jr., from the play, "Square Crooks" by James P. Judge. Directed by Harry Lachman. *Cast:* James Dunn, Claire Trevor, Shirley Temple, Alan Dinehart, Ray Walker, Dorothy Libaire, Ralf Harolde, James Flavin, Lillian D. Strart, Paul McVey, Howard Hickman, Eddie Hart, Guy Usher, Olive Tell, Tichard Tucker, Samuel S. Hinds, One Reed, Garland Weaver, Marily Granas, Gordon Carveth, W. Laverick, Chick Collins.

Now and Forever (Paramount, 1934). Screenplay by Vincent Lawrence from the novel, "Honor Bright," by Jack Kirkland. Directed by Henry Hathaway. *Cast:* Gary Cooper, Carole Lombard, Shirley Temple, Sir Guy Standing, Charlotte Granville, Gilbert Emery, Henry Kolker, Tetsu Komai, Jameson Thomas, Harry Stubbs, Egon Brecher, Ynez Seabury, Buster Phelps, Richard Loo.

Bright Eyes (20th Century Fox, 1934). Screenplay by William Conselman from the story by Edwin Burke. Directed by David Butler, *Cast:* James Dunn, Shirley Temple, Judith Allen, Lois Wilson, Jane Withers, Dorothy Christy, Theodor Von Eltz, Chares Sellon, Jane Darwell, Brandon Hurst, Walter Johnson, Dave O'Brien, Frank Moran, Earle Foxe, James Flavin, Paul McVey, Wade Boteler, Selmer Jackson, Rodney Hildebrand, Sam Labrador, George Irving, Sunny Ingram, Gardner James.

The Little Colonel (20th Century-Fox, 1935). Screenplay by William Conselman from the novel by Annie Fellows Johnston. Directed by David Butler. *Cast:* Shirley Temple, Lionel Barrymore, Evelyn Venable, John Lodge, Bill Robinson, Hattie McDaniel, William Burress, Alden Chase, Sidney Blackmer, Avonne Jackson, Myamaza Potts, Dave O'Brien, Geneva Williams, Lillian West, Robert Warwick, Harry Strang.

Our Little Girl (20th Century-Fox, 1935). Screenplay by Stephen Avery, Allen Rivkin and Jack Yellen from the story, "Heaven's Gate," by Florence Leighton Pfalzgraf. Directed by John Robertson. *Cast:* Shirley Temple, Rosemary Ames, Joel McCrea, Lyle Talbot, Erin O'Brien-Moore, Poddles Hanneford, Margaret Armstrong, Rita Owen, Leonard Carey, J. Farrell MacDonald, Jack Baxley.

Curly Top (20th Century-Fox 1935). Screenplay by Patterson McNutt and Arthur Beckhard from the novel by Jean Webster. Directed by Irving Cummings. *Cast:* Shirley Temple, John Boles, Rochelle Hudson, Jane

The Littlest Rebel (20th Century Fox, 1935). Screenplay by Edwin Burke from the play by Edward Peple. Directed by David Butler. *Cast:* Shirley Temple, John Boles, Jack Holt, Karen Morley, Bill Robinson, Guinn Williams, Willie Best, Frank McGlynn Sr., Bessie Lyle, Hannah Washington.

Captain January (20th Century-Fox, 1936). Screenplay by Sam Hellman, Gladys Lehman and Harry Tugend from the novel by Laura E. Richards. Directed by David Butler. *Cast:* Shirley Temple, Guy Kibbee, Slim Summerville, Buddy Ebsen, June Lang, Sara Haden Jane Darwell, James Farley, Si Jenks, Nella Walker, George Irving, Jerry Tucker, Gladden James, Geneva Sawyer, William Benedick, Mary McLaren, Frank Darien.

Poor Little Rich Girl (20th Century-Fox, 1936). Screenplay by Sam Hellman, Gladys Lehman and Harry Tugend from the stories of Eleanor Gates and Ralph Spence. Directed by Irving Cummings. *Cast:* Shirley Temple, Alice Faye, Gloria Stuart, Jack Haley, Michael Whalen, Sara Haden, Jane Darwell, Claude Gillingwater, Paul Stanton, Henry Armetta, Charles Coleman, Arthur Hoyt, John Kelly, John Wray, Tyler Brooke, Mathilde Comont, Leonard Kilrick, Dick Webster, Bill Ray.

Dimples (20th Century-Fox, 1936). Screenplay by Arthur Sheekman and Nat Perrin. Directed by Nunnally Johnson. *Cast:* Shirley Temple, Frank Morgan, Helen Westley, Burton Churchill, Robert Kent, Delma Bryon, Astrid Allwyn, Julius Tannen, Paul Stanton, Stepin Fetchit, Bill McClain, Robert Murphy, Jack Clifford, Betty Jean Hainey, Francis MacDonald, John Carradine, Douglas Fowley, Herbert Ashley, Fred Silva, Fred Wallace, Margaret Bloodgood.

Stowaway (20th Century-Fox, 1936). Screenplay by William Conselman, Arthur Sheekman and Nat Perrin from the story by Sam Engel. Directed by William A. Seiter. *Cast:* Shirley Temple, Robert Young, Alice Faye, Eugene Pallette, Helen Westley, Arthur Treacher, J. Edward Bromberg, Astrid Allwyn, Allen Lane, Robert Greig, Jayne Regan, Julius Tannen, Willie Fung, Philip Ahn, Paul McVey, Helen Jerome Eddy, William Stack, Honorable Wu.

Wee Willie Winkle (20th Century-Fox, 1937). Screenplay by Ernest Pascal and Julien Josephson from the story by Rudyard Kipling. Directed by John Ford. *Cast:* Shirely Temple, Victor McLaglen, C. Aubrey Smith, June Lang, Michael Whalen, Cesar Romero, Constance Collier, Douglas Scott, Gavin Muir, Willie Fung, Lionel Pape, Brandon Hurst, Clyde Cook, Lauri Beatty, Mary Forbes, George Hassell, Lionel Braham, Cyril McLaglen, Pat Sommerset, Hector V. Sarno, Noble Johnson.

Heidi (20th Century-Fox, 1937). Screenplay by Walter Ferris and Julien Josephson from the novel by Johan Spyri. Directed by Allan Dwan. *Cast:* Shirley Temple, Jean Hersholt, Arthur Treacher, Helen Westley, Pauline Moore, Thomas Beck, Mary Nash, Sidney Blackmer, Mady Christians, Sig Ruman, Marcia Mae Darwell, Rafaela Ottiano, Esther Dale, Etienne Girardot, Arthur Treacher, Maurice Murphy. Jones, Delmar Watson, Egon Brecher, Christian Rub, George Humbert.

Rebecca of Sunnybrook Farm (20th Century-Fox, 1938. Screenplay by Karl Tunberg and Don Ettlinger from the novel by Kate Douglas Wiggin. Directed by Allan Dwan. *Cast:* Shirley Temple, Randolph Scott, Jack Haley, Gloria Stuart, Phyllis Brooks, Helen Westley, Slim Summerville, Bill Robinson, J. Edward Bromberg, Alan Dinehart, Raymond Scott Quintet, Dixie Dunbar, Paul Hurst, William Demarest, Ruth Gillette, Paul Harvey.

Little Miss Broadway (20th Century-Fox, 1938). Screenplay by Harry Tugend and Jack Yellen. Directed by Irving Cummings. *Cast:* Shirley Temple, George Murphy, Jimmy Durante, Phillis Brooks, Edna May Oliver, George Barbier, Edward Ellis, Jane Darwell, El Brendel, Donald Meek, Patricia Wilder, Claude Gillingwater, Russell Hicks, Brian Sisters, George and Olive Brasno.

Just Around the Corner (20th Century-Fox, 1938). Screenplay by Ethel Hill, J.P. McEvoy and Darrel Ware from the novel, "Lucky Penny" by Paul Gerard Smith. Directed by Irving Cummings, *Cast:* Shirley Temple, Charles Farrell, Joan Davis, Amanda Duff, Bill Robinson, Bert Lahr, Franklin Pangborn, Cora Witherspooon, Claude Gillingwater Sr., Bennie Barlett, Hal K. Dawson, Charles Williams, Eddy Conrad, Marilyn Knowlden, Tony Hughes, Orville Caldwell.

The Little Princess (20th Century-Fox, 1939). Screenplay by Ethel Hill and Walter Ferris from the novel, "The Fantasy," by Frances Hodgson Burnett. Directed by Walter Lang. *Cast:* Shirley Temple, Richard Greene, Anita Louise, Ian Hunter, Cesar Romero, Arthur Treacher, Mary Nash, Sybil Jason, Miles Mander, Marcia Mae Jones, Beryl Mercer, Deirdre Gale, Ira Stevens, E.E. Olive, Eily Malyon, Kenneth Hunter, Lionel Braham, Clyde Cook, Holmes Herbert, Olaf Hytton, Rita Page.

Susannah of the Mounties (20th Century- Fox, 1939). Screenplay by John Tainter Foote and Philip Dunne. Directed by Sidney Lanfield. *Cast:* Shirley Temple, Randolph Scott, Margaret Lockwood, Martin Goodrider, J. Farrell MacDonald, Maurice Moscovich, Moroni Olsen, Victor Jory, Leyland Hodgson, Herbert Evans, Charles Irwin, John Sutton, Jack Luden, Chief John Big Tree, Larry Dods, Harold Goodwin, Tom Spotted Eagle, John Little Blaze, Victor Chief Coward, Turtle, Albert Mad Plume, Night Shoots.

The Blue Bird (20th Century-Fox, 1940). Screenplay by Ernest Pascal from the play by Maurice Maeterlinck with additional dialogue by Walter Bullock. Directed by Walter Lang. *Cast:* Shirley Temple, Spring Byington, Nigel Bruce, Gale Sondergaard, Eddie Collins, Sybil Jason, Jessie Ralph. Helen Ericson, Johnny Russell, Laura Hope Crews, Russell Hicks, Cecilia Loftus, Al Shean, Gene Reynolds. Leona Roberts, Stanley Andrews, Frank Dawson, Thurston Hall, Edwin Maxwell, Dorothy Dearing, Sterling Holloway, Scotty Beckett, Dickie Moore, Edward Earle, Eddie Waller, Imboden Parrish, Otto Hoffman, Ann Todd, Eric Wilton, Alec Craig, Brandon Hurst, Dewey Robinson, Alice Armand, Claire DuBrey.

Young People (20th Century-Fox, 1940). Screenplay by Edwin Blum and Don Ettlinger. Directed by Allan Dwan. *Cast:* Shirley Temple, Jack Oakie, Charlotte Greenwood, Arleen Whelan, George Montgomery, Kathleen Howard, Minor Watson, Frank Swann, Frank Sully, Mae Marsh, Sarah Edwards, Irving Bacon, Charles Halton, Arthur Aylsworth, Olin Howland, Harry Tyler, Darryl Hickman, Diane Fisher, Robert Shaw, Syd Saylor, Dell Henderson, Ted North, Evelyn Beresford, Bill Benedict.

Kathleen (20th Century-Fox, 1941). Screenplay by Mary McCall Jr., from the story by Kay Van Riper. Directed by Harold S. Buquet. *Cast:* Shirley Temple, Laraine Day, Herbert Marshall, Gail Patrick, Felix Bressart, Nella Walker, Lloyd Corrigan, Guy Bellis, Fern Emmett, Charles Judels, Wade Boteler, Else Argal, Margaret Bert, James Flavin, Monty Collins, Joe Jule.

Miss Annie Rooney (United Artists, 1942). Screenplay by George Bruce. Directed by Edwin L. Marin. *Cast:* Shirley Temple, William Gargan, Guy Kibbee, Dickie Moore, Peggy Ruan, Roland DuPree, Gloria Holden, Jonathan Hale, Mary Field, George Lloyd, Jan Buckingham, Selmer Jackson, June Lockhart, Charles Coleman, Edgar Dearing, Virginia Sale, Shirley Mills, Noel Neill, Byron Foulger, Wilson Benge.

Since You Went Away (Selznick International - United Artists, 1944). Screenplay by David O. Selznick from the novel by Margaret Buell Wilder. Directed by John Cromwell. *Cast:* Claudette Colbert, Jennifer Jones, Joseph Cotten, Shirley Temple, Monty Woolley, Lionel Barrymore, Robert Walker, Hattie McDaniel, Agnes Moorehead, Guy Madison, Craig Stevens, Keenan Wynn, Albert Basserman, Nazimova, Lloyd Corrigan, Jackie Moran, Gordon Oliver, Jane Devlin, Ann Gillis, Dorothy (Cindy) Garner, Andrew McLaglen, Jill Warren, Helen Koford (Terry Moore), Robert Johnson, Dorothy Dandridge, Johnny Bond, Irving Bacon, George Chandler, Addison Richards, Barbara Pepper, Byron Foulger, Edwin Maxwell, Florence Bates, Theodor Von Eltz, Adeline de Walt Reynolds, Doodles Weaver, Warren Hymer, Jonathan Hale, Eilene Janssen, William B. Davidson, Ruth Roman, Rhonda Fleming.

I'll Be Seeing You (United Artists, 1944). Screenplay by Marion Parsonnet from a story by Charles Martin. Directed by William Dieterle. *Cast:* Ginger Rogers, Joseph Cotten, Shirley Temple, Spring Byington, Tom Tully, Chill Wills, Dare Harris (John Derek), Kenny Bowers.

Kiss and Tell (Columbia, 1945). Screenplay by F. Hugh Herbert from his play. Directed by Richard Wallace. *Cast:* Shirley Temple, Jerome Courtland, Walter Abel, Katherine Alexander, Robert Benchley, Porter Hall, Edna Holland, Virginia Welles, Tom Tully, Mary Philips, Darryl Hickman, Scott McKay, Scott Elliott, Kathryn Cord, Darren McGavin, Jessie Arnold, Frank Darien, Isabel Withers.

Honeymoon (RKO, 1947). Screenplay by Michael Kanin from the story by Vicki Baum. Directed by William Keighley. *Cast:* Shirley Temple, Franchot Tone, Guy Madison, Lina Romay, Gene Lockhart, Corinna Mura, Grant Mitchell, Julio Villareal, Mauel Arvide, Jose R. Goula, Carol Forman, Charles Trowbridge, John Parrish, Forbes Murray, Franklin Farnum, Rodolpho Hoyos Sr., Mario Santos.

The Bachelor and the Bobby-Soxer (RKO, 1947). Screenplay by Sidney Sheldon. Directed by Irving Reis. *Cast:* Cary Grant, Myrna Loy, Shirley Temple, Rudy Vallee, Ray Collins, Harry Davenport, Johnny Sands, Don Beddoe, Lillian Randolph, Veda Ann Borg, Dan Tobin, Ransom Sherman, William Bakewell, Irving Bacon, Ian Bernard, Carol Hughes, William Hall, Gregory Gay, Marilyn Mercer, Kay Christopher, Myra Marsh, Ellen Corby, J. Farrell MacDonald.

That Hagen Girl (Warner Brothers, 1947). Screenplay by Charles Hoffman from the novel by Edith Kneipple Roberts. Directed by Peter Godfrey. *Cast:* Ronald Reagan, Shirley Temple, Rory Calhoun, Lois Maxwell, Dorothy Peterson, Charles Kemper, Conrad Janis, Penny Edwards, Jean Porter, Harry Davenport, Nella Walker, Winifred Harris, Moroni Olsen, Frank Conroy, Kathryn Cord, Douglas Kennedy, Barbara Brown, Tom Fadden, Jane Hamilton, William B. Davidson, Virginia Farmer, Constance Purdy, Milton Parson, Guy Wilkerson, Dania Bussey, Rex Downing, Frank Meredith.

Fort Apache (RKO, 1948). Screenplay by Frank S. Nugent from the novel, "Massacre" by James Warner Bellah. Directed by John Ford. *Cast:* John Wayne, Henry Fonda, Shirley Temple, John Agar, Pedro Armendariz, Ward Bond, Irene Rich, George O'Brien, Anna Lee, Victor McLaglen, Dick Foran, Jack Pennick, Guy Kibbee, Grant Withers, Miguel Inclan, Mae Marsh, Mary Gordon, Movita, Hank Warden, Francis Ford, Cliff Clark, Fred Graham, Frank Ferguson, William Forrest.

Mr. Belvedere Goes To College (20th Century-Fox, 1949). Screenplay by Richard Sale, Mary Loos and Mary McCall Jr., from characters created by Gwen Davenport. Directed by Elliott Nugent. *Cast:* Clifton Webb, Shirley Temple, Tom Drake, Alan Young, Jessie Royce Landis, Kathleen Hughes, Taylor Holmes. Alvin Greenman, Paul Harvey, Barry Kelly, Bob Patten, Jeff Chandler, Clancy Cooper, Lotte Stein, Sally Forest, Peggy Call, Kathleen Freeman.

Adventure in Baltimore (RKO, 1949). Screenplay by Lionel Houser from the story by Christopher Isherwood and Lesser Samuels. Directed by Richard Wallace. *Cast:* Robert Young, Shirley Temple, John Agar, Albert Sharpe, Josephine Hutchinson, Charles Kemper, Johnny Sands, John Miljan, Norma Varden, Carol Brannan, Charles Smith, Josephine Whittell, Patti Brady, Gregory Marshall, Patsy Creighton, Dorothy Vaughn, Charles Evans, Regina Wallace, Ann O'Neal.

The Story of Seabiscuit (Warner Brothers, 1949). Screenplay by John Taintor Foote from his story. Directed by David Butler. *Cast:* Shirley Temple, Barry Fitzgerald, Lon McCallister, Rosemary DeCamp, Donald McBride, Pierre Watkin, William Forrest, Sugarfoot Anderson, William M. Cartledge, Forbes Murray, Edward Keane, Lou Harvey, Herman Kantor, Gertrude Astor, Creighton Hale, Ray Erlenborn, Gil

Warren, Jack Lomas, Alan Foster, James Simmons.

A Kiss For Corliss (United Artists, 1949). Screenplay by Howard Dimsdale from characters created by F. Hugh Herbert. Directed by Richard Wallace. *Cast:* Shirley Temple, David Niven, Tom Tully, Virginia Welles, Darryl Hickman, Robert Ellis, Richard Gaines, Kathryn Cord, Gloria Holden, Roy Roberts.

APPENDIX I - Miscellaneous Selznick Players

Rory Calhoun

In January 1944, Rory Calhoun was visiting Los Angeles where his grandmother lived. One morning he was horseback riding in the Hollywood Hills and met a fellow rider, Alan Ladd. Ladd introduced him to his agent-wife, Sue Carol, who sent the young man to screen test at 20th Century-Fox.

Calhoun was born Francis Timothy Durgin in Hollywood on August 8, 1922. He had led a desultory and deliquent childhood which led to his arrest for automobile theft. He was imprisoned at the El Reno Federal Reformatory in Oklahoma, and after escaping from that institution, was sent to prison in Springfield, Missouri. He served a total of seven-and-a-half years in prison, and after being released in 1939, he worked variously at bronco busting, hard-rock mining, camp logging, and as a forest ranger in San Jose, California. While working on the latter job, he went to Los Angeles to visit his grandmother and there met Alan Ladd.

20th Century-Fox was not interested in signing Calhoun to a long-term contract, but when he came to the attention of Henry Willson, head of Selznick's Talent Department, Willson suggested they sign him. Selznick agreed, and they changed his name to Rory Calhoun.

Selznick failed to find a place for Calhoun in his Selznick Players, but to help him gain some acting experience he loaned him to other studios for small roles in *Something For the Boys* (1944-20th Century-Fox), *Nob Hill* (1945-20th Century-Fox), *The Red Horse* (1947-United Artists), and *That Hagen Girl* (1947-Warner Brothers). Calhoun later recalled, "While I didn't make any pictures for Selznick, I didn't worry about it, because it was like a long vacation with pay, and I was busy doing lots of things I'd always wanted to do and couldn't afford."

When Selznick ended production in 1948, the remainder of Calhoun's contract was sold to Warner Brothers. Calhoun said of his former boss, "I loved that man. He knew all about my record, but he went all out to help me. It was while I was with Selznick that I met Guy Madison, my closest friend, and another pal Howard Hill, the famous archer."

Warner Brothers did not renew Calhoun's option, and he was signed by a now-interested 20th Century-Fox. At that studio he appeared in increasingly larger roles as a leading man for some of their most beautiful women—*I'd Climb the Highest Mountain* (1951) opposite Susan Hayward, *Meet Me After the Show* (1952) opposite Betty Grable, *With a Song in My Heart* (1952) opposite Susan Hayward, *How to Marry a Millionaire* (1953) with Miss Grable and Marilyn Monroe, and *River of No Return* (1954) with Miss Monroe.

However, by the middle Fifties it became apparent that his career was not a lasting one, and the remainder of it was spent in B westerns and occasional appearances on television.

On August 29, 1948, he had married Lita Baron, a singer-dancer who was born in Madrid. Her real name was Isabel Beth Castro, and under the name of Isabelita, she sang with the Xavier Cugat orchestra. Their marriage seemed a very happy one, until surprisingly in 1969, Lita sued him for divorce claiming he had committed adultery with at least seventy-nine women, one of whom included his former co-star, Betty Grable. Their divorce became final on January 19, 1970.

Rory Calhoun visiting the set of *Duel in the Sun* (1946).

Rhonda Fleming

From cheesecake starlet to character roles early in her career, to "Queen of Technicolor" and a string of B's, statuesque redhead, Rhonda Fleming's healthy voluptuousness has carried her through nearly thirty years of motion pictures, night clubs, television, summer stock, and most recently, Broadway. Today she says, "I want to keep learning, I want to keep working; and most of all I want to be independent."

She was born Marilyn Louise Louis in Los Angeles, California, on August 10, 1933, the daughter of Harold and Olivia Louis. Her father was an insurance broker and her mother, under the stage name of Effie Graham, was a musical comedy star who had appeared on Broadway in Al Jolson's "Dancing Around." Mrs. Graham had her daughter begin studying singing and dancing and acting at an early age. Miss Fleming told the author, "I was groomed for New York. My mother set the goals. I did not. I studied light opera for ten years." She was a semifinalist along with Linda Darnell in Jesse Lasky's Hollywood Gateway contest at fifteen, but as she says, "often losers are winners." Shortly after that contest, Henry Willson, head of Selznick's Talent Department, followed the beautiful young redhead in his car when he saw her walking to the Beverly Hills High School. Both her mother and Willson thought she was too young to begin a career in motion pictures at that time and she stayed to finish high school.

After graduation, she did a brief stint as a showgirl in Ken Murray's "Blackouts," and as a result was signed to a six-month contract by 20th Century-Fox, under the name Marilyn Lane. At age seventeen, Miss Fleming had married interior decorator Thomas Wade Lane and bore him a son named Kent in 1941. Miss Fleming said she and her son grew up together and today they have a marvelous mother-son friendship. She divorced Lane in 1947.

20th Century-Fox used her only in publicity

photographs. Miss Fleming recalls that the studio's general production manager, Lois Schreiber, did not think the name Marilyn was commercial. Ironically, a few years later one of that studio's all-time "commercial" stars was a blonde named Marilyn Monroe. One day while at the studio she met Henry Willson in the parking lot, and he arranged a luncheon for the starlet with his boss, David O. Selznick. During that luncheon, Willson proposed they change her name to Ronda Fleming. Selznick liked the sound, but said the name should be spelled with a "h" — Rhonda. Before the lunch was over, Selznick leaned over to her and whispered that she would be signed without a screen test, a most unusual practice for Selznick in hiring new talent.

Selznick cast her in a bit part as a dancer in *Since You Went Away* (1944) and assigned her to the tutelage of Anita Colby, his Feminine Director, who taught the untrained actress how to walk, dress, present herself at interviews, etc. Miss Colby says that Miss Fleming was one of the most grateful of stars for her assistance and eagerly followed her guidance.

Selznick thought enough of her to assign her as the nymphomaniac in the sanatorium in *Spellbound* (1945), which was directed by Alfred Hitchcock. Miss Fleming says, "Hitch was at his peak. He had magnificent humor which I could not really appreciate at the time. He would walk on the set and tease me by asking, 'How is your sex life?' I would turn green. One day he led me into the projection room to view the rushes of *Spellbound* and I didn't believe what I saw. I thought I was awful, but he was pleased. I also sang the words of the *Spellbound* theme for Selznick but it was not used in the picture." During this production, because of her height, Hitchcock used her as a stand-in for the picture's star, Ingrid Bergman.

She was loaned to RKO for *The Spiral Staircase* (1946) in another good part — as the secretary who is murdered by George Brent. After these two roles, Selznick, involved in other productions and with the career of Jennifer Jones (whom, Miss Fleming maintains had "set her sights on Selznick"), seemed to lose interest in her career and loaned her out for three B's — *Abilene Town* (1946-United Artists) with Randolph Scott, *Adventure Island* (1947-Paramount) with another Selznick contractee, Rory Calhoun, and *Out of the Past* (1947-RKO) with Robert Mitchum. He then loaned her to Paramount for a first-rate production and her first on-screen singing assignment — *A Connecticut Yankee in King Arthur's Court* (1948)

Rhonda Fleming in a studio publicity shot.

— and as a result she was named the "Queen of Technicolor." She says, "I remember Deanna Durbin fled to Europe and never came back to Hollywood. They were looking for a girl to replace her with Bing (Crosby). Out of 250 girls, I won. I could sing, and Bing liked me. Bing never liked his name alone over the picture and that's how I got co-star billing. And then Bob Hope (Crosby's best friend and another Paramount star) said, "If Bing's gonna use her, so am I." Hope used her as the fake heiress in *The Great Lover* (1949) after which she stayed on at Paramount for a third loan-out — *The Eagle and the Hawk* (1950) starring John Payne.

At this point Selznick had shut down the Selznick Culver City studio and Miss Fleming's lawyer, Greg Bautzer, arranged for her to buy the remainder of her contract with Selznick for $25,000 in June 1950.

Of Selznick she recalls, "He was a genius, the captain of the ship; he ruled."

For the next decade-and-a-half, Rhonda Fleming appeared in over thirty pictures — "some good, some money-making B's. It was a while before I realized that without a Selznick I was on my own. I made some mistakes."

Her pictures during this time included *The Red-*

head and the Cowboy (1951) with Glenn Ford; *Pony Express* (1953) with Charlton Heston; *Yankee Pasha* (1954) with Jeff Chandler; *Gunfight at the O.K. Corral* (1957) with Burt Lancaster and Kirk Douglas; *Home Before Dark* (1958) with Jean Simmons; and *Alias Jesse James* (1959) with Bob Hope. She also appeared in a singing quartet with Jane Russell, made recordings, appeared in night club revues, and on television, her buxom figure often provided Red Skelton with some of his best *double entendres*.

After her divorce from Lane in 1947, she married a surgeon, Dr. Lewis V. Morrill on July 11, 1952. They were divorced on July 8, 1958, after which she married television western actor, Lang Jeffries in 1960. They divorced on January 11, 1962. She married for a fourth time on March 27, 1966, to producer Hal Bartlett and retired from acting. That marriage ended in a bitter divorce in February, 1972, awarding her $1,000,000 in community property and $2,500 monthly alimony for three years. She says, "Everything fell apart after the divorce. I hadn't worked for eight years except for cerebral palsy. It was a nervous time, but I was determined. I had to lose twenty pounds and reactivate my mind and my body."

She signed with the William Morris Agency, made an appearance on the Merv Griffin television show, appeared in an episode of NBC television's "Search," and landed the role of Miriam Aarons, the worldly-wise divorcee in the Broadway revival of "The Women" in 1973. (That role was played by Paulette Goddard in the 1939 screen version). She says of New York, "This city is a big hunk of life. It strengthens you."

Today Rhonda Fleming wishes to continue her career and is studying singing and drama again. She is also an active exponent of the metaphysical positive side of spiritual living. She says, "Life has to knock you down to wake you up." She goes on, "Acting careers build you into someone else and you lose your identity. I kept asking myself, 'Who was I?' It was a struggle. But one must be strong with oneself and not allow the negatives to enter. It is a difficult world and life is a challenge, but I am receptive."

Recently Miss Fleming filmed a television commercial for Pepsodent toothpaste, and played the malevolent head of a ring of smugglers in a two-hour segment of television's "Macmillan and Wife" (NBC - 17th February 1974) starring Rock Hudson, and has begun a whole new career doing guest spots on television series. Her positive thinking is paying off and she has never looked better.

Kim Hunter

In the early Forties, Selznick attended a stage production of "Arsenic and Old Lace" at the Pasadena Playhouse and as a result, signed a young actress named Janet Cole. Miss Cole had been born in Detroit, Michigan, on November 12, 1922, and as a teenager began a career on the stage.

Selznick put her under contract to his Vanguard Productions in association with Dore Schary, and she recalls, "Selznick told me Janet Cole could be anyone, but that Kim Hunter had individuality and would go far as an actress." Renamed, she debuted in RKO's *The Seventh Victim* (1943) and after small roles in *Tender Comrades* (1944-RKO), *When Strangers Marry* (1944-Monogram), and *You Came Along* (1945-Paramount), Alfred Hitchcock, who was then under contract to Selznick, suggested her to J. Arthur Rank for the role opposite David Niven in *Stairway to Heaven* (1947). While in England making that picture, she also appeared in *A Canterbury Tale* (1949), whereupon she returned to the United States.

Free of her contract with Selznick, she went back to the theatre. When Irene Mayer Selznick was readying her stage production of Tennessee Williams' "A Streetcar Name Desire," a theatrical agent suggested that she consider Miss Hunter for the role of Stella. Remembering her husband's early enthusiasm over Miss Hunter, Mrs. Selznick endorsed her for the role. The play opened to smashing success in 1947, and ran for two-and-a-half years, earning Miss Hunter the Donaldson and Critics Circle Awards. It also led to her being cast in the motion-picture version of that play for which she received the Academy Award as Best Actress in a Supporting Role.

Since that time she has alternated her career between motion pictures and the stage and is frequently seen on television. Her films include *Storm Center* (1956), *Lilith* (1964), *Planet of the Apes* (1968), *The Swimmer* (1969) and *Beneath the Planet of the Apes* (1969). She has been married to Robert Emmett since December 20, 1951.

Kim Hunter with David Niven in *Stairway to Heaven* (1947). (GB title *"A Matter of Life and Death"*).

Louis Jourdan

For years Louis Jourdan has fought being typecast as the elegant, suave, accented, romantic leading man — the perfect French lover — but for the most part it has been a losing battle and his most popular film roles have kept him in the eyes of the audience as our younger version of Charles Boyer.

He was born Louis Gendre in Marseilles, France, on June 19, 1920. His father was one of the promoters of the Cannes Film Festival and while in his teens, he studied drama in Paris under Rene Simon. He became for a short time assistant director to Marc Allegret, but because of his good looks he was earning more money as an actor. When he first began acting, in *Le Corsaire* (1939) with Charles Boyer, he took his mother's maiden name, Jourdan, as his stage name.

When World War II erupted in France, he was too young to enlist, and was put on a work gang for one year by the Nazis. When they demanded he make non-political films for them, he escaped and joined the French underground. There he met his future wife, Berthe Fréderique (called Quique), whom he married on March 11, 1946. They have a son Louis Henry Georges Jourdan, born October 6, 1951.

After the Nazis left France, he returned to motion pictures and when an American talent scout sent some film clips of the young Frenchman to producer David Selznick, Selznick signed him to play the tormented, guilt-ridden valet in his production of *The Paradine Case* (1947). Selznick introduced him to the American public with considerable publicity hoopla, announcing him as the new French lover, and when that picture was released, Bosley Crowther in the New York "Times" called him "electric."

Selznick loaned Jourdan to RKO for *Letter From an Unknown Woman* (1948) with Joan Fontaine, and to M-G-M for *No Minor Vices* (1949). Each time Selznick suggested another romantic role to Jourdan, he balked and as a result was suspended four times. Jourdan says, "I didn't want to be perpetually cooing in a lady's ear. There's not much satisfaction in it." Selznick loaned him to M-G-M to star opposite Jennifer Jones in *Madame Bovary* (1948) and he was excellent as the aristocratic Rodolphe Boulanger.

After Selznick closed his studio in 1948, Darryl F. Zanuck bought his contract from Selznick for $50,000, and brought him to 20th Century-Fox, where Jourdan continued to battle against typecasting. He lost the battle when cast in the overly-romantic *Bird of Paradise* (1951) with Debra Paget, but was happier as the wastrel in *The Happy Time* (1952). More typecasting had him as the Italian prince in *Three Coins in the Fountain* (1954), and he was the royal tutor in *The Swan* (1956) with Grace Kelly. A role he liked better than most was the psychopathic-killer husband of Doris Day in *Julie* (1956).

Jourdan faired a little better on stage, earning

Louis Jourdan with Gregory Peck in *The Paradine Case* (1947).

excellent reviews as the homosexual archeologist in Andre Gide's "The Immoralist" in New York in 1954, opposite Geraldine Page. And on French television, he played with Claude Dauphin in twenty-six episodes of a series called "Paris Precinct" (1955).

His most popular role, for which he was perfectly cast, was Gaston in *Gigi* (1958), after which he played the judge in *Can-Can* (1960), and the gigolo who makes love to Elizabeth Taylor in *The V.I.P.'s*.(1963).

In 1965, he appeared in the out-of-town, pre-Broadway engagement of Lerner and Loewe's musical "On a Clear Day You Can See Forever," but clashed with Lerner over the script and was fired. He had signed a run-of-the-play contract and continued to be paid $4,000 weekly after his release.

The handsome, six-foot actor, continues to appear in motion pictures and on stage, and after years of living in Hollywood, has recently returned to Paris. He assesses his career with typical French *insouciance,* "If I was not a great success in American films, neither was I a failure. I've been working for years without setting the world on fire, but managing to keep Quique, my wife, in caviar and champagne."

Guy Madison

In 1943, talent scout, Helen Ainsworth, saw a photograph of a boyishly-handsome sailor on the cover of a Naval magazine and signed him to play a bit part in David Selznick's production of *Since You Went Away* (1944). The young man's name was Robert Ozell Mosely and he was born in Bakersfield, California, on January 19, 1922.

His part in *Since You Went Away* was a three-minute scene in which he heckles Jennifer Jones at a bowling game. Henry Willson, head of Selznick's Talent Department and famous for creating such movie names as Rory Calhoun, Rock Hudson, and Tab Hunter, changed Mosely's name to Guy Madison and the young sailor completed his part in the picture while on a three-day pass from the San Diego Naval post where he was stationed.

Guy Madison with Dorothy McGuire in *Till the End of Time* (1946).

When the picture was released the following year, his brief appearance elicited an unprecedented fan-mail response — 43,000 letters — proclaiming him the bobby-soxers' delight. When he was discharged from the Navy in 1945, Selznick put him under contract at $600 a week and loaned him to RKO as the lonely, ex-Marine who falls in love with Dorothy McGuire in *Till the End of Time* (1946). His popularity was greatly increased by this sympathetic role and Selznick loaned him to RKO a second time for *Honeymoon* (1947) opposite Shirley Temple and to United Artists for *Texas, Brooklyn and Heaven* (1948) co-starring Diana Lynn, and for these loan-outs, Selznick reaped $150,000.

When Selznick disbanded his stock company in 1948, Madison went on to appear in a few westerns, most notably, *The Charge at Feather River* (1953), but his adult career never got off the ground. He signed a contract with 20th Century-Fox in 1954, but it was really his playing Wild Bill Hickock on radio (300 episodes) and television (125 episodes) that gained him a wide following and financial security. Tallulah Bankhead, an avid television fan during her lifetime, quipped, "He made all the other cowboys look like fugitives from Abercrombie and Fitch."

By the Sixties, his career was over except for a few westerns made in Italy, and in 1972, he was quoted as saying he no longer received any picture offers.

He was married to actress Gail Russell from July 31, 1949, to October 26, 1954, and in 1954, he married actress Sheila Connolly.

Hildegarde Neff (Knef)

In 1947, "Life" magazine published a cover story about actress Hildegard Knef proclaiming her as the first new star to come out of Germany since the war, and hinting at her being a possible successor to Marlene Dietrich. David Selznick saw that article and invited her to come to the United States to star in motion pictures. Since Miss Knef was married to Kurt Hirsch, a U.S. Information officer from Queens, she decided to accept Selznick's offer.

She was born Hilde Knef on December 28, 1925, in Ulm, a manufacturing town in Wurttemberg, and as a teenager had appeared in two films. When the war interrupted her career, she joined her film producer-lover in the fight for Germany and ended up being captured by the Russians. She managed

***Hildegarde Neff* (Hildegard Knef).**

to escape their brutality and at the end of the war moved to the Allied section of Berlin, married Hirsch, and resumed her career.

She achieved stardom in Germany as Hildegard Knef in *Murderers Are Amongst Us* (1946) and *Film Without Title* (1947); and when she arrived in the United States in 1948, Selznick changed the spelling of her name to Hildegarde Neff. However, Selznick was no longer producing pictures when she arrived and she spent two fruitless years under contract to him. She says, "Mr. Selznick was not producing movies at the time. For two years I sat around doing nothing except to learn English. Then 20th Century-Fox asked Mr. Selznick if he would loan me to that studio to appear in *The Big Lift*, which was to be made in Germany. He agreed and I flew to Berlin, so happy about a job at last. But as I arrived, I learned that changes had been made in the film story and one of those changes concerned me. I was out of the cast. Oh, I was terribly disappointed."

Finally, when it became apparent that Selznick was not going to use her in any pictures, she dissolved her contract with him and was hired by 20th Century-Fox to appear in *Decision Before Dawn* (1951), *Diplomatic Courier* (1952), and *The Snows of Kilimanjaro* (1952). In the latter, as Countess Liz, she sang two Cole Porter songs — "You Do Something to Me" and "Just One of Those Things."

She returned to live in her native Germany, but when Cole Porter began working on a stage musical version of the motion picture *Ninotchka* (1939), which had starred Greta Garbo, he remembered Miss Knef singing his songs in *The Snows of Kilimanjaro* and suggested her for the lead in the musical which was to be called "Silk Stockings." She was cast in the play which enjoyed excellent reviews and a two-and-a-half year run.

When "Silk Stockings" closed, she once again returned to Germany, where she became less and less interested in a motion-picture career and began to build a reputation as a *chanteuse*. In 1970, she published a book of memoirs called "The Gift Horse." It became a best-seller both in Europe and the United States and gained her laudatory reviews for her frank recall of her sometimes brutal and frequently unhappy life. In one chapter she recalls being summoned to Selznick's office at ten o'clock one night. Selznick kept her waiting two hours then admitted her to his office. Selznick questioned her about her life and she revealed only those facets of her life which she thought he should know. Then she described the following:

"He wrote something down on one of the many pads which were lying around. 'Could make a good story,' he said and went into the bathroom. I heard the shower gushing, heard gasps and gargling, when he returned his hair was wet and his shirt fresh. 'You're an interesting girl,' he said standing directly before me, 'a pretty, interesting girl.' I thought it was wiser to stand up but the edge of the seat pressed against the backs of my knees, and I plopped down again. This stimulated his sense of humor. 'Do you like me a little?' he asked, pulling me up.

'I don't know you very well' I said idiotically, near panic.

"That could be changed," Stiff spikes of hair waggled over his brow like chrysanthemum leaves, I stared at the wide neck, the tight smile, a smile that meant power, full power, 'You're mine to do with as I please' power. 'I don't know any German girls,' he said and tugged at my jacket. Two buttons sprang away like flat stones that one flips over water. The man, smelling of mouthwash and after-shave, was more menacing than the Russians, incalculable like the Mongolians, more foreign than Martians, revenge unknown.

'I feel sick,' I said, because I felt sick, and ran for the bathroom. I couldn't find the toilet so I vomited into the basin, looked at myself across the bottles and tubes. I was without fury, had changed, fury and rage lost on the way.

When I went back he was telephoning. As I crossed to the door, he called out: 'Nine o'clock tomorrow at M-G-M, they want to test you for a new film. If you get the part, I'll loan you out'."

Miss Knef had divorced Hirsch in 1952 and on June 30, 1962, married David Anthony Palastanga, who is an actor under the name of David Cameron. They have a daughter, Christina, born May 17, 1968. Palastanga translated his wife's book into its English version. Today her career as writer-*chanteuse* interests her far more than motion pictures. Her last feature film appearance was in *The Lost Continent* (1968) and she says, "I shall never do another movie unless poverty forces me to."

Joan Tetzel

A dark-haired patrician beauty, actress Joan Tetzel has appeared in only five motion pictures, two of which were produced by David O. Selznick — *Duel In the Sun* (1946) and *The Paradine Case* (1947).

She was born on June 21, 1921, in New York City, and as a child attended the Professional School for Children and began her acting career as a child actress on radio and in the theatre and as a child model for the John Powers Agency. As an ingenue in the theatre she played in "Lorelei" (1938) with Philip Merivale and was the daughter of Ingrid Bergman and Burgess Meredith in "Liliom" (1940).

Joan Tetzel with Charles Coburn in *The Paradine Case* (1947).

In 1942, while playing in "The Damask Check" with Flora Robson, she was signed to a motion-picture contract by David Selznick. Miss Tetzel was at the time committed to the stage and did not arrive in Hollywood until three years later.

In the interim, she was signed to play her first leading role on Broadway in Zoe Akins's "The Happy Days," which also starred a young Diana Barrymore, and two years later, she was cast in her most important Broadway role, that as Katrin, the daughter in "I Remember Mama" (1944).

After that successful play, Selznick brought her to Hollywood where she played Otto Kruger's daughter in *Duel In the Sun* (1946). She stayed on to play the sophisticated daughter of barrister Charles Coburn in *The Paradine Case* (1947), after which she returned to Broadway where she starred with Charles Boyer in "Red Gloves" (1948).

One of her co-stars in "I Remember Mama," was Oscar Homolka, twenty years her senior, who had played the role of Uncle Chris, and with whom Miss Tetzel fell in love. Preceding their marriage in 1949, Miss Tetzel appeared in another picture, *The File of Thelma Jordan*, and at the time she said, "He wouldn't marry me until I got out of my Hollywood contract."

By this time her contract with Selznick had expired and she and Homolka were married in 1949. Miss Tetzel had been married at age nineteen to CBS radio executive, John E. Mosman, whom she had met while appearing in two CBS soap-operas in 1940 — "When A Girl Marries" and "Woman of Courage." Since her marriage to Homolka, she has appeared in only two films — *Hell Below Zero* (1954) and *Joy in the Morning* (1965) — but she continues to do stage work, sometimes opposite her husband. They appeared together in 1955 in "The Master Builder." Her most recent Broadway appearance was opposite Kirk Douglas in "One Flew Over the Cuckoo's Nest" in 1961. The Homolkas live in London.

Alida Valli

Once touted as Europe's most beautiful woman, the shy, enigmatic Alida Valli was born Alida Altenburgher in Pola, Italy, on May 31, 1921. Her father was a professor of philosophy at the Milan University and at age fifteen, she enrolled in the Motion Picture Academy in Rome. Success in motion pictures came to her in her teens, most notable of which were *Manon Lescaut* (1939) and *Piccolo Mondo Antico* (1941). For the latter she won the Venice Film Festival Award.

In 1943, in Nazi-occupied Italy, the Gestapo summoned her to make pictures for the Germans. She refused, went into hiding, saying she was ill, and was no longer going to be an actress. She remained incommunicado until April, 1945, when the German's left her country, at which time she resumed her career.

David Golding, managing editor of the "Stars and Stripes" magazine, published a photograph of her which came to the attention of David Selznick. Selznick invited her to come to the United States, and with some thirty-four pictures to her credit in Italy, she arrived in Hollywood in January, 1947.

Selznick put her under the tutelage of Anita Colby and advised Miss Colby to coach her in English and to have her lose some weight. He decided, like Garbo, she would henceforth be known by one name — Valli — but, she says, "He was the first around the studio to call me Alida."

Selznick groomed his new find for stardom by casting her in his production of *The Paradine Case* (1947) in which she played the nymphomaniac-murderer. He loaned her to RKO, where she starred with Frank Sinatra in the *Miracle of the Bells* (1948) and with Joseph Cotten in *Walk Softly, Stranger* which was made in 1948-49, but not released until 1950.

Selznick closed down his studio, and after two years in Hollywood and three pictures, Miss Valli moved to New York City, with three years remaining on her contract. Selznick used her in his English co-production of *The Third Man* (1950) and loaned her to RKO for *The White Tower* (1950) opposite Glenn Ford, after which her contract ended.

Always a private person who never fitted into the hoopla of Hollywood stardom, Miss Valli says, "Hollywood is much less the picnic than I

Alida Valli in *The Paradine Case* (1947).

thought. It is a factory town where people dedicate themselves to the motion picture. It's the life, the talk, the everything.''

She returned to Italy where she pursued her life as an actress in both motion pictures and on the stage, but she never sought out the publicity that surrounds the lives of most actors and actresses, and which Selznick had begun when she was under contract to him.

In one of her most recent performances, she was strikingly and unglamorously fresh and mature as the ageing mistress in Bernardo Bertolucci's *The Spider's Stratagem* (1970). When Miss Valli arrived in the United States she was married to composer-pianist, Oscar de Mejo, by whom she has two sons. They have since divorced.

APPENDIX II - Academy Award Nominations of David O. Selznick Productions

*Denotes Academy Award Winners

1936 — *The Garden of Allah*
Best Musical Score — Max Steiner
Best Assistant Director — Eric G. Stacy
Special Award — to W. Howard Greene and Harold Rosson for the color cinematography of the Selznick International Production, *The Garden of Allah.*

1937 — *A Star Is Born*
Best Picture
Best Direction — William A. Wellman
Best Actor — Fredric March
Best Actress — Janet Gaynor
Best Original Story — William A. Wellman and Robert Carson
*Best Screenplay — Alan Campbell, Robert Carson and Dorothy Parker
Best Assistant Director — Eric G. Stacey
*Special Award — to W. Howard Green for the Color Photography of *A Star Is Born.*

1937 — *The Prisoner of Zenda*
Best Art and Set Direction — Lyle Wheeler
Best Musical Score — Alfred Newman

1938 — *The Young In Heart*
Best Cinematography — Leon Shamroy
Best Musical Score — Franz Waxman

1939 — *Intermezzo: A Love Story*
Best Musical Score — Lou Forbes

1939 — *Gone With the Wind*
*Best Picture
*Best Director — Victor Fleming
Best Actor — Clark Gable
*Best Actress — Vivien Leigh
Best Supporting Actress — Olivia de Havilland
*Best Supporting Actress — Hattie McDaniel
*Best Screenplay — Sidney Howard
*Best Art and Set Direction — Lyle Wheeler
*Best Cinematography — Ernest Haller and Ray Rennahan
*Best Editing — Hal. D. Kern and James E. Newcom
Best Sound Recording — Thomas T. Moulton
*Best Special Effects — John R. Cosgrove, Fred Albin and Arthur Johns
*Special Award — to William Cameron Menzies for outstanding achievement in the use of color for the enhancement of dramatic mood in the production of *Gone With the Wind*
*Scientific Achievement — to Don Musgrave and Selznick International Pictures, Inc., for pioneering in the use of the coordinated equipment in the production of *Gone With the Wind*
*Irving G. Thalberg Memorial Award — David O. Selznick.

1940 — *Rebecca*
*Best Picture
Best Director — Alfred Hitchcock
Best Actor — Laurence Olivier

Best Actress — Joan Fontaine
Best Supporting Actress — Judith Anderson
Best Screenplay — Robert E. Sherwood
Best Art and Set Direction — Lyle Wheeler
*Best Cinematography — George Barnes
Best Editing — Hal C. Kern
Best Musical Score — Franz Waxman
Best Special Effects — Photographic: John R. Cosgrove
Sound: Arthur Johns

1944 — *Since You Went Away*
Best Picture
Best Actress — Claudette Colbert
Best Supporting Actor — Monty Woolley
Best Supporting Actress — Jennifer Jones
Best Art and Set Direction — Mark-Lee Kirk and Victor A. Gangelin
Best Editing — Hal C. Kern and James E. Newcom
Best Cinematography — Stanley Cortez and Lee Garmes
*Best Musical Score — Max Steiner
Best Special Effects — Photographic: John R. Cosgrove
Sound: Arthur Johns

1945 — *Spellbound*
Best Director — Alfred Hitchcock
Best Supporting Actor — Michael Chekhov
Best Cinematography — George Barnes
*Best Musical Score — Miklos Rozsa
Best Special Effects — Photographic: John R. Cosgrove

1946 — *Duel in the Sun*
Best Actress — Jennifer Jones
Best Supporting Actress — Lillian Gish

1947 — *The Paradine Case*
Best Supporting Actress — Ethel Barrymore

1948 — *Portrait of Jennie*
Best Cinematography — Joseph August
*Best Special Effects — Visual: Paul Eagler Jr., J. McMillan Johnson, Russell Shearman and Clarence Slifer
Audible: Charles Freeman and James G. Stewart
1950 — *The Third Man*
Best Director — Carol Reed
*Best Cinematography — Robert Krasker
Best Editing — Oswald Hafrenrichter

1957 — *A Farewell To Arms*
Best Supporting Actor — Vittorio de Sica

APPENDIX III - Academy Award Nominations of The Selznick Players

(*Denotes Academy Award Winners)

INGRID BERGMAN—
1943—Best Actress — *For Whom the Bells Toll*
*1944—Best Actress — *Gaslight*
1945—Best Actress — *The Bells of St. Mary's*
1948—Best Actress — *Joan of Arc*
*1956—Best Actress — *Anastasia*
*1974—Best Supporting Actress — *Murder on the Orient Express*

JOAN FONTAINE—
1940—Best Actress — *Rebecca*
*1941—Best Actress — *Suspicion*
1943—Best Actress — *The Constant Nymph*

JENNIFER JONES—
*1943—Best Actress — *The Song of Bernadette*
1944—Best Supporting Actress — *Since You Went Away*
1945—Best Actress — *Love Letters*
1946—Best Actress — *Duel in the Sun*
1955—Best Actress — *Love Is A Many-Splendored Thing*

VIVIEN LEIGH—
*1939—Best Actress — *Gone With the Wind*
*1951—Best Actress — *A Streetcar Named Desire*

DOROTHY McGUIRE—
1947—Best Actress — *Gentlemen's Agreement*

GREGORY PECK—
1945—Best Actor — *The Keys of the Kingdom*
1946—Best Actor — *The Yearling*
1947—Best Actor — *Gentlemen's Agreement*
1949—Best Actor — *Twelve O'Clock High*
*1962—Best Actor — *To Kill a Mockingbird*

SHIRLEY TEMPLE—
*1934—Special Award — in grateful recognition of her outstanding contribution to screen entertainment during the year of 1934.

APPENDIX IV - All-Time Top Grossing Motion Pictures of David O. Selznick and The Selznick Players.

Gone With the Wind	$77,900,000
How the West was Won	$24,269,000
Swiss Family Robinson	$16,500,000
Tora! Tora! Tora!	$14,500,000
The Guns of Navarone	$13,000,000
Duel in the Sun	$11,300,000
Old Yeller	$ 8,200,000
The Bells of St. Mary's	$ 8,000,000
To Kill a Mockingbird	$ 7,200,000
For Whom the Bell Tolls	$ 7,100,000
David and Bathsheba	$ 7,100,000
The Greatest Story Ever Told	$ 7,000,000
The Snows of Kilimanjaro	$ 6,500,000
The Yellow Rolls Royce	$ 6,000,000
The Valley of Decision	$ 5,560,000
The Yearling	$ 5,250,000
Friendly Persuasion	$ 5,050,000
A Farewell to Arms	$ 5,000,000
Anastasia	$ 5,000,000
Island in the Sun	$ 5,000,000
The Song of Bernadette	$ 5,000,000
Three Coins in the Fountain	$ 5,000,000
On the Beach	$ 5,000,000
Spellbound	$ 4,975,000
Since You Went Away	$ 4,950,000
Notorious	$ 4,800,000
A Streetcar Named Desire	$ 4,800,000
Moby Dick	$ 4,800,000
A Summer Place	$ 4,700,000
The Bachelor and the Bobby-Soxer	$ 4,500,000
The Inn of the Sixth Happiness	$ 4,400,000
The Man in the Gray Flannel Suit	$ 4,350,000
Saratoga Trunk	$ 4,250,000
Joan of Arc	$ 4,100,000
The Emperor Waltz	$ 4,000,000
Love is a Many-Splendored Thing	$ 4,000,000
Summer Magic	$ 4,000,000
Captain Newman M.D.	$ 4,000,000
Arabesque	$ 4,000,000

These figures represent the amounts paid in rentals by U.S. and Canadian distributors and do not include total box-office takings or earnings outside North America.

BIBLIOGRAPHY

Books

James Agee, "Agee On Film" (McDowell Obolensky, 1958)

Felix Barker, "The Oliviers" (Lippincott, 1953).

Rudy Behlmer, "Memo From David O. Selznick" (Viking, 1972).

Gary Carey, "Cukor and Co." (Museum of Modern Art, 1971).

Bosley Crowther, "The Great Films" (G.P. Putnam, 1967).

Bette Davis, "The Lonely Life" (G.P.Putnam, 1962).

Graham Greene, "Graham Greene on Film" (Simon and Schuster, 1972).

John Gruen, "Close-Up" (Viking Press, 1968).

Charles Higham and Joel Greenberg, "The Celluloid Muse" (Signet, 1969).

Hedda Hopper and James Brough, "The Whole Truth and Nothing But" (Doubleday, 1962).

John Houseman, "Run-Through" (Simon and Schuster, 1972).

Pauline Kael, "Kiss Kiss Bang Bang" (Little, Brown, 1968).

Hildegard Knef. "The Gift Horse" (McGraw-Hill, 1971).

Gavin Lambert, "On Cukor" (G.P. Putnam, 1971).

Gavin Lambert, "The Making of Gone With the Wind" (Atlantic-Little, 1973).

James Robert Parish, "The Fox Girls" (Arlington House, 1971).

George Perry, "The Films of Alfred Hitchcock" (Dutton Vista, 1965).

Gwen Robyns, "Light of a Star" (Leslie Frewin, 1968).

David Shipman, "The Great Movie Stars" (Crown, 1970).

David Shipman, "The Great Movie Stars" (St. Martin's, 1972).

Bob Thomas, "Selznick" (Doubleday, 1970).

Robert Wilson, "The Film Criticism of Otis Ferguson" (Temple University Press, 1971).

Norman Zierold, "The Moguls" (Coward McCann, 1969).

Periodicals and Newspapers

"Cinema"
"Films In Review"
"Kaleidoscope"
The New York "Times"
"Variety"
" Screen Facts"

INDEX